DR JEKYLL AND MR HYDE
AFTER ONE HUNDRED YEARS

DR JEKYLL AND MR HYDE
AFTER ONE HUNDRED YEARS

Edited by William Veeder and
Gordon Hirsch

The University of Chicago Press
Chicago and London

The University of Chicago Press, Chicago 60637
The University of Chicago Press, Ltd., London

LIBRARY OF CONGRESS CATALOGING-IN-PUBLICATION DATA

Dr Jekyll and Mr Hyde after one hundred years.

Bibliography: p.
1. Stevenson, Robert Louis, 1850–1894.   Strange
case of Dr Jekyll and Mr Hyde.   I. Veeder, William R.
II. Hirsch, Gordon.
PR5485.D7   1988   823'.8   87-19033
ISBN 0-226-85228-8
ISBN 0-226-85229-6 (pbk.)

Contents

Illustrations

Introduction

I

In 1950, C. Keith observed: "it is now a hundred years since, on a bleak Edinburgh November, Robert Louis Stevenson was born. The east wind was blowing. . . . A city in fine to shrink from. . . . And yet, you had only to turn the other way to see, looming through those same grey clouds, the romantic magnificence of the Castle on her towering rock, and Arthur's Seat vivid against the sullen sky." Edinburgh has her glories and her weather still. And in 1986, Robert Louis Stevenson has another centenary. *Strange Case of Dr Jekyll and Mr Hyde* is one hundred years old. We again face the question posed by one of the 1950 commentators, Leslie Fiedler. "One hundred years after the birth of Stevenson, the question of his worth as a writer remains very much at issue." For Fiedler and most readers then and now, the question is not why we have read Stevenson but why we should reread him. Can the man who speaks so well to children have much to say to adults?

Inevitably, perhaps, most of the critics who have taken the trouble to pose this question in print have answered it in the affirmative. But less inevitably, critics support their affirmations with quite diverse arguments. Keith celebrates Stevenson the storyteller. "So, after a hundred years, there is still much to keep Stevenson's name fresh, for those that love literature. . . . For in all that prolific century [since Stevenson's birth] we've not had a second *Treasure Island,* nor are like to. And over the winter's fire, there's still no rival to *Kidnapped*." Espousing a different novel—"*The Master of Ballantrae* is a splendid book, Stevenson's only truly embodied tragedy"—Fiedler emphasizes Stevenson the mythographer. "It is in the realm of myth, which sometimes overlaps but is not identical with literature, that we must look for clues to the meaning and unity of Stevenson's work." A third testament has been offered recently by Graham Good:

> Stevenson rediscovered the free individual in the open air and in
> the open world, grappling actively with the unexpected, rather

than being passively determined by heredity, habit and social circumstance. . . . This is the core of Stevenson's importance for the next generation of writers. . . . in an era which saw man as the passive servant of great abstractions like Progress, Evolution, or Capital, Stevenson maintained an image of man as an individual, free agent.

Critics today are impelled to raise and answer the question of Stevenson's value because his reputation has fluctuated so steeply during our century. After a quite protracted apprenticeship (even *A Child's Garden of Verses* did not sell well initially), Stevenson achieved with *Jekyll and Hyde* a popularity with adult readers that grew steadily until 1894. Untimely death, combined with Stevenson's qualities as storyteller, stylist, and moralist, elevated him to virtually iconic status in the later 1890s. Reaction quickly set in, however. William Ernest Henley's "seraph in chocolate" essay of 1901, Frank Swinnerton's devastating book in 1914, and several subsequent reappraisals prompted Leonard Woolf to say in 1924: "there never has been a more headlong fall in a writer's reputation than there was in Stevenson's after his death." For many Edwardian intellectuals, Stevenson's fiction never got beyond childish escapism, his morality echoed with "Victorian" falseness, and, as for his style, Woolf asserted that "a false style tells most fatally against a writer when, as with Stevenson, he has nothing original to say." Stevenson's fall has, moreover, been as protracted as it was steep. More than forty years after Woolf's remarks, Stevenson was excluded from the 1966 edition of *Victorian Fiction: A Guide to Research*, "in spite of his influence on romantic fiction, because his adult novels are few and of debatable rank."

Critical disparagement extended to *Jekyll and Hyde*. By 1947, the novella's stock was so low in the academy that it was accorded only seven lines in F. E. Baily's chapter on Stevenson in *Six Great Victorian Novelists*. The fifties tended to accept Walter Allen's verdict in *The English Novel*: "*Jekyll and Hyde* is a crude morality." For Fiedler, "*Jekyll and Hyde* is a tragedy . . . but its allegory is too schematic, too slightly realized in terms of fiction and character . . . while its explicit morality demands that evil be portrayed finally as an obvious monster." Keith agreed:

. . . had not the book a moral? (Oh, but a blatant one!) If you weren't careful, the evil in you would swallow up the good, as the wicked Hyde does to Dr. Jekyll. And you'd be lost. So be careful! Nearly as crude as that! But with the subtler psychologists of to-day, *Dr. Jekyll* has faded out. And you'll turn with relief to Scott's novels.

The fact that Stevenson's decline among intellectuals did not extend to the general public is important. Both groups had initially joined in his celebration. Henry James, Edmund Gosse, and Andrew Lang echoed and amplified praises by readers everywhere. That these general readers remained loyal as their more "serious" brethren turned away from Stevenson indicated the enduring power of his best work and made inevitable a critical re-turn to him. Reappraisal is now underway, led by the Scots. In 1979 came Ian Campbell's *Nineteenth-Century Scottish Fiction* and Jenni Calder's biography of Stevenson. In addition to her collections of essays (*Robert Louis Stevenson: A Critical Celebration* and *Stevenson and Victorian Scotland*) in the 1980s, there is Swearingen's excellent bibliography of Stevenson's prose writings, Noble's recent book of critical essays, Menikoff's edition of "The Beach of Falesa," and the promise of both the long-awaited edition of the complete letters from Mehew and a new biography from Swearingen. The most recent edition of *Victorian Fiction: A Guide to Research* devotes a chapter to Robert Louis Stevenson.

The renewal of attention to *Jekyll and Hyde* inevitable with a renaissance of interest in Stevenson is being complemented by a larger scholarly phenomenon. Gothic literature in general is at last receiving substantial, serious critical attention. Overviews by Kiely, Levy, MacAndrew, Punter, Sedgwick, Wilt, and Day have been supplemented by studies focused on specific texts or issues: book-length works on *Frankenstein* (*Ariel Like a Harpy* [1972], *The Endurance of Franken-stein* [1979], *Mary Shelley and Frankenstein: The Fate of Androgyny* [1986]); numerous essays on *Frankenstein* and *Dracula;* ongoing concern with "sensation" fiction; feminist recognition of the importance of gothic for women writers (from Ann Radcliffe to Flannery O'Connor); and Lawler's forthcoming edition of *Dorian Gray.* Clearly scholars are moving beyond condescension and cliché to detailed, serious analyses of the nature and force of gothic. *Jekyll and Hyde* has not yet received the attention accorded to *Frankenstein* or even to *Dracula,* but Geduld's recent collection, plus work by Fraustino, Hennelly, Nabokov, Saposnik, and others, indicate that Stevenson's novella is beginning to attract the study due to one of the greatest gothic texts of the nineteenth century. Such study is the goal of our volume.

II

Philip Fisher, in *Hard Facts,* makes a distinction between popular and high art that helps locate the aesthetic value of *Jekyll and Hyde.*

> In popular forms images outrun analysis. The opposite is true in high art. . . . The works of George Eliot, James, Conrad, and

Faulkner epitomize the modern ideal of the novel because within the novels themselves can be found the secondary analysis of their own exhausted categories—heroism, manners, self-ishness, marriage. They are themselves disquisitions, critical speculation of a profound kind, about their own material. The popular forms, sentimental, historical, and naturalistic, often seem, when quoted in moments of self-analysis, stupid, obtuse, commonplace. . . . Instead it is the picture-making, the configurations and patterns themselves, that are entirely fresh and particularly in need of later, external analysis because, by being so striking, they quickly become settled in the language and in the perceptual frame of their civilization.

Jekyll and Hyde fits awkwardly between Fisher's categories of popular and high art. The novella is "popular" insofar as it refuses to analyze itself. Or rather, it engages in self-analysis as inept as anything Fisher finds in popular authors. Jekyll's "Full Statement of the Case," plus local comments by Utterson and Lanyon, are often "stupid, obtuse, commonplace." Placing *Jekyll and Hyde* with Fisher's "popular" fictions immediately reveals, however, a distinction between Stevenson and his best-selling brethren. The self-analytic ineptitudes in his novella derive not from the author (or "the text"), but from the characters. *Jekyll and Hyde* engages ineptly in self-analysis in order to call into question the very possibility of such analysis and to complicate comparable analytical moves by readers. Stevenson's novella further problematizes Fisher's categories because it combines analytic reticence with the formal perfection of "high art." *Jekyll and Hyde* exhibits the economy of means, the multivalence of language, and the intricate patterning of imagery that marks such gothic masterpieces as James's *The Turn of the Screw,* Conrad's *Heart of Darkness,* and Faulkner's "A Rose for Emily."

To account for this combination of artistic and popular features is the challenge of our volume. The complexity of Stevenson's novella is reflected in the diversity of responses to it over the past century. Illustrators and cinematographers, actors and script writers, professional and general readers have for one hundred years attested to the power of *Jekyll and Hyde* by reinterpreting it every decade. Our volume attempts to study, reflect, and contribute to this variegated response.

The diverse visual appeal of *Jekyll and Hyde* is reflected in the plates that we have selected for inclusion. The first Jekyll/Hyde to tread the boards, Richard Mansfield (1886), his principal British successor, H. B. Irving (1910), and his first screen counterpart, James Cruz (1912), constitute both a study in themselves and a context for the great cinema performers after World War I—Barrymore (1920), March (1932),

Tracy (1941), and the underrated Ralph Bates and Martine Beswick of *Dr. Jekyll and Sister Hyde* (1971). (The editors are particularly grateful to Professor Virginia Wright Wexman for her erudition and savvy in obtaining movie stills.) Three of these photographs are particularly valuable. For fear of compromising Spencer Tracy's reputation as a matinee idol, MGM refused to release in America any press stills of him as Hyde. The studio was less anxious, apparently, about releases in Britain. Through the good offices of the National Film Archive, we can present— in a press still rather than an inevitably fuzzier frame enlargement—a moment of Tracy as Hyde. In addition, thanks to the help of Professor Richard Koszarski, Professor Wexman has come upon something still rarer: a press still of Fredric March as Hyde in makeup that Paramount experimented with but never actually employed in the film. Finally, we present a press still that could not be matched by any frame enlargement. Paramount took two moments from its film—March as Jekyll meditating by the fire and as Hyde raging forth—and superimposed them. The consequence is more than a representation of dual identity. This identity is articulated in terms of its cause and effect—the flames of desire and of retribution.

In selecting illustrations from five different editions of *Jekyll and Hyde,* we have emphasized diversity of interpretation and technique by counterpointing representations of crucial moments in the plot—Gillet and Wilson on Hyde's trampling of the little girl, Beaman and MacCauley on Hyde's killing of Carew. We have also included particularly graphic representations of narrative situations—Beaman's and Wilson's visions of the bystreet setting of Jekyll's rear door, and MacCauley's location of Utterson in that setting as the lawyer awaits Edward Hyde. A last illustration is of a very different type. The *Punch* cartoon by John Tenniel of a member of Parnell's Irish National League who pretends to be a respectable, Jekyll-like member of Parliament while he is really a murderous, Hyde-like radical in league with the Phoenix Park assassins shows Stevenson's creations extending beyond the literary and psychological life of the times and becoming political emblems.

The diverse literary aspects of *Jekyll and Hyde* offer challenges both scholarly and critical. Two long-neglected projects of scholarship are undertaken in our volume. The surviving fractions of the manuscript drafts of Stevenson's novella are brought together and collated. An introduction presents the history (so far as it can be pieced together) of the composition of *Jekyll and Hyde* and suggests a controversial interpretation of the creative process that Stevenson underwent between his seminal dream and his novella's publication. A second scholarly project is the bibliography of critical titles pertaining to *Jekyll and Hyde.*

These are complemented by selected titles that either provide readers with information basic to Stevenson's life and work or constitute important moments in the development of his reputation.

The principal enterprise of our volume is critical. Eight essays reflect in their diverse interests and tactics the breadth of appeal that has made *Jekyll and Hyde* a force in our culture for one hundred years. These essays employ such divergent methodologies as deconstruction, feminism, psychoanalysis, intellectual and cultural history, and genre study, as well as close textual analysis. They evoke diverse theorists: Bakhtin, Barthes, Derrida, and Foucault; Marx, Lukacs, and Jameson; Freud, Lacan, and Kristeva. The essays move from formal to contextual questions in a four-part sequence. In the opening section, "Questions of Voice," Peter K. Garrett and Ronald R. Thomas combine various poststructuralist strategies with close analysis in their attention to formal complexities. Garrett traces the intricate interplay between "voices" or positions of narration and reading in *Jekyll and Hyde*. He shows how a conservative logic that bases meaning on traditional moral oppositions and organizes narrative as a disclosure of truth is confronted and subverted by more radically plural and unstable effects. Inevitably the reader's demands for narrative coherence become implicated in the spreading violence which the novella both represents and enacts. Thomas examines "voice" in *Jekyll and Hyde* in a quite different way, reading the novella as an enactment of the modern critical notion of "the death of the author." The estrangement of a speaker from his own voice and of a writer from what he has written are reflected in what Thomas defines as the novella's opposing plots of exclusion and escape. Thomas then goes on to relate Stevenson's oppositions to an important strain in modernist fiction as exemplified in Samuel Beckett. In the "schizo-text," the subject is alienated from his own voice, and both character and narrative are marked by unavoidable disintegration and breakdown.

In the section, "Questions of Repression," William Veeder and Jerrold E. Hogle combine feminist, psychoanalytic, deconstructive, and Marxist interests to explore the latent and occluded forces that drive Stevenson's characters. Veeder moves beyond the generally held view that *Jekyll and Hyde* is an indictment of Victorian repression of "pleasure" and sees the novella indicting patriarchy for repressing its own oedipal rages and sibling rivalries. Locating his psychoanalytic reading in culture by defining patriarchy in terms of the rise of professionalism in late-nineteenth-century Britain, and extending his reading to the issue of woman's virtual exclusion from the novella, Veeder defines misogynistic and homoerotic impulses that prevent patriarchs from marrying and drive them to narcissistic isolation. Hogle draws on Kristeva, Marx, Derrida, and Foucault to define what Jekyll and many of his critics repress in their assertions of a dual personality—the frightening possibility that the "self" may have multiple personalities. "Identity" may be based upon the movement of a multidimensional body language into public discourse where bounded texts attempt to repress more basic and visceral levels of figural play. This repressive process is, Hogle argues, one result of the human birth process in a patriarchal world where man must throw off ("abject") the feminine in himself in order to seem "a man."

In the section "Questions of Genre," Gordon Hirsch and Donald Lawler read *Jekyll and Hyde* in terms of common origins and divergent developments in the tradition of fiction. Hirsch begins with *Frankenstein* and traces the development of the detective story from its gothic origins. The epistemological radicalness of Stevenson's novella becomes particularly clear in immediate juxtaposition to the paramount model of ratiocination, Sherlock Holmes, who first debuts one year after Jekyll and Hyde. Holmes has his foil in Dr. Watson, as Poe's Dupin did in the Prefect of Police, but, as Hirsch establishes, the equally inept inspector in *Jekyll and Hyde,* Scotland Yard's Newcomen, is paired not with an analytic genius but with an amateur detective who is ultimately as obtuse as himself, Gabriel John Utterson. Stevenson's refusal to endow Utterson with the effective reason of Holmes and Dupin reveals the subversive psychology of his novella's gothic origins. Lawler also begins with *Frankenstein,* from which he traces the gothic roots of another genre produced by the nineteenth century, science fiction. As Hirsch sees the ratiocinative pretensions of detection undermined by the gothic unconscious, Lawler sees a similar fate for science itself. Gothic science fiction reveals the connection between the unrepresented forces of the unconscious and the equally unrepresented and equally real forces of nature. Gothic conventions and transformations can thus symbolize that deconstruction of the ruling Newtonian paradigms which was effected by the implications of recessive Darwinism, entropy, and molecular randomness. For Lawler, *Jekyll and Hyde* is important to the development of nineteenth-century science fiction because Stevenson's novella mythologizes those discontinuities of nature and those contradictions of empiricism that were beginning to undermine the progressive, scientific optimism of the Victorian period.

The section "Questions of Context" presents essays by Patrick Brantlinger and Richard Boyle and by Virginia Wright Wexman, which share a concern with audiences and examine art in terms of modes of production. Brantlinger and Boyle see *Jekyll and Hyde* in light of the new literacy that transformed the industry of British bookmaking between 1850 and 1900. Like many of his cultural peers, Stevenson was disturbed by what seemed to be a lowering of taste to the standards or the appetites of millions of new readers, yet he was willing to write for this audience and to accept wealth and adulation from it. For Brantlinger and Boyle, slum-dwelling Hyde represents both these masses and Stevenson's capacity to appease them with "Shilling Shockers," even as upper-class Jekyll with his readings in divinity represents Stevenson's attempts to produce "high art" through the allegorization of *Jekyll and Hyde*. Wexman too is interested in the "political" aspects of the Jekyll/Hyde story, as she expands the notion of context to include another medium and another century. Rouben Mamoulian's great film of *Jekyll and Hyde* rearticulates Stevenson's concern with human devolution in terms of the racial anxieties of the 1930s. The presentation of the human body, which is so important to Stevenson, is also made central by Mamoulian, as the economic tensions of the Depression era are expressed in terms of sexuality. Hollywood's star system facilitates both the equation of "white" with "beautiful" and the reinforcement of the angel/whore dichotomy. The social repression of blacks and women, which is implicit in Stevenson's treatment of the underclassed, becomes central to what Wexman sees as the twentieth century's myth of "natural" morality.

Especially given the brief compass of Stevenson's novella, the contributors to this collection have inevitably tended to emphasize certain key words, passages, and themes. These emphases serve as markers in two different ways. On the one hand, they situate our volume at a moment in the evolution of critical concerns; they indicate the analytical interests of a time in the history of criticism when psychoanalysis and continental theories have pervaded the academy and when "history" has regained the prominence lost during the New Critical years. On the other hand, such shared foci attest to the diversity that is Stevenson's enduring strength. Specific details and features of his text have the power to take on diverse meanings when viewed from diverse perspectives. Handwriting in *Jekyll and Hyde,* for example, is seen by Hirsch in terms of detection, by Brantlinger and Boyle in terms of the new literacy, by Garrett and Hogle in terms of the inextricable association of writing and identity, by Thomas in terms of the ultimate inseparability of text and voice. Another node of critical interest is devolution. Lawler finds this theory central to both Stevenson's view of character and the whole enterprise of post-Darwinian science; Wexman views it in terms of the racism that permeates Anglo-American culture from the 1860s through the 1930s; Brantlinger and Boyle focus on political cartoons that articulate British anti-Fenian sentiments in terms of devolutionary caricatures of "Paddy"; and Veeder defines Dr. Denman as the primal father from whom Victorian patriarchy ultimately derives. These and other textual foci (such as Jekyll's striking denial/affirmation "He, I say—I cannot say I") call forth from the contributors that variegated response which Stevenson himself insisted upon when he rejected the very possibility of exhausting a subject. "To 'say all'? Stay here. All at once? . . . We say each particular thing as it comes up."

III

For clarity, the contributors all refer to the same, readily available text of *Jekyll and Hyde:* Jenni Calder's Penguin edition (*The Strange Case of Dr Jekyll and Mr Hyde and Other Stories* [Harmondsworth, England, 1979]), set directly from the first edition of the novella. In addition, we all use the same conventions in referring to this text and to others. Parenthetical numbers signify pages in Calder's edition of *Jekyll and Hyde;* parenthetical numbers preceded by an L and a numeral refer to the four-volume 1911 edition of Stevenson's letters (*The Letters of Robert Louis Stevenson,* ed. Sidney Colvin [New York: Charles Scribner's Sons]); parenthetical numbers preceded by an author's name refer to texts listed in the bibliography (when it is clear from the immediate context which author is referred to, the name is omitted). Other texts by Stevenson and other authors' works are specified in the contributors' footnotes, and thereafter cited parenthetically in the text, except in the case of well-known and widely available essays of Stevenson (such as "A Chapter on Dreams") that are cited in the text by title alone. Finally, among the many variations that the novella's title has assumed throughout the years— with and without the initial *The,* with and without periods after *Dr* and *Mr,* with and without both *Strange Case of* and *Strange Case of Dr . . . Mr*—we use the least cumbersome, *Jekyll and Hyde,* except when full formal recognition of the title is required. Then we adopt the title that Stevenson himself designated: *Strange Case of Dr Jekyll and Mr Hyde.* The only exception to this practice is our own title, which was dictated by various factors and which features the middle-length version, *Dr Jekyll and Mr Hyde.*

For their help with the illustrations for this volume, the editors would like to thank Mary Corliss and the Museum of Modern Art for the press stills of John Barrymore as Hyde and of Ralph Bates and Martine Brunswick as Dr. Jekyll and Sister Hyde, Tim Hawkins and the Wisconsin Center for Film and Theater Research for the composite still of Fredric March as Jekyll contemplating himself as Hyde, Richard Koszarski and the Museum of the Moving Image for the still of March in experimental makeup for Hyde, Jenny Sussex and the Nation Film Archive of Britain, for the press still of Spencer Tracy as Hyde, and BBC Hulton Picture Library for the photographs of the 1910 Queen's Theatre and 1931 Savoy stage productions of *Dr. Jekyll and Mr. Hyde.* The illustrations by S. G. Hulme Beaman, Frank Gillet, Mervyn Peake, and

Edward A. Wilson of scenes from editions of Stevenson's novella are reprinted by kind permission of their respective publishers, the Bodley Head Limited, Collins Publishers, the Folio Society, and the Limited Editions Club.

Contributors

RICHARD BOYLE: Ph.D. from Indiana University. He has done the entry on Stevenson for the *Dictionary of Literary Biography* and is now at work on a critical study, *Stevenson and Realism*.

PATRICK BRANTLINGER: professor of English at Indiana University and editor of *Victorian Studies*. He is the author of *The Spirit of Reform: British Literature and Politics, 1832–1867* (1977) and *Bread and Circuses: Theories of Mass Culture as Social Decay* (1983). He has recently completed *Rule of Darkness: British Literature and Imperialism, 1830–1900*.

PETER K. GARRETT: professor of English at the University of Illinois at Urbana-Champaign. He is the author of *Scene and Symbol from George Eliot to James Joyce: Studies in Changing Fictional Mode* (1969) and *The Victorian Multiplot Novel: Studies in Dialogical Form* (1980). He is now writing a book on varieties of narrative reflection, with several chapters on nineteenth-century gothic fiction.

GORDON HIRSCH: associate professor of English at the University of Minnesota. He has published essays on Dickens, Lawrence, Carroll, Carlyle, Tennyson, J. S. Mill, and Mary Shelley. He is now working on other Stevenson texts.

JERROLD E. HOGLE: associate professor of English at the University of Arizona. He has published essays on Romantic poetry, gothic fiction, the theory of metaphor, deconstructive criticism, Shakespeare, and Marxist/feminist theory. His *Shelley's Process: Radical Transference and the Development of His Major Works* is now in press.

DONALD LAWLER: professor of English at East Carolina University and editor of *Victorians Institute Journal*. He has edited a collection of essays on Vonnegut (1977) and a critical anthology of science fiction (1978); his edition of *The Picture of Dorian Gray* appeared in 1987. He is now working on a study of fantasy and science fiction as modern genres.

RONALD R. THOMAS: assistant professor of English at the University of Chicago. He has published on Dickens (and on Stevenson in an earlier version of his essay for this volume). He is currently completing *Dreams of Authority*, a book on dreams in nineteenth-century fiction.

WILLIAM VEEDER: professor of English at the University of Chicago. He has written books on Yeats (1968), Henry James (1975), and Mary Shelley (1986), has coauthored a three-volume study of Anglo-American feminism (1983), and has coedited a collection of James's criticism of fiction (1986). He is currently writing *The Serpent's Tale: Anglo-American Gothic Fiction: 1885–1914.*

VIRGINIA WRIGHT WEXMAN: associate professor of English at the University of Illinois at Chicago and editor of *Cinema Journal*. She has written *Robert Altman: A Guide to References and Resources* (1982) and *Roman Polanski* (1985) and has edited a critical edition of the screenplay of *Letter from an Unknown Woman* (1986). She is now completing a book on screen acting.

I
QUESTIONS OF TEXT

The Texts in Question

WILLIAM VEEDER

The burning of the original draft of *Strange Case of Dr Jekyll and Mr Hyde* assures that certain questions about the novella's genesis and Stevenson's intentions can never be answered. Collating the fractions of the surviving manuscripts allows, however, for a more complete narrative than any told before. I will address first the history of composition, then the contents of the drafts.

I

Two months after the publication of *Jekyll and Hyde*, Robert Louis Stevenson wrote to F. W. H. Myers that " 'Jekyll' was conceived, written, re-written, and re-re-written, and printed inside ten weeks" (L2, 325). Was Stevenson speaking literally here? Swearingen, in his excellent review of the evidence, answers yes (98–99). I agree, but with one qualification. Stevenson family accounts of the novella's genesis all attest that *Jekyll and Hyde* grew out of a dream, was "written" in three days, and was burned by Louis in response to Fanny's criticism. The fractions of the two subsequent drafts that survive today suggest that the novella as we have it was "re-written" quickly after the burning of the original, and was then "re-re-written" at some leisure thereafter. What collation also reveals, however, is that Stevenson's words to Myers and Swearingen's characterization of the second manuscript as "final" (98) must be qualified. Although the "re-re-written" draft is indeed the printer's text (revealing compositor's marks in various hands), this draft does not reproduce exactly the first printed edition of the novella. Stevenson undoubtedly took advantage of galley proofs to make numerous last-minute alterations. *Jekyll and Hyde* was thus re-re-re-written as well.

In referring to the surviving manuscripts, I will follow Swearingen in calling the earlier one the "Notebook Draft," but I will name the later manuscript the "Printer's Copy" since it was not "final." The Notebook Draft is on copybook paper (6¼-inch × 7⅞-inch, lined), with twenty or twenty-one lines per page, and with catchwords at the bottom of most, though not all, of the pages. Pages 58, 67, 69–84, 86–90, and 103 are preserved at the Beinecke Rare Book and Manuscript Library at Yale University; pages 33 and 48, at Princeton University Library; and page 68, at the Silverado Museum in St. Helena, California. The overall length of the Notebook Draft cannot be determined. Page 103 is unquestionably not the end, since it recounts nocturnal adventures of Hyde. The page is, moreover, anomalous in the draft. It breaks off in the middle of the nineteenth line, without a catchword. Did Stevenson pause here in his white-hot labors and resume on page 104? Or did he stop here and begin a whole new draft? The lack of any indication of such a draft inclines me to the former explanation. Although no other page of the Notebook Draft shows Stevenson resuming his labors by skipping to a new leaf, page 39 of the Printer's Copy evidences precisely this phenomenon.

The Printer's Copy is written on foolscap paper (8-inch × 13-inch, lined), with thirty-six lines per page, and with catchwords on most pages. Pages 1–8A, 10–14, and 43–62 are preserved at the Pierpont Morgan Library; page 9, at Silverado. The overall length of the Printer's Copy can be determined precisely, since page 62 ends with both the last words of the first printed edition and the signature of Robert Louis Stevenson. Limedorfer is incorrect, however, in listing the length of this draft as sixty-two pages (52). Sometime after completing page 9, Stevenson inserted a page numbered 8A, changing accordingly the catchword on page 8 and adding after it "\to p 8A." Stevenson apparently added a page 8B as well, since there is a catchword at the bottom of page 8A and the direction "to p. 8B." This direction was subsequently canceled, however, and replaced by "to p 9," presumably because 8B was deleted entirely along with the first fifteen and one-half lines of page 9. The catchword on page 8A was accordingly altered to correspond to the first surviving word on page 9. The Printer's Copy of *Jekyll and Hyde* thus consisted of sixty-four pages. Only one of these is anomalous. Page 39 contains fifteen and one-quarter lines. The entire page is canceled, and its sixteenth line breaks off in midthought.

The provenance of neither of the surviving drafts can be established fully. The Notebook Draft was broken up by 1898, for at the bottom of the Silverado Museum's page 68 are typed the words, "Presented by Mrs Robert L. Stevenson to J. E. Schermerhorn/May 6, 1898." The Pierpont Morgan archives preserve a memo written by the curator, Mr. George K. Boyce, on 5 May 1952, to the director, Mr. Frederick B. Adams, Jr.:

> In the files I find a letter from Luther S. Livingston of Dodd & Livingston, 9 June 1911, addressed to Miss Greene [first director of the Morgan]; he offers the Dr. Jekyll MS thus,
> "A few days ago we received from Mrs. Strong [Stevenson's stepdaughter], another Stevenson Manuscript, being 24 pages

of an early draft of 'Dr. Jekyll & Mr. Hyde.' This she said she found in an old trunk which had not been opened for a long time. The sheets are not quite consecutive, but show considerable variations from the first edition of the book. We must ask $1500, for the 24 leaves. . . ."

Why the Morgan declined to purchase the leaves is not explained. They are the fraction of the Notebook Draft that was given years later to Yale University by Mr. Edwin J. Beinecke. He has left a two-page description of the Yale fraction, but has not detailed his acquisition of the pages either here or in a 5 February 1951, letter to the Pierpont Morgan Library in which he presents page 52 of the Printer's Copy to Mr. Adams. A book plate with "Ex libris Harry Glemby" in the Yale fraction indicates that Mr. Glemby, who amassed a substantial collection of Stevensoniana, owned or may even have been the original purchaser of the twenty-four leaves from Dodd & Livingston. The Silverado page 68 was purchased in 1983 by its curator, Miss Ellen Shaffer.

The Printer's Copy was apparently intact until at least 1900, for Limedorfer expresses his "thanks . . . to Mrs. Isobel Strong, who very kindly and courteously put the whole manuscript at my disposition" (52). By 1909, however, the pages had been dispersed, for Mr. Boyce's 1952 memo records that the thirty-page fraction "was sold to Mr. Morgan on December 8 1909, and the bill for $1500 paid on 14 July 1910," presumably to Dodd & Livingston. Pages 43 and 52 were given to the Morgan Library by Mr. Beinecke in 1951, page 47 in 1960. The Silverado page 9 was received as a gift in 1970.

A last aspect of the Printer's Copy, or rather of the history of commentary on the draft, should be mentioned. Limedorfer's account, in addition to frequent small errors in reading Stevenson's hand and transcribing his words, presents three puzzling features relevant to the composition of *Jekyll and Hyde*. Limedorfer records what he calls "Stevenson's characteristic marginal notes" (54).

> Only toward the end of it [chapter 1] is one of Stevenson's characteristic marginal notes. He gives us the conversation between Enfield and Utterson, and originally Utterson is made to say: ". . . The fact is I know something about this other party," and here the chapter ended. When the author revised his manuscript he put down on the margin, "Must be extended," and at some later day he added the rest of the chapter. . . . In the original manuscript we find these words: "And still there was no rest for the solicitor, and instead of taking his place by the fire," then comes an abrupt end and the remark, "Too copious," the sentence is struck and instead of it he writes: "With that he blew out his candle, put on a great-coat." . . . At the end of the

paragraph there is one word in parenthesis, "Better." Whether this means that the changed form appeared to the author as being better than the original one, or whether he meant it as a sort of reminder that he ought to make it better we do not know. . . . Proceeding farther on, we find another of Stevenson's marginal remarks, not intended for the printer. In the part which contains the conversation between Hyde and Utterson the manuscript runs in this way: " 'Good God,' thought Utterson, 'can he too have been thinking of the will, discounting the inheritance?' But he merely thanked the other and promised to remember it." "That's bad," says the marginal note, and at a subsequent reading probably the author crossed out the end of that paragraph, substituting for "discounting the inheritance . . ." "But he kept his feelings to himself and only grunted in acknowledgment of the address."

In the description of Hyde's appearance there is a slight but significant change made in the text. Originally the sentence read: ". . . He had borne himself to the lawyer with a *somewhat* murderous mixture of *cowardice and savagery* . . .": a marginal note says: "I have to make that more smooth," and then came the alteration by substituting "sort of" for "somewhat," and "timidity and boldness" for "cowardice and savagery." Another similar remark is on the next page. Says the author in a marginal note: "Threw him out of gear.' I do not like that phrase." And acting upon his own remark, he changes the sentence "his encounter with Hyde had thrown him out of gear" into "the face of Hyde sat heavy on his memory." . . . Another interesting sentence that caused a marginal note is: "Into the details of this fad I will not enter." Marginally the author says: "Must omit that, may have to add a few hundred words." [54, 56, 58]

No marginalia occur in the Printer's Copy. Since Limedorfer maintains that "every correction in the manuscript is in ink" (52), any erasures would be unmistakable on foolscap paper. (There is also no indication of the penciled marginalia that Limedorfer discusses: "On the margin [of page 1] there is a pencil note reading: 'Dedication?' This goes to prove that the four lines 'To Katherine De Mattos' were an afterthought" [52].) The absence of erasure marks raises the possibility of a third draft of *Jekyll and Hyde.* But this possibility must be discounted, at least in terms of Limedorfer's commentary. The three manuscript pages that he photoduplicated in his essay are absolutely identical—down to the smallest cancellations and irregularities—with pages 9, 45, and 61 of the Printer's Copy.

A second problem concerns page 39 of the draft. The final sentence of the page breaks off with the words "worthy of the cells of Bedlam, the sight of this so . . ." Limedorfer quotes the entire page and records as its final words a completed sentence: ". . . the sight of this unnerved Utterson." Even if Stevenson added the words "unnerved Utterson" on page 40, no cancellation of the "so" on page 39 warrants Limedorfer omitting the word from his transcription of the sentence.

This passage also points to the final troubling feature of Limedorfer's commentary. In quoting page 39, he begins with the words, "There were all signs of a man having made experiments." Page 39 in fact begins with the word "experiments." An obvious explanation of the preceding nine words in Limedorfer's transcription is that he found them on the now-lost page 38. But if this is so, the words "There . . . made," plus "unnerved Utterson" at the end of last sentence from page 39, are the only ones in Limedorfer's entire essay that lie outside the fraction of the Printer's Copy that survives today. Swearingen in a note left with the Pierpont Morgan manuscript observes (in addition to the absence of the marginalia) that "Limedorfer also implies (p. 56) that he has seen the missing pp. 14–42 of this Ms. and that these 'show very little alterations' but he quotes nothing from them and in his specific comments goes from Ms. p. 13 to deleted 39 (verso of p. 43). This makes one think that he never saw any other pages than are in this manuscript." The words "There . . . made" and "unnerved Utterson" protect Limedorfer from Swearingen's conclusions somewhat. But if the final words of Limedorfer's transcription of page 39 are suspect, the initial words may also be.

Limedorfer's account is, then, troubling on various grounds. If he did not, in fact, see "the whole manuscript," we cannot certify that it remained intact until 1900. If he did see marginalia, was he, as Swearingen suggests in his Morgan note, dealing with "some sort of transcript of the MS. with these marginalia," which Limedorfer had "mistaken . . . for Stevenson's"? Swearingen adds, "if so this transcript is unknown to me." I have found no evidence of it. Thus the two features that make Limedorfer's essay valuable to readers studying the surviving pages of the Printer's Copy—information about its provenance and help with supplementary wording—are both called seriously into question.

II

In terms of the contents of the Notebook Draft and the Printer's Copy, the changes within each draft, between them, and between them and the first printed edition are so numerous that I must leave it to each reader to draw the conclusions appropriate to individual interests and perspectives. I will concentrate on four changes in events and characters. Compare Jekyll's accounts of Hyde's 3 A.M. altercation:

> detected in an act of infamy, I had to bribe a party of young fools
> to set me free. [Notebook Draft]

> An act of cruelty to a child aroused against me the anger of a
> passer by, (whom I recognized but the other day in the person of
> your kinsman); the doctor and the child's family joined him.
> [Printer's Copy]

In the latter passage (which corresponds, except for one minor word, to
the first printed edition of the novella), neither Enfield nor the others who
confront Hyde can be characterized as "young fools." Does the change to
professional men and neighbors indicate that the event that generated the
confrontation was itself different in the Notebook Draft?

A second, potentially more important change occurs in the name and
character of the murder victim of Edward Hyde. In the Printer's Copy,
the victim is the distinguished M.P., Sir Danvers Carew, "an aged
beautiful gentleman with white hair" whose face "seemed to breathe
such an innocent and old-world kindness of disposition, yet with
something high too, as of a well-founded self-content." In the Notebook
Draft, the murder victim is a "Mr. Lemsome." (On page 33, Stevenson's
handwriting allows for the possibility that the spelling is "Lensome," but
on page 88 the third letter of the name is clearly an *m*.) He appears only on
the isolated page 33 (Jekyll mentions his death on page 88), so the genesis
of Lemsome and the details of his dire fate remain mysterious. What we
do know from page 33 is that lawyer Utterson receives his first independent corroboration of Edward Hyde's existence from Lemsome, "a
creature who had come to him bleating for help under the most ignoble
and deserved misfortunes." Page 33 does not reveal what these
misfortunes are, but it does reveal a character very different from Sir
Danvers. Lemsome is

> a man of about twenty-eight, with a fine forehead and good
> features; anoemically pale; shading a pair of suffering eyes
> under blue spectacles; and dressed with that sort of outward
> decency that implies both the lack of means and a defect of taste.
> By his own confession, Mr. Utterson knew him to be a bad
> fellow . . . an incurable cad.

Utterson accepts Lemsome as a client, presumably to discover more
about Edward Hyde. Why Hyde murders Lemsome (whom, unlike Sir
Danvers, he knows beforehand) is not revealed in the surviving pages of
the Notebook Draft. Why Stevenson initially envisioned Hyde's victim
as a character like Lemsome, and why he changed the character so
dramatically in the Printer's Copy, are ripe subjects for speculation. Mine
appear in my essay on the novella, so I will not rehearse them here.

A third intriguing passage deleted from the printed text appears in the
Printer's Copy and relates to Gabriel John Utterson. The lawyer's obsessive fascination with Edward Hyde is Stevenson's subject here. Having

initially presented this fascination in the paragraph extending from the bottom of page 8 to the middle of page 9, Stevenson canceled this passage and inserted page 8A, which corresponds to the printed sequence "Hitherto it had troubled him. . . . on his chosen post." Since this sequence includes a version of the sentence about Utterson visiting the door "in the morning . . . at noon . . . at night," we can see that Stevenson canceled the passage on pages 8–9 not because he disliked the materials but because, on the contrary, he felt the need to expand them. This decision gives the lost page 8B all the more interest. Since Stevenson returned to the "morning . . . afternoon . . . night" materials at the bottom of 8A, did he continue to expand on the rest of the original materials on 8B? Did Stevenson, in particular, do more with the scene of Utterson looking in the cookshop's and perfumer's windows? This question is important because, if I am correct in my essay that the windows scene reveals much about the repressed desires of Mr. Utterson, page 8B may well have taken us still deeper into his consciousness, one of the most important and most occluded in *Jekyll and Hyde.*

Why, in turn, did Stevenson cut page 8B *and* the windows scene? Here we come to the most speculative—but potentially most important—of the issues raised by the two surviving drafts. In 1950, Malcolm Elwin called into question the traditional explanation of the burning of the original version of *Jekyll and Hyde*—that Stevenson had missed the allegorical point of the story.

> From Stevenson's own account in "A Chapter on Dreams," it appears unlikely that he 'missed' the point of the allegory in writing the first draft. The allegory was the germ of the story, and he had in fact already attempted the theme in *The Travelling Companion*. Suspicion arises that Fanny's criticism [of *Jekyll and Hyde*] was inspired by reasons which she preferred to conceal. *The Travelling Companion* was rejected by an editor as "a work of genius and indecent"; was the anonymous editor to be identified with Fanny herself? Remarking that "their discussions over the work [*Jekyll and Hyde*] were sometimes hot and protracted," her sister quotes a letter from Fanny to Stevenson's mother:
>
>> If I die before Louis, my last earnest request is that he shall publish nothing without his father's approval. I know this means little short of destruction to both of them, but there will be no one else. The field is always covered with my dead and wounded, and often I am forced to compromise, but still I make a very good fight.
>
> Her suggestion of Stevenson's father as suitable mentor indicates the direction of Fanny's censorship; less than a year before, Thomas Stevenson had protested, "with his usual

vehemence of feeling and expression," against the stage confrontation in *Admiral Guinea* "of profane blackguardry in the person of Pew with evangelical piety in that of the reformed slaving captain," evoking from Stevenson the rejoinder 'My Dear Father,—Allow me to say, in a strictly Pickwickean sense, that you are a silly fellow.' There seems reason to suspect that, in the first draft of *Jekyll and Hyde*, Stevenson drew upon his own experiences of the double life to describe more realistically the excesses indulged by Jekyll in the character of Hyde. Little more than a year later, George Moore was writing in *Confessions of a Young Man:* 'If any man living in this end of the century needed freedom of expression for the distinct development of his genius, that man was R. L. Stevenson.' [201–2]

In the thirty-five years since Elwin's *The Strange Case of Robert Louis Stevenson*, critics and biographers have not tended to follow his line of speculation. They have usually retold the family account of the burning incident, despite the fact that the only two narratives that purport to be eyewitness accounts, Fanny's and Lloyd's, differ widely. The collated fractions of the surviving manuscripts do not support Elwin unequivocally or call the family account into serious question. But the drafts will provide some encouragement for readers troubled by Stevenson's burning of the first draft of *Jekyll and Hyde*.

What accounts for the *intensity* of the reactions of Fanny and Louis? Why did she object so strenuously? She had not, apparently, objected to "Markheim," which was also a "crawler" depicting "the old war in the members." She knew well that Louis was sorely pressed for funds in the fall of 1885 and that Longmans had asked expressly for a crawler. Why, in turn, did Louis react to Fanny's critique so violently that he burned on the spot a manuscript that he had just proclaimed "the best thing he had ever done" (Sanchez, 118)? Sanchez's explanation—that "he was afraid of being influenced by the first writing and preferred to start anew, with a clean slate" (118–19)—may not satisfy readers troubled by Stevenson's subsequent reference to the novella's "moral, worse luck" ("A Chapter on Dreams").

Did Robert Louis Stevenson, as Elwin suggests, present in the original pages of *Jekyll and Hyde* an adult view of sexuality, which Fanny perceived as potentially threatening to his public image as author of children's books? The surviving fractions reveal a steady occlusion of outré materials that some readers will see as vestiges of an original concern with the sexual sources of human motivation. ". . . if Hyde was Jekyll's son, why the provision of the disappearance?" Was this sentence deleted because it raised expressly the forbidden subject of illegitimacy?

WILLIAM VEEDER

There is unquestionably a steady toning down of Jekyll's discussion of his turpitude. In the Notebook Draft, Jekyll says, "From a very early age, however, I became in secret the slave of disgraceful pleasures." The word *disgraceful* is weighty in our language. What disgraceful pleasures could a small boy be guilty of? The Printer's Copy presents the sentence in already milder form: "From a very early age, however, I became in secret the slave of certain appetites." This is then revised in the Printer's Copy to read, "and indeed the worst of my faults was a certain impatient gaiety of disposition, such as has made the happiness of many." Not only has Stevenson toned down the sentence overall; he has changed the focus to adulthood. The early childhood sources of Jekyll's adult dilemmas are thus obscured in revision. The *connection* between boy and man is further emphasized in the Notebook Draft as we read on down the passage in question. "The iron hand of indurated habit plunged me once again into the mire of my vices. I will trouble you with these no further than to say that they were at once criminal in the sight of the law and abhorrent in themselves." Readers who see in the "disgraceful pleasures" of Jekyll's "very early" years a suggestion of masturbation may feel that the "iron hand" indicates some type of regressive recurrence in adulthood. More complicated behavior must be indicated now, however, since criminality has become an issue. What is the connection between boyhood and adult practices? Again, revision involves effacement. The Printer's Copy retains the earlier wording of the sentence down to "they were" and then continues, "at that period, no worse than those of many who have lived and died with credit." The whole passage is then deleted and replaced with the still milder "Many a man would have even blazoned such irregularities as I was guilty of."

Are the staying hand of Fanny, the strident voice of Thomas, and the cautionary glance of Victorian propriety operative in these and other revisions? Can the alterations be seen as germane in any way to the foregrounding of the story's moral? The surviving fractions do not provide a decisive answer. But for readers troubled by the official account, the drafts give some indication of a steady movement away from outré materials. Surely, one side of Robert Louis Stevenson yearned mightily to join Henry James, George Moore, George Gissing, and other novelists of the 1880s who were attacking Mrs. Grundy and Mr. Mudie and were refashioning British fiction into an adult depiction of the human condition. Another side of Stevenson, however, shared Fanny's reverence for the proprieties and her concern for the practical aspects of authorship and reputation. To what extent did this old war in the members contribute to the genesis and the thematic concerns of *Jekyll and Hyde*?

III

In preparing the fractions for publication, I have not attempted a diplomatic transcript. But I have tried to give as complete a representation of compositional processes as possible. The objection that such a text makes for difficult reading—as Edmund Wilson and others have lamented—seems less relevant in the present instance because I am not offering a *reader's* text. There are a dozen available editions of *Jekyll and Hyde*. A scholarly collation is offered to people interested in what might be revealed of Stevenson's mind and compositional habits.

I have retained oddities of Stevenson's spelling: "mischeif," "carying," "here" for "hear," and repeatedly "nieghbourhood" and "niether." I have not, on the other hand, reflected his frequent tendency to cross the *h* rather than the *t* of *th* words. I have recorded inconsistencies of punctuation: Stevenson often, but not always, inserts a hyphen between the prefix *dis-* and the succeeding syllables; he frequently places a hyphen in *by-street,* though he sometimes writes *bystreet* and sometimes *by street;* he occasionally includes a period with *Mr.* or *Dr.,* but usually does not, and at least once spells out *Doctor* with a proper name.

I represent Stevenson's various types of changes by the following typographic devices:

/	A slash through a letter or punctuation mark indicates deletion.
———	A single line through a word or words indicates deletion; a single line through part of a word indicates that Stevenson made one word into another by crossing out part of the initial word.
═══	Two lines through part of a word indicate that Stevenson changed one word to another by writing over part of the original word.
⟨ ⟩	Angle brackets indicate that the enclosed word(s) appear above what Stevenson initially wrote.
⟨/ ⟩ ⟨^ ⟩	A slash or a caret within the angle brackets indicates the mark that Stevenson used to signal the presence of the added word(s) above the line.
[ ]	Square brackets indicate that a second change was set above the one marked by angle brackets.
{ }	Curved brackets indicate that part of an added item intrudes horizontally into the left margin.
iIt	A lowercase letter followed by its uppercase counterpart indicates that Stevenson initially wrote the word in lowercase and then superimposed a capitalization on the initial letter, usually when he changed a preceding

	semicolon to a period and began a new sentence with the word in question.
1	Footnotes indicate alterations unusual or complicated enough to require further explanation.
\?/	Inverted slashes around a question mark indicate illegible letter(s) or word(s).

IV

For their permission to publish the various pages collated here, I wish to express my gratitude to the Beinecke Manuscript and Rare Book Library, the Pierpont Morgan Library, the Princeton University Library, and the Silverado Museum. My debts, moreover, go far beyond acts of permission. Calling on librarians for assistance with aspects of Stevenson's fractions and practices, I have been answered with a patience, expertise, and good humor that have left me both with increased knowledge and without adequate words of thanks. I would in particular like to acknowledge Miss Marjorie G. Wynne, Mr. Stephen Parks, and their staff at the Beinecke, Mr. Herbert Kahoon and Mr. Kurt W. Hettler at the Morgan, Miss Jean F. Preston at Princeton, and Miss Ellen Shaffer at Silverado. My colleague at the University of Chicago, Professor Bruce Redford, has assisted in every phase of the project; I thank him both for his help with specific textual difficulties and for the more general example of his editorial probity. I would also like to thank my research assistants, Mr. Timothy Child and Ms. Karen Rosenthal, whose contributions have exceeded the mechanics of text preparation. With young eyes and bright minds they have taken on problems readily and have solved them repeatedly. Finally, I am grateful to two of Stevenson's most dedicated scholars, Mr. Ernest Mehew and Mr. Roger G. Swearingen, who have commented helpfully on various aspects of this introduction and partake in none of its heresies.

T W O

Collated Fractions of the Manuscript Drafts
of *Strange Case of Dr Jekyll and Mr Hyde*

WILLIAM VEEDER

PRINTER'S COPY

[1] Strange Case of Dr Jekyll and Mr Hyde

Story of the door.

Mr Utterson the lawyer was a man of a rugged countenance, ~~and~~ that ⟨/was⟩ never lighted by a smile; cold, scanty and embarrassed in dis-course; backward in sentiment; lean, long, dusty, dreary and yet somehow loveable. At friendly meetings, and when the wine was to his taste, something ~~evid~~ eminently human beaconed from his eye; something indeed which never found its way into his talk, but which spoke not only in these silent symbols of the afterdinner face, but more often and loudly in the acts of his life. He was austere with himself; drank gin when he was alone, to mortify a taste for vintages; and though he enjoyed the theatre, had not crossed the doors of one for twenty years. But he had an approved tolerance for others, sometimes wondering, almost with envy, at the ⟨/high⟩ pressure of ~~high~~ spirits involved in their misdeeds, and in any extremity inclined to help rather than to reprove. "I rather incline to Cain's heresy," he used to say quaintly: "I let my brother go to the devil in his own way." In this character, it was frequently his fortune to be the last reputable acquaintance and the last good influence in the lives of down-going men. And to these, as long as they came about his chambers, he never marked a shade of change in his demeanour.

No doubt the feat was easy to Mr Utterson, for he was undemonstrative at the best, and even his friendships seemed to be founded in a similar catholicity of good nature. It is the mark of a modest man to accept his friendly circle ready-made from the hands of opportunity; and that was the lawyer's way. His friends were those of his own blood or those whom he had known the longest; his affections, like ivy, were the growth of time, ~~and~~ they implied no aptness in the object. Hence, no doubt, the bond that united him to Mr Richard Enfield, his distant kinsman, the well known man about town. It was a nut to crack for many, what these two could see in each other or what subject they could find in common. It was ~~encountered~~ ⟨reported⟩ by those who encountered them in their

14

Sunday walks, that they said nothing, looked singularly dull, and would [2] hail with obvious relief the appearance of a friend. For all that, the two men set the greatest store by these excursions, counted them the chief jewel of each week, and not only set ⟨/aside⟩ occasions of pleasure, but even resisted the calls of business, that they ⟨^might⟩ enjoy them uninterrupted.

It ~~changed~~ ⟨chanced⟩ on one of these rambles that their way led them down a by-street in a busy quarter of London. The street was small and what is called quiet, but it drove a thriving trade on the weekdays. The inhabitants were all doing well, it seemed, ⟨/and all⟩ emulously hoping to do better still, and laying out the surplus of their gains in coquetry; so that the shop fronts ⟨/stood⟩ along that thoroughfare with an air of invitation, like rows of smiling saleswomen. Even on Sunday, when it veiled its more florid charms and lay comparatively empty of passage, the street shone out, in contrast to its dingy nieghbourhood, like a fire in a forest; and with its freshly painted shutters, well polished brasses, and general cleanliness and gaiety of note, instantly caught and pleased the eye of the passenger.

Two doors from one corner, on the left hand going east, the line was broken by the entry of a court; and just at that point, a certain sinister block of building thrust forward its gable on the street. It was two storeys high; showed no window, nothing but a door on the lower storey and a blind forehead of discoloured wall on the upper; and bore in every feature, the marks of ⟨/prolonged and⟩ sordid negligence. The door, which was equipped with niether bell nor knocker, was blistered and distained. Tramps slouched into its shelter and struck matches on the panels; children kept shop ~~on~~ ⟨upon⟩ the steps; the schoolboy had tried his knife on the mouldings; and for close on a generation, no one had appeared to drive away these random visitors or to repair their ravages.

Mr Enfield and the lawyer were on the other side of the bystreet; but when they came abreast of the entry, the former lifted up his cane and pointed.

"Did you ever remark that door?" he asked; and when his companion had replied in the affirmative, "It is connected in my mind," added he, "with a very odd story."

"Indeed?" said Mr Utterson, with a slight change of voice. "And what was that?"

"Well, it was this way," returned Mr Enfield: "I was coming home [3] from some place at the end of the world, about three o'clock of a black winter morning, and my way lay through a part of town where there was literally nothing to be seen but lamps. Street after street, and all the folks asleep—street after street, all lighted ~~t~~ up as if for a procession and all as empty as a church—till at last I got into that state of mind when a man listens and listens and begins to ~~weary~~ ⟨long⟩ for the sight of a policeman. All at once, I saw two figures: one a little man who was stumping along eastward at a ~~d~~ good walk, and the other a girl of maybe eight or ten who was running ~~down~~ ⟨as⟩ hard as she was able down a cross street. Well, sir, the two ran into one another naturally enough ⟨/at the corner⟩; and then came the horrible part of the thing; for the man trampled calmly over the child's body and left her screaming on the ground. It sounds nothing to hear, but it was hellish to see. ⟨{It wasn't li}ke a man; it was like some damned Juggernaut⟩ I gave a view halloa, took to my heels, collared ~~the~~ ⟨my⟩ gentleman, and brought him back to where there was already quite a group about the screaming child. He was perfectly cool and made no resistance, but gave me one look so ugly that it brought out the sweat on me like running. The people who had turned out were the girl's own family; and pretty soon, the doctor, for whom she had been sent, put in his appearance. Well, the child was not much the worse, more frightened, according to the sSawbones; and there you might have supposed would be an end to it. But there was one curious circumstance. I had taken a loathing to my gentleman at frist sight; so had the child's family, which was only natural. But the doctor's case was the what struck me. He was the usual cut and dry apothecary, of no particular age and colour, with a strong Edinburgh accent, and about as emotional as a bagpipe. Well, sir, he was like the rest of us; everytime he looked at my prisoner, I saw that Sawbones turn sick and white with the desire to kill him. I knew what was in his mind, just as he knew what was in mine; and killing being out of the question, we did the next best. We told him ⟨/the man⟩ we could and would make such a scandal out of this, as should make his name stink from one end of London to the other. If he had any friends or any credit, we undertook that he should lose them. And all the time, as we were pitching it in red hot, we were keeping the women off him as best they ⟨we⟩ could, for they were as wild as harpies. All th I never saw a circle of such hateful faces; I declare we looked like fiends and there was the [4] man in the middle, with a kind of black, sneering coolness. that—frightened⁄too, I could see that—but carying it off, sir, really like Satan. ⸲'If you choose to make capital out of this accident,' ⸲said he, ⸲'I am naturally helpless. No gentleman but wishes to avoid a scene,' ⸲says he. 'Name your figure.' Well, we screwed him do up to a thousand ⟨hundred⟩ pounds for the child's family; he would have dearly liked to stick out; but there was something about the lot of us that meant mis-cheif, and at last he struck. The next thing was to get the money; and where do you think he carried us but that place with the door? I pointed out—whipped out a key, went in, and presently came back with the matter of fifty ⟨ten⟩ pounds in gold and a cheque for the balance on Coutts's, drawn payable to bearer and signed with a name that I can't mention, though it's one of the points of my story, but it was a name at least very well known and often printed. The figure was stiff; but the signature was good for more than that, if it was only genuine. I took the liberty of pointing out to my gentleman that the whole business looked apocryphal, and that a man does not, in real life, walk into a cellar door at four in the morning and come out of it with another man's cheque for close upon a thousand ⟨hundred⟩ pounds. But he was quite easy and sneering. 'LSet your mind at rest,'' says he. 'I will stay with you till the banks open and cash the cheque myself.' So we all went ⟨set⟩ off, the doctor, and the child's father, and our friend and myself, and passed the rest of the night in my chambers; and next day, when we had breakfasted, set off ⟨went⟩ in a body fro ⟨to⟩ the bank. I gave in the cheque myself, and said I had every reason to believe it was a forgery. Not a bit of it, sir. The cheque was genuine."

"Tut-tut," said Mr Utterson.

"I see you feel as I do," said Mr Enfield. "Yes, it's a bad story. For my man was a fellow that nobody could have to do with, a really damnable man; and the person that drew the cheque is the very pink of the proprieties, celebrated too, and (what makes it worse) one of your fellows who do what they call good. Black mail, I suppose: an honest man paying ~~for~~ through the nose for some of the capers of his youth. Black Mail House is what I call that place with the door, in consequence. Though/even that, you know, is far from explaining all," he added, and with the words fell into a vein of musing.

[5] From this he was recalled by Mr Utterson asking rather suddenly: "And you don't know if the drawer of the cheque lives there?"

"A likely place, isn't it?" returned Mr Enfield. "But I happen to have noticed his address; he lives in some square or other."

"And you never asked about—the place with ~~a~~ ⟨the⟩ door?" said Mr Utterson.

"No, sir: I had a delicacy," was the reply. "I feel very strongly about putting questions; it partakes too much of the style of the day of judgement. You start a question, and it's like starting a stone. You sit quietly on the top of a hill; and away the stone goes, starting others; and presently some bland old bird (the last you would have thought of) is knocked on the head in his own back garden and the family have to change their name. No, sir, I make it a rule of mine: the more it looks like Queer Street, the less I ask."

"A very good rule, too," said the lawyer.

"But I have studied the place for myself," continued Mr Enfield. "It seems scarcely a house. There is no other door, and nobody goes in or out of that one but, once in a great while, ~~my~~ ⟨the⟩ gentleman of my adventure. There are three windows looking on the court on the first floor; none below; the windows are always shut ~~and wonderfully dirty~~ ⟨but they're clean⟩. And then there is a chimney which is generally smoking; so somebody must live there. And yet it's not so sure; for the buildings are so packed together about that court, that it's hard to say where one ends and another begins."

The pair walked on again ⟨/for a while⟩ in silence; and then "Enfield," said Mr Utterson, "that's a good rule of yours."

"Yes, sir, I think it is," returned Enfield.

"But for all that," continued the lawyer, "there's one point I want to ask: I want to ask the name of that[1]⟨t⟩ man who walked over the child."

"Well," said Mr Enfield, "I can't see what harm it would do. It was a man of the name of Hyde."

"Hm," said Mr Utterson. "What sort of a man is he to see?"

"He is not easy to describe. There is something wrong with his appearance; something displeasing, something downright detestable. I never saw a man I so disliked, and yet I scarce know why. He must be deformed somewhere; he gives a strong feeling of deformity, although I couldn't specify the point. He's an extraordinary looking man, and yet I really can name nothing out of the way. No, sir; I can make no [6] hand of it; I can't describe him. And it's not want of memory; for I declare I can see him this moment."

Mr Utterson again walked some way in silence and obviously under a weight of consideration. "You are sure he used a key?" he inquired at last.

"My dear sir . . ." ~~cried~~ ⟨began⟩ Enfield, surprised out of himself.

"Yes, I know," said Utterson; "I know it must seem strange. The fact is, ~~I~~

---

1. Stevenson canceled "that," wrote above it "t" (for "the"?) then canceled the "t" and put three dots under the "that" to indicate its reinstatement.

~~know something about this~~ (if I do not ask you the name of the) other party, it is because I know it already. You see, Richard, your tale has gone home. If you have been inexact in any point, you had better correct it."

"I think you might have warned me," returned the other with a touch of sullenness. "But I have been pedantically exact, as you call it. The fellow had a key; and what's more, he ~~must have~~ (is) ~~been in the habit of using it, for I have seen him go in again in the same way.~~ he has it still. I saw him use it, not a week ago."

Mr Utterson sighed deeply but said never a word; and the young man presently resumed. "~~This~~ (Here) is another lesson to say nothing," said he. "I am ashamed of my long tongue. Let us make a bargain never to refer to this again."

"With all my heart," said the lawyer. "I shake hands on that, Richard."

Search for Mr Hyde

That evening, Mr Utterson came home to his bachelor house in sombre spirits and sat down to dinner without relish. It was his custom of a sunday, when this meal was over, to sit close by the fire, a volume of some dry divinity on his reading desk, until the clock of the nieghbouring church rang out the hour of twelve when he would go soberly and gratefully to bed. On this night, however, as soon as the cloth was taken away, he took up a candle and went into his business room. There he opened his safe, took from the most private part of it a document endorsed on the envelope as Dr Jekyll's Will, and sat down with a clouded brow to study its contents. The will was holograph, for Mr Utterson, though he took charge of it now that it was made, had refused to lend the least assistance in the making of it; and it provided [7] not only that, in case of the decease of Henry Jekyll, M.D., D.C.L., L.L.D., F.R.S., &c, all his possessions were to pass into the hands of his "friend and benefactor Edward Hyde," but that in case of Dr Jekyll's "disappearance or unexplained absence for any period exceeding three calendar months," the said Edward Hyde should step into the said Henry Jekyll's shoes without further delay and free from any burthen or obligation, beyond the ~~immediate~~ payment of ~~the~~ a few small sums to the members of the doctor's household. This document had long been the lawyer's eyes~~ha~~ore. It offended him as a lawyer and as a lover of the sane and customary sides of life, to whom the fanciful was the immodest. And hitherto it was his ignorance of Mr Hyde that had swelled his indigation; now, by a sudden turn, it was his knowledge. It was already bad enough/when the name was but a name, of which he could learn ~~nothing further~~ (no more)/. iIt was worse when it began to be clothed upon with detestable attributes; and out of the shifting, insubstantial mists that had so long baffled his eye, there leaped up the sudden, definite presentment of a fiend.

"I thought it was madness" he said, as he replaced the obnoxious paper in the safe. "and now I begin to fear it is disgrace."

~~And still there was no rest for the solicitor; and instead of taking his place by the fire,~~ (And thereupon) (With that he blew out his candle,) he put on ~~his~~ (a) great coat and set forth in the direction of Cavendish Square, (/that citadel of medicine,) where his friend, the great Dr. Lanyon, had his house and received his crowding patients. "If anyone knows, it will be Lanyon," he (˄had) thought.

The solemn butler ~~received~~ (knew and) welcomed him; he was subjected to no stage of delay, but ushered direct from the door to the dining room where Dr Lanyon sat alone over his wine. This was a hearty, healthy, dapper, red-faced gentleman, with a shock of hair prematurely white ⟨/, and a boisterous and decided manner⟩. At sight of Mr Utterson, he sprang up from his chair and welcomed him with both hands. The geniality, as was the ~~manners~~ ⟨way⟩ of the man, was somewhat theatrical to the eye; but it reposed on genuine feeling. For these two were old friends, old mates both at school and college, both thorough respecters of themselves and of each other, and, ⟨t⟩ what does not always follow, men who thoroughly enjoyed each other's company.

[8] After a little rambling talk, the lawyer led up to the subject which so disagreeably preoccupied his mind.

"I suppose, Lanyon," said he "you and I will be the two oldest friends that Henry Jekyll has?"

"I wish the friends were younger," chuckled Dr Lanyon. "But I suppose we are. And what of that? I see little of him now."

"Indeed?" said Utterson. "I thought you had a bond of ⟨/common⟩ interest."

"We had," was the reply. "But it is more than ten years since Henry Jekyll became too fanciful for me. He began to go wrong, wrong in mind; and though of course I continue to take an interest in him for old sake's sake as they say, I see and I have seen devilish little of the man. Such unscientific balderdash," added the doctor, flushing suddenly purple, "would have estranged Damon and Pythias."

This little spirt of temper was somewhat of a relief to Mr Utterson. "They have only differed on some point of science," he thought; and ~~even~~ ⟨being⟩ a man of no scientific passions (except in the matter of conveyancing) he even added: "It is nothing worse than that!" He gave his friend a few seconds to recover his composure, and then approached the question he had come to put. "Did you ever come across a protégé of his—one Hyde?" he asked.

"Hyde?" repeated Lanyon. "No. Never heard of him. Since my time."

That was the amount of information that ~~the lawyer~~ [2]⟨Mr Utterson⟩ carried back with him to the great, dark bed on which he tossed to and fro, until the small hours of the morning began to grow large. It was a night of little ease to his toiling mind, toiling in mere darkness and besieged by questions. How[3] could such a man as Henry Jekyll be bound up with such a man as Edward Hyde? How should he have chosen as his heir one who was unknown to his oldest intimates? If it were a case of terrorism, why the will? Or again, if Hyde were Jekyll's son, why the proviso of the disappearance? Six o'clock struck on the bells of the church that was so conveniently near to Mr Utterson's dwelling, and still he was digging at the problem. ∫ and[4] for all that, he had no sooner swallowed his breakfast, than he

2. After canceling "the lawyer" and replacing it above the line with "Mr Utterson," Stevenson deleted the replacement and put five short strokes under "the lawyer" to reinstate it.

3. The passage from "How" through "disappearance?" is canceled by a single loop which runs through line 26 down the right margin to line 29, then back through the last ten words of the line, then down to line 30 where it continues back toward the left margin, canceling the initial two words of this line, and then turning up the left margin until it returns to its beginning at line 26.

4. The passage from "and" through "knocker" is canceled by a loop like the one sentence in the passage above.

must put on his hat and great coat and set forth eastward of a ⟨in⟩ the teeth of a fine, driving rain, coming iced out of Siberia, with no more sensible purpose than to stand awhile on the opposite pavement and look awhile at the door without the knocker. This⁵ [8A] Hitherto the matter ⟨it⟩ had touched him on the intellectual side alone; but now his imagination also was engaged or rather enslaved; and as he lay and tossed in the gross darkness of the night and the curtained room, Mr Enfield's tale went by before his mind in a scroll of lighted pictures. He would see ⟨be aware of⟩ the great field of lamps of the nocturnal city; then of the figure of a man walking swiftly; then of a child running from the doctor's; and then these met, and that human Juggernaut trod the child down and passed on regardless of her screams. Or else he would see a room in a rich house, where his friend lay asleep, dreaming and smiling at his dreams; and then the door of that room would be opened, the curtains of the bed plucked apart, the sleeper recalled, and lo! there would stand by his side a figure to whom power was given, and even at that dead hour of the night, he must rise and do its bidding. The figure in these two faces ⟨phases⟩ haunted the lawyer all night; and if at any time he dozed over, it was but to see it glide ⟨stalk⟩ ⟨/glide⟩ more stealthily through sleeping houses, or move the more swiftly, and still the more swiftly, even to diziness ⟨dizziness⟩, through wider labyrinths of lamplighted city, and at any street corner, crush a child and leave her screaming. Still ⟨And still⟩ the figure had no face by which he might know it; even in his dreams, it had no face, or one that baffled him and melted before his eyes; and thus it came ⟨was⟩ that, whether he was asleep or awake ⟨there sprang up and grew apace in⟩ the lawyer's mind, a singularly strong, ⟨^and⟩ almost ⟨^an⟩ inordinate, curiosity to behold the features of the real Mr Hyde. If he could but once set eyes on him, he thought the mystery would lighten and perhaps roll altogether away, as was the habit of mysterious things when well examined. He might see a reason for his friend's strange preference or bond⟨/a⟩ge (call it which you please) and even for the startling clauses of the will. And at least it would be a face worth seeing: the face of a man who was without bowels of mercy: a face which ⟨/had⟩ but to show itself to raise up, in the mind of the unimpressionable Enfield, a spirit of enduring hatred.

From that time forward, Mr Utterson began to haunt the door in the bystreet of shops. In the morning before office hours, at noon when time ⟨business⟩ was scarce ⟨plenty⟩ and business plenty ⟨time scarce⟩, at night under the fogged⁶ face of the city moon, by all lights and at all hours of solitude or of concourse, the lawyer was to be found on his chosen post. Now he⁷ "If [9] . . . . This⁸ excursion, once taken, seemed to have laid a spell on the methodical gentleman. In the morning before office hours, at noon when business was plenty and time scarce, at night under the glimpses of the fogged city moon or by the cheap glare of the lamps, a spirit in his feet kept still drawing and guiding the lawyer to that door

5. Catchword deleted on the insertion of page 8A.
6. Appears in ms. thus: the fogged̮face of the̮city moon,
7. Catchword deleted (along with the preceding word "now") upon the removal of page 8B. "If" was then inserted as the catchword for page 8A.
8. The passage from ". . . . This" through "Hyde" is canceled both by a loop like the one on page 8 and by a large X inscribed within the loop and extending almost to its four corners.

WILLIAM VEEDER

in the by street of shops. ~~He saw it thus under all sorts of illumination, and occupied by all kinds of passing tenants.~~ He made long stages on the pavement opposite, studying the bills of fare stuck on the sweating windows of the cookshop, reading the labels on the various lotions or watching the bust of the proud lady swing stonily round upon him on her ⟨/velvet⟩ pedestal at the perfumers; but ~~all the time~~ ⟨still⟩ with one eye over his shoulder, spying at the door. And all the time the door remained inexorably closed; none entered in, none came ~~forth; it~~ the high tides of the town swarmed close by, but did not touch it. Yet the lawyer was not to be beaten. He had made a solemn agreement with himself, ~~and~~ ⟨to⟩ penetrate this mystery of Mr Hyde. "If he be Mr Hyde," he had thought ⟨/with grim pleasantry⟩, "I shall be Mr Seek." ~~Let him but set eyes upon the man, and he could judge him.~~

And at last his patience was rewarded. It was a fine dry night; frost in the air; the streets as clean as a ballroom floor; the lamps, unshaken by any wind, drawing a regular pattern of light and shadow. By ten o'clock, when the shops were closed, the bystreet was very solitary and, in spite of the low growl of London from all round, very silent ~~to the ear~~. Small sounds carried far; domestic sounds out of the houses were clearly audible on either side of the roadway; and the rumour of the approach of any passenger preceded him by a long ~~way~~ ⟨time⟩. Mr Utterson had been some minutes at his post, when he was aware of an odd, light footstep drawing ~~rapidly~~ near. In the course of his nightly patrols, he had long grown accustomed to the quaint effect with which the footfalls of a single person, while he is still a great way off, ~~spring~~ ⟨suddenly⟩ spring out distinct from the vast hum and clatter of the city. Yet his attention had never before been so sharply and decisively arrested; and it was with a strong, superstitious prevision of success that he withdrew into the entry of the court.

The steps drew swiftly nearer, and swelled out suddenly louder as they turned the end of the street. The lawyer, looking forth from the [10] entry, could soon see what manner of man he had to deal with. He was small and very plainly dressed, and the look of him, even at that distance, went ~~st~~ somehow strongly against the watcher's inclination. But he made straight for the door, crossing the roadway to save time; and as he came, he drew a key from his pocket like one approaching home.

Mr Utterson stepped out and touched him on the shoulder as he passed. "Mr Hyde, I think?"

Mr Hyde shrank back with a hissing intake of the breath. But his fear was only momentary; and though he did not look the lawyer in the face, he answered cooly enough: "That is my name~~, said he.~~ ⟨What do you want?"

"I see you are going in," returned the lawyer. "I am an old friend of Dr Jekyll's—Mr Utterson of Gaunt Street—you must have heard my name; and meeting you so conveniently, I thought you might admit me."

"You will not find Dr Jekyll; he is from home," replied Mr Hyde, blowing in the key. And then suddenly, but still without looking up, "How did you know me?" he asked.

"On your side," said Mr Utterson, "will you do me a favour?"

"With pleasure," replied the other. "What shall it be?"

"Will you look me in the face?" asked the lawyer.

Mr. Hyde appeared to hesitate, and then, as if ~~op~~ upon some sudden reflection, fronted about with an air of defiance; and the pair stared at each other pretty fixedly for ~~some~~ ⟨a few⟩ seconds. "Now I shall know you again," said Mr Utterson. "It may be useful."

"Yes," returned Mr Hyde, "⟨/it is as well we have met;⟩ and à propos, you should have my address." And he gave a number of a street in Soho.

"Good God," thought Mr Utterson, "can he too have been thinking of the will,?" ~~discounting the inheritance~~ ~~But he merely thanked the other and promised to remember it~~ ⟨But he kept his feelings to himself and only grunted in acknowledgment—of the address.⟩

"And now," said the other, "how did you know me?"

"By description," was the reply.

"Whose description?"

"We have common friends," said Mr Utterson.

"Common friends?" echoed ⟨^Mr⟩ Hyde, a little hoarsely. "Who are they?"

"Jekyll, for instance," said the lawyer.

"He never told you," cried Mr Hyde, "never, never told you. I [11] ~~Id~~ did not think you would have lied."

"Come, ~~come,~~" said Mr Utterson, "that is not fitting language."

The other ~~laugh~~ snarled aloud into a savage laugh; and the next moment, with extraordinary quickness, he had unlocked the door and disappeared into the house.

The lawyer stood awhile when Mr Hyde had left him, the picture of disquietude. Then he began slowly to mount the street, pausing every step or two and putting his hand to his brow like a man in mental perplexity. The problem he was thus debating as he walked, was one of a class that is rarely solved. Mr Hyde was pale and dwarfish, he gave an impression of deformity without any nameable malformation, he had a displeasing smile, he had borne himself to the lawyer with a ~~somewhat~~ ⟨sort of⟩ murderous ~~mixture of cowardice and savagery~~ {/mixture} ⟨of timidity and boldness⟩, and he spoke with a husky, whispering and somewhat broken voice; all these were points against him, but not all of these together could explain the hitherto unknown disgust, loathing and fear with which Mr Utterson regarded him. "There must be something else," said the perplexed gentleman. "There is something more, if I could find a name for it. God bless me, the man seems hardly human! Something troglodytic, shall we say? or can it be the old story of Dr. Fell? or is ⟨/it⟩ the mere radiance of a foul soul that thus transpires through, and transfigures, its clay continent? The last, I think; for O my poor old Harry Jekyll, if ever I read Satan's signature upon a face, it is on that of your new friend.

Round the corner from the bystreet, there was a square of ancient, handsome houses, now for the most part decayed from their high estate and let in flats and chambers to all sorts and conditions of men: map-engravers, architects, shady lawyers and the agents of obscure enterprises. One house, however, second from the corner, was still occupied entire; and at the door of this, which wore a great air of wealth and comfort, though it was now plunged in darkness except for the fanlight, Mr Utterson stopped and knocked. A well-dressed, elderly servant opened the door.

"Is Dr. Jekyll at home, Poole?" asked the lawyer.

"I will see, Mr Utterson," said Poole, admitting the visitor, as he spoke, into a large, low-roofed, comfortable hall, paved with flags, warmed (after the fashion of a country house) by a bright, open [12] fire, and furnished with costly cabinets of oak. "Will you wait here by the fire, sir? or shall I give you a light in the dining room?"

"Here, thank you," said the lawyer, and he drew near and leaned on the tall fender. This hall, in which he was now left alone, was a pet fancy of his friend the doctor's; and Utterson himself was wont to speak of it as the pleasantest room in London. But tonight there was a shudder in his blood; ~~his encounter with~~ (the face of) Hyde ~~had thrown him out of gear~~ (sat heavy on his memory); he felt (what was rare with him) a nausea and distaste of life; and in the gloom of his spirits, he seemed to read a menace in the flickering of the firelight on the polished cabinets and the uneasy starting of the shadow on the roof. He was ashamed of his relief, when Poole presently returned to ~~say~~ (announce) that Dr Jekyll was gone out.

"I saw Mr Hyde go in by the old dissecting room door, Poole," he said. "Is that right, when Dr Jekyll is from home?"

"Quite right, Mr Utterson, sir," replied the servant. "Mr Hyde has a key."

"Your master seems to repose a great deal of trust in that young man, Poole," resumed the other musingly.

"Yes, sir, he do indeed," said Poole. "We have all orders to obey him."

"I do not think I ever met Mr Hyde?" asked Utterson.

"O, dear no, sir. He never <u>dines</u> here," replied the butler. "Indeed we see very little of him on this side of the house; he mostly comes and goes by the laboratory."

"Well, good night, Poole."

"Good night, Mr Utterson."

And the lawyer set out homeward with a very heavy heart. "Poor Harry Jekyll," he thought, "my mind mis-gives me ~~you are~~ (he is) in deep waters! ~~That could never be the face of his son, never in this world. No, there is a secret at the root of it; Jekyll~~ (He) was wild when he was young; a long while ago to be sure; but in the law of God, there is no statute of limitations. Ay, it must be that; the ghost of some old sin, the cancer of some concealed disgrace; punishment coming, <u>pede claudo,</u> years after memory has forgotten and self-love condoned the fault." And the lawyer, scared by the [13] thought, brooded awhile on his own past, groping in all the corners of memory, lest by chance some Jack-in-the-Box of an old iniquity should leap to light there. His past was fairly blameless; few men could read the rolls of their life with less apprehension; yet he was humbled to the dust by the many ill things he had done, and raised up again into a sober and fearful gratitude by the many that he had so near to doing yet avoided. And then by a return on his former subject, he conceived a spark of hope. "This Master Hyde, if he were studied," thought he, "must have secrets of his own: black secrets, by the look of him; secrets compared to which poor Jekyll's worst would be like sunshine. ~~I think we might turn the tables; I am sure, if Harry will but let me, that I ought to try. For~~ tThings cannot continue as they are. It turns me cold to think of this creature stealing like a thief to Harry's bedside ~~and~~; poor Harry, what a wakening! And the danger of it; for if this Hyde suspects the existence of the will, he may grow impatient to inherit. Ay, I must put my hand ⟨shoulder⟩ to the wheel, if Jekyll will but let me," he added, "if Jekyll will only let me." For once more he saw before his minds eye, as clear as a transparency, the strange clauses of the will.

~~But he made up his mind to even to stretch friendship in so good a cause, and on the first occasion~~

Dr Jekyll was quite at ease

A fortnight later, by excellent good fortune, the doctor gave one of his pleasant dinners to some five or six old cronies, all intelligent, reputable men and all judges of good wine; and Mr Utterson so contrived that he remained behind after the others had departed. This was no new arrangement, but a thing that had befallen many scores of times. Where Utterson was liked, he was liked well. Hosts loved to detain the dry lawyer, when the light-hearted and the loose-tongued had already their foot on the threshold; they liked to sit awhile in his unobtrusive company, practising for solitude, sobering their minds in the man's rich silence after the expense and strain of gaiety. To this rule, Dr Jekyll was no exception; and as he now sat on the opposite side

NOTEBOOK DRAFT

[33] ten[9] years old. For ten years he had kept that preposterous document in his safe; and here was the first ~~external proof~~ ⟨independent sign⟩ that such a man as Mr Hyde existed.—here, ~~on~~ ⟨from⟩ the lips of a creature who had come to him bleating for help under the most ignoble and deserved misfortunes, he ~~found~~ ⟨heard⟩ the name of the man to whom Henry Jekyll had left everything and whom, ~~in that~~ he named his "friend and benefactor." He studied Mr Lemsome covertly. He was ~~still~~ a ~~youngish~~ man of about twenty eight, with a fine forehead and good features; anoemically pale;[10] shielding a pair of ~~faint~~ suffering eyes under blue spectacles; and dressed with that sort of ~~external~~ ⟨outward⟩ decency that implies ⟨/both⟩ a lack of means and a defect of taste. By his own confession, Mr Utterson knew him to be a bad fellow; ~~and in this short scrutiny, he read him through and through~~ ⟨made[11] out very plainly that⟩ ~~him out to be a bad fellow of the~~ he now saw for himself that he was an incurable cad.

"Sit down," said ~~M~~he, "I will take your business."

No one was more astonished than the client; but as he had been speaking uninterruptedly for some three minutes, he set down the success to the score of his own eloquence~~;~~. ~~and~~ There never was a client who did less credit to his lawyer;

9. Stevenson drew a large X from the top to the bottom of this page, canceling the whole passage from "ten" through "might."

10. There is a unique series of nineteen strokes over the first three words of lines 11–13 (shielding . . . means), extending slightly into the left margin. Stevenson seems to have been testing or honing his pen, since pairs of lines are joined on the right side of the configuration, making narrow horizontal V's, in effect, down the passage.

11. Stevenson deleted "read . . . through" and replaced it with "made . . . that"; then he canceled everything from "in" through "the" and continued to the end of the sentence.

WILLIAM VEEDER

but still Mr Utterson stuck to him on the chance that something might
[48] Thereupon,[12] Mr Utterson, conceiving he had done ~~the~~ all and more than could be asked of him, went home to his rooms and lay down upon his bed, ~~mentally~~ ⟨like one⟩ sick. The[13] last words of the public officer had been the last straw on his overtaxed endurance; there was something in the heaving air, ⟨/as of a man who said a pleasant and witty thing⟩ with which that deadly truth had been communicated ~~that~~ finally unmanned the lawyer. He had been dragged all day through scenes and among characters that made his gorge rise; hunting a low murderer, and himself hag-ridden by the thought that this murderer was the chosen heir ⟨^and⟩ the secret ally ~~and the so-called benefactor of the good learned and well-beloved Henry Jekyll~~ ⟨of his friend⟩; and now, at the end of that experience, an honest man and active public servant ⟨/spoke out in words what had been for Mr Utterson the haunting moral and unspoken refrain of the day's journeyings:⟩ ~~tells him with a smile~~ that all men, high and low, are of the same ⟨/pattern⟩. He lay on the outside ~~side~~ ⟨of⟩ his bed in the fall of the foggy night; and ~~he~~ heard the pattering of countless thousands of feet, all, as he now told himself, making haste to do evil, and the rush of the wheels of countless cabs and carriages conveying men ~~to deadly yet~~ ⟨still yet⟩ more expeditiously to sin and punishment; and the horror of that monstrous seething mud-pot of a city, and of that kindred ~~monster~~ monster-man's soul, rose up within ⟨/him⟩ to the

NOTEBOOK DRAFT	PRINTER'S COPY
[58] alive.	
"He must be buried underneath the flags," said Poole.	
~~"He may,"~~ replied the lawyer[14]; "or he may have fled. ~~O!" he cried suddenly, "in what blindman's buff is this in what~~ This is beyond me, Poole. Let us return to the cabinet." ~~They mounted~~	
~~Upstairs, all was as it was~~	
They mounted the star in silence, and looked on every side. At a long table, there were traces of chemical experiments.	[38] There[15] were all signs of a man having made[16] [39] ~~experiments~~ ⟨work⟩,

12. Stevenson drew a single vertical line from the upper right to the lower left of this page, canceling the whole passage from "Thereupon" through "the."

13. Prior to canceling the whole page, Stevenson deleted the sentence from "the" through "lawyer" with horizontal strokes through each line and vertical strokes down both margins.

14. Around the words "replied . . . lawyer" Stevenson has drawn a loop one line of which extends down to the space after "fled," indicating where Stevenson wished the words placed after he deleted "He may."

15. The words preceding "experiments" in this sentence occur on the lost page 38 of the printer's copy, and are recovered from Limedorfer's essay. Readers should be apprised that his transcriptions are not always accurate.

16. The sixteen lines of this page are canceled by a large X extending to the four corners of the passage.

Various measured heaps of some ⟨/white⟩ salt, apparently the same, were laid out on glass saucers a and, these Poole recognized as if for some purpose in which the unhappy man had been interrupted.

various measured heaps of some white salt, apparently the same, being laid out on glass saucers, as if for some ⟨an⟩ experiment in which the unhappy man had been prevented. At another, as has been said, tea was set out The kettle had by this time boiled over; and they were obliged to take it off the fire; but the tea things were still set forth with a comfort and orderliness that was in strange contrast to the tumbled corpse upon the floor. Indeed the Several books were on a shelf beside ⟨near⟩ the fire; one lay beside ⟨beside⟩ the tea things openʝ, and Utterson was amazed ⟨/somewhat surprised [amazed]⟩ to find it /?\ ⟨pious⟩. Next, in the course of their review of the chamber, the searchers came to the cheval glass.

"This glass has seen some queer doings, ⟨sir,⟩ no doubt," whispered Poole.

"And none stranger than itself," echoed the lawyer ⟨/in the same tones⟩. "What did—what did Jekyll do with a glass?"

"I can't tell you ⟨That's what I have⟩ often asked myself," returned the butler.

When they found a prayer in the doctor's writing, very eloquently put in words, but breathing a spirit of despair and horror worthy of the cells of Bedlam, and the sight of this so

On the desk of the business table, among the n/?\i neat array of papers, a very large envelope was uppermost and bore, in Doctor Jekyll's hand, the name of Mr Utterson. The lawyer tore it open, Then and as his hand was shaking with emotion, the enclosures fell to the floor. The first that he was a will, drawn in the same strange terms as the first one, to act as a testament in case of [67] conclusion of what still appeared to me a thing too freakish and irrational ⟨the adventure. As the hours dragged on, and I sat alone in⟩ my consulting room, trying to compose my spirits over a medical journal, an odd I found myself grow steadi more and more attracted to the drawer and at last, undoing the

[43] Square.

sheet, I proceeded to examine the contents. There was first of all a considerable number of powders, ~~neatly~~ ⟨securely⟩ enough made up but ~~still~~ not with the nicety of ~~a~~ ⟨the⟩ dispensing chemist; it was therefore plain that they were of Jekyll's private manufacture; and when I opened the wrappers ⟨~~I qu~~⟩, I found what seemed to me a simple crystalline salt of a white colour. The only other objects in the drawer ~~was~~ ⟨were⟩ a small phial, about half filled with a ⟨/blood⟩ red liquor, and a paper {book} with a series of dates. I took out the glass stopper of the phial and smellt ⟨/, ~~tasted~~⟩ the contents; it was highly pungent, aromatic and burning, ~~too strong a~~ and I seemed to detect the presence of ⟨/both⟩ ether and phosphorous: ~~of~~ ⟨at⟩ the other ingredients I ~~had~~ could make no guess. The dates in the version ⟨book⟩ covered ~~a consider~~ many years, fifteen I think or twenty, but I observed that they had ceased [68] some months before ⟨/that day, or about April 1884⟩. Here and there ~~there~~ were remarks appended, usually not longer than a word: "Double" occurring perhaps six times ~~out~~ ⟨in the course⟩ of several hundred entries; and once very early in the list, and followed by several marks of exclamation, "Total Failure!!!" All this, though I confess it whetted my curiosity, told me little that was definite. If[17] the book were not left in the drawer by

Here I proceeded to examine its contents. The powders ⟨/⟨~~of which there were but 3 or 4~~⟩⟩ were neatly enough made up, but not with the nicety of the dispensing chemist; so that it was plain they were of Jekyll's private manufacture; and when I opened one of the wrappers, I found what seemed to me a simple, crystalline salt of a white colour. The phial, to which I next turned my attention, might have been about half-full of a blood-red liquor, which was highly pungent to the sense of smell and seemed ⟨/to me⟩ to contain phosphorous and some volatile ether. At the other ingredients, I could make no guess. The book was an ordinary version book and contained little but a series of dates. These covered a period of many years, but I observed that the entries ceased nearly a year ago and quite abruptly. Here and there a brief remark was appended to a date, usually no more than a single word: "double" occuring perhaps six times in a total of several hundred entries; and once very early in the list and followed by several marks of exclamation, "total failure!!!" All this, though it whetted my curiosity, told me little that was definite.

17. The cancelation from "If" through "engaged" is a single serpentine line that moves horizontally from "If" through "left," then drops along the right margin to the end of the

accident, it ~~see~~ seemed to prove ⟨/indeed⟩
that Jekyll had been long engaged ~~What~~

could

⟨Here ~~was~~ were⟩ a phial of some tincture, a   Here were a phial of some tincture, a
few papers of salts, and a record   papers of some salt, and a ⟨the⟩ record
apparently of a series of experiments   of a series of experiments
that had ⟨/~~probably~~⟩ led (like too ~~my~~ ⟨many⟩   that had led (like too many
of Jekyll's investigations) to no end of   of Jekyll's investigations) to no end of
practical uselesfulness.~~;~~ ~~but~~ hHow could the   practical usefulness. How could the
presence of these articles in my house   presence of these articles in my house
affect either the honour, the sanity or   affect either the honour, the sanity or
the life of my flighty colleague?   the life of my flighty colleague? ~~and~~ if
I own I began to have misgivings that I had   his messenger could go to one place, why
been wrong directed, and had brought a   could he not go to another? and even
different drawer from the one required.   granting some impediment ~~to that~~, why was
                                                          this gentleman to be received by me in
                                                          secret? The more I reflected, the more
                                                          convinced I grew that I was dealing with a
                                                          case of cerebral disease; and though I
                                                          dismissed my servants to bed, I loaded an old
                                                          revolver that I might ⟨/be found⟩ be in some
                                                          posture of self-defence.

Two o'clock had scarce ~~struck before~~   Twelve o'clock had scarce rung out

rung

over London, ere the ~~bell~~ knocker sounded   over London, ere the knocker sounded
very gently on [69] the door~~;~~ ~~and I, when I~~   very gently on the door. I

had

~~opened it found myself~~ According to my   opened it, of course, myself, and found
reading   ~~almost~~ ⟨a
of Jekyll's letter I had long ago   small man⟩ crouching against the
sent the servant's   pillars
to bed, ~~and was alone~~ and I now ~~anse~~   of a ⟨the⟩ portico.

answered
the summons myself   "Are you come from Doctor Jekyll?" I
                                                          asked
                                                              He told me "yes" by a constrained
                                                          gesture; and when I had bidden him enter, he
                                                          did not obey me without a search backward
                                                          glance into the darkness of the square. There
                                                          was a policeman not far off, advancing with
                                                          his bull's eye open; and at the sight, I
                                                          thought my visitor started and made greater
                                                          haste.

---

line below, then proceeds back along this line from "that" to "in," and then drops along the
left margin to the start of the line below, whence it proceeds forward from "Jekyll" through
"engaged."

and led into the light of the
consulting room, a small man whom

I had certainly never seen before that night.
He was small,
I have said;
he had besides a slight shortening of some of
the cords of the neck which tilted his head
upon one side;
I was struck by his disagreeable
expression,
by the great ⟨his⟩ remarkable combination
of ⟨/great⟩ muscular activity
and ⟨/great, apparent⟩
constitutional debility⌿,
and, ⟨—⟩ last but not least, —
by the curio odd subjective disturbance
caused by his nieghbourhood.
I do not quite kn This ma bore some
resemblance to incipient rigor,

and it was accompanied by a marked
sinking of the pulse; and at the time,
I set it down to some idiosyncratic
personal distaste, and merely wondered
at the acuteness of the symptoms; but
                                    ⟨though⟩
I have now ⟨since had⟩ reason to believe
that the cause to lie much deeper in the
nature of man, and to turn on ⟨some⟩
nobler principles than hinge than the
principle of hatred.
    [70] This person⌿(who had, from
the first moment of his entrance,
fascinated me ⟨^with⟩ what I can only
                                    describe
as a disgustful curiosity) was dressed
in a fashion that would have made an
ordinary person laughable: his clothes,
that is to say, ⟨/although they were made of
the richest and soberest materials,⟩ were
enormously too large for him in every
measurement—the trousers hanging about
his legs and turned ⟨rolled⟩ up to keep them

[44] These particulars struck me, ⟨/I
confess,⟩ dis-agreeably; and as I
followed him into the bright light of the
consulting room, I kept my hand ready on
my weapon. Here, at last, I had the ⟨a⟩
chance of clearly seeing him.
I had never set eyes on him before, so
much was certain. He was small,
as I have said;

I was struck besides with the shocking
expression of his face,
with his remarkable combination
of great muscular activity and lightness
⟨and great,⟩ apparent
debility of constituon,
and—last but not least—
with the odd, sujective disturbance
caused by his nieghbourhood.
This bore some
resemblance to incipient rigor
or what is called goose-flesh;
it ⟨and⟩ was accompanied by a marked
sinking of the pulse⌿. aAt the time,
I set it down to some idiosyncratic,
personal distaste, and merely wondered
at the acuteness of the symptoms; but

I have since had reason to believe
the cause to lie much deeper in the
nature of man, and to turn on some
nobler hinge than the
principle of hatred.
    This person (who had thus, from
the first moment of his entrance, ·
struck in me what I can only describe

as a dis-gustful curiosity) was dressed
in a fashion that would have made an
ordinary person laughable: his clothes,
that is to say, although they were of
rich and sober fabric, were
enormously too large for him in every
measurement—the trouses hanging on
his legs and rolled up to keep them

from the ground—the waist of his coat
below his haunches and the collar ~~low down~~
⟨sprawling wide⟩ upon his shoulders.
Strange to ~~say~~ ⟨relate⟩, this ludicrous
accoutrement ~~was~~ did not
tickle in my chest the nerves of laughter.
Rather, as there was something
abnormal and misbegotten in the very
essence of the creature that now faced
me,—something seizing, surprising
and revolting—this ~~second~~ fresh
disparity seemed but to fit in with and
to reinforce it; {/so that,} to
~~the curiosity as to my visitor's~~ ⟨any
interest in the man's⟩ nature and
character, ~~this even~~ ⟨was now⟩ added
a curiosity as to his origin, his life,
his fortune and his status in the world.

These observations, ~~flashed across me~~
⟨though they have taken so great a space⟩
to be set down in, were yet the work
of a few seconds. My visitor was,
indeed, ~~aflame~~ ⟨on fire⟩ with sombre
excitement.

[71] "Have you got it?" he cried.
"Have you got it?"
and so lively was his impatience that
he even laid his hand upon my sleeve
and tried to shake me.

I put him back; conscious, at his
touch, of a certain icy pang along my
blood. "Come, sir," said I.
"I have not yet
the pleasure of your acquaintance.
Be seated, if you please." And I
showed him an example and sat
down myself in my customary seat
and with as fair an imitation of my
ordinary bearing to a patient,
as the lateness of the hour, the nature
of my preoccupations, and the
horror I had of my visitor, would
suffer me to muster.

"I beg your pardon, Dr Lanyon,"
he replied civilly enough.

"My impatience has shown its heels

from the ground, the waist of the coat
below his haunches, and the collar
sprawling wide upon his shoulders.
Strange to relate, this ludicrous
accoutrement ~~f~~ was far from
tickling the cacchinatory impulse.
Rather, as there was something
abnormal and misbegotten in the very
essence of the creature that now faced
me—something seizing, surprising
and revolting—this fresh
disparity seemed but to fit in with and
to rëinforce it; so that to
my
interest in the man's nature and
character, there was added
a curiosity as to his origin, his life,
his fortune and status in the world.

These observations,
though they have taken so great a space
to be set down in, were yet the work
of a few seconds. My visitor was,
indeed, on fire with sombre
excitement.

"Have you got it?" he cried,
"Have you got it?"
And so lively was his impatience that
he even laid his hand upon my arm
and sought to shake me.

I put him back, conscious at his
touch of a certain icy pang along my
blood. "Come, sir," said I.
"You forget. ⟨/that⟩ I have not yet
the pleasure of your [45] acquaintance.
Be seated, if you please." And I
showed him an example, and sat
down myself in my customary seat
and with as fair an imitation of my
ordinary manner to a patient,
as the lateness of the hour, the nature
of my prëoccupations, and the
horror I had of my visitor, would
suffer me to muster.

"I beg your pardon, Dr Lanyon,"
he replied civilly enough.
"What you say is very well founded;
and my impatience has shown its heels

to my politeness. I come here
~~on behalf~~ ⟨at the instance⟩
of your colleage, Dr Henry Jekyll,
on a piece of business
of very considerable moment,
and I understood—" he paused and
put his hand to his throat, and I
could see, in spite of his very
collected manner, that he was wrestling
aginst the approaches of
~~globus hystericus~~ ⟨the hysteric ball⟩—
"I understood, a drawer . . ."
    [72] ~~I declare~~ But here I took pity
on ~~the v~~ my visitor's suspense, and
some perhaps on my own growing
curiosity "There it is, sir," said I,
pointing to the drawer where it lay
~~still ⟨on the floor again and co⟩~~
~~covered by the sheet~~ on the floor
behind a table and once again covered
with the sheet.
    He ~~ran~~ ⟨sprang⟩ to it, and then
paused, and laid his hand upon his heart;
I could hear his teeth grate together
/?\ ~~in his jaws~~ with the
⟨/convulsive action⟩ of his jaws; and
his face was ghastly to see.

    "Compose yourself," ~~said~~ I cried.
He turned a dreadful smile to me,
and ~~plucke~~ as if with the decision
of despair, plucked away the sheet.
At the sight of the contents, he uttered
one loud sob of such immense
relief that I sat petrified; and
the next moment, in a voice which was
already fairly well under control,
"Can you lend me a graduated glass?"
he asked.
    I rose from my place with something
of an effort, and gave him what he asked.
    He thanked me with a smiling nod,
~~and poure~~ ⟨measured⟩
[73] out a few minims of the red
tincture, and added one of the powders.
~~The mixture ha ⟨which was at first of a~~

to my politeness. I come here
at the instance
of your colleague, Dr Henry Jekyll,
on a piece of business
of some moment;
and I understood . . ." he paused and
put his hand to his throat, and I
could see, in spite of his
collected manner, that he was wrestling
against the approaches of
the hysteric ball—
"I understood, a drawer . . ."
    But here I took pity
on my visitors suspense, and
some perhaps on my own growing
curiosity. "There it is, sir," said I,
pointing to the drawer, where it lay

on the floor
behind a table and still covered
with ~~a~~ the sheet.
    He sprang to it, and then
paused, and laid his hand upon his heart;
I could here his teeth grate
with the
convulsive action of his jaws; and
his face was ⟨/so⟩ ghastly to see
that I grew alarmed both for his life
and reason.
    "Compose yourself," said I.
He turned a dreadful smile to me,
and as if with the decision
of despair, plucked away the sheet.
At sight of the contents, he uttered
one loud sob of such immense
relief that I sat petrified. And
the next moment, in a voice that was
already fairly well under control,
"Have you a graduated glass?"
he asked
    I rose from my place with something
of an effort and gave him what he asked.
    He thanked me with a smiling nod,
measured
out a few minims of the red
tincture and added one of the powders.

reddish co⟩ ~~effervesced and threw off a little~~
~~vapour, while ⟨and⟩ he stood and looked~~
~~watched its metama~~
The mixture,
which was at first of a reddish ~~colour~~
⟨hue⟩, began, in proportion as the
crystals melted, to e brighten in colour,
to effervesce ⟨/audibly⟩, and to throw
off small fumes of vapour↕. sSuddenly,
⟨^and⟩ at the same moment, the
ebullition ceased and the compound
changed to a dark purple, which faded
again more slowly to a waterish green.
My visitor, who had watched these
metamorphoses with a keen eye,
smiled, set down the glass upon the
table, and then turned and looked at
me with a great air of scrutiny
and hesitation.
 "And now," said he, "to settle what
remains. Will you be wise? will you be
guided ~~by m~~? will you suffer me to
take this glass in my hand and
to go forth from your house without
more parley? or has the ~~evil~~ greed of
curiosity too much command ⟨/of⟩ you?
~~Spea~~ Think before you answer, for it shall
be done as you decide↕. aAs you shall
decide, you shall be left here ⟨/as you were
before ~~and~~ and⟩ niether wiser nor

      ~~unhappier,~~
⟨richer,⟩ ~~as you may~~ ⟨unless the sense⟩
[74] {~~the~~} of a great service ⟨/rendered⟩
to a man in mortal distress may be
counted as a kind of riches of the soul↕
oOr, if you shall so prefer to choose,
a new province of knowledge and new
avenues to power and fame shall be laid
open to you here, in this room, ~~and~~ upon the
instant, and your sight shall be blasted
by a ⟨/prodigy to⟩ stagger the unbelief
of Satan."
 "Sir," said I, ⟨I⟩a affecting a coolness
that I was far from ~~really~~ ⟨truly⟩ possessing.

The mixture,
which was at first of a reddish
hue, began, in proportion as the
crystals melted, to brighten in colour,
to effervesce audibly, and to throw
off small fumes of vapour. Suddenly
and at the same moment, the
ebullition ceased and the compound
changed to a dark purple, which faded
again more slowly to a watery green.
My visitor, who had watched these
metamorphoses with a keen eye,
smiled, set down the glass upon the
table, and then turned and looked upon
me with an air of scrutiny.

 "And now," said he, "to settle what
remains. Will you be wise? will you be
guided? will you suffer me to
take this glass in my hand and
[46] to go forth from your house without
further parley? or has the greed of
curiosity too much command of you?
Think before you answer, for it shall
be done as you decide. As you
decide, you shall be left as you were
before, and niether richer nor

wiser, unless the sense
of ~~a great~~ service rendered
to a man in mortal distress may be
counted as a kind of riches of the soul.
Or, if you shall so prefer to choose,
a new province of knowledge and new
avenues to fame and power shall be laid
open to you, here, in this room, upon the
instant; and your sight shall be blasted
by a prodigy to stagger the unbelief
of Satan"
 "Sir," said I, affecting a coolness
that I was far from truly possessing,
"you speak enigmas, and you will perhaps
not wonder that I hear you with no very
strong impression of belief↕. But

"I have gone rather too far in this most inexplicable piece of work, to pause before I see the end."

"It is well⁄," replied my visitor. "Lanyon, you remember
your vows: what follows is under the seal of our profession. And now, sir, you who have been so long bound to the most narrow and material views, you who have so obstinat denied the virtue of transcendental medicine, you ⟨/who⟩ have derided your superiors—behold!"

He put the glass to his lips and drank at one gulp. A cry followed,
he reeled, staggered, clutched at the table and held on, staring before [75] him with
congested ⟨injected⟩ eyes, gasping with open mouth; and as I looked, there came, I thought, a change—he seemed to swell— his face became suddenly black and the features seemed to melt and change— and the next moment, I had sprung to my feet and leaped ⟨staggered⟩ back against the wall, with my arm raised as if to shield me from that prodigy, my mind submerged in consternation and. "O God!" I screamed and "O God!" again and again; for there before my eyes, a little ⟨—⟩ pale, and shaken, and half fainting, and goping before him with his hands, like a man restored from death—there stood with his firm stature and Henry Jekyll! The other, the ghost, the double, the unutterable spectre that had drunk the potion, was gone from before me, and there, in his place, was Henry Jekyll!

What he told me in the next hour, I cannot bring my mind to place on paper. In spite of what I saw, my mind revolts from against belief; the shock of that moment has, I feel sure,

struck at the very roots of my life, but it has not a

I have gone too far in the way of inexplicable services, to pause before I see the end.

"It is well," replied my visitor, with a kind of "Lanyon, you remember your vows: what follows is under the seal of our profession. And now, you who have so long been bound to the most narrow and material views, you who have denied the virtue of transcendental medicine, you who have derided your superiors—behold!"

He put the glass to his lips and drank at one gulp. A cry followed;
he reeled, staggered, clutched at the table and held on, staring with

congested ⟨injected⟩ eyes, gasping with open mouth; and as I looked there came, I thought, a change—he seemed to swell— his face became suddenly black and the features seemed to melt and alter— and the next moment, I had sprung to my feet and leaped back against the wall, my arm raised to to shield me from that prodigy, my mind submerged in consternation ⟨terror⟩. "O God!" I screamed, and "O God!" again and again; for there before my eyes—pale and shaken, and half fainting, and groping before him with his hands, like a man restored from death—there stood Henry Jekyll!

What he told me in the next hour, I cannot bring my mind to set on paper. I saw what I saw, I heard what I heard, and my soul sickened at it; and yet now when that sight has melted from my eyes, I ask myself if I believe it, and I cannot answer. My life is shaken to its roots;
sleep has left me; the deadliest terror

bowed the pride of my [76] scepticism;

I shall die,
but I shall die incredulous.
As for the moral turpitude that man
unveiled to me,

it is matter that I disdain
to handle.
He found me an elderly, a useful and a
happy man; that he has blighted and
shortened what remains to me of life,
is but a small addendum to the monstrous
tale of his misdeeds.

Hastie Lanyon.

Henry Jekyll's Full Statement of the Case

======================

I was born in the year 1830 to a good
fortune, endowed ⟨/besides⟩ with
good parts and much application,
but with such as might justify the highest
flights of ambition,
inclined by nature to industry, fond
of the respect of my fellow m ⟨the wise
and good⟩ among cree ⟨my⟩ fellow men,
and thus, ⟨/as⟩ it might have been
supposed, with every g promise and
                                    guarantee
of an honourable and distinguished future.
From a very early age, however, I became
add ⟨/in secret⟩ the slave of
disgraceful pleasures;
my life was double; outwardly absorbed
in scientific toil, and, not ju?
never indifferent to any noble opinion cause
an

of the sits by me at all hours of the day and
night; I feel that my days are
numbered, and that I shall ⟨must⟩ die;
and yet I shall die incredulous.
As for the moral turpitude that man
unveiled to me,
even with tears [47] of penitence, even
kneeling at my feet, and covering my hands
with his abhorred caresses,
I cannot, even in memory, dwell on it
without a start of horror.
I will say but one thing, Utterson,
and that (if you can bring your mind to
credit it) will be more than enough.
The creature who crept into my house
that night was, on Jekyll's own confession,
known by the name of Hyde and now
hunted for in every corner of the land as the
murderer of Carew.

Hastie Lanyon.

Henry Jekyll's Full Statement of the Case

======================

I was born in the year 18— to a large
fortune, endowed besides with
excellent parts,

inclined by nature to industry, fond
of the respect of the wise
and good among my fellow men,
and thus, as might have been
supposed, with every guarrantee

of an honourable and distinguished future.
From an early age, however, I became
in secret the slave of
certain appetites
⟨/¹⁸ and indeed the worst of my faults
was a certain impatient gaiety of
disposition, such as has made the
happiness of many, but such as I found it

18. The words "and . . . pleasures" are written in a six-line vertical block down the
upper third of the left margin.

and when I f reached years of
reflection, and began to look
round me and [77] take note of my
progress and position in the world, I
found myself stood al deeply committed
to a profound duplicity of life. On the
one side, I was what you have known
me,
a man of distinction, immersed in toils,
open to generous sympathies,
never slow to befriend struggling
virtue,
never backward in an honourable
cause; on the other,
as soon as night had fallen

and I could shake off my
friends, the iron hand of
indurated habit plunged me once again
into the mire of my vices. I will
trouble you with these no further than
to say that they were at once
criminal in the sight of the law and
abhorrent in themselves. They cut me
off from the sympathy of those whom I
otherwise respected;

and with even a deeper trench than in
the majority of men, severed the
⟨those⟩ provinces of good and ill which

---

hard to reconcile with my imperious desire
to carry my head high, and wear a more than
commonly grave countenance before the
public. Hence it came about that I concealed
my 'pleasures');
and ⟨/that when⟩ I reached years of
reflection, and began to look
round me and take note ⟨stock⟩ of my
progress and position in the world, I
stood already committed
to a profound duplicity of life. On[19] the
one side, I was what you have known
me,
a man of some note, immersed in toils,
open to ⟨/all⟩ generous sympathies,
never slow to befriend struggling
virtue,
never backward in an honour
⟨the cause⟩ of honour; on the other,
as soon as night released me
from my engagements and covered ⟨hid⟩
me from the espial ⟨notice⟩ of my
friends, the iron hand
indurated habit plunged me again
into the mire of my vices. I will
trouble you with these no further than
to say that they were, at that period,
no worse than those of many who have
lived and died with credit. It was rather
the somewhat higher aspirations of my
life by daylight ⟨/[20]Many a man would have
even blazoned such irregularities as I was
guilty of; but from the high views of conduct
[that I had] set before me I regarded and hid
them with an almost morbid sense of shame,
and it was thus rather the exacting nature of
my aspirations⟩ than any particular
degradation in my faults, that made me what
I was;
and with even a deeper trench than in
the majority of men, severed ⟨/in me⟩
those provinces of good and ill which

---

19. The passage from "On" through "aspirations" is canceled both by a loop like those
on preceding pages and by an X extending almost to the four corners of the passage.

20. The words "Many . . . aspirations" are written in a six-line vertical block down the
middle third of the left margin.

divide and compound man's dual nature.
In thiese case, I was driven to reflect ~~more~~
deeply and inveterately upon that hard
law of life, which lies at the root of all
religions and is the
spring of all suffering. Though so
profound
a double-dealer, I was in no sense a
hypocrite; Both sides of me were in
dead
earnest; I was no more [78] myself when I
~~fing~~ laid aside restraint and wallowed in
shame, than when I laboured, in the eye
of day, at the furtherance of knowledge
or the relief of sorrow and suffering.
And it chanced that the ~~very~~ direction of
my scientific investigations, which led
~~entirely~~ ⟨wholly⟩ towards the
transcendental and the mystic,
reacted and shed a strong light on this
consciousness of the perennial war
among my members. With every day,
and from both sides of my intelligence,
the moral and the intellectual, I
drew steadily nearer to that great truth,
by ~~whose~~ ⟨whose⟩ partial discovery
~~of which~~ I have been ~~sent~~ ⟨doomed⟩
to such a dreadful shipwreck:
that man is not truly one, but truly
two.
I say two, because ⟨/the state of⟩ my ⟨/own⟩
knowledge does not pass beyond that point;
others will follow, others will outstrip
me on the same lines; and I hazard the
guess that man will be ultimately
known for a mere polity of multifarious
~~and,~~ incongruous and independent
denizens.
I, ~~upon~~ ⟨for⟩ my part, under the impulse of
~~my own~~ experiences and sufferings, ~~leaned~~
to ~~the moral side,~~
~~and leaned~~ ⟨advanced⟩ infallibly
in one direction ⟨/and in one direction
only:⟩ɟ
[79] it was on the moral side ⟨/and in my
own
case,⟩ that I ⟨/learned to⟩ recognized the

divide and compound man's dual nature.
In this case, I was driven to reflect
deeply and inveterately on that hard
law of life, which lies at the root of
religion and is t one of the most plentiful
springs of distress. Though so
profound
a double-dealer, I was in no sense a
hypocrite; both sides of me were in
dead
earnest; I was no more myself when I
laid aside restraint and plunged in
shame, than when I laboured, in the eye
of day, at the furtherance of knowledge
or the relief of sorrow and suffering.
And it chanced that the direction of
my scientific studies, which led
wholly towards [48] the
mystic and the transcendental,
rëacted and shed a strong light on this
consciousness of the perennial war
among my members. With every day,
and both sides of my intelligence,
the moral and the intellectual, I ⟨/thus⟩
drew steadily nearer to that truth,
by whose partial dis-covery
I have been doomed
to such a dreadful shipwreck:
that man is not truly one, but truly
two.
I say two, because the state of my own
knowledge does not pass beyond that point.
Others will follow, others will outstrip
me on the same lines; and I hazard the
guess that man will ⟨^be⟩ ultimately ~~be~~
known for a mere polity of multifarious,
incongruous and independent denizens.

I for my part, from the nature of
my life,

advanced infallibly
in one direction and in one direction only.

It was on the moral side, and in my own

person, that I learned to recognize the

thorough and primitive duality of man;
I saw that, of the two natures that
contended in the field of my
consciousness, even if I could be rightly
said to be either, it was only because
I was radically both; and from an
early date, even before the course of my
scientific dis-coveries had begun to
suggest the ~~most~~ ⟨/most naked⟩ possibility
of such a miracle, I had ~~begun~~ ⟨learned⟩
to dwell with pleasure ⟨/as a beloved
day-dream⟩ on the thought of the
separation of these elements. If each,
I told myself, could but be housed in
separate identities, life would be
relieved of all that was unbearable;
the unjust might go his way, delivered
from the aspirations and the remorse
of his more perfect twin; and the just
could walk steadfastly and securely on
his upward path,
~~no longer~~ doing the good things
in which he found his pleasure, and no
longer exposed to disgrace and penitence
~~through~~ ⟨by⟩ the hands of this extraneous
                                    evil.
It was the curse of mankind that these
incongruous faggots were thus bound
together—that, in the ~~sensitive~~ ⟨agonised⟩
womb of /?\ consciousness, these polar
twins should be continuously struggling.
How, then, were they [80] dissociated?
    I was so far in my reflections when,
as I have said, a side-light began to shine
upon the subject from ~~my~~ ⟨the⟩ laboratory
table. I began to perceive, more deeply
than it has ever yet been stated, the
trembling immateriality, the
mist-like transience, of this seemingly
so solid body in which we /?\ walk attired.
Certain ~~potent~~ agents I found to have the
power to ~~make~~ shake and to pluck back that
fleshly vestment, even as a wind might
toss the curtains of a ~~tent~~ pavilion. For
two good reasons, I will not enter
deeply into this scientific branch of
my confession. First, because I have

thorough and primitive duality of man;
I saw that, of the two natures that
contended in the field of my
consciousness, even if I could rightly be
said to be either, it was only because
I was radically both; and from an
early date, even before the course of my
scientific dis-coveries had begun to
suggest the most naked possibility
of such a miracle, I had learned
to dwell with pleasure, as a beloved
daydream, on the thought of the
separation of these elements. If each,
I told myself, could but be housed in
separate identities, life would be
relieved of all that was unbearablɇ;
the unjust might go his way, delivered
from the aspirations and remorse
of his more upright twin; and the just
could walk steadfastly and securely on
his upward path,
doing the good things
in which he found his pleasure, and no
longer exposed to disgrace and penitence
by the hands of this extraneous evil.

It was the curse of mankind that these
incongruous faggots were thus bound
together—that in the agonised
womb of consciousness, these polar
twins should be continuously struggling.
How, then, were they dissociated.
    I was so far in my reflections when,
as I have said, a side light began to shine
upon the subject from the laboratory
table. I began to perceive more deeply
than it has ever yet been stated, the
trembling immateriality, the
mist-like transience, of this seemingly
so solid body in which we walk attired.
Certain agents I found to have the
power to shake and to pluck back that
fleshly vestment, even as a wind might
toss the curtains of a pavilion. For
two good reasons, I will not enter
⟨/deeply⟩ into this scientific branch of
my confession. First, because I have

been made to learn that the doom and
burthen of our life is riveted
forever on man's shoulders, and ~~that~~
when the attempt is made to cast
it off, it but returns upon us with
more unfamiliar and more awful
pressure. Second, because, as my
narrative will make alas! too evident,
my dis-coveries were incomplete./
~~and my action~~
Enough, then, that I not [81] only
recognized my natural body for the mere
aura and effulgence of certain of the
powers that made up my spirit, but
dis-covered an agent
by which these powers might be
dethroned from their supremacy, and a
second form and countenance substituted,
none the less natural to me/although
it was the expression, and bore the
mark, of lower elements in my soul.
~~The efficacy of this drug was but to shake the~~
~~immaterial and ineffable~~

    I hesitated long before I put this theory
to the dire test of practise. I knew well
that I risked death, for any drug
that so potently controlled and shook
the ~~immaterial~~ ⟨frail⟩ pillars of identity,
might, ~~at~~ ⟨by⟩ the least scruple of an
overdose or at the least inopportunity
in the ~~th~~ moment of exhibition, utterly
~~destroy~~ ⟨/blot out⟩ that ~~thin~~ ⟨immaterial⟩
tabernacle which I looked to it to change.
But the temptation was too great.

I had long since prepared my tincture~~s~~,
though it was the work of years of killing
            study;
I purchased at once from a ~~great~~ ⟨firm of⟩
wholesale chemists, a large quantity of a
particular salt which I knew, by my
[82] experiments to be the last ingredient
⟨/required⟩; and late one accursed night, I
compounded the elements, watched them
boil and smoke together in the glass,
and when the ebullition had subsided,

been made to learn that the doom and
burthen of ~~man's~~ ⟨our⟩ life is bound
forever on man's shoulders, and [49]
when the attempt is made to cast
~~if~~ ⟨it⟩ off, it but returns upon us with
more unfamiliar and more awful
pressure. Second, because as my
narrative will make alas! too evident,
my dis-coveries were incomplete.

Enough, then, that I not only
recognized my natural body for the mere
aura and effulgence of certain of the
powers that made up my spirit, but
managed to compound a drug
by which these powers should be
dethroned from their supremacy, and a
second form and countenance substituted,
none the less natural to me because
they were the expression, and bore the
stamp, of lower elements in my soul.

    I hesitated long before I put this theory
to the test of practise. I knew well
that I risked death; for any drug
that so potently controlled and shook
the very fortress of identity,
might by the least scruple of an
overdose or at the least inopportunity
in the moment of exhibition, utterly
blot out that immaterial
tabernacle which I looked to it to change.
But the temptation of a dis-covery so
singular and profound, ⟨/at last⟩ overcame
the suggestions of alarm.
I had long since prepared my tincture;

I purchased at once, from a firm of
wholesale chemists, a large quantity of a
particular salt which I knew, from my
experiments, to be the last ingredient
required; and late one accursed night, I
compounded the elements, watched them
boil and smoke together in the glass,
and when the ebullition had subsided,

with a strong glow of courage, drank
off the potion.

    The most ~~deadly~~ ⟨racking⟩ pangs
                       succeeded:
a grinding in the bones,
~~an unexampled sickness~~
deadly nausea, ⟨/and⟩ a horror of the spirit
that cannot be exceeded at the hour of
birth or death; then these agonies began
rapidly to subside, and I came to myself,
as if out of a great sickness~~,~~. There was
something strange in my sensations,
something incredibly new~~,~~ and, from
its very novelty, incredibly sweet.
I felt ~~youngest~~ younger, ~~I felt~~
lighter, happier in body; ~~in mind~~ ⟨within⟩,
I was conscious of a heady recklessness,
a current of disordered ⟨/sensual⟩ images
running like a mill race ⟨/in my
~~imagination~~ fancy⟩, a solution of the bonds
                             of
obligation, an unknown but not an
innocent freedom of the soul. I knew
myself, at the first touch of this new
life, to be more wicked, tenfold more
wicked, sold a slave to my original evil;
and the thought, in that moment, braced
[83] and delighted me like wine. I stretched
out my hands,

and ~~lo~~ then I was suddenly
aware that I had lost in stature.

    There was no mirror, at that date,
in my cabinet; but the night was far gone

~~into~~ into the morning~~,~~—the morning,
black as it was, was nearly ripe for
the conception of the day—the inmates
of my house were locked in the most
rigorous ~~hours~~ ⟨hours⟩ of slumber; and I
determined, flushed as I was with hope
and triumph, to venture in my new shape
~~into~~ ⟨/as far as to⟩ my bedroom. I crossed the
yard, ~~and I remember well with what a~~

with a strong glow of courage, drank
off the potion.

    The most racking pangs succeeded:

a grinding in the bones,

deadly nausea, and a horror of the spirit
that cannot be exceeded at the hour of
birth or death. Then these agonies began
swiftly to subside, and I came to myself
as if out of a great sickness. There was
something strange in my sensations,
something indescribably new and, from
its very novelty, incredibly sweet.
I felt younger,
lighter, happier in body; within
I was conscious of a heady recklessness,
a current of disordered sensual images
running like a mill race in my
fancy, a solution of the bonds of

obligation, an unknown but not an
innocent freedom of the soul. I knew
myself, at the first breath of this new
life, to be more wicked, tenfold more
wicked, sold a slave to my original evil;
and the thought, in that moment, braced
and delighted me like wine. I stretched
out my hands, exulting in the freshness
of these sensations;
and in the act, I was suddenly
aware that I had lost in stature.

    There was no mirror, at that date,
in my room; ~~but the night was far gone~~ ⟨that
which stands beside [50] me⟩ as I write,
was brought there later on and for the
very purpose of these transformations.
The night, however, was far gone
into the morning—the morning,
black as it was, was nearly ripe for
the conception of the day—the inmates
of my house were locked in the most
rigorous hours of slumber; and I
determined, flushed as I was with hope
and triumph, to venture in my new shape
as far as to my bedroom. I crossed the
yard,

wherein the constellations looked down
upon me, I could have thought, with
wonder, the first creature of the sort
that their eternal vigilance
had yet dis-closed to them; I stole through
the corridors, a thief in my own house;
and coming ~~at last~~ to my room, I saw
for the first time the appearance of
Edward Hyde.

I speak now by theory.

The evil side of my nature, to which I
had now transferred the stamping
efficacy, was probably less robust and less
developed [84] than the good, which I had
just

deposed⌐. ~~that~~ On the other hand, in my
life which had been, after all, nine tenths
a life of effort, virtue and control, it had
been much less exercised and much less
exhausted. And hence, as I think, it came
⟨/about⟩ that Edward Hyde was so much
smaller, slighter and younger than
Henry Jekyll. Even as ~~the~~ good shone upon
the countenance of the one, evil was
~~written~~ written broadly and plainly on the
face
of the other. Evil⌐besides,—which I must
still believe to be the infernal and the
~~mortal~~ ⟨lethal⟩ side of man—had ~~presented~~
⟨left⟩
on ~~the~~ ⟨that⟩ body ~~the~~ evidences of
deformity
and decay. And yet when I looked upon that
ugly ~~and image~~ ⟨idol⟩ in the glass, I was
conscious of no repugnance, rather of a
⟨/leap of⟩ welcome.⌐ ⌐This, too, was myself⌐
i⌐It seemed natural and human⌐. ~~to me~~ i⌐In my
eyes, it ~~was ⟨bore⟩, and I still consider it to be~~
bore ~~an~~ a livelier image of the spirit, it
seemed more express and single, than the
imperfect and divided countenance ~~that~~ I
~~was~~ had been hitherto accustomed to call
mine.

wherein the constellations looked down
upon me, I could have thought, with
wonder, the first creature of that sort
that their ~~eternal~~ ⟨unsleeping⟩ vigilance
had yet dis-closed to them; I stole through
the corridors, a stranger in my own house;
and coming to my room, I saw
for the first time the appearance of
Edward Hyde.

~~What here follows is not so much a
narrati~~ ⟨I must here speak by theory alone,
saying not that which⟩ I know, but that
which I suppose to be most probable.
The evil side of my nature to which I
⟨^had⟩ now transferred the stamping
efficacy was less robust and less
developed than the good which I had just

deposed. And again, in the course of my
life which had been after all, nine tenths
a life of effort, virtue and control, it had
been much less exercised and much less
exhausted. And hence, as I think, it came
about that Edward Hyde was so much
smaller, slighter and younger than
Henry Jekyll. Even as good shone upon
the countenance of the one, evil was
written broadly and plainly on the
face
of the other. Evil, besides (which I must
still believe to be the
lethal side of man) had left

on that body an imprint of deformity

and decay. And yet when I looked upon that
ugly idol in the glass, I was
conscious of no repugnance, rather of a
leap of welcome. This, too, was myself.
It seemed natural and human. In my
eyes it
bore a livelier image of the spirit, it
seemed more express and single, than the
imperfect and divided countenance, I had
been hitherto accustomed to call mine.

And in so far I was doubtless
[85 missing]

And in so far I was doubtless right, I
have observed that when I wore the
semblance of Edward Hyde, none could
come near to me at first without a visible
mis-giving of the flesh. This, as I take it, was
because all human beings, as we meet them,
are commingled out of good and evil; and
Edward Hyde, alone in the ranks of
mankind, was pure evil.

I lingered but a moment at the mirror: the
second and conclusive experiment had yet to
be attempted; it yet remained to be seen if I
had lost my identity beyond redemption and
must flee before daylight from a house that
was no longer mine; and hurrying back to
my cabinet, I once more prepared and drank
the cup, once more suffered [51] the pangs of
dissolution, and came to myself once more
with the character, the stature and the face
of Henry Jekyll.

That night I had come to the fatal
crossroads. Had I approached my dis-covery
in a more noble spirit, had I risked the
experiment while under the empire of
generous or pious aspirations, all ~~might~~
⟨must⟩ have been otherwise, and from these
agonies of death and birth, I had come forth
ian angel instead of a fiend. The drug had no
dis-criminating action; it was niether
diabolic ~~and~~ nor divine; it but shook the
doors ~~of the prison and let forth (and broke
the seals, and)~~ of the prisonhouse of my
disposition; and like the ~~prisoners~~ ⟨captives⟩
of Philippi, that which ~~lay~~ ⟨stood⟩ within ~~in
tr~~ ran forth. At that ~~time~~ ⟨hour⟩ my virtue
slumbered; my evil, kept awake by ambition,
was alert and swift to seize the occasion; and
the thing that was projected was ~~thus~~
Edward Hyde. Hence, although I had now
two characters as well as two
appearances, one was wholly evil, and
the other was still
the old Henry Jekyll,
that incongruous compound of whose
reformation and improvement I had
already learned to despair.

[86] side unchastened;
and although I had now indeed
two characters as well as two
appearances, the one was wholly evil, and
the other was still
the old Henry Jekyll of the past,
that incongruous compound of whose
reformation and improvement I had
already learned to despair.

You can see now what
was the result; for days, I would, /?\ /?\
⟨as of yore,⟩ pursue and obey
my better ~~nature~~ ⟨instincts⟩; and
then when evil triumphed, I would again
                                    drink
the cup and, impenetrably disguised as
                        ~~Henry~~
⟨Edward⟩ Hyde, pass ⟨/privately⟩ out of the
laboratory door and roll myself in infamy.
    The temptation of my present
power can hardly
be overestimated. As ~~Henry~~ ⟨Edward⟩
                        Hyde/(for
I had so dubbed ~~myself~~ ⟨/my second self
                        (—God
help me!—⟩ in pleasantry), I was secure of
an immunity that never ~~man~~ before was
attained by any criminal/. tThink of it—I
did not exist! Let me but escape into my
laboratory door, give me but a second to
                        ⟨/mix &⟩
swallow ~~that~~ the draught that I had always
standing ready, and whatever I~~he~~ had done,
                        Edward
Hyde had vanished like a wreath of smoke,
and there, in his stead, quietly at home and
                        ~~burning~~
[87] trimming the midnight lamp in his
laborious study, was the well-known, the
spotless, the benevolent and the beloved
Do~~e~~⟨r⟩ Jekyll!
    I made my preparations with the most
studious care.

I announced to my servants that a Mr.
Hyde ~~had full li~~ (whom I described) had
full liberty and power about the house;
and to parry mishaps,
I even called and introduced ~~myself~~
⟨/and made myself a familiar object,⟩
in my second character. I drew up
the will to which you so much objected;

The
movement was thus wholly toward the
worse.
    Even at that time, I had not yet
conquered my aversion to the dryness

of a life of study. I would still be

merrily disposed at times; and as my
pleasures were (to say the least)
undignified, ~~they had become~~ ⟨and I was

~~both~~ [not only] well known⟩ and highly

considered, but growing towards the

elderly man, this incoherency of my life
was daily growing more unwelcome.
It was ~~by this that~~ ⟨on this side⟩ that my
new power tempted me until I fell in
slavery. ~~I had now at hand an

impenetrable disguise;~~ I had but to drink
~~my~~ ⟨the⟩ cup, to doff at once the ~~too well

known and too~~ ⟨body of the noted

professor⟩, and to assume ~~that~~, like a
thick cloak, that of Edward Hyde. I
smiled at the notion; it seemed ~~at~~ to me at
the time to be humourous;
and
I made my preparations with the most
studious care.
I took ~~th~~ and furnished that house in Soho,
to which Hyde was tracked by the police;
and engaged as housekeeper a creature
whom I well knew to be silent and
unscrupulous. On the other side, ~~to parry~~
⟨I announced⟩ to my servants that a Mr
Hyde (whom I described) was to have
full liberty and power about my house
in the square; and to parry mishaps,
I even called
and made myself a familiar object,
in my second character; I next drew up
that will to which you so much objected;

so that if anything befell me in the character of Doctor Jekyll, I could enter upon that of Edward Hyde without pecuniary loss. And thus fortified as I

                proudly
supposed on every side, I began to plunge into a career of cruel, soulless and degrading vice.

so that if anything befell me in the person of [52] Doctor Jekyll, I could enter on that Edward Hyde without pecuniary loss. And thus fortified, as I

supposed, on every side, I began to profit by the strange immunities of my position.

Men have before hired bravos to transact their crimes, while their own person and reputation sat under shelter. I was the first that ever did so for his pleasures⟨. I was the first that reconciled liberty and respectability ⟨plodding [/the while] in the public eye, with my load of respectab [/genial]⟩. I was the first that could thus plod in the ⟨/public⟩ eye with a load of genial respectability, and in a moment, like a schoolboy, strip off these lendings and spring headlong into the sea of liberty. But for me, in my impenetrable mantle, the safety was complete, and I could snap my fingers at the. Think of it—I did not even exist! Let me but escape into my laboratory door, give me but a second or two to mix and swallow the draught that I had always standing ready; and whatever he had done, Edward Hyde would pass away like the stain of breath upon a mirror, and there in his stead, quietly at home and, trimming the midnight lamp in his laborious study, a man who could afford to laugh at suspicion, would be Henry Jekyll.

The pleasures which I made haste to seek in my disguise⟨were, as I have said, undignified. But I was now trusting ⟨to the guidance⟩ the foul part of me abroad I would scarce use a harder term; but in the hands of Edward Hyde, they soon began to turn towards the monstrous. Into the details of this fall, I will not When I returned ⟨/would come back⟩ from these excursions, I soon began to be plunged into a kind of wonder at my vicarious depravity. This familiar that I called out of my own soul, and sent forth alone to ⟨^do⟩ his good good pleasure, was a being inherently malign and villainous; his

every act and thought self centered/ and that
on the lowest ⟨on self; drinking pleasure⟩
with bestial avidity from any degree of
torture to another; relentless like a man of
stone. I cannot deny that Henry Jekyll was
⟨stood⟩ at times aghast before and at times
secure to ⟨the acts of Edward Hyde;⟩ but the
situation was apart from ordinary laws/,
and as time went I grew more and more
⟨insidiously relaxed the grasp of conscience⟩.
It was Hyde, after all, and Hyde alone, that
was guilty. Jekyll was no worse; he awoke
again to his good qualities seemingly
unimpaired; he woke to a fresh ⟨would even
make⟩ haste, where it was possible, to rep
undo the evil of the other ⟨/done by Hyde⟩.
And thus his conscience slumbered.

Into the details of this my shame,

Into the details of the infamy at which I
thus connived (for even [53] now I can
scarce grant that I committed it)

I scarce to enter; I mean but
to point out the warnings and the
⟨/successive⟩ steps of my chastisement with
which my chastisement approached me.

I have no design of entering; I mean but
to point out the warnings and the
successive steps with
which my chastisement approached/
and the halter of moral responsibility, which
I had so long eluded, ⟨was⟩ once more
tightened about my neck.

I met with an accident/which I, as it
brought on no consequence, I mention
only in passing: detected in an act of
infamy, I had to bribe a party of young
fools to set me free,

I met with one accident which, as it led to
⟨brought on⟩ no consequence, I mention
only in passing. An act of cruelty to a
child aroused against me the anger of a
passer by, {whom I recognized but the other
day in the person of your kinsman}; the
doctor and the child's family joined him \?/;
there were moments when I feared for my
life; and

and in order to paid
the money ⟨\satisfy their demands,⟩[21]
[88] I had Edward Hyde had to bring them
                                        to the
door, and pay them with a cheque
drawn in the name, of Henry Jekyll.
But this danger was easily eliminated

at last, in order to pacify their too just
resentment,
Edward Hyde had to bring them to the

door, and pay them in a cheque
drawn in the name, of Henry Jekyll.
But this danger was easily eliminated

21. The words "satisfy their demands" appear below this line, the last on the page;
Stevenson drew around them a loop whose top side is the cancellation of "paid the money."

WILLIAM VEEDER

from the future, by opening an account
at another bank in the name of Edward
Hyde himself. And my true punishment
lay in a far different direction.

    About ~~five~~ ⟨a⟩ months before the
Lemsome murder, I had been out
on one of my excursions, ⟨^and⟩ had
returned ~~about three in the morning~~
at a late hour,
and woke the next day in my bed with
somewhat strange sensations. It was in
vain I looked about me; in vain I saw the
handsome furniture and tall proportions
of my room in the square, in vain that I
recognized the ~~carving~~ pattern of the ⟨/bed⟩
curtains and the carving of the ~~bed of~~
~~Henry Jekyll's bed~~ ⟨mahogany posts⟩;
something still kept insisting that I was
not where I thought I was, that I had not
awakened where I seemed to be, but in
the ł iron bed and the somewhat dreary
and exiguous rooms off Gray's Inn Road,
where I was sometimes accustomed to sleep
in my character of ~~Henry Jekyll~~ Edward
                              Hyde.
I smiled [89] to myself and, in my
psychological way, began lazily to
examine into the elements of this ~~ił~~ illusion,
~~dropp~~ occasionally,
even as I did so, dropping
back into a comfortable morning doze.
I was still so engaged when, in one of my
more wakeful moments, my eyes fell upon
my hand. Now the hand of Henry Jekyll,
as we have often jocularly said, was
                         eminently
professional in shape and size; it was
large, firm, white and comely,
the hand of a lady's doctor, in a word.
~~Now~~ ⟨But⟩ the hand which I now saw,
                         clearly
enough, in the yellow light of a
mid-London morning, laying half-shut
~~on~~ among the bed clothes, was lean,

from the future, by opening an account
at another bank in the name of Edward
Hyde himself; and when, by sloping my
own hand backward, I had supplied my
double with a signature, ~~me~~ ⟨I⟩ thought I sat
beyond the reach of fate.
    Some two months before the
murder of Sir Danvers, I had been out
~~for so~~ ⟨on one⟩ of my adventures, had
returned
at a late hour,
and woke the next day in bed with
somewhat odd sensations. It was in
vain I looked about me; in vain I saw the
decent furniture ⟨^and⟩ tall proportions
of my room in the square; in vain that I
recognized the pattern of the bed
curtains and the design of the
mahogany frame;
something still kept insisting that I was
not where I was, that I had not
wakened where I seemed to be, but in

the little room ~~where~~ in ~~the~~ Soho
where I was accustomed to sleep
in the ~~character~~ ⟨body⟩ of Edward Hyde.

I smiled to myself and ~~began~~, in my
psychological way, began lazily to
~~exin~~quire into the elements of this illusion,
occasionally,
even as I did so, dropping
back into a comfortable morning doze.
I was still so engaged when, in one of my
more wakeful moments, my eye fell upon
my hand. Now the hand of Henry Jekyll
⟨as you have often remarked⟩ was

professional in shape and size; it was
large, firm, white and comely.

But the hand which I now saw, clearly

enough, in the yellow light of a
mid-London morning, lying half shut
~~upon~~ ⟨on⟩ the bed clothes, was lean,

corded, knuckly, of a dusky pallour and thickly shaded with a swart growth of hair. It was the hand of Edward Hyde.

I think I must have stared upon it for near a minute, sunk as I was into the mere stupidity of wonder; before terror woke up in my breast ⟨^as⟩ sudden and startling as the crash of cymbals; and bounding from my bed, I rushed to the mirror.
My blood was changed into something [90] exquisitely cold and yet alive.
Yes: I had
gone to bed Henry Jekyll, I had awakened

up²²

Edward Hyde. How was this to be explained? I asked myself; and then, with a another bound of terror—how was it to be remedied? It was well on in the morning; the servants were up; and all my drugs were in the cabinet ⟨^—a long journey⟩ down two pair of stairs, through the back passage, across the open court and through the anatomical theatre, from where I was then standing, horror-struck.
To conceal my face was ⟨/might, indeed, be⟩ possible; but of what use was that, when I was unable to dissemble the alteration in my stature? And then

I remembered (and how I thanked God for it!) that I had prepared ⟨accustomed⟩ my servants to the haunting presence of my second self. I had soon dressed,

had soon passed through the house (where Bradshaw stared and drew back to see the eternal Mr. Hyde at such an hour)

and ten minutes later Dr Jekyll had returned to his own shape and was sitting down to breakfast

corded, knuckly, of a dusky pallor and thickly shaded with a swart growth of hair. It was the hand of Edward Hyde.

I must have stared upon it for near half a minute, sunk as I was in the mere stupidity of wonder, before terror woke up in my breast [54] as sudden and startling as the crash of cymbals; and bounding from my bed, I rushed to the mirror. At the sight that met my eyes, my blood was changed into something exquisitely thin and icey.
Yes, I had
gone to bed Henry Jekyll, I had awakened

Edward Hyde. How was this to be explained? I asked myself; and then, with another bound of terror—how was it to be remedied. It was well on in the morning; the servants were up; all my drugs were in the cabinet—a long journey, down two pair of stairs, through the back passage, across the open court and through the anatomical theatre, from where I stood ⟨was⟩ then standing horror-struck.
It might indeed be possible to hide cover my face; but of what use was that, when I was unable to conceal the alteration in my stature? And then with an overpowering sweetness of relief, it came back upon my mind that the servants were already used to the coming and going of my
second self. I was ⟨had soon⟩ dressed, as well as I was able, in clothes of my own size: had soon passed through the house, where Bradshaw stared and drew back at seeing Mr Hyde at such an hour and in such a strange array;
and ten minutes later, Dr Jekyll had returned to his own shape and was sitting down,

---

22. After deleting "up," Stevenson went back and added an initial "a" to the "wakened."

with a darkened brow,
to make a feint of breakfasting.
Small

with a darkened brow,
to make a feint of breakfasting.
Small [91–102 missing]

Printer's Copy

indeed was my appetite. This inexplicable incident, this reversal of my previous experience, seemed, like the Babylonian finger on the wall, to be spelling out the letters of my judgement; and I began to reflect more seriously than ever before on the issues and possibilities of my double existence. That part of me which I had the power of projecting, had lately been much exercised and nourished; it had seemed to me of late as though the body of Edward Hyde had grown in stature, as though (when I wore that form) I were conscious of a more generous tide of blood; and now began to spy a danger that, if this were much prolonged, the balance of my nature might be permanently overthrown, the power of voluntary change be forfeited, and the character of Edward Hyde become irrevocably mine. The power of the drug had not been always equally displayed. Once, very early in my career, it had totally failed me; since then I had been obliged on more than one occasion to double, and once, with infinite risk of death, to treble the amount; and these rare uncertainties had cast hitherto the sole shadow on my contentment. Now, however, and in the light of that morning's accident, I was led to remark [55] that whereas, in the beginning, ~~the sy~~ ⟨the⟩ difficulty had been to throw off the body of Jekyll, it had ~~lately,~~ ⟨of late,⟩ gradually but decidedly transferred itself to the other side All things therefore seemed to point to this: that I was slowly losing hold of my original and better self, and becoming slowly incorporated with my second and worse.

Between these two, I now felt I had to choose. My two natures had memory in common, but all other faculties were most unequally shared between them. Jekyll⟨,⟩ (who was composite) now with the most sensitive apprehensions, now with a greedy gusto, projected and shared in the pleasures and adventures of Hyde; but Hyde was indifferent to Jekyll, or but remembered him as the mountain bandit remembers the cavern in which he conceals himself from pursuit. Jekyll had more than a father's interest; Hyde had more than a son's indifference. To cast in my lot with Jekyll, was to die to those ~~pleasures~~ ⟨appetites⟩ ~~for~~ which I had long secretly ~~I allowed myself and which had~~ ⟨indulged and ~~recently~~ had of late begun⟩ to pamper. To cast it in with Hyde, was to die to a thousand interests and aspirations, and to become, at a blow and forever, despised and friendless. The bargain might appear unequal; but there was still another consideration in the scales; for while Jekyll would suffer smartingly in the fires of abstinence, Hyde would be not even conscious of all that he had lost. Strange as my circumstances were, the terms of this debate are as old and commonplace as man; much the same inducements and alarms cast the die for every tempted and trembling sinner; and it fell out with me, as it falls with so vast a majority of my fellows, that I chose the better part and was found wanting in the strength to keep it.

Yes, I preferred the elderly and discontented doctor, surrounded by friends and cherishing honest hopes; and bade a resolute farewell to the liberty, the comparative youth, the light step, leaping pulses and ~~cherished~~ ⟨secret⟩ pleasures, that I had enjoyed in the disguise of Hyde. ⟨/²³I made this choice perhaps with some unconscious reservation, for I niether gave up the house in Soho, ~~discharged~~ ⟨nor destroyed⟩ the clothes of Edward Hyde, which still lay ready in my cabinet.⟩ For two months, ⟨/however,⟩ I was true to ~~these~~ ⟨my⟩ determinations; for two months, I led a life of such severity as I had never before attained to, and ~~infor~~ enjoyed the compensations of an approving conscience. But ~~the pas~~ time began at last to obliterate the freshness of my alarm; the praises of conscience began to grow into a thing of course; ⟨/I began to ~~grow~~ be tortured with throes and ~~tor~~ longings as [as] of Hyde struggling after freedom⟩ ~~and the clamour of mortified appetites to grow more instant~~; and at last, in an hour of moral weakness, I once again compounded and swallowed the transforming draught.

[56] I do not suppose that, when a drunkard reasons with himself upon his vice, he is once out of five hundred times affected by the dangers that he runs through his brutish, physical insensibility,; N neither had I, long as I had considered my position, made enough allowance for the complete moral insensibility and insensate readiness to evil, which were the leading characters of Edward Hyde,. and ⟨Yet⟩ it was by ~~that~~ ⟨these⟩ that I was punished. ~~My devil, having been long caged, was in perhaps a stormier disposition (the more inclined to).~~ My devil had been long caged, he came out roaring. I was conscious, even when I took the draught, of a more unbridled, a more furious propensity to ill. It must have been this, I suppose, that ~~rage up~~ ⟨raged [stirred]⟩ in my soul that tempest of impatience with which I listened to the civilities of ~~that~~ ⟨my⟩ unhappy ~~man.~~ victim; I declare at least, before God, ~~th~~ no man morally sane could have been guilty of that crime upon so pitiful a provocation; and that I struck in no more reasonable spirit than that in which ~~the~~ ⟨a⟩ sick child may break a plaything. But I had voluntarily stripped myself of all those balancing instincts, by which even the worst of us continues to walk with some degree of steadiness among temptations; and in my case, to be tempted however slightly, was to fall.

~~With the first blow,~~ ⟨Instantly⟩ the spirit of hell awoke in me and raged. With a transport of glee, I mauled the unresisting body, tasting delight from every blow; ~~until~~ and it was not till weariness had begun to succeed, that I was suddenly ~~pierced~~ ⟨struck⟩ through the heart, in the top fit of my delirium, by a cold thrill of terror. ~~Hyde was quick enough to fear I~~ A mist dispersed dispersed; I saw my life to be forfeit; and fled from the scene of these excesses, ~~glorying in my act and trembling for the in the joys of cruelty~~ ⟨at once glorying and trembling, ~~at once~~ reveling my lust of evil gratified⟩ and stimulated, my love of life screwed to ~~its~~ ⟨the⟩ topmost peg. I ran to the house in Soho,, and (to make assurance doubly sure) destroyed my papers; thence I set out through the lamplit streets, in the same divided ecstasy of mind, gloating ~~ion what I~~ ⟨my crime⟩ ~~and~~, light-headedly devising others ⟨/in the future⟩, and yet still hastening and still ~~glancing~~ ⟨hearkening⟩ ~~behind me~~ ⟨in my wake for⟩ the steps of the avenger. Hyde had a song upon his lips as he compounded the draught, and as he drank it, pledged the

23. The words "I . . . cabinet" are written in a three-line vertical block down the lower half of the left margin.

WILLIAM VEEDER

dead man by name. The pangs of transformation had not done tearing him, before Henry Jekyll, with streaming tears of gratitude and remorse, had fallen upon his knees and lifted his clasped hands to God. The veil of self-indulgence was ~~thus~~ rent from head to foot, ~~and I beheld, in the holy place of~~ I saw my life as a whole: [57] I followed it ⟨/up⟩ from the days of ~~my~~ childhood, when I had walked with my father's hand, ~~to the damned incident ⟨horrors⟩ of that night, and~~ and through the self-denying days of my professional life, to arrive again and again, with the same sense of unreality, at the damned horrors of the evening. I could have screamed aloud; I sought with tears and prayers to smother down the crowd of hideous images and sounds with which my memory swarmed against me; and still, between ~~my~~ ⟨the⟩ petitions, the ugly face of my iniquity stared into my soul. As the acuteness of this remorse began to die away, it was succeeded by a sense of joy.~~; Hyde was thenceforth impossible~~ ⟨The problem of my conduct was solved;⟩. Hyde was thenceforth impossible; whether I would or not, I was compelled to ~~the~~ ⟨my⟩ better life; and O, how I rejoiced to think it! ~~how~~ with what willing humility, I embraced anew the restrictions of natural life! with what sincere renunciation, I locked the door by which I had so often |come| and |gone|, and ~~broke~~ ⟨ground⟩ the key under my heel!

~~And t~~The next day, ~~with~~ ⟨came⟩ the news that the murder had been overlooked, that the guilt of Hyde was patent to the world, and that the victim was a man ~~of~~ ⟨^high in⟩ public estimation. It was not only a crime, it had been a tragic folly. I think I was glad to know it; I think I was glad to have my better impulses thus buttressed and guarded by the terrors of the scaffold.~~—for what temptation could now avail to make me choose the body~~ Jekyll was now my city of refuge; let but Hyde peep out an instant, and the hands of all men ~~were~~ ⟨would be⟩ raised to take ~~him~~ and slay him. ~~The long drawn hum of anger and horror that sounded through society upon the fall of their favorite crew, was~~

I resolved in my future conduct to redeem the past; and I can say with honesty that my resolve was fruitful of some good. You know yourself how earnestly, in the last months of last year, I laboured to relieve suffering; you know that much was done for others, and that the days passed quietly, almost happily for myself. Nor can I truly say that I wearied of this benificent and innocent life; I think instead that I daily enjoyed it more completely; but I was still cursed with my ~~infirmity~~ ⟨duality⟩ of purpose; and as the first edge of my penitence wore off, the lower side of me, so long indulged, so recently chained down, began to growl for license. Not that I dreamed of rescussitating Hyde; the bare idea of that would startle me to frenzy: no, it was in my ⟨/own⟩ person that I was once more tempted to ~~condescend with baser instinc~~ ⟨trifle with my conscience; and it was⟩ as an ordinary secret sinner, ~~and~~ that I at last fell before the assaults of temptation.

[58] There ~~is~~ ⟨/comes⟩ an end ~~of~~ ⟨to⟩ all things; the most capacious measure is filled at last; ⟨/and⟩ this ~~last condescension to~~ ⟨brief condescension to⟩ my evil finally destroyed the balance of my soul. And yet I was not alarmed; the fall seemed natural, like a return to the old days before I had made my discovery. ~~I sat on a~~ ⟨It was a fine,⟩ ~~clear winter's~~ ⟨clear January⟩ day, wet underfoot where the frost had melted ⟨/but cloudless overhead⟩; and the ~~r~~Regent's park was full of winter chirruppings and ⟨/sweet with⟩ Spring odours. I sat in the sun on a bench; the animal within me licking the chops of memory; the spiritual side a little

drowsed, promising subsequent penitence, but not yet moved to begin. After all, I reflected I was like my nieghbours; and then I smiled, comparing myself with other men, comparing my active goodwill with the lazy cruelty of their neglect. And at the very moment of that vainglorious thought, a qualm came upon me, a horrid nausea and the most deadly shuddering. These past away, and left me faint; and then as the in its turn the faintness subsided, I began to be aware of a change in the temper of my thoughts, a greater boldness, a contempt of danger, a solution of the bonds of obligation. I looked down; my clothes hung formlessly on my shrunken limbs; the hand that lay on my knee was corded and hairy. I was once more Edward Hyde. A moment before I had been safe of all men's respect, wealthy, beloved—the cloth laying for me in the dining room at home; and now I was the common quarry of the mankind, hunted, houseless, a known murderer, thrall to the gallows.

My reason wavered, but it did not fail me utterly. I have more than once observed that, in my second character, my faculties seemed sharpened to a point and my spirits more tensely elastic; thus it came about that, where Jekyll perhaps might have succumbed, Hyde rose to the importance of the occasion. My drugs were in one of the presses of my cabinet; how was I to reach them? That was the problem that/ (crushing my temples in my hands) I set myself to solve. The laboratory door I had closed/. iIf I sought to enter by the house, my own servants would consign me to the gallows. I saw I must employ another hand, and thought of Lanyon. How was he to be reached? how persuaded? Supposing that I escaped capture in the streets, how was I to make my way into his presence? and how should I, an unknown and displeasing visitor, prevail on the famous physician to rifle the study of his colleague, Dr Jekyll? Then I remembered that of my original character, one part remained to me: I could write my own hand; and once I had conceived that kindling spark, the way that I must follow became [59] lighted up from end to end.

Thereupon, I arranged my clothes as best I could, and summoning a passing hansome, drove to an hotel in Portland street, the name of which I chanced to remember. At my appearance (which was indeed comical enough, however tragic a fate these garments covered) the driver could not conceal his mirth. I gnashed ⟨/my teeth⟩ upon him with a gust of devilish fury; that and the smile withered from his face, happily for him, yet more happily for myself, for in another instant I had certainly dragged him from his perch. At the inn, as I entered, I looked about with me with so black a countenance as turned ⟨made⟩ the attendants tremble; not a look did they exchange in my presence; but obsequiously took my orders, led me to a sid private room, and brought me wherewithal to write. Hyde in danger of his life was a creature new to me: shaken with inordinate anger, strung to the pitch of murder, lusting to inflict pain. Yet the creature was astute; mastered his fury with a great effort of the will; composed his two important letters, one

NOTEBOOK DRAFT

[103] misfitting clothes rendered me so marked an object that in the streets, that the danger of recognition was increased to

PRINTER'S COPY

to Lanyon and one to Poole; and that he might receive actual evidence of their being posted, sent them out with

WILLIAM VEEDER

something

close on certainty; and it was thus my wish to stay as long as possible in the hotel⸝.

~~where~~ But at length I began to fear ~~that I was~~ shuld be judged excentric, ~~and the~~ ⟨/formed another plan,⟩ called for my bill, ~~paid it,~~ ordered a four wheeler ⟨/to the door⟩, and ~~concealing myself~~ ⟨sitting back⟩ in the ~~darkest~~ corner, had myself driven to a remote part of London.

~~where~~ ⟨Here⟩ I stopped ⟨^the driver⟩ at a door, asked for the first name that came into my head, was of course refused admittance, and was then driven back to the nieghborhood of Cavendish Square not very long before the hour of my appointment.

You know already what occurred.

Lanyon threw me off from him with horror; it scarcely moved

me; I was still so full of my immediate joy. l was already so conscious of the perpetual doom that hung above my head;

and when I returned home, carrying with me my precious drugs

directions that they should be registered.

Thenceforward, he sat all day over the fire in the private room, gnawing his nails; there he dined, sitting alone with his fears, the waiter visibly quailing before his eye; and thence, when the

night was fully come, he set forth in the corner of a closed cab, and was driven to and fro about the streets of the city. He, I say—I cannot say, I. That child of Hell had nothing human; nothing lived in him but fear and hatred. And when at last, thinking the driver had begun to grow suspicious, he discharged the cab and ventured on foot, attired in his misfitting clothes, an object marked out for observation, into the midst of the nocturnal passengers, these two base passions raged within him like a tempest. He walked fast, hunted by his ~~alarms~~ ⟨fears⟩, chattering to himself, skulking through the less frequented thoroughfares, counting the minutes that still divided him from midnight. Once a woman spoke to him, offering, I think, a box of lights. He smote her in the face, and she fled.

When I came to myself at Lanyon's, the

horror of my old friend perhaps affected

me somewhat: I do not know; it was at least but a drop in the sea to the abhorrence ~~w~~ with which I looked back upon th~~is~~ese hours. A [60] change had come over me. It was no longer the fear of the gallows, it was the horror of being Hyde, that racked me. I received Lanyon's condemnation partly in a dream; it was partly in a dream that I came home to my own house and ~~went to~~ ⟨got into⟩ bed. I slept after the

PRINTER'S COPY

prostration of the day, with a stringent and profound slumber⸝which not even the nightmares that wrung me could avail to break. I awoke in the morning shaken, weakened, ~~still haunted by the~~ ⟨but refreshed. I still⟩ hated and feared the thought of the brute that slept within me ~~and; I still,~~ and I had not of course forgotten the appalling dangers of the day before; but I was once more at home, in my own house ⟨^and⟩ close to my drugs; ~~close to the~~ ⟨and gratitude⟩ for my escape ~~was~~ ⟨shone⟩ so strong ~~within me~~ ⟨in my soul⟩ that it almost ~~wore~~ ⟨/rivalled⟩ the brightness of hope.

I was stepping liesurely across the court after breakfast, drinking the chill of the air with pleasure, when I was siezed again with those indescribable sensations that heralded the change; ⟨/and⟩ I had but the time to ~~fly~~ gain the shelter of my cabinet, before I was once again raging and freezing with the passions of Hyde. It took on this occasion a double dose to recall me to myself; and alas, six hours after, as I sat looking sadly in the fire, ~~lashed~~ the pangs returned, and the drug had to be re-administered. In short, from that day forth it seemed only ~~In sh~~ by a great effort as of gymnastics, and only under the immediate stimulation of the drug, that I was able to wear the countenance of Jekyll. ~~Whe~~ At all hours of the day and night, I ~~was~~ ⟨would be⟩ taken with the premonitory shudder; above all, if I slept, or even dosed for a moment in my chair, it was always as Hyde that I awakened. ~~This condemned me to vigils in~~ ⟨Under the strain of this continually⟩ impending doom and by the sleeplessness to which I now condemned ⟨myself⟩, ay, even beyond ~~the~~ /?\ what I had thought possible, ~~Jekyll fell into a state of dazed~~ ⟨to man, I became, in my own person, a creature eaten⟩ up and ~~exhausted~~ ⟨emptied⟩ by fever, languidly weak ⟨^both⟩ in body and mind, and solely occupied by one thought: the horror of my other self. But when I slept, or when the virtue of the medicine wore off, I would leap ~~{almost without transition (for the pangs of transformation grew daily less marked) into~~ ~~that~~ the ~~uncontrollable energies, terrors and angers of that rent~~ possession of a fancy brimming with images of terror, a soul boiling with causeless hatreds, and a body that seemed not strong enough to contain the raging energies of life. The powers [61] of Hyde seemed to have grown with the sickliness of Jekyll. And certainly ~~if~~ the hate that now divided them was equal on each side. With Jekyll, it was a thing of vital instinct~~/~~. ~~h~~He had now seen the full deformity of that creature that shared with him some of the phenomena of consciousness, and was coheir with him to death: ~~more bonds he could not now recognise; the thought of him, like the sight of something odious,~~ ⟨and beyond these links of community, ~~he did not stoop to recognise him⟩⟨killing smell of ammonia⟩~~ which were in themselves ⟨made⟩ the most poignant ⟨/part⟩ of his distress ~~and horror,~~ he ~~but~~ thought of Hyde, for all his ~~ecstasy~~ ⟨energy⟩ of life, as ⟨/of⟩ something ⟨/not only hellish but⟩ inorganic. This was the ~~horror~~ ⟨/shocking thing⟩; that the slime of the pit seemed to utter cries and voices; that the amorphous dust gesticulated and sinned; that what ~~ha~~ was dead, and had no shape, ~~shuld~~ ⟨should⟩ ~~usurped~~ the offices of life. And this again, that that insurgent horror was knit ~~by~~ ⟨to⟩ him closer than a wife, ⟨/closer than an eye⟩; a ⟨and⟩ ~~went to and fro~~ ⟨lay caged⟩ in his ~~bosom~~ ⟨flesh⟩, where he heard it ~~growl~~ ⟨mutter⟩ and felt it ~~wrest~~ struggle to be born; ~~and was at all points conterminous with his life.~~ ⟨and at every hour of weakness, and in the confidence of slumber,⟩ prevailed against him, and deposed him out of life. The hatred of Hyde for Jekyll, was of a different order. His terror of the gallows drove him continually to

WILLIAM VEEDER

commit ~~that~~ temporary suicide, and return to his subordinate station ~~as~~ of a part instead of a person; but he ~~go~~ loathed the necessity, he loathed the despondency into which Jekyll ~~had~~ ⟨was⟩ now fallen, ⟨and⟩ he resented the dislike with which he was ⟨/himself⟩ regarded. Hence the apelike tricks that he would play me, scrawling in my own hand blasphemies ~~upon~~ ⟨on⟩ the pages of my books, burning the letters and destroying the portrait of my father; and indeed, had it not been for his fear of death, he would long ago have ruined himself in order to involve me in the ruin. But his ~~fear~~ ⟨love⟩ of ~~death~~ ⟨life⟩ is wonderful; I go further: ~~I think it touching~~ I, who sicken and freeze at the mere thought of him, when I recall the abjection and passion of this attachment, and when I know how he fears my power to cut him off by suicide, I find it in my heart to pity him.

~~W~~ It is useless, ~~it is loathsome,~~ ⟨/and the time awfully fails me,⟩ to prolong this ~~picture~~ description; no one has ever suffered such ~~a~~ torments, let that suffice; and yet even to this ~~there time~~ ⟨habit⟩ brought—no, not alleviation—but a certain callousness of soul, a certain acquiesence of despair; and my punishment might have gone on for years, but for the last calamity which has now fallen, and which has finally [62] severed me from my own face and nature. My provision (^of) the salt, ~~had~~ which had never been renewed since the ⟨/date of⟩ first experiment, began to run low. I sent out for a fresh supply, and mixed the draught; the ebullition followed, and the first change of colour, not the second; I drank it and it was without efficiency. You will learn from Poole how I have had London ransacked; it was in vain; and I am now persuaded that my first supply was impure, and that it was that unknown impurity which leant efficacy to the draught.

~~Nearly a week has~~ ⟨I hav About a week has⟩ passed, and I am now finishing this statement under the influence of the last of the old powders. This, ⟨/then,⟩ is the last time, short of a miracle, that Henry Jekyll can think his own thoughts or see his own face (now how sadly altered!) in the glass. Nor must I delay too long to bring my writing to an end; for if ~~this~~ ⟨my⟩ narrative has hitherto escaped destruction, it has been only by a combination of great prudence and great good luck. Should the throes of change take me in the act of writing it, Hyde ~~would~~ ⟨will⟩ tear it in pieces; but if some time shall have elapsed after I have laid it by, his wonderful selfishness and circumscription to the moment will probably save it once again from ~~destruction~~ ⟨the action of⟩ his apelike spite. And indeed the doom that is closing on us both, has already changed and crushed him. Half an hour from now, when I shall again and forever reindue that hated personality, I know how I shall sit shuddering and weeping in my chair, or continue, with the most strained and fearstruck ecstasy of listening, to pace up and down this room, (my last earthly refuge) and give ear to every sound of menace. Will Hyde die upon the scaffold? or will he find the courage to release himself at the last moment? God knows; I am careless; this is my true hour of death, and what is to follow concerns another than myself. ~~and this moment when I shall~~ Here then, as I lay down the pen and proceed to seal up my confession, I bring the life of that unhappy Henry Jekyll to an end.

Robert Louis Stevenson.

Textual Variants: Printer's Copy and First Printed Edition

(Numbers refer to page and line. Page numbers given for the printer's copy are those in the present volume.)

PRINTER'S COPY	FIRST PRINTED EDITION
14:12. I rather incline	29:15. I incline
14:15. And to these	29:19. And to such as these
15:2. set	30:5. put
15:23. into its shelter	30:30. into the recess
15:32. Indeed?	31:3. Indeed!
15:32. voice. "And	31:3. voice, 'and
16:8. frist sight; so	31:31–32. first sight. So
16:12. turn	31:37. turned
16:27. but that	32:17. but to that
16:42. it, sir.	32:35. it.
17:28. "Yes, sir, I	34:1. 'Yes, I
18:22–23. it; and it	35:14. it; it
19:12. I will	36:24. I must
20:19. any	37:36. every
20:34–35. the fogged face of the city moon	38:16. the face of the fogged city moon
20:35. or of concourse	38:17. or concourse
21:47. "Will you look me in the face?"	39:22. 'Will you let me see your face?'
22:17. cried Mr Hyde, "never, never told you. I	40:2. cried Mr Hyde, with a flush of anger. 'I
23:12. rare with him	41:13. rare in him
23:32. Ay	41:37. Ah
23:40. had so near	42:9. had come so near
23:45. turns me cold	42:14. turns me quite cold
25:31–26:32. There were all signs of a man having made work, various measured heaps of some white salt, apparently the same, being laid out on glass saucers, as if for an experiment in which the unhappy man had been prevented.	71:11–72:1. At one table, there were traces of chemical work, various measured heaps of some white salt being laid on glass saucers, as though for an experiment in which the unhappy man had been prevented. 'That is the same drug that I was always bringing him,' said Poole; and even as he spoke,
The kettle had by this time boiled over; and they were obliged to take it off the fire;	the kettle with a startling noise boiled over. This brought them to the fireside, where the easy chair was drawn cosily up,

but the tea things were still set
forth with a comfort and orderliness
that was in strange contrast to the
tumbled corpse upon the floor.
Several books were on a
shelf near the fire; one lay beside the tea
things open, and Utterson was
amazed to find it pious.

Next, in the course of their
review of the chamber, the
searchers came to the
cheval glass.

"This glass has seen some
queer doings, sir, no doubt," whispered
Poole.
    "And none stranger
than itself," echoed the
lawyer in the same tones. "What
did—what did Jekyll do with a glass?"

"That's what I have often asked
myself," returned the butler.
    When they found a prayer in the
doctor's writing, very eloquently
put in words, but breathing a spirit of
despair and horror worthy of the cells of
Bedlam, and the sight of this so

and the tea things stood ready
to the sitter's elbow, the very
sugar in the cup.

There were several books on a
shelf; one lay beside the tea
things open, and Utterson was
amazed to find it a copy of a pious work for
which Jekyll had several times expressed a
great esteem, annotated, in his own hand,
with startling blasphemies.
    Next, in the course of their
review of the chamber, the
searchers came to the
cheval-glass, into whose depth they looked
with an involuntary horror. But it was so
turned as to show them nothing but the rosy
glow playing on the roof, the fire sparkling
in a hundred repetitions along the glazed
front of the presses, and their own pale and
fearful countenances stooping to look in.
    'This glass has seen some
strange things, sir,' whispered
Poole.
    'And surely none stranger
than itself,' echoed the
lawyer, in the same tone.
    'For what did Jekyll'—he caught himself up
at the word with a start, and then
conquering the weakness: 'what could
Jekyll want with it?' he said.
    'You may say that!'
said Poole.
    Next they turned to the
business table. . . .

28:12. colleague? if
28:26–28. I opened it, of course, myself,
28:38. search
30:5–6. from tickling the cacchinatory
                                                        impulse.
31:11. the hysteric ball—
32:7. melted
32:20. now
40:19. And again

76:38. colleague? If
77:9–10. I went myself at the summons,
77:14. searching
78:5. from moving me to laughter.

78:32. the hysteria—
80:23. faded
80:34. *deleted*
84:25. Again

44:29–30. I mention only in passing
49:3. hands
49:5. days
49:14. thenceforth
49:14–15. was compelled to my better life

49:15. O
50:4. upon
50:17. occasion
52:44. confidence
53:14. this

87:12–13. I shall no more than mention
91:15. hand [typo?]
91:19. toils
91:27. henceforth
91:28. was now confined to the better part
of my existence

91:29. oh
92:32. over
93:10. moment
96:1. confidences
96:20. these

I I

QUESTIONS OF VOICE

THREE

Cries and Voices: Reading *Jekyll and Hyde*

PETER K. GARRETT

"Is *Dr. Jekyll and Mr. Hyde* a work of high philosophic intention, or simply the most ingenious and irresponsible of fictions?" Henry James's question (Maixner 308) is no easier to answer now than a hundred years ago; it is if anything harder, since we are no longer sure that its terms can be so "simply" opposed. James acquits Stevenson of irresponsibility ("There is a genuine feeling for the perpetual moral question"), but he is more concerned with fictional craft. "It is . . . not the profundity of the idea which strikes me so much as the art of the presentation—the extremely successful form." Genuine feeling and irresponsibility, the philosophic and the fictive, idea and form: such are the oppositions from which James's tentative appreciation is constructed, and which may still seem pertinent as we try to decide how seriously to take *Jekyll and Hyde*.

Readers more concerned with the tale's philosophic intention are likely to focus on the general pronouncements in "Henry Jekyll's Full Statement of the Case," which also deal with oppositions. "I thus drew steadily nearer to that truth, by whose partial discovery I have been doomed to such a dreadful shipwreck: that man is not truly one but truly two" (82). Like his psychological investigations, Jekyll's scientific experiments in "transcendental medicine" are also based on duality.

> I not only recognized my natural body for the mere aura and effulgence of certain of the powers that made up my spirit, but managed to compound a drug by which these powers should be dethroned from their supremacy, and a second form and countenance substituted, none the less natural to me because they were the expression, and bore the stamp of lower elements in my soul. [83]

Good and evil, higher and lower, spirit and matter, soul and body: such are the oppositions from which Jekyll's philosophic discourse is constructed, and which may seem to underlie the whole tale.

They are also the concern of another book, of indisputably high

59

philosophic intention, also published in 1886, Nietzsche's *Beyond Good and Evil,* which begins by exposing and questioning precisely such assumptions. "The fundamental faith of the philosophers is *the faith in opposite values.*"[1] Nietzsche's polemical "Prelude to a Philosophy of the Future" strives to discredit this faith, as well as "the soul superstition which, in the form of the subject and ego superstition, has not even yet ceased to do mischief" (2), and "the worst, most durable and dangerous of all errors . . . Plato's invention of the pure spirit and the good as such" (3). To confront Jekyll's voice with Nietzsche's helps to bring out the strong conservative strain in Jekyll's "Statement," his efforts to make sense of his terrible experience in conventional moral terms and as the reenactment of a traditional story. "Strange as my circumstances were, the terms of this debate are as old and commonplace as man . . . and it fell out with me, as it falls with so vast a majority of my fellows, that I chose the better part and was found wanting in the strength to keep to it" (89).

Jekyll's voice is, of course, only one among the many that compose the tale, but none of the others challenges his conservatism or opens up conflicting perspectives. What is most striking about them is, rather, the ways they are all shaped to fit together like the pieces of a puzzle or mechanism. Thus the first narrative segment, Enfield's "Story of the Door," meshes with Utterson's knowledge of both Jekyll's house and will to trigger his "Search for Mr. Hyde." Coincidences help assemble information efficiently: the murder of Carew is quickly assimilated because the maid who witnesses it can identify Hyde and because the victim was carrying a letter addressed to Utterson, who, having already encountered Hyde, can provide *his* address. Just as these contrivances work to make connections, others work to avoid redundancy: Lanyon's narrative reveals the identity of Jekyll and Hyde, leaving to Jekyll's the task of explanation. (It is also necessary for Jekyll to know of Lanyon's letter, so he can instruct Utterson to read that account before his own.) Such devices not only serve to accelerate the narrative and make it the "masterpiece of concision" that James admired (Maixner 308); they also implement a drive toward an all-inclusive coherence.

The form of that coherence, the mystery plot so tightly strung between the initial enigma of the relation between Jekyll and Hyde and its final solution, works by foregrounding what Barthes calls the hermeneutic code, the narrative structure of questions and (delayed) answer. (Its prominence is clearly shown by Kaja Silverman's use of *Jekyll and Hyde* to illustrate each of this code's "morphemes" [257–62].) Barthes's five codes are conceived as interwoven textual voices, of which the hermeneutic code is the "Voice of Truth," a purely formal truth of coherence produced by deferral, by prolonged expectation, and established by

60   PETER K. GARRETT

ultimate disclosure. "Truth is what completes, what closes."[2] For Barthes, this closure is a mainstay of the classic, "readerly" text, in whose "circle of solidarities . . . 'everything holds together'" (156). Along with the "proairetic" code of actions, the linear, irreversible structure of the hermeneutic code works to constrain possibilities of reading, and "*it is precisely this constraint which reduces the plural of the classic text*" (30).

As in its thematic oppositions, so again in the narrative form of *Jekyll and Hyde* we encounter a strong conservative strain, a force that marshalls the voices of the tale so that "everything holds together." It is necessary to recognize the strength of this force in order to appreciate the factors that resist it and to realize possibilities of reading that might lead beyond good and evil or toward greater plurality.

We can begin to locate those possibilities interwoven with the voice that tells the truth of plot and theme in Jekyll's "Full Statement." Even as he announces his rediscovery of "the thorough and primitive duality of man," confirming the traditional notion that "man is . . . truly two," Jekyll goes on to offer his own speculative philosophy of the future. "I say two, because the state of my knowledge does not pass beyond that point. Others will follow, others will outstrip me on the same lines; and I hazard the guess that man will ultimately be known for a mere polity of multifarious, incongruous and independent denizens" (82). Such a plural, disunified model of the self displaces traditional dualities and seems to anticipate the decomposition of the unitary subject by several modern heirs of Nietzsche.[3] As the ostensible guide to the philosophic intention of the tale, Jekyll himself becomes multifarious.

Providing the last pieces of the narrative puzzle, Jekyll's "Statement" claims final authority, but the thrust of the mystery plot that it completes also works against his assertions of duality. As Chesterton observes, in terms that apply to plotting as well as theme, "The real stab of the story is not in the discovery that the one man is two men; but in the discovery that the two men are one man" (50). One discovery contests the conclusiveness of another; the narrative drive toward closure itself becomes divided.

As hermeneutic denouement, Jekyll's "Statement" gathers up the threads of the preceding episodes—the encounter with Enfield, the murder of Carew, the appeal to Lanyon—and joins them in a continuous, intelligible sequence. Its disclosures offer "a final nomination, the discovery and uttering of the irreversible word," (Barthes 210), a finality that governs not only events but the self. "Because the hermeneutic code moves toward disclosure, it . . . projects a stable subject about whom things can ultimately be discovered although the process may be painstaking and full of delays—a subject, in short, who can be defined and known" (Silverman 262). Yet at the same time that the "Statement" discloses and defines its divided subject, it also reopens the questions it claims to answer. It begins a new narrative: "I was born in the year 18— . . ." (81), presenting the relation of Jekyll and Hyde not as an established fact but as a developing story. This sequence opens in a mood of unqualified identification as Jekyll observes his new form: "I was conscious of no repugnance, rather of a leap of welcome. This too was myself. It seemed natural and human" (84), and it moves toward equally unqualified denial and dissociation: "He, I say—I cannot say I. That child of Hell had nothing human; nothing lived in him but fear and hatred" (94).

These instances show how the drama of shifting relations between Jekyll and Hyde is played out in terms of grammatical and narrative positions, the permutations of "I," "he," and "it." As narrator and author of his "Statement," Jekyll is "I," but as protagonist or object of his narrative he is sometimes "I," sometimes "he" or "Jekyll," while "Hyde" is sometimes replaced by "I." Observe how quickly these positions shift in this summary of the early stages of divided existence:

> The pleasures which I made haste to seek in my disguise were, as I have said, undignified; I would scarce use a harsher term. But in the hands of Edward Hyde, they soon began to turn toward the monstrous. When I would come back from these excursions, I was often plunged into a kind of wonder at my vicarious depravity. This familiar that I called out of my own soul, and sent forth alone to do his good pleasure, was a being inherently malign and villainous; his every act and thought centered on self; drinking pleasure with bestial avidity from any degree of torture to another; relentless like a man of stone. Henry Jekyll stood at times aghast before the acts of Edward Hyde; but the situation was apart from ordinary laws, and insidiously relaxed the grasp of conscience. It was Hyde, after all, and Hyde alone, that was guilty. Jekyll was no worse; he woke again to his good qualities seemingly unimpaired; he would even make haste, where it was possible, to undo the evil done by Hyde. And thus his conscience slumbered. [86–87]

Tension between the splitting and joining of persons is both represented in the narrative and enacted in the narration of this passage. The "I" who seeks pleasures and wonders at his vicarious depravity is replaced by the formally distanced "Henry Jekyll"; the "I" who judiciously describes Jekyll's pleasures modulates into an unmarked "omniscient" voice that judicially condemns Hyde's and, like a typical Victorian authorial narrator, both ironically represents Jekyll's rationalizations and irresponsibility in indirect discourse and adds a summary moral comment.

PETER K. GARRETT

Like Jekyll in his role as protagonist, the narrative voice of his "Statement" often refuses identification with Hyde, as in skirting "the details of the infamy at which I thus connived (for even now I can scarcely grant that I committed it)" (87). But this voice can also merge completely with Hyde, even in the account of his most extreme action, the assault on Carew. "With a transport of glee, I mauled the unresisting body, tasting delight from every blow" (90). The unnamed narrator who can speak for either Jekyll or Hyde is matched within the story by an indeterminate figure who is neither: "Between these two I now felt I had to choose" (89). Who is this anonymous agent? Who writes "Henry Jekyll's Statement"? The more we ponder its disclosures, the more mysterious and unstable it becomes.

We may wish to say, like Jekyll, that, strange as the circumstances are, the source of these uncertainties is as old and commonplace as narrative, the doubling of the subject that is always produced by telling one's story. That is already saying a great deal, since it suggests how Stevenson's tale discloses the actual strangeness of the commonplace, including the commonplace notion of human duality. But more is at stake in this multiplication and interweaving of voices. It not only disrupts the projection of a stable subject; it makes speech and writing irresponsible by preventing us from determining their origins. Such undecidability is just what the conservatism of opposite values and final disclosures cannot admit. It is what scandalizes Jekyll when, imagining Hyde as utterly alien, "not only hellish but inorganic," he also senses a force that transgresses fundamental oppositions and subverts responsible utterance. "This was the shocking thing: that the slime of the pit seemed to utter cries and voices" (95).

As his "Statement" nears its end, Jekyll reasserts his separation from Hyde by identifying himself with his narrative, its last words with his death. "Will Hyde die upon the scaffold? or will he find courage to release himself at the last moment? God knows; I am careless; this is my true hour of death, and what is to follow concerns another than myself. Here, as I lay down the pen and proceed to seal up my confession, I bring the life of that unhappy Henry Jekyll to an end" (97). As the last words of *Jekyll and Hyde,* these produce a poignant effect of narrative reflexivity, in which Jekyll's life is doubled and replaced by "the life of . . . Henry Jekyll," the written account. But we can also reconstruct a different story, with rather different last words, from the narrative that precedes Jekyll's "Statement" and presents the events that follow its writing, a story that reaches its climax as Utterson stands before the door of Jekyll's cabinet and insists on being admitted.

"Jekyll," cried Utterson, with a loud voice, "I demand to see you." He paused a moment, but there came no reply. "I give you

fair warning, our suspicions are aroused, and I must and shall see
you," he resumed; "if not by fair means. then by foul—if not of
your consent, then by brute force!"

"Utterson," said the voice, "for God's sake have mercy!"

"Ah, that's not Jekyll's voice—it's Hyde's!" cried Utterson.
"Down with the door, Poole!" [69]

The desperate plea for mercy could well be taken for Jekyll's last words,
addressed to his old friend and the man who has replaced Hyde as his heir.
But Utterson believes he can identify the true source of these words, and
this confident certainty authorizes the violence of foul means and brute
force. In place of verbal dialogue, the crash of the axe against the door is
answered by "a dismal screech, as of mere animal terror" (69). The "real
stab of the story" may be neither the discovery that one is two nor that
two are one but the discovery of the violence entailed in assigning any
univocal meaning to these cries and voices.

Here we begin to move from the instabilities of Jekyll's "Full Statement" to those of the fuller narrative context and from the formal aspects
of voice and person to the representation of character and action. The
tension between splitting and joining reappears here as the basis of
Jekyll's scientific project, his sense of the continuous struggle between his
"two natures" as a curse, which leads to his dream of "the separation of
these elements" as in a process of chemical purification (82). He claims to
have succeeded; Hyde's singular purity is shown by the invariable response he provokes in others.

> I have observed that when I wore the semblance of Edward
> Hyde, none could come near me at first without a visible misgiv-
> ing of the flesh. This, as I take it, was because all human beings,
> as we meet them, are commingled out of good and evil; and
> Edward Hyde, alone in the ranks of mankind, was pure evil. [85]

The accounts of Enfield's, Utterson's, and Lanyon's responses to Hyde
seem consistent with this explanation, but there the stress is on the
mysterious and disturbing quality of his effect on them. As that effect is
repeated and elaborated a different perspective emerges, in which we
can see their unsuccessful efforts to describe, name, and analyze as
failed rites of purification. Though Enfield declares he "can see him at
this moment," he cannot describe him.

> There is something wrong with his appearance; something
> displeasing, something down-right detestable. I never saw a
> man I so disliked, and yet I scarce know why. He must be
> deformed somewhere; he gives a strong feeling of deformity,
> although I couldn't specify the point. He's an extraordinary
> looking man, and yet I really can name nothing out of the way.
> [34]

Utterson goes home to dream repeatedly of Hyde, but "the figure had no face, or one that baffled him and melted before his eyes; and thus it was that there sprang up and grew apace in the lawyer's mind a singularly strong, almost an inordinate curiosity to behold the features of the real Mr. Hyde" (37–38).

Yet when Utterson at last sees Hyde face to face, the effect of indescribability is not removed but intensified.

> Mr. Hyde was pale and dwarfish, he gave an impression of deformity without any namable malformation, he had a displeasing smile, he had borne himself to the lawyer with a sort of murderous mixture of timidity and boldness, and he spoke with a husky, whispering and somewhat broken voice; all these were points against him, but not all these together could explain the hitherto unknown disgust, loathing and fear with which Mr. Utterson regarded him. [40]

The effort to resolve this enigma here becomes precisely what Barthes describes as the goal of the hermeneutic code, an attempt at "a final nomination" (210). " 'There must be something else,' said the perplexed gentleman. 'There *is* something more, if I could find a name for it.' " He tries a series of descriptions: "hardly human . . . troglodytic . . . the mere radiance of a foul soul," and ends not by describing Hyde's appearance but by reading it as a sign, "Satan's signature upon a face" (40).

With Lanyon, we get not the lawyer's attempt at accurate testimony but a more clinical account that dwells on Hyde's effect,

> the odd, subjective disturbance caused by his neighbourhood. This bore some resemblance to incipient rigour, and was accompanied by a marked sinking of the pulse. At the time, I set it down to some idiosyncratic, personal distaste, and merely wondered at the acuteness of the symptoms; but I have since had reason to believe the cause to lie much deeper in the nature of man, and to turn on some nobler hinge than the principle of hatred. [77]

All of these passages can be read as components of a hermeneutic sequence that concludes with Jekyll's "discovery and uttering of the irreversible word" (Barthes 210), the explanation that Hyde is "pure evil." But we can also observe the repeated struggle to master "subjective disturbance" through the power of naming, and we may question how successfully it is resolved. Hyde remains as faceless for us as he is in Utterson's nightmares, a blank to be filled in by each interpreter who encounters him. His significance depends less on some pure essence within him than on the purifying effect of considering him wholly other, the flattering effect of considering hatred for him a confirmation of "nobler" human instincts.

Believing he has succeeded in separating and projecting his evil nature, Jekyll describes an asymmetrical relation between his "two characters . . . one was wholly evil and the other was still the old Henry Jekyll, that incongruous compound" (85). His later account of their attitudes toward each other elaborates this pattern.

> My two natures had memory in common, but all other faculties were most unequally shared between them. Jekyll (who was composite) now with the most sensitive apprehensions, now with a greedy gusto, projected and shared in the pleasures and adventures of Hyde; but Hyde was indifferent to Jekyll, or but remembered him as the mountain bandit remembers the cavern in which he conceals himself from pursuit. Jekyll had more than a father's interest; Hyde had more than a son's indifference. [89]

Here there is no overt attempt at dissociation, but the sense of separation is clear; little of Jekyll but a vague memory remains in Hyde. The action of the story, however, displays a much more complicated relation and a stronger mix of memories, as in the episode of Jekyll's appeal to Lanyon, of which each gives a partial account.

Jekyll's account in his "Statement" explains how the spontaneous transformation that produces this crisis arises from the slackening of his penitence and "fall" into the indulgences of "an ordinary secret sinner" (92). It is not deeds but impure thoughts, "the animal within me licking the chops of memory," that trigger the change into his more bestial form: "the hand that lay on my knee was corded and hairy" (92). (One may recall Victorian cautionary tales about the consequences of sexual impurity.) Escape from the plight of being Hyde, "the common quarry of mankind, hunted, houseless, a known murderer, thrall to the gallows," also depends on memory. "I remembered that of my original character, one part remained to me: I could write my own hand" (93). Who owns the "hand" is a recurrent question that links the themes of identity and writing, from the check Hyde signs as Jekyll to the signature Jekyll creates for Hyde by "sloping my own hand backward" (87) to the "startling blasphemies" written in Jekyll's pious books "in his own hand" (71; cf. 96).[4] Here the letter to Lanyon is written by Hyde, but its voice, as we can observe from its transcription in Lanyon's narrative (74–75), seems entirely and convincingly Jekyll's. Whether we consider Hyde capable of extraordinary ventriloquism or rather suppose that much of Jekyll subsists within him, their relation hardly matches Jekyll's description. It is precisely while telling of Hyde's journey to Lanyon's house that Jekyll's "Statement" pauses to insist on their radical separation—"He, I say—I cannot say I. That child of Hell had nothing human; nothing lived in him but fear and hatred" (94)—precisely at the point where we are best able to sense how much more lives in him.

PETER K. GARRETT

Lanyon's account of their interview strengthens this sense. Once Hyde's desperation subsides and the potion is ready, he speaks in tones we do not hear elsewhere in the tale, offering a fateful choice between ignorance and "a new province of knowledge and new avenues to fame and power," and then, binding Lanyon by the "vows . . . of our profession," triumphantly displaying that power. "And now, you who have so long been bound to the most narrow and material views, you who have denied the virtue of transcendental medicine, you who have derided your superiors—behold!" (80). Not only are these words spoken as if by Jekyll but their melodramatic intensity offers a glimpse of the pride and ambition, as well as the desire for irresponsible pleasure, that went into the making of Edward Hyde, and that live in him as well. On the level of character and action as well as on the level of narration, we find neither unity nor purified duality but a complex weave of voices that resists conservative simplifications.

A reading that dwells on such tensions and discrepancies does not simply replace a classic, readerly coherence in which everything holds together with a writerly plurality in which nothing does. Such a symmetrical reversal, still governed by a faith in opposites, would do little to account for the power of *Jekyll and Hyde,* which depends to a large extent on holding together what both characters and readers try to separate.[5] Jekyll realizes at the end that his supposed success in separating the elements so painfully mixed within him and in projecting a purified essence of evil depended on a crucial "unknown impurity" in one of the ingredients of the potion (96). This ironic discovery applies to the tale as well, which achieves its most impressive and unsettling effects by compounding an impure, murderous mixture of motives.

Like Jekyll, several of the other characters try to dissociate themselves from Hyde, but the "instinctive" repulsion they feel toward him also binds them to him, as Lanyon is held by "a disgustful curiosity" (77). This fascination is presented most fully in Utterson's response to Enfield's story.

Hitherto it had touched him on the intellectual side alone, but now his imagination was also engaged, or rather enslaved; and as he lay and tossed in the gross darkness of the night and the curtained room, Mr. Enfield's tale went before his mind in a scroll of lighted pictures. He would be aware of the great field of lamps of a nocturnal city; then of the figure of a man walking swiftly; then of a child running from the doctor's; and then these met and that human Juggernaut trod the child down and passed on regardless of her screams. Or else he would see a room in a rich house, where his friend lay asleep, dreaming and smiling at his dreams; and then the door of the room would be opened, the curtains of the bed plucked apart, the sleeper recalled, and lo!

there would stand by his side a figure to whom power was given, and even at that dead hour, he must rise and do its bidding. [37]

The two scenic images of the faceless Hyde are repeated and multiplied obsessively in Utterson's troubled dreams. Enfield has said of the scene he witnessed, "It sounds like nothing to hear, but it was hellish to see" (31); here the vision is recreated by Utterson's enslaved imagination ("in a scroll of lighted pictures," which prefigures cinematic versions) and complemented by another that we will eventually realize to be literally impossible but an accurate prefiguration of Hyde's ascendance. The images both represent and exercise power, figured in an interplay of accelerating movement and compulsive repetition, as Utterson sees "the figure . . . move the more swiftly, and still the more swiftly, even to dizziness, through wider labyrinths of lamp-lighted city, and at every street corner crush a child and leave her screaming." Utterson's efforts to break the spell that has enslaved his imagination lead him to replace these repeated images with his own purposeful movement, the search for Hyde, but that project also binds them together in complementary roles ("If he be Mr. Hyde . . . I shall be Mr. Seek" [38]). It leads not just to their encounter by the outer door where the tale began but to their final dialogue through the door of Jekyll's cabinet, where it will be Utterson who presses on, "regardless of [the other's] screams." Narrative movement yields in turn to an uncanny repetition of violence and domination as these two exchange places.

The opposition between Hyde and others repeatedly begins to blur as soon as it is posited. In the account of his trampling the child, as in the later account of his attack on Carew, his evil is presented as uniquely gratuitous, violent aggression, which Jekyll amplifies by describing the monstrous turn of Hyde's depravity as "drinking pleasure with bestial avidity from any degree of torture to another" (86). But from the beginning there is a sense of him not just as an isolated embodiment of rage and cruelty but also as the occasion of them in others. Enfield tells how, after he has captured Hyde, he, the child's family, and even the unemotional doctor become possessed "with desire to kill him. . . . I never saw a circle of such hateful faces" (32). Those who confront and oppose Hyde seem to turn into his doubles.

This effect of contamination takes a more complex course with Utterson, who at the outset displays a milder form of Jekyll's vicarious depravity, denying himself pleasures while maintaining "an approved tolerance for others; sometimes wondering, almost with envy, at the high pressure of spirits involved in their misdeeds; and in any extremity inclined to help rather than to reprove" (29). His investigations turn this tendency into a source of guilt, which arises first through identification

PETER K. GARRETT

with Jekyll; supposing Hyde to be connected with "the ghost of some old sin," he uneasily broods on his own "fairly blameless" past and "the many ill things he had done" (42). After the murder of Carew, his anxieties implicate him more with Hyde. Driving with the officer seeking Hyde through fog-darkened Soho, "like a district of some city in a nightmare," he is "conscious of some touch of that terror of the law and the law's officers, which may at times assail the most honest" (40). At the end, however, Utterson betrays no sign of any such disturbing identifications, and it is he, rather than the more single-minded and self-righteous Enfield or Lanyon, who at last discharges the violence that has gathered around Hyde throughout the tale. Breaking down the door is justified by considering Hyde as completely other, deserving no mercy, but this outburst of brute force actually removes the separation between them.

Similar effects of contamination can be traced in the motives of the tale itself and the ways they implicate the reader, as the taint of sadistic aggression spreads from Hyde to other, opposed figures and at last to the whole narrative. Wherever we locate the real stab of the story, we should recognize that it really means to stab. It may arouse guilty identification like Utterson's, the sense of a corresponding doubleness ("You are certainly wrong about Hyde being overdrawn," Hopkins wrote to Bridges: "my Hyde is worse" [Maixner 229].) But even without or apart from such recognition, there is a covert cruel streak in the narrative that also seeks to implicate us. It appears most clearly in the presentation of the maid who views the encounter between Hyde and Carew, "brilliantly lit by the full moon."

> It seems she was romantically given; for she sat down upon her box, which stood immediately under the window, and fell into a dream of musing. Never (she used to say, with streaming tears, when she narrated that experience), never had she felt more at peace with all men or thought more kindly of the world. [46]

As Carew approaches he becomes the focus of this romantic reverie, "an aged beautiful gentleman with white hair . . . the moon shone on his face as he spoke, and the girl was pleased to watch it, it seemed to breathe such an innocent and old-world kindness of disposition." Hyde's ferocious attack on Carew also violates the maid's moony dreams with an insistent demonstration of human evil. She too is a victim: "At the horror of these sights and sounds, the maid fainted," but we are induced not to sympathize but to participate in her victimization. By focusing the account through her and alluding to her subsequent tearful narration, the passage makes her a kind of unreliable narrator from whose naive innocence the superior, knowing tone of the enclosing narrative ("It seems she was romantically given") invites us to separate ourselves. We are offered instead the vicarious depravity of a philosophical rape.[6]

The impulse to violate and destroy innocence or optimistic contentment finds other victims, and in each case the reader is nudged into alignment with that impulse. After his first encounter with Hyde, Utterson feels "a nausea and distaste of life" (41), and this effect is carried further in the mortally shaken Lanyon. " 'I have had a shock,' he said, 'and I shall never recover. It is a question of weeks. Well, life has been pleasant; I liked it; yes sir, I used to like it. I sometimes think if we knew all, we should be more glad to get away' " (57). The implied reader's position is less clearly marked here. We may only register the excitement of increasing threat and mystery, but we may also sense the savage pleasure of sharing in dark knowledge that the mystery plot promises. As the repeated pattern of devastating experiences allows us to assume a privileged detachment instead of sharing shock and nausea, the narrative drive to destroy complacency again proposes a conspiracy of aggression.

It may seem that this violence is contained and redefined within the tale's larger moral purpose, in which the insistence on evil and its inseparability from human existence opposes Jekyll's mistaken project of purification. His own scientific optimism has been harshly refuted: "I have been made to learn that the doom and burthen of our life is bound forever on man's shoulders, and when the attempt is made to cast it off, it but returns upon us with more unfamiliar and more awful pressure" (83). But the logic of the cautionary tale, with its insistence on the appropriateness of the retribution that overtakes him ("If I am the chief of sinners, I am the chief of sufferers also. I could not think that this earth contained a place for sufferings and terrors so unmanning" [58]), is produced by a punitive impulse that is the respectable double of Hyde's pleasure from torture to another. The tale provides no position, no point of identification, that is not implicated in some form of victimization and violence.[7]

To consider whether any conception of *Jekyll and Hyde*'s moral purpose can contain and stabilize its tensions is to return to our initial question. The possibilities of reading we have been exploring suggest that the tale's greatest power and interest derive less from any high philosophic intention we may ascribe to it than from its fictional irresponsibility, its refusal or failure to offer any secure position for its reader or to establish any fixed relation between its voices. The conservative, ordering force of its moral oppositions and the constraining coherence of its mystery plot lose their grip on a reading that recognizes the insidious, subversive effects we have traced. We may wonder, however, whether such a reading necessarily loses its own grip on the most obvious and fundamental features of the tale, the elements preserved by the perpetuation of its story as popular myth and its title as byword. A certain estrangement from the obvious and the popular does indeed seem necessary; stage, film, and television versions, as well as commonplace allusions (all the available ways of "knowing" *Jekyll and Hyde* without reading it), tend not only to reproduce but to exaggerate its dualism by making its moral oppositions more symmetrical. To undermine those oppositions is to challenge the common understanding of the tale.

But there is another way in which a subversive or sceptical reading can rejoin and reinterpret the common sense. Like any popular tale of terror, *Jekyll and Hyde* exploits the drama of uncertain control, of mysterious threat, the struggle for mastery, and the spectacle of victimization. As Jekyll's triumphant discovery of "a new province of knowledge and new avenues to fame and power" leads to utter and terrifying loss of control, we recognize an appeal to impulses and anxieties more powerful than the tale's moral framework, to fantasies and fears of releasing desire from social restraints and responsibilities. Gothic fiction depends at least as much on producing such disturbance as on containing it; its characteristic complication of narrative form and multiplication of voices, whether in conflict or complementarity, always express the effort required to establish control of meaning and often suggest its uncertain success. The narrative of *Jekyll and Hyde* advances precisely through a series of such efforts, through Utterson's quest and Enfield's, Lanyon's, and Jekyll's narratives, and through the larger development of the mystery plot that includes them. To observe how the voices and positions of the tale shift and blur is to see how these efforts all fail. Like Jekyll, the tale releases a force that cannot be mastered—not because it simply overwhelms all resistance but because all efforts at resistance or containment themselves become further instances of its cruel logic.

Our own efforts as readers join this series of struggles by the enslaved imaginations of the characters. Our position may be best indicated by the way the account of Utterson is suspended on the threshold of a scene of reading, as he "trudged back to his office to read the two narratives in which this mystery was now to be explained" (73). That reading, left unrecorded, becomes our own, since we never return to Utterson or learn what he makes of those two narratives. Would he have recognized his own role in the destruction of his friend, the way he had become identified with what he opposed, and the violence produced by his demand for explanation? But we hardly care to be shown Utterson's response to what he has read, any more than we care to reflect on our own complicity. That, perhaps, would be too cruel.

NOTES

1. Friedrich Nietzsche, *Beyond Good and Evil,* tr. Walter Kaufmann (New York: Vintage Books, 1966), 10.

2. Roland Barthes, *S/Z,* tr. Richard Miller (New York: Hill and Wang, 1974), 76.

3. Compare Ronald Thomas's discussion of the ways *Jekyll and Hyde* anticipates the dissolution of the self in modern writers such as Beckett.

4. The relation between identity and writing is explored much more fully by Thomas, whose account of the "death or disappearance of the author" develops the radical implications of Jekyll's unsuccessful efforts to maintain control through writing.

5. This is where my concern with reading differs most from other approaches, such as Thomas's, which also stress the subversion of a coherent self or story. The contending impulses that produce and disrupt readerly coherence also deny the reader any secure position, including that of detached writerly sophistication.

6. Compare the earlier female victim, the girl Hyde tramples. That scene may also be read as an equivalent for sexual assault, which seems to be the way Hopkins read it: "The trampling scene is perhaps a convention: he was thinking of something unsuitable for fiction" (Maixner 229). The maid's "dream of musing," loss of consciousness, and distraught retellings also recall Utterson's nightmares and his efforts to regain control. In these repetitions the tale seems to be retelling the story of its own origination in dreams, retracing the links between its active and passive voices or the suffering and infliction of narrative violence.

7. Claims have recently been made in feminist film theory that all narrative entails such domination. Laura Mulvey declares that "Sadism demands a story, depends on making something happen, forcing a change in another person, a battle of will and strength, victory/defeat, all occurring in a linear time with a beginning and an end" ("Visual Pleasure and Narrative Cinema," *Screen* 16, no. 3 [Autumn 1975]: 14). This equation of narrative and sadism is elaborated in terms of the Oedipal structures of patriarchy in Teresa de Lauretis, *Alice Doesn't: Feminism, Semiotics, Cinema* (Bloomington: Indiana University Press, 1984), 103–57. One need not accept such a comprehensive indictment to recognize how narrative always involves questions of power, or how, in a tale so insistently concerned with the infectious transfer of violence, the effort to impose narrative order itself becomes contaminated. In reading *Jekyll and Hyde,* and many other gothic tales, we are confronted with a troubling representation of our own demand for narrative intelligibility.

PETER K. GARRETT

The Strange Voices in the Strange Case: Dr. Jekyll, Mr. Hyde, and the Voices of Modern Fiction

RONALD R. THOMAS

Like the voices and personalities in its title, *Strange Case of Dr Jekyll and Mr Hyde* contains encased within it two opposing texts with two opposing plots: a plot of exclusion and a plot of escape. It recounts the estrangement of a speaker from his own voice and a writer from what he has written, while it also declares the independence of the text from the mastery and intentionality of its author. This double plot enacts two of the central problems of modern fiction: the "death" or "disappearance of the author" and the taking on by the text of a life of its own. The act of self-narration is revealed in *Jekyll and Hyde* to be a ritual act of self-estrangement rather than the act of self-discovery that it purports to be in the case of a traditional autobiographical novel such as *Jane Eyre* or *David Copperfield,* for example. The end of *Jekyll and Hyde* is the fragmenting of the self into distinct pieces with distinct voices, not the bringing together of those pieces into some unified character who speaks with a single voice. This accomplishment brings Stevenson's work closer to that of Beckett than that of Dickens, and it opens the door to the modernist claim that the self is not represented at the scene of writing. It is reinvented there.

Even before the end of the book, the voice of Jekyll is silenced, replaced by the texts he has written. And even before his voice is suppressed, it is exposed as a form of writing itself—as a sign of Jekyll's absence rather than his presence. On the night before Dr. Jekyll disappears for the last time, his lawyer, Utterson, is summoned by Jekyll's butler. The butler is disturbed because his master has mysteriously withdrawn into his laboratory for several days. But he is more deeply disturbed by the voice that issues from behind the locked door of the laboratory: it sounds strange and unfamiliar to him. Utterson agrees when he listens that the voice is strange, that it is "much changed," and that it could not be the voice of "the master." The lawyer's concern over the mystery is deepened when he reads the "strange note" that Jekyll had apparently written to a druggist, franticly pleading for certain chemicals to be delivered to him.

The note is even stranger than Utterson and the butler realize, and its implications are more far-reaching; written in it is the formula that Jekyll had used to regain his identity after having lost it for a time to Hyde. The reason that Jekyll has disappeared and his voice is so strange is that his identity no longer conforms to that formula. He no longer fits the text by which he defined himself. Nor does Hyde's identity continue to be contained within the formula Jekyll had written for him. While Jekyll cannot return to the text that defines him, Hyde keeps uncontrollably breaking out of his.

The novel has always been a form in which an individual's image of himself is reexamined and restructured, where the misrepresentations of a self are tested, uncovered, and replaced with a more authentic self-integration.[1] In the modern novel, however, this restructuring of the image of the individual calls for a restructuring of the whole notion of individuality and the form of the novel in which it is contained. The novel is no longer the scene of self-possession; it has become a sign of the self's dissolution. My argument here is that *Jekyll and Hyde* announces this development by launching an elaborate assault on the ideals of the individual personality and the cult of character that dominated the nineteenth century, striking at the heart of that ideology: the life story. Moreover, this case is in its narrative form as well as its content at the beginning of a tradition subversive to conventional self-narration, a tradition that can be traced through the central modernist English writers of fictional autobiography—Conrad, Joyce, and, most prominently, Beckett. A further claim is that *Jekyll and Hyde* is ultimately concerned with fundamental questions about the authority of texts and the power of language to represent human life—the very questions that preoccupy much of modern fiction and criticism as well.[2]

It is a critical commonplace to regard the novel as "essentially biographical" (Lukacs 77).[3] A novel's plot traditionally centers around the story of a single life, usually mapped from adolescence to adulthood, representing figuratively (and in some cases literally) the beginning and the end of a human life. From *Robinson Crusoe* to *Emma* to *Great Expectations,* the novel traces a movement across the critical arc from a state of dependence or isolation to a state of independence or inclusion. It stresses the processes of growth, education, judgment, and progress that enable that movement and lead to the individual's accession to power in the world by the forging of a will, the articulation of a voice. There are many cases (such as *The Mill on the Floss, The Portrait of a Lady,* and *Jude the Obscure*) where the outcome of that process is made problematic; but the progressive, biographical form remains intact even if the hero becomes a victim in the course of that progress.

In *Jekyll and Hyde,* however, we are presented with a strange case.

RONALD R. THOMAS

Rather than a character's gradual integration, we witness his sudden disintegration. Rather than progress, regression. Dr. Jekyll's story begins with his preparations for its end; the first thing we know about him is that he has written a will and that it is written in his own hand. He is at the outset already a respected member of his society, a professional man of character and reputation. But over the course of his story we watch him become a recluse, a murderer, and finally a suicide. And this breakdown is more than a moral, social, and psychological one; it is a philosophical one as well. Not only does the main character disintegrate over the course of this text, but the whole notion of character is undermined. "Character" dissolves into what Jekyll calls an "incongruous compound" of "dissociated," and "independent," "elements" (82, 85). "Think of it," Jekyll claims in his "full" statement, "I did not even exist!" (86). And by the end of the book he does not exist. He has lost his will, surrendered his moral agency, and "shaken" the "very fortress of identity" (82). In fact, before anyone even reads his narrative, Jekyll has literally and permanently disappeared.

This is not just a story of the exposure of a hypocrite or an account of the explosive return of a repressed past. It enacts the withdrawal of the articulating self from the text—the disappearance of the author. By the end of the narrative, Jekyll can only speak of another, no longer himself: "He, I say—I cannot say I" (94). He cannot take authority for his own actions or even for his own words. Subject and object split apart in *Jekyll and Hyde,* and the writer is eradicated by the thing he has written. The text ends, in fact, as a detective novel customarily begins—with the disappearance of a body and the appearance of an enigmatic text (a will clouded by uncertain intentions, disputed authenticity, and an alteration of the name of the heir). The absent body, in this case, happens to be that of the text's author. In the place of that absence there remains an inexplicable mystery: the mute corpse of the violent and disfiguring force Jekyll called Hyde.

The breakdown of the conventions of character in this text corresponds to a breakdown of narrative conventions as well. The absence of a coherent self here is joined by the absence of a coherent plot. The "case" is composed not of chapters but of ten disparate documents identified only as letters, incidents, cases, and statements. These parts never succeed in becoming a whole story that makes sense out of events; like Jekyll's character, they fray into "elements" that have less and less connection. The first of the pieces of this case is auspiciously titled, "The Story of the Door." But the story referred to is called a "bad story" by its teller, Enfield, because it is "far from explaining" the mystery it raises (32–33). It is the first account we have of the actions of Mr. Hyde and yet in the story itself, Hyde is not even named. Enfield "can't mention" the name, he says, even "though it is one of the points of my story" (32). Presumably, this omission is made out of a sense of respect for Dr. Jekyll's privacy. But in fact, the point of this story cannot be named because it has no single point. The personalities in it cannot be clearly connected to one another and the events cannot be explained. Enfield's story presents an enigma that baffles him as its teller and baffles his listener, Utterson, as well. The remainder of the text is merely a repetition of this "story" gone "bad." Whereas Garrett sees narrative intelligibility as something that is posed and then undercut in this tale, I see it as already deeply devalued and suspect when it is set into place.[4] Enfield's is the last piece of the case even to be called a story. We move through its secret door into a world where names cannot be named, points cannot be reached, stories cannot be told. That world is one of vain searches, unexplained disappearances, random incidents, and incomplete statements. The psychological infirmities with which the text is manifestly concerned always express themselves as narrative infirmities in *Jekyll and Hyde,* a correlation that Freud would take note of in his case histories and regard as possessing "great theoretical significance." "The patient's inability to give an ordered history of their life," Freud would say in his analysis of the Dora case, "coincides with the history of their illness" and is "characteristic of the neurosis."[5] But narrative and psychological disorder may be regarded as symptomatic of each other, and there may be as much "theoretical significance" for the history of narrative as there is for the history of medicine in the disorder that characterizes *Jekyll and Hyde.*

The narrative disintegration in the Jekyll and Hyde case is not achieved all at once. Rather, as is true in Freud's cases, it has a history. The confusion at the beginning of the text appears at first to resemble that of the traditional detective novel. Along with the detective figure Utterson, we are presented with a series of enigmatic scenes and incidents—a mystery that needs solving. His interest aroused, Utterson resolves to be the "Mr. Seek" to Jekyll's "Mr. Hyde" and to investigate the strange events that have taken place. After a series of mistaken explanations are made and the final disappearance of Dr. Jekyll occurs, Utterson is presented with the two documents that he presumes will provide the necessary links between the conflicting pieces of evidence: the written testimony of the key witness (Dr. Lanyon's letter) and the "confession" of the criminal ("Henry Jekyll's Full Statement of the Case"). Thus far, the tale conforms to the pattern of the detective story where a confused narrative of a crime is set right at last by the explanation of the detective figure.[6] The final act performed in *Jekyll and Hyde* is Utterson's withdrawal into his office "to read the two narratives in which this mystery was to be explained" (73).

But these expectations are soon cancelled by the narratives them-

RONALD R. THOMAS

selves. Lanyon's account begins by referring to the assurance Jekyll had given him that, if he obeyed the bizarre instructions contained in Jekyll's letter, the mystery would "roll away like a story that is told" (75). This was, of course, false assurance because the story never does get fully told. And Utterson's expectations of the mystery's explanation will be as disappointed as Lanyon's were. Within Lanyon's narrative is an account of his own disappointed reading of an enigmatic text—the confused notebooks belonging to Dr. Jekyll—in which Lanyon recalls reading only the recurrence of the word "double" and the emphatic exclamation "total failure!!!" (76). He mentions them perhaps because they come to characterize his own "explanatory" text as well as Jekyll's. At the crucial moment, when he is about to reveal how Jekyll and Hyde are connected, Lanyon duplicates Jekyll's secrecy and his failure to explain the mystery. The essential information that Jekyll had related about his relationship to Hyde, Lanyon says, "I cannot bring my mind to set [it] on paper" (80).

"Henry Jekyll's Full Statement of the Case" is no more satisfactory in setting down on paper the explanation that binds pieces of this story together than Lanyon's. Jekyll refers to his document as his confession, and he begins it by promising that it will be comprehensive, as any confessional life story would be: "I was born in the year 18— to a large fortune . . ." (81). Jekyll's first words echo the opening words of life stories such as *David Copperfield*, and his description of himself as being composed of a "dual nature" is reminiscent of Augustine's candid accounting of himself in the *Confessions*. But by the third page of this "full" confession, Jekyll admits that it cannot be full because even his own knowledge of what he has done is "incomplete" (83). And unlike David Copperfield, this narrator will surely not turn out to be the hero of his own life story because the story told here finally denies the existence of the one telling it: "I had lost my identity. . . . I did not even exist!" (83). As a confession, it seems to be one uttered in bad faith since this penitent casts the blame for his sins on "another than myself"—Hyde (97). It is as if Jekyll's narrative has dramatized what Foucault has called the medicalization and legalization of the confessional act. Rather than revealing the speaker's error or sin, this confession has value only as a legal or therapeutic operation intended to elucidate a case of law or medicine.[7]

As Jekyll's statement progresses, the events described become more uncontrollable and inexplicable, the transformations between Jekyll and Hyde more random and unpredictable. Simultaneously, Jekyll's text shifts from an examination of a moral dilemma (how should I behave?) to a confrontation with an ontological impasse (do I exist?). It changes from the story of a man making his life to the account of his breaking it apart. In the course of that shift, the narrator's authority and the character's coherence have both been undermined. "As I lay down the pen," Jekyll says at the end of his text, "I bring the life of that unhappy Henry Jekyll to a close" (97). What remains, he says, does not concern him; it "concerns another than myself." His life is not his own in his writing. "That" life is closed to him. And at its closing, he does not even die; he vanishes.

Two objects remain behind to take the place of the vanished narrator: the text of the narrative itself and the "body of the self-destroyer" called Hyde (70). The two are, in important ways, the same thing. In fact, Hyde embodies the text's escaping from Jekyll's control. The strange voice that Utterson and the butler hear speaking from Jekyll's laboratory after the doctor disappeared is, of course, Hyde's. As Jekyll's narrative ends, it predicts just this eventuality. Jekyll recounts two fears about Hyde: first, the fear that "the cries and voic s" of Hyde would at any moment "usurp" his own speaking voice and force him to "give ear to every sound of menace" that Hyde would utter; and second, that "the throes of change [should] take me [Jekyll] in the act of writing" this statement, and that Hyde would proceed to "tear it in pieces" (95, 97). It is important that Jekyll fears Hyde's "voices" and his reappearance "in the act writing"; he is afraid of his own "fearstruck ecstasy of listening" to Hyde, and of Hyde's destruction of the text he is writing. He is not fearful of the cry itself, but of the fact that the cries and voices are in the plural. They defy identity, definability, univocality. Jekyll's deepest fear about Hyde is that he will usurp his authority as the master and definer of his own identity—take from him the power he has wielded through his voice and pen.

This fear is of particular interest because Hyde is from the outset the product of Jekyll's pen. Not only does Hyde begin his existence as the chemical formula Jekyll writes out in his notebook; he is sustained by the banknotes and account books Jekyll writes for him. He even has his future provided for by the will that names him heir—again, in Jekyll's own handwriting. Lanyon is first introduced to Hyde by way of a letter written (apparently) by Jekyll, and Utterson learns of Hyde's existence from the text of the controversial will. But while Hyde's existence depends on these texts, his existence also seems bent on destroying, altering, or disfiguring them. Along with Utterson, we have seen the charred remains of the account books in the fireplace of Hyde's abandoned rooms, and have learned directly from Jekyll of Hyde's practice of defacing the crucial texts of Jekyll's life: "scrawling in my own hand blasphemies on the pages of my books, burning the letters and destroying the portrait of my father" (96). When Jekyll strives to counteract Hyde's undermining of his authority at the end, he does so by appealing to the authority of his original text of himself—by trying to replicate the formula that "blots out" Hyde. His failure to do so, he speculates, comes about because the original batch of chemicals must have been "impure"

RONALD R. THOMAS

and therefore must not have corresponded precisely to the formula (96). The larger point that Jekyll misses here is that he fails because any text is "impure" in the sense that it is never a perfect representation of what it seeks to represent. The representation is always something else; it always takes on a life of its own. Jekyll's hidden self cannot be contained in any text without something being lost and something else being found—or unleashed. The compound—and its effects—are never fully contained within the formula that expresses them.

Like the unstable impure element in a compound, Hyde continually gives the lie to Jekyll's fictions, breaking out of the formulaic plot in which he is to remain hidden. Each time Jekyll attempts to put an "end" to Hyde, to "be done" with him, to suppress this text of himself, Hyde bursts out and exposes him for being something else (52). The most important text in which this escape takes place is Dr. Jekyll's will, the other document that survives him and in the end is left in Utterson's hands to read. The authority and authorship of the will is the first problem Utterson confronts in the case, and it remains the last. The will is described by Utterson as a "holograph" text; it is written in Jekyll's own hand because the lawyer has refused to endorse its unusual provisions, which call for Hyde's inheritance of Jekyll's estate in the event of Jekyll's "unexplained absence or disappearance" (35). Utterson could not give his official legal sanction to this document because its contents "offended" his sense of "the sane and customary" and because the heir (Hyde) was nothing "but a name" to him (35). For the lawyer, the will's authority was a suspect—or at least an "impure"—representation of his client's intentions, just as for the doctor, the chemical formula was an impure representation of his patient's (his own) intentions.

Utterson will eventually learn that Jekyll's handwriting is identical to Hyde's, that the suspect will and the suspect notes to the chemist were both written by the same hand. The very action that separated Jekyll from Hyde in the first place (the writing out of the formula), also binds them inextricably together. But the sticking point for Utterson is not so much the matter of the handwriting (which he misinterprets as Hyde's forgery), but the wording of the will that provides for its author's "disappearance." When Utterson is instructed later that the letter he receives from Lanyon is to be opened only in the case of Jekyll's "death or disappearance," he becomes concerned that "the idea of disappearance and the name of Henry Jekyll" always seemed to be "bracketed" together in these texts (58–59). Finally, appended to Jekyll's "Full Statement" is a note from Jekyll addressed to Utterson declaring that when *this* text falls into Utterson's hands, "I shall have disappeared" (72). Inscribed in each of Jekyll's texts, then, is the impending disappearance of its author, along with the implication that the author is not so much represented by his text as he is replaced—and victimized—by it.

Jekyll's consistent absenting of himself from his own texts accords with his purpose in creating Hyde in the first place: to deny himself moral agency, to cease being an "I." This intention is fulfilled at the end of Jekyll's statement in the hopeless confusion with which the first- and third-person pronouns are used; the writer finally begins referring to both Jekyll and Hyde as "them," as autonomous, in other words (95). Both become third persons—strangers—and the author is shocked that what he has written about should speak and act with an agency of its own:

> This was the shocking thing; that the slime of the pit seemed to utter cries and voices; that the amorphous dust gesticulated and sinned; that what was dead, and had no shape, should usurp the offices of life. [95]

Hyde lives on and speaks out of the text Utterson holds and reads. He is both what is produced by Jekyll's utterances and what cannot be contained in them. The strange case that *Jekyll and Hyde* finally makes is a case for the estranging yet enduring power of language to make of ourselves something totally other, something with a voice—and a life—of its own that replaces rather than represents the life of its author.

The case may be made that this surrendering of the authorial voice to the text itself is the main action of the central modernist works of prose fiction. "If we wish to know the writer in our day," Foucault claims about all of modern literature, "it will be through the singularity of his absence and in his link to death, which has transformed him into a victim of his own writing."[8] Foucault points out a fundamental shift in modern literature from a conception of writing as a means of conferring immortality on the author to a means of eliminating him. "Writing is now linked to sacrifice and to the sacrifice of life itself; it is a voluntary obliteration of the self . . ." (117). The void left by this "disappearance or death of the author" is filled by "the concept of the work," the autonomous existence of the text itself. I have argued that this is precisely what *Jekyll and Hyde* has enacted: "As I lay down the pen," Jekyll says, "and proceed to seal up my confession, I bring the life of that unhappy Henry Jekyll to an end" (97). The life is a function of the pen that writes it. Here, the text of the "confession" remains and the life of Jekyll ends, "sealed up" in the text itself, and the corpse of Hyde remains as a sign of the author's sacrifice of his life to the body of his work.

This disappearance might be compared to Marlow's at the end of *Lord Jim*. There, after telling the "incomplete story" of Jim, Marlow's narration withdraws into the text of the letter he writes to the one

RONALD R. THOMAS

"privileged man" who "showed an interest in him that survived the telling of his own story."[9] Like Jekyll, Marlow withdraws from the scene of narration and leaves behind a letter and a group of documents to replace him. For the Marlow who acts as the narrative voice of *Heart of Darkness,* the object of his narration—Kurtz—was himself "little more than a voice."[10] And it is Kurtz's voice, not Marlow's, that continues "speaking" at the end of this text, "from beyond the threshold of eternal darkness" (108). Not unlike Jekyll's Hyde, Kurtz is Marlow's "nightmare" with whom he has an "unforeseen partnership" of words—words that both appall and fascinate him (97). The partnership to which Marlow refers is based on his fear that at the moment of death he, unlike Kurtz, "would have nothing to say"; so he takes refuge in the voice of this strange other whose "words will remain" when Marlow has become "indistinct and silent" (101, 109, 111). For Marlow, as for the Stephen Dedalus of *A Portrait,* "the personality of the artist passes into the narration itself" and "refines itself out of existence."[11] This takes place at the end of *A Portrait* in the form of Stephen's withdrawal into the text of his diary, where he gives himself over to the "the spell" of "voices" from which he earlier tried to distinguish himself. At the end they "call" to him as his "kinsmen" (252). When they call, the diary reads, "the air is thick with their company"—a company into which the call of Stephen's own voice becomes merged.

Bakhtin has described the novel as a "multivoiced" form, the object of which is "precisely the act of passing the themes through many and varied voices"; it is a form in which the hero's paradoxical problem is to "separate [his] voice from another voice with which it is inseparably merged. . . ."[12] The writers of modern fiction have made this formal matter the central thematic of their novels as well. The prose of Samuel Beckett explores this territory intensely and repeatedly. Beckett's trilogy of *Molloy, Malone Dies,* and *The Unnamable* fulfills the prophecy Jekyll had made: the self is not one but many—an incongruous compound of forces and voices without any real coherence. The trilogy maps this development in a complex movement outward by a succession of narrators through the concentric circles of their own fictions. Each of Beckett's narrators generates a new name to distinguish itself from the voice of its predecessors and exposes the inadequacies of the earlier attempts to represent the speaker's experience. And each of them acknowledges that this narrative will mean the death of them. Molloy regards his narrative as his attempt to "finish dying," and Malone only tells himself these stories "while waiting" to be "quite dead."[13] Finally, the Unnamable voice speaks in order to silence the "lies" of the others. But even this is not the end. The speaking continues though the speaker cannot be named. Each subsequent narrator inherits his predecessor's words, words that figure and disfigure the discourse of the one speaking: "I'm in words, made of words, others' words," the Unnamable says.[14] "If I could only find a voice of my own in all this babble, it would be the end of their troubles and of me" (84–85).

Like Beckett's other recent prose, *Company* begins in the babble of this narrative impasse, the same impasse in which *Jekyll and Hyde* ended. In *Company*, "a voice comes to one in the dark" and "tells of a past." Here it is the unrecognizable, disembodied "voice" that performs the action, that comes to "the one" who can only be an object of discourse, never a speaking subject, never a "first person":

> Could he speak to and of whom the voice speaks there would be a first. But he cannot. He shall not. You cannot. You shall not.[15]

The confusion of personal pronouns that marked the end of the narrative of Dr. Jekyll marks the beginning of this one; it has become the subject of the narrative itself. The absence of the first person from the text with which *Jekyll and Hyde* ended is the first problem here. Like Jekyll speaking of Hyde, the voice in *Company* also "speaks of himself as of another" (26). And the past the voice speaks of is not even "the past" or "your past," but "a past" that may or may not be connected to the "you" the voice addresses. Most of *Company* is made up of labored meditations seeking to establish some connection between the one who does the speaking in the text and the one to whom the voice refers. It cannot even determine who it is that inquires into these matters:

> Who asks in the end, Who asks? And in the end answers as above? And adds long after to himself, Unless another still. Nowhere to be found. Nowhere to be sought. The unthinkable last of all. Unnamable. Last person. I. Quick leave him. [24]

Like Jekyll's disowning of himself in his own text, *Company*'s voice always concerns "another than myself"; it leaves the "I" behind. And like Hyde's rejection of Jekyll's past and his destruction of its traces, the "you" of *Company* does not recognize as his own the past the voice speaks about and ascribes to him.

Allen Thiher's study of postmodern fiction claims that Beckett's earlier prose "ushers in the era of the schizo-text that is perhaps the postmodern text par excellence." He says that Beckett's work "gives full expression to the voice alienated from itself, the voice for which the first- and the third-person pronouns are a matter of indifference."[16] Although I agree that Beckett gives this form its "fullest expression," the era was ushered in much earlier. *Jekyll and Hyde* may not be the first "schizo-text" in the language either, but it is arguably the one most fundamental to the modern era. It has thematized and enacted the issue, and it has

RONALD R. THOMAS

entered our vocabulary as a sign of this challenge to our own subject-hood. To say that this is a "matter of indifference" in any of these texts is misleading. For Beckett's *Company* in particular it is a matter of profound importance. That text exists to question the possibility of self-representation; it may not be an answerable question, but *Company* demands that it be raised again and again.

We might look back to the gothic tradition's doppleganger tale as a source for *Dr. Jekyll and Mr. Hyde* and for the schizo-text in general. *Frankenstein, Melmoth the Wanderer, Caleb Williams,* and *Private Memoirs and Confessions of a Justified Sinner* are all concerned with the loss of personal authority in a character (and narrator) divided against itself. In each case, the denial of a repressed, hidden self leads to the formation of a destructive, monstrous version of it. But what distinguishes these "double-texts" from texts like *Jekyll and Hyde* or *Company* is that the earlier gothic forms retain an implicit confidence in the ideal of a unified self, however threatened it may be. The assumption behind *Frankenstein,* for example, is that Dr. Frankenstein's monstrous self-division is caused and maintained because of his silence, his refusal to give an account of his secret self. It is figured in his withdrawal from social (and sexual) intercourse. The division within himself also divides him from the world. When Frankenstein says in his narrative, "By the utmost self-violence I curbed the imperious voice of wretchedness, which sometimes threatened to declare itself to the whole world," he indicates, if unconsciously, that his repression—his silence—is what has performed the violence in this text.[17] He also indicates quite explicitly that the violence is directed against his own conception of himself—his wholeness, his integrity. But the monster's narrative testifies against its creator's, insisting of Frankenstein that he recognize his own creation. This distinguishes him from the more purely subversive figure of Hyde. Frankenstein's monster desires society, discourse, and integration as Frankenstein flees them. The effect of Frankenstein's narrative is a self-indictment, just as the effect of the monster's narrative is a self-exoneration. Frankenstein's story only confirms the very thing that he tries to deny in it: the self cannot be divided. Despite his casuistry, the monster is himself.

The force of a "schizo-text" such as *Jekyll and Hyde* or *Company* moves in the opposite direction. Here the issue is not that the subject denies his connection with the "other" self, nor that he refuses to articulate that connection. In the schizo-text, the subject cannot maintain any connection between the contrary aspects of the self once they are seen as in "contention." Nor is his text able to make them converge regardless of how persistent the attempt or how deep the desire to do so. "Of the two natures that contended in the field of my consciousness,"

Jekyll admits, "I was radically both" (82). When Jekyll confesses to Dr. Lanyon his relation to Hyde, it doesn't alter Jekyll's ability to control his transformations or restrict Hyde's activities, any more than his written confession to Utterson does. Unlike *Frankenstein*, the text does not accomplish even an implicit reunion of the aspects of the self. This essential difference deeply qualifies the analogies that Hirsch draws between the monsters created by Frankenstein and Jekyll.[18] The estrangement of the author from what he writes is, in the schizo-text, a sign of a genuine estrangement within himself. In the double-text, it is a sign of a lie, a denial of the true unity of the self.

Stevenson himself calls attention to his famous novella as a representation of this division within the author and this separation from his own text in an essay in which he describes his method of composition in a rather schizophrenic way. The essay, "A Chapter on Dreams," begins with Stevenson's description of the scenes of two recurring dreams dreamt by a friend of his when they were both students at Edinburgh College. The first scene was of a "surgical theatre" in which the dreamer witnessed the most "monstrous malformations and the abhorred dexterity of surgeons." The second consisted of a long staircase that the dreamer was doomed to climb unendingly, "stair after stair in endless series." The student soon became unable to distinguish his waking life from his dream life and began to "lead a double life—one of the day, one of the night—one that he had every reason to believe was the true one, another that he add no means of proving to be false." Eventually, the student was driven to seek the help of a doctor who, Stevenson claims, "with a single draught" "restored" the student to "the common lot of man."

Stevenson then explains his interest in this student's dreams as being rooted in two facts. First, he confesses that the student was really himself. Second, he was impressed by the fact that regardless of how many times he dreamed these dreams, they never reached a narrative conclusion, but remained in fragmentary form. "My imperfect dreamer," Stevenson says—speaking of himself again in the third person—was "unable to carry the tale to a fit end." By referring to himself in these pages as another, Stevenson seems in the writing of the essay to be reenacting the inevitable alienation of the writer from his text and from his own past as well. His remarks take on further interest in this connection when later in the same essay Stevenson describes how his own tale, *Strange Case of Dr Jekyll and Mr Hyde,* had its origin in another fragmentary dream that he had dreamed on the eve of his writing it. Like the student's, this dream was also divided into two distinct scenes: the first, in its incarnation in the story, pictures Jekyll at the window of the laboratory that had once been a "surgical theatre"; the second shows the figure who would become Mr.

RONALD R. THOMAS

Hyde being "pursued for some crime" and then taking the powder that transforms him in the presence of his pursuers. These scenes have obvious similarities to those of the earlier dreams that the dreamer was unable to bring "to a fit end." But these later dreams' portrayals of two different figures, one of which undergoes a split in personality within the dream, also echoes Stevenson's description of the student's "double life," anticipates his concern with the "double being" of Henry Jekyll in the tale, and sets up Stevenson's account in this same essay of his own "double life" as an author. "For myself—what I call I, my conscience ego," Stevenson goes on to say, "I am sometimes tempted to suppose he is no story-teller at all." Rather than being the "teller" of the story, Stevenson suspects that when he writes, he may simply be the agent of some "unseen collaborator, whom I keep locked in a back garret." The shift between the first- and third-person pronouns when Stevenson refers to himself as an author-agent in this statement, enacts his uncertainty about his control over his own texts, and it directly echoes Jekyll's inability to speak confidently about himself in the first person in his narrative. Like the Hyde that is hidden in Jekyll's back garret, Stevenson's texts seem to spring from the dream of a split ego. They are the expression of a double life, belonging not to himself but to some hidden "collaborator" who robs him of his own authority in the very act of writing. According to Stevenson, "I" am only a name.

Beckett's novels seem to spring out of the confusion of these same dreams. "There were times when I forgot not only who I was," says Molloy (echoing the ontological uncertainty of both Stevenson and Jekyll), "but that I was, forgot to be." "You have to be careful," he continues, "ask yourself questions, as for example whether you still are, and if no when it stopped, and if yes how long it will still go on, anything at all to keep you from losing the thread of the dream" (65). *Molloy*, the first volume in Beckett's trilogy, may be seen as existing on the frontier between the double-text and the schizo-text seeking to bring the fragmentary dream of life to some "fit end." The novel's two narrators—Molloy and Moran—may be the same person or they may be unwitting "collaborators." The novel itself is divided on this question. Its two halves may or may not be "doubles" of each other—two different versions of the same events. The reader cannot decide, nor can the narrator(s). "Between the Molloy I stalked within me thus and the true Molloy, after whom I was soon to be in full cry," says Moran, "the resemblance cannot have been great" (157). "For what I was doing I was doing neither for Molloy who mattered nothing to me, nor for myself, of whom I despaired, but on behalf of a cause which . . . was in its essence anonymous . . ." (156–57). The cause to which both Molloy and Moran are bound is the cause of this text. Its writing divides them as it brings them together; it makes self-possession ("myself") a thing to be despaired of, and it makes the project of the "I" into something "anonymous" in its essence.

The anonymity and absence of the author and the failure to make complete stories are the threats that the double-text resists. They become the inescapable fact with which the schizo-text contends. Nevertheless, rather than accepting those conditions unconditionally, Beckett's novels are constantly contending with those limitations, resuming over and over again the unfinished tale they have renounced. The other side of a world where there are no life stories is a world in which only stories have life, only the "fable," as *Company* calls it, that never ends. "The process continues none the less lapped as it were in meaninglessness," the voice of *Company* says. "Supine now you resume your fable where the act of lying cut it short" (61–62). Like Jekyll's, Beckett's fabling both is and is not an act of "lying." It is always and only a "conjuring out of nothing," an expression of the speaker that becomes a strange "creature" as soon as the words are spoken (43, 53). In *Company*, the fable's "end" never lies down within it, but is constantly getting up and moving—or crawling—outside of its indistinct boundaries.[19] "Crawling in the dark in the way described was too serious a matter and too all-engrossing to permit of any other business were it only the conjuring of something out of nothing" (*Company* 53). *Company's* conjuring of something else out of the nothing that the self has become is an extension of the nightmare of Henry Jekyll and the unending dreams of Stevenson. Jekyll's increasingly frequent and uncontrollable acts of transformation supplanted the purpose for which they were begun, eventually permitting him the freedom of no business other than the fear of being overtaken by the creature of his fable while he was in the act of writing about him.

Company is not made up entirely of speculations about its speaker and the one to whom and of whom it speaks. These speculations are interrupted by a series of other voices and a set of other words that presumably issue from "a past," providing, like the handwriting in *Jekyll and Hyde,* the single connection between "the voice" and "the one" of whom it speaks. Those voices are of three kinds: first, the supposed memory of the voices of "your mother" and "your father" along with those of a beggar-woman and a midwife; second, direct quotations from Beckett's previous narratives; and finally, allusive words and phrases from a larger literary past. Together, these voices and the words they speak implicitly provide the connections to a family and a society and a past that are explicitly absent or unattainable in the text. The sense of a personal, historical identity and the assurance of a natural or real presence that can be verified by a biological family or a familiar society are replaced here by a conversation between literary texts. The voices of family and society

RONALD R. THOMAS

become indistinguishable from written words in *Company,* just as Hyde's past exists only in the notebooks and formulae written by Jekyll.

In *Company,* the alternating words of rebuke and encouragement offered by "your mother" and "your father" enact an almost archetypal drama of isolation and reunion, punishment and reward, fall and redemption (11, 18, 22). They are joined by the one word spoken in the text by the midwife when he announces that the mother's labor is "Over!" Out of that one word, signalling both an ending and a starting over, the other words in the text are born. In *Company,* the words themselves become companions for the listener, relieving momentarily the fear of his own "fabling in the dark." There is endurance in these words; they suggest a "then" distinct from a "now," yet somehow joined to it (16). They lend what Heidegger calls "presence" to what is otherwise in *Company* a void that cannot be filled:

> The speaking does not cease in what is spoken. Speaking is kept safe in what is spoken. In what is spoken, speaking gathers the ways in which it persists as well as those which persist by it—its persistence, its presence.[20]

Like the other modernist texts we have referred to here, *Company* is about the words and voices that do not pass away. It is in this sense a life story—an almost unrecognizable one, but one with the essential characteristic: the "labored" tracing of an arc from birth to an almost death. As is true of *Jekyll and Hyde,* the life story is parodied and almost expires here. It is just barely sustained in the words of these "unstillable" voices from "a past" that offer the temporal and spatial presence that are lost to the one whose imagination is so "ill," so "reason-ridden" (*Company* 23, 33). This life story makes explicit what was implicit in *Jekyll and Hyde:* the self is not a natural production nor a private possession. It is a collaborative creation. It does not speak; it is written.

This is the reason that the echoes of a physical family in *Company* resonate in the echoes of a family of texts. Beckett's habitual self-referencing, his continual recasting of his own material, is frequently noted in his work. The references to *Watt,* the trilogy, *How It Is,* and several other previous novels are unmistakably important to the listening and remembering that are at the center of this text as well. They help establish a past for the "author" of this text, even if the past of its narrative voice is in question. *The Unnamable* seems to anticipate its fathering of *Company* in its opening pages:

> I am of course alone. Alone. That is soon said. Things have to be soon said. And how can one be sure, in such darkness? I shall have company. In the beginning. A few puppets. Then I'll scatter them, to the winds, if I can. [3]

But still more striking than the companionship of Beckett's own literary past in *Company,* however, is the presence a deeper literary past in the voices of other writers that cannot be forgotten, the buried allusions that haunt the text as persistently as the recurring ghost of the father does. Just before the recollection of a scene of his playing in the garden, for example, the "one on his back in the dark" notes the occurrence of an unidentifiable "odd sound" that immediately becomes identifiable to us as the presence of another author's voice in this text:

> Some soft thing softly stirring soon to stir no more. To darkness visible to close the eyes and hear if only that (*Company* 19).

We hear only Milton in the words "darkness visible"; stirring softly in that odd sound we see the figure of the fallen archangel also lying on his back in the dark, also haunted by the voices of a lost past. "By the voice," the next paragraph in *Company* begins, "a faint light is shed" (19). The shedding of the light is both a bestowal of the angel's remembered glory and a casting off of the serpent's deceptive skin. It is, for the one who listens, a remembering and an opening up into another world. The rebuke he recalls on the following pages, spoken by his mother when he falls from a fir tree in the garden, becomes framed within the story of this other fall in this other garden.

The faint light and the odd sound of Hamlet's ghost also gleam in the dark voices of *Company.* When the voice speaks again and again of "the shade of your father" and by its "repetitiousness" pressures the hearer to say "Yes I remember," the insistent voice of Hamlet's father's ghost seems to be dimly present as well, repeatedly demanding the prince to "Remember me" (I, v, 91). Even when denying it, the appearance and disappearance of the father's ghost haunts the pages of *Company* much as it does *Hamlet:*

> Your father's shade is not with you any more. It fell out long ago. You do not hear your footfalls any more. Unhearing unseeing you go your way. Day after day. The same way. As if there were no other any more. You used never to halt except to make your reckoning. [37]

It is difficult not to hear the voice of Hamlet's father and his bitter complaint that his life was halted with "No reckoning made" (I, iv, 76). Perhaps the ghost of Prince Hal's false father Falstaff and his "trim reckoning" of "a word" also live on in these words. It is as true for the one who listens in *Company* as it was for Hamlet that these dying, ghostly words must be reckoned with, and that they "Shall live / Within the book and volume of my brain" (I, v, 102–3). All of these voices belong to sons cut off from their fathers, fathers cut off from their sons, heirs cut off from

RONALD R. THOMAS

their inheritance. And the words they invoke compose a literary legacy, rewritten and relived in the mind of "the one" in this book.

The ghostly company Beckett's allusions call up is a bleak group; but in their bleakness is their force. What Christopher Ricks has said of Tennyson's use of allusion is as true, I believe, of Beckett's:

> His allusions rise when they speak not of a fullness reasserted, but of an emptiness encouragingly peopled from the past, an emptiness defied by a poetic solidarity.[21]

"Defiance" and "solidarity" may be too-solid characterizations for the faint poetic voice of Beckett's *Company*, this "devised deviser devising it all for company" (46). But like Chaucer's description of Dante—to whom *Company* also alludes by name—each of Beckett's lonely voices "can al devyse."[22] The way mortals speak, Heidegger says, is by "responding" to language, by "listening" to what is already present in the words: "Every word of mortal speech speaks out of such a listening, and as such a listening." The important thing, he adds, is "learning to live in the speaking of language" (209–10). In Beckett, a great company seems to be gathered into and living within each word; and even if he does not speak, the one on his back in the dark learns to listen to the company that is already present in the words and to devise for himself the pages of a past that he can occupy.

In the work of Beckett, as well as that of Conrad and Joyce, the author withdraws but does not quite disappear; he lives, if faintly, in the listening to and the speaking of language. Stevenson's *Jekyll and Hyde* prepares the way for this near disappearance and for the modernist notion of the autonomy of the text independent of the intentions of its author. Jekyll—as author—says he could only listen to the voices of his "text"—Hyde—in a "fearstruck ecstasy of listening"; he compares his alienation from his own actions to the watching of "the Babylonian finger on the wall . . . spelling out the letters of my judgment . . ." (88). His own hand becomes unrecognizable to him and stands in judgment as he writes his own story, just as his voice becomes unrecognizable when he hears it speaking out of his hidden self. For Beckett and his narrators, however, the speaking self's estrangement within its own multiplicity disturbs but does not terrify. Such "events" bring with them their own consolation, upsetting the paralyzing force of habit that deceives us into thinking of our "succession of selves" as one.[23] But they also bring the consoling presence of a "past" closer. "Listen to the leaves," a beloved voice murmurs in *Company*, alluding, perhaps, to the pages of many texts that can be heard within its own. "Eyes in each other's eyes you listen to the leaves" (48).

Both of these expressions of "schizotextuality" are responses to a larger cultural concern of the modern era that extends beyond the boundaries of literary theory and criticism. The development of psychoanalytic, sociological, and anthropological discourses about the self around the turn of the century codified a general cultural unease about the nature of the human self. These discourses raised to official and professional status the very questions that Dr. Jekyll investigated privately in his laboratory: the conflict among the elements and agencies of personality, the constitution of the "individual" in a social setting, and the persistence of past cultural formations within the psyche. Literary production, and in particular, what Bakhtin called "novelized" literary production, takes a kind of pleasure in generating these schizo-texts that function as acts of liberation from a script, violations of the boundaries in which "the text" circumscribes the self. Bakhtin's description of the "dialogical" in the novels of Dostoevsky speaks of this force as a "profound communication" that enacts a continual critique and reconceptualizing of the self:

> Man has no internal sovereign territory; he is all and always on the boundary; looking within himself, he looks *in the eyes of the other or through the eyes of the other.* . . . I cannot do without the other; I cannot become myself without the other; I must find myself in the other, finding the other in me. . . .[24]

We should read *Jekyll and Hyde* and *Company* not only as accounts of the self's entrapment within the leaves of a text or within the words of a language, then, but as narratives of self-discovery, of escape into an "other." The escape takes place not in the action of a potion or the completion of a story but in the mystery with which the texts conclude by refusing to conclude, in the discovery of a stranger within the self that may destroy the identity of the subject as we know it, but may also provide some company in its place. The self cannot be found if it is looked for in one place; it refuses to be only an "I" or a "you" or a "he" in these texts. Rather, the self exists on the boundaries between them, in the play of relational forces between father and son, doctor and patient, past and present, speaker and listener, writer and reader.

NOTES

1. Implicit to the genre, says Bakhtin, is "the radical restructuring of the image of the individual"; in the novel, he continues, "man ceased to coincide with himself, and consequently men ceased to be exhausted by the plots that contain them." See M. M. Bakhtin, *The Dialogic Imagination,* ed. Michael Holquist, tr. Caryl Emerson and Michael Holquist (Austin: University of Texas Press, 1981), 35. This account of the novel corresponds to similar claims made by Ian Watt in *The Rise of the Novel* (London: Chatto and Windus, 1957); Edward Said in

Beginnings: Intentions and Method (New York: Basic Books, 1975); and George Lukacs in *The Theory of the Novel,* tr. Anna Bostock (Cambridge, Mass.: MIT Press, 1971). Perhaps the most relevant for the purposes of this paper is Lukacs's analysis: "as the objective world breaks down, so the subject, too, becomes a fragment; only the 'I' continues to exist, but its existence is then lost in the insubstantiality of its self-created world of ruins" (53). In such a description of the novel, it becomes clear that the prose works of Beckett, for example, could not be considered "anti-novels." Like *Jekyll and Hyde,* they extend the subversive tradition of the novel by exposing the inadequacies of man's fictions about himself.

2. The importance of this matter is suggested not only in the way these texts work but in their autobiographical nature as well. Stevenson's essay "A Chapter on Dreams" offers a specific account of the composition of *Jekyll and Hyde* in the context of a larger discussion of how he writes his fiction. There, Stevenson refers to a set of unforgettable dreams he had as a student, dreams that had him living a "double life" (significantly, he presents them first as if they were the dreams of an acquaintance, and later reveals the acquaintance to be himself). Those dreams correspond directly to specific scenes in *Jekyll and Hyde,* as I make clear later in this essay. See Stevenson's "A Chapter on Dreams."

Beckett's *Company* also draws from events in its author's life to confront the problematics of authorship. John Pilling's review of the book says that it "gravitates more openly towards the genre of autobiography than anything [of Beckett's] before it," giving expression to several of the crucial childhood events Deirdre Bair speaks about in her biography of Beckett (127). See Deirdre Bair, *Samuel Beckett* (New York: Harcourt Brace Jovanovich, 1978); and John Pilling, "Review Article: 'Company,'" *Journal of Beckett Studies* 7 (1982): 127–31.

3. See also Lukacs 80: "The inner form of the novel has also been understood as the process of the problematic individual's journeying towards himself, the road from dull captivity within a merely present reality—a reality that is heterogeneous in itself and meaningless to the individual—towards clear self-recognition." The action of Stevenson's text (and later of Beckett's) is to fulfill this novelistic tradition by breaking novelistic conventions that "captivate" the self in cliché. Beckett's essay on Proust is virtually a manifesto on Proust's development of this tradition.

4. See Peter K. Garrett's essay in this volume on the general issue of narrative cohesion and the subversion of duality in *Jekyll and Hyde.*

5. Sigmund Freud, *Dora: An Analysis of a Case of Hysteria,* ed. Philip Rieff (New York: Collier Books, 1963), 30–31.

6. Cawelti defines the crime in a detective novel as representing "not only an infraction of the law but a disruption of the normal order of society" (83). He says that the announcement of the crime's solution is generally more important than the apprehension of the criminal because the explaining narrative reestablishes the threatened order and reassures the society of its cohesion. "The classical detective story," he claims, "offered a temporary release from doubt" for a society deeply troubled about its ideology of individualism and its moral and social repressiveness (105). See John G. Cawelti, *Adventure, Mystery, and*

Romance (Chicago: University of Chicago Press, 1976). I maintain that *Jekyll and Hyde* exposes early on the fragile and temporary quality of that release in its parody of detective story conventions.

7. Michel Foucault, *The History of Sexuality, Volume I: An Introduction,* trans. Robert Hurley (New York: Vintage Books, 1978) 58–67.

8. Michel Foucault, "What Is an Author?" in *Language, Counter-Memory, Practice,* tr. Donald R. Bouchard and Sherry Simon, ed. Donald R. Bouchard (Ithaca, N.Y.: Cornell University Press, 1977), 117.

9. Joseph Conrad, *Lord Jim* (Harmondsworth, England: Penguin Books, 1957), 253–54.

10. Joseph Conrad, *Heart of Darkness* (Harmondsworth, England: Penguin Books, 1973), 69.

11. James Joyce, *A Portrait of the Artist as a Young Man,* ed. Chester G. Anderson (Harmondsworth, England: Penguin Books, 1968), 215.

12. M. M. Bakhtin, *Problems of Dostoevsky's Poetics,* tr. R. W. Rostel (Ann Arbor, Mich.: Ardis Publishers, 1976), 201, 226.

13. Samuel Beckett, *Molloy* (New York: Grove Press, 1955), 7; and *Malone Dies* (New York: Grove Press, 1956), 1.

14. Samuel Beckett, *The Unnamable* (New York: Grove Press, 1958), 13.

15. Samuel Beckett, *Company* (New York: Grove Press, 1980), 8.

16. Allen Thiher, *Words in Reflection: Modern Language Theory and Postmodern Fiction* (Chicago: University of Chicago Press, 1984), 131.

17. Mary Shelley, *Frankenstein,* in *Three Gothic Novels,* intro. Mario Praz, ed. Peter Fairclough (Harmondsworth, England: Penguin Books, 1968), 458.

18. See Gordon Hirsch's essay in this volume for further consideration of *Jekyll and Hyde*'s debt to the gothic, and in particular to *Frankenstein.*

19. Bakhtin calls the novel an essentially unfinished form—an "unfolding genre" (*Dialogic Imagination,* 7); and Lukacs refers to it as "something in the process of becoming" (*Theory of the Novel,* 72–73). As such, the novel is the appropriate genre for an epoch like our own when, as Kermode says in his discussion on ending in the novel, "we move from transition to transition" in the absence of positive absolute truths. When Kermode says that in modern life "we exist in no intelligent relation to the past, and no predictable relation to the future," he echoes what these theorists of the novel have said about what characterizes a whole genre (Frank Kermode, *The Sense of an Ending* [New York: Oxford University Press, 1976], 101–2).

20. Martin Heidegger, "Language," in *Poetry, Language, Thought,* tr. Albert Hofstadter (New York: Harper and Row Publishers, 1975), 194.

21. Christopher Ricks, "Tennyson Inheriting the Earth," *Studies in Tennyson,* ed. Hallam Tennyson (Totowa, N.J.: Barnes and Noble Books, 1981), 81. Ricks's essay, along with John Hollander's *The Figure of Echo* (Berkeley: University of California Press, 1981), opens up important matters for a larger consideration of the whole subject of allusion. The importance of allusion to *Company* is suggested on its first page. The voice that speaks persistently of "a past" in *Company* (7–8) is said to make "occasional allusion to a present and more rarely to a future." It is to the past that the voice alludes with more frequency, urging "the one" to say, "Yes I remember," trying to convince

him to recognize those "allusions" to the past: "As if willing him by this dint to make it his" (16). John Pilling's review of *Company* regards it as a "palimpsest" (*Journal of Beckett Studies* 7 [1982], 129). He points out possible allusions to *The Merchant of Venice, A Midsummer Night's Dream, Love's Labour's Lost,* and "Dover Beach." His analysis of the text is primarily concerned, however, with seeing *Company* as a "compendium" of "self-plagiarism"—that is, as a series of Beckett's allusions to his own work.

22. Geoffrey Chaucer, *The Complete Works of Geoffrey Chaucer,* ed. Walter W. Skeet (Oxford: Clarendon Press, 1894), 149.

23. Samuel Beckett, *Proust* (New York: Grove Press, 1958), 8.

24. M. M. Bakhtin, "Toward a Reworking of the Dostoevsky Book," quoted by Tzvetan Todorov, *Mikhail Bakhtin: The Dialogical Principle,* tr. Wlad Godzich (Minneapolis: University of Minnesota Press, 1984), 96.

ILLUSTRATORS' INTERPRETATIONS

"A certain sinister block of building." *The Strange Case of Dr. Jekyll and Mr. Hyde,* illustrated by S. G. Hulme Beaman, frontispiece. London, Bodley Head, 1930.

"Did you ever remark that door?" *Strange Case of Dr. Jekyll and Mr. Hyde,*
illustrated by Edward A. Wilson, p. 5. New York: Limited Editions Club, 1952.

Utterson awaiting Hyde. *The Strange Case of Dr. Jekyll and Mr. Hyde,*
illustrated by Charles Raymond Macaulay, facing p. 42. New York: Scott-Thaw
Company, 1904. Photo, Library of Congress.

Hyde with beaker of potion. *Dr. Jekyll and Mr. Hyde,* illustrated by Mervyn Peake, p. 110. London: Folio Society, 1948.

"The man trampled calmly over the child's body." *The Strange Case of Dr. Jekyll and Mr. Hyde,* illustrated by Frank Gillet, R.I., p. 66. London: Collins' Cleartype Press, n.d.

"Trampling calmly over the child's body." *Strange Case of Dr. Jekyll and Mr. Hyde,* illustrated by Edward A. Wilson, p. 12. New York: Limited Editions Club, 1952.

Hyde killing Carew. *The Strange Case of Dr. Jekyll and Mr. Hyde,* illustrated by Charles Raymond Macaulay, facing p. 62. New York: Scott-Thaw Company, 1904. Photo, Library of Congress.

"Fled from the scene of these excesses, at once glorying and trembling." *The Strange Case of Dr. Jekyll and Mr. Hyde,* illustrated by S. G. Hulme Beaman, facing p. 122. London, Bodley Head, 1930.

DR. M'JEKYLL AND MR. O'HYDE.

"Dr. M'Jekyll and Mr. O'Hyde." *Punch*, 18 August 1888, p. 79.

III
QUESTIONS OF REPRESSION

FIVE

Children of the Night: Stevenson and Patriarchy

WILLIAM VEEDER

So I sidled up to the old gentleman, got into conversation with him and so with the damsel; and thereupon, having used the patriarch as a ladder, I kicked him down behind me.

Stevenson

I wonder why my stories are always so nasty.

Stevenson

The psychoanalytic critic is a literary historian.

William Kerrigan

My study of *Jekyll and Hyde* began as an attempt to answer two questions. Why are there, for all practical purposes, no women in Stevenson's novella? And why are the major characters, Jekyll, Utterson, and Lanyon, all professional men as well as celibates? These specific questions lead me toward the larger concerns, the enduring power, of *Jekyll and Hyde*. Since defining this power has become my project—in which answering the two questions about gender and profession plays a part—I should begin with what I take to be the overall concern of the novella. *Jekyll and Hyde* dramatizes the inherent weakness of late-Victorian social organization, a weakness that derives from unresolved pre-oedipal and oedipal emotions and that threatens the very possibility of community. Since these emotions appear in Stevenson's life, as well as in his novella and his culture, I will examine all three nodes in my study of the power of *Jekyll and Hyde*.

I will first set forth the social, psychological, and critical elements deployed in this study.

> It seems to me that the story of Jekyll and Hyde, which is presumably presented as happening in London, is all the time very unmistakably happening in Edinburgh. [Chesteron 51]

> The most important focus in the story, as we might expect, will be on Jekyll's attitude toward his double. [Eigner 145]

What these two sensible observations do not account for is what I want to explore. The site of *Jekyll and Hyde* is, I feel, not simply London or Edinburgh but the larger milieu of late-Victorian patriarchy; the focus of the story is less on Jekyll's attitude toward Hyde than on the way that the Jekyll/Hyde relationship is replicated throughout Jekyll's circle. Lanyon, Enfield, and Utterson participate so thoroughly in Jekyll/Hyde that they constitute an emblematic community, a relational network, which reflects—and thus allows us readers a perspective on—the network of male bonds in late-Victorian Britain.[1] This network marks a psychological condition as a cultural phenomenon. The cultural and psychological come together in Stevenson's famous statement of theme: "that damned old business of the war in the members" (L2, 323). Because members of the psyche are at war, other members must be— family members, members of society, genital members. The resulting casualty is not simply Jekyll/Hyde but culture itself.

Focusing on society might seem to ally me with the many critics who interpret *Jekyll and Hyde* as an indictment of Victorian repressiveness, a tale of decorum and desire. "[Jekyll's] society . . . refuses to recognize or accept the place of pleasure in identity" (Day 92).[2] Repression is indeed important in *Jekyll and Hyde*, but what is being repressed is not *pleasure*. Victorian culture *fosters* as well as represses pleasure in *Jekyll and Hyde*. To call Stevenson's men "joyless" (Miyoshi 471) is to overstate. "All intelligent, respectable men, and all judges of good wine" (43), Utterson and his peers are capable of genuine friendship (the word "friend" appears at least thirty-three times)[3] that expresses itself in "pleasant dinners" (43), particularly those hosted by Henry Jekyll, who entertains "five or six old cronies" early in the story (43), celebrates his return from reclusion by becoming "once more their familiar guest and entertainer" (56), and sees Utterson for the last time at "the doctor's . . . small party" on January 8 (56). The pleasure of these gatherings is enhanced by their domestic nature. Rather than entertaining at clubs, old friends invite one another home. Again Jekyll is the model. His entrance hall is called by Utterson "the pleasantest room in London" (41).

Especially considering how much of Robert Louis Stevenson is invested in these companionable pleasures—his love of wine and boon fellowship—why does he include such pleasures in what I will argue is an ultimately damning presentation of Jekyll's circle? He could easily have satirized this group as he did other bourgeois males who "had at first a human air/ In coats and flannel underwear./ They rose and walked upon their feet/ And filled their bellies full of meat./ They wiped their lips when they had done,/ But they were Ogres every one" (Calder 152). Stevenson foregoes so complete an indictment because society is

WILLIAM VEEDER

not completely odious, pleasure not entirely interdicted. Of course, Stevenson wishes in his life and in *Jekyll and Hyde* that society were less hypocritical about pleasures natural and healthy, and even pleasures unnatural and unhealthy. But the companionable pleasures in *Jekyll and Hyde* function less by implicit contrast with outré desires than as emblems of promise tragically unfulfilled. Though boon fellowship should combine with public service to constitute the rewards of a professional life, the combination in fact constitutes a threat to society itself.

This threat cannot be explained by an interpretation that locates the novella's paramount tension between decorum and desire. Jekyll himself points to such a tension, and surely it is an awkward one: men who officially embody and articulate orthodoxy incline to violate it. This awkwardness is, however, not sufficient to account for Jekyll's anguish or Stevenson's novella. Established men have long since discovered how to mediate between decorum and desire. The old boys cover for one another. Lanyon will get Jekyll the chemicals regardless of what the night and secrecy may be hiding; Enfield will handle Hyde's trampling of the child without calling in the police. If, however, the repression of *pleasure* is not the principal dilemma in *Jekyll and Hyde,* another sort of repression is at work. Males use traditionally sanctioned social "forms"— friendship and professionalism—to screen subversive drives directed *at one another.* The dual roles of friend and attorney allow Utterson to express his own private anxiety about Jekyll's will; Lanyon uses his professional "services" to excuse his curiosity about Edward Hyde. "Under the seal of our profession" (80) rage what I will argue are the regressive emotions of oedipal sons and sibling rivals.

At stake in *Jekyll and Hyde* is nothing less than patriarchy itself, the social organization whose ideals and customs, transmissions of property and title, and locations of power privilege the male. Understanding the Fathers in *Jekyll and Hyde* is helped by seeing patriarchy both traditionally and locally: first in terms of its age-old obligations, then in terms of its immediate configuration in late-Victorian Britain. Traditionally the obligations of patriarchs are three: to maintain the distinctions (master-servant, proper-improper) that ground patriarchy; to sustain the male ties (father-son, brother-brother) that constitute it; and to enter the wedlock (foregoing homosexuality) that perpetuates it.[4] Exclusion and inclusion are the operative principles. Men must distinguish the patriarchal self from enemies, pretenders, competitors, corruptors; and they must affiliate through proper bonds at appropriate times. What Stevenson devastatingly demonstrates is that patriarchy behaves exactly counter to its obligations. Distinctions that should be maintained are elided, so that bonds occur where divisions should obtain; and affiliations that should be sustained are sundered, so that males war with one another and refuse to wed.[5]

As his love of boon fellowship indicates, Robert Louis Stevenson respects the bonds traditional with patriarchy even as he rages against the failures of patriarchs. He faults established men not only for being Fathers (dictatorial, repressed, hypocritical) but also for *not* being Fathers (rigorous, supportive, procreative). The author who within seven years of *Jekyll and Hyde* ensconced himself firmly, if wryly, as the patriarch of Vailima, who put the Athenaeum on his calling cards and was called by Gosse "the most clubbable of men" (Furnas 99), who quipped sincerely, "Let us hope I shall never be such a cad any more as to be ashamed of being a gentleman" (L2, 131), and who was increasingly moved by Thomas Carlyle ("the old man's style is stronger on me than it ever was" [L2, 28]), this author is finally closer in social vision to Carlyle than to, say, J. S. Mill. Despite fashionable nods to socialism, Stevenson inclines not to a Mill-like reorganization of society but to a Carlylean nostalgia for earlier probities.[6] Stevenson hates for the Fathers to be overbearing, but he hates still more for the Fathers to be weak. He criticizes his own father's presidential address to the Royal Society of Edinburgh for being "so modest as to suggest a whine"; he calls Thomas Stevenson's gloominess "plaguey peevishness"; and he adds, "My Dear Father,—Allow me to say, in a strictly Pickwickian sense, that you are a silly fellow" (L2, 243, 244).

Breakdowns in the three traditional obligations of patriarchy are so important to *Jekyll and Hyde* that I will structure my analysis of the novella in terms of them. But before undertaking that analysis, I must set forth the equally important role of patriarchy as an immediate presence in late-Victorian Britain. In the household of Thomas Stevenson, the patriarchal was inseparable from the professional. Engineering and medicine were, like law, "eminently respectable and had contributed much to Edinburgh's wealth and status" (Calder 2). The emergence of the professions as one of the major forces in social organization had occurred in Stevenson's own century. "Before the Industrial revolution," Larson establishes,

> even the profession of law . . . had not yet developed the stable
> and intimate connection with training and examination that
> came to be associated with the professional model in the nine-
> teenth century. . . . Professions are, therefore, relatively recent
> social products. . . . In England, of the thirteen contemporary
> professions . . . ten acquired an association of national scope
> between 1825 and 1880.[7]

WILLIAM VEEDER

Upper-middle-class professional men are for Robert Louis Stevenson the principal expression of the patriarchal tradition in the Victorian period, despite the lingering presence of a landed, titled aristocracy and Stevenson's nostalgia for the gentry Balfours of his mother's line. Patriarchy, as Stevenson considers it, is essentially *bourgeois*. These men are not the products of ancient families and land tenure. Their bonds are formed through the educational process ("old mates both at school and college" [36]), which prepares men not for the aristocratic pleasures of leisure and sport but for the middle-class ideals of hard work and public service. "Name" is important because it constitutes not continuity of title but hard-earned respect.

As a third-generation professional, Robert Louis Stevenson has a rare perspective on patriarchy. In addition to the Fathers' egregious hypocrisies—leading citizens who go wenching on Saturday night and show up at church hungover provoke Stevenson to rage—there are subtler, finally more threatening disparities between roles and realities. Professions can function as empty forms that Fathers deploy to make sons conform to paternal wills and dreams. Stevenson feels particularly threatened because he is in part recoiling from the impact of professionalism upon his own father who wanted so intensely to place him in engineering or law. Thomas himself was coerced by *his* father into a profession for which he had no special aptitude. He admitted that he never mastered the formulae basic to structural engineering. Despite his dedicated scrutiny of nature, Thomas's mind proceeded by intuitive leaps; his true gifts were, like Louis's, literary and existential. He was a gifted storyteller, a sincere lover of reading, and a man graced with a tremendous if inhibited capacity for sensuous experience. In indicting the professions, Louis is thus doing more than striking back against paternal domination. He is trying to save himself from his father's fate.

The professions have additional moment for Robert Louis Stevenson because they relate to father in a second way. To explain this, I must posit what I will argue for in detail in section 2: Stevenson is, as Kanzer and Fiedler have maintained, a man torn by oedipal emotions. Although such emotions may seem a long way from Stevenson's concern with the professions in late-Victorian Britain, the two relate directly. Freud argues that desire, which is directed toward mother initially and is interdicted at the oedipal moment, can reappear under the pressures of adolescence—in its initial triangular configuration. Mother is again the object of desire, and father again the rival. Now, however, desire can be managed outside strictly domestic confines, in the realm of public action and career choice. (Work is the one outlet of human energy that Freud ranks along with sex.) Father-son quarrels over careers are thus often restagings of childhood antagonisms. Even a biographer as wary of Freudianism as Furnas attests that Louis's famous battles with Thomas over profession (and religion) are inseparable from the men's fierce possessiveness toward Margaret. In turn, a resolution of oedipal antagonisms through professional achievement becomes possible. The very fact that the Fathers' professional inadequacies are so present to Stevenson means that he is characterized by an adult awareness denied to patriarchs hypocritical or complacent. If Louis can go on to express this awareness in fiction, if he can indict fathers as Fathers by revealing the inadequacy of their professionalism, he will write the book that constitutes him professionally. By revealing in the fathers an unresolved oedipal rage that he himself is resolving in the revelation, Stevenson will extend the old war among the members from the domestic to the professional front and will thus have a chance for victory. But things, alas, are not this simple.

For one thing, awareness of patriarchal failure threatens the son. If he cannot respect the father's masculinity and achievement, the son cannot negotiate either the pre- or the postlatency stages of oedipal conflict; he cannot effect that bonding with the father that will confirm his own sense of sexual adequacy and will encourage him to contribute to society's welfare. Worse still, Stevenson knows that most of his indictment of patriarchal inadequacy can be turned back on himself. Not only is he too racked by unresolved oedipal rages, but he has not achieved by 1885 what he respects professionally—the writing of great books, which alone, despite the puffs of his friends, constitutes true professionalism in letters. Even hypocrisy can also be charged against Stevenson, too. His terrible quarrels with Thomas do not prevent him from continuing to accept his father's money.

Another problem for Louis is that fighting on two fronts—the professional as well as the domestic—has not shaped his art up through the middle of 1885. He has tended to configure himself as only, as still, a son. Besides the *Garden of Verses,* there is "Markheim," where the "war in the members" ends with the son surrendering to the (bad) father. *Jekyll and Hyde* was apparently conceived in the same spirit, but, quite astonishingly, Stevenson effects—between the Notebook Draft and the Printer's Copy—a change that enables him to fight both the domestic and the professional wars in his life. Discussing the novella's genesis, Stevenson lists first among the incorporated dream episodes "the scene at the window" ("A Chapter on Dreams"). Killing, in other words. Who is killing whom? In the Notebook Draft, Hyde's victim is "Lemsome." Lemsome incorporates Stevenson's worst fears about himself as a weak, grown-up son. "A youngish man of about twenty-eight, with a fine forehead and good features; anoemically pale; shielding a pair of suffering eyes under blue spectacles," Lemsome is called "an incurable cad" by the young author whom we have seen promise never to be "a cad any more." In killing Lemsome/Stevenson, Hyde/Stevenson is only visiting once more upon himself the anger that psychic health and maturity require him to direct outward at the fathers. By belaboring himself as failed son, Louis remains a failure; by not waiting for confrontation with the father, he precludes a therapeutic working through of oedipal emotions; by not directing anger at a patriarch, he prevents his feelings about professionalism from becoming central.

Stevenson escapes sonship by changing the character of Hyde's victim. Lemsome, the paradigm failed son of the Notebook Draft, becomes in the Printer's Copy the paradigm patriarch, Sir Danvers Carew. Carew, the only "Sir" in a novel filled with "sir"s, is essentially bourgeois: he is affiliated with the House of Commons, not the House of Lords; he lives in a London square, not a country house. Killing Carew means that Stevenson's self-hate is turned outward in an act of violence therapeutic both domestically and professionally. Carew is both a father surrogate and a Father. Since Carew as "an aged beautiful gentleman with white hair" (46) can stand in for the aging but still strikingly handsome Thomas Stevenson, Louis can deploy literary patricide to murder his "father" rather than himself. He can, moreover, enlist Carew in the other war in his life—the professional. Carew points Stevenson's rage toward the Fathers as well as toward father. Lemsome, whose suit "implied both a lack of means and a defect of taste," is "a bad fellow" of the lower middle class, whereas Carew is a distinguished man who contributes the professional initials "M.P." (53) to the long list set forth with Jekyll: "M.D., D.C.L., LL.D., F.R.S., &c." (35). Carew focuses Stevenson's rage at the patriarchs as professionals.

Stevenson's capacity to see what the fathers overlook and to announce what they hide does not, of course, result in any overnight change in him psychologically. But *Jekyll and Hyde* does constitute a milestone. The novella brings professional presence to Stevenson for the first time. The fame and the revenue that he needs so desperately begin to flow in, and they remain with him until death. He can, in turn, especially after the death of his father ("I almost begin to feel as if I should care to live; I would, by God! and so I begin to believe I shall" [Furnas 263]), take a less hostile stance against the patriarchy, a stance more in keeping with his essentially conservative nature. What happens is not that Stevenson comes to countenance all that he had once indicted in contemporary professionalism. Rather, with the passing years and increasing successes, Stevenson, like Carlyle, exercises a nostalgic return to an earlier, more feudal type of patriarchy that, in Louis's case, can mediate between the rigorous professionalism of the Stevensons and his historical fascination with the Balfours. I agree with Harvie that "we must see *Weir of Her-miston* . . . as a conservative parable of law and duty. . . . Weir towers over every other character in the book. . . . Climbing 'the great staircase of his duty' he, in a social context, is a figure . . . powerfully and sympathetically symbolic" (122, 123). Harvie is equally persuasive when he finds in Stevenson's own life a comparable move to nostalgic patriarchy. "Ultimately Stevenson's political creed is authoritarian but—unlike Kipling's—feudal and familial rather than technocratic. Weir is an image of the power of the legal system which underlay the Scots enlightenment, yet which was drawn from a pre-existent social state not unlike that which Stevenson himself tried to recreate in Samoa: a charismatic authority now being sapped by imperialist bureaucrats as much as by socialistic bureaucrats at home" (124).

Stevenson's involvement in *Jekyll and Hyde* means that the very psyche I am examining is not easy to define. On the one hand, the childhood into which the patriarchs of the novella regress can be seen as ultimately Stevenson's own. The "brown" fog that enwraps Utterson's world (48) is the farthest emanation of Louis's terrors, which emerged first as a childhood nightmare about the color brown, then reemerged as a boyhood nightmare about a brown dog, and eventually shaped itself into the Brownies who personified for him the unconscious processes themselves.[8] Likewise, the nighttime in which every violent event of *Jekyll and Hyde* occurs is a protraction of the long nights of fear that Louis endured as a sickly boy. "All night long in the dark and wet,/ A man goes riding by./ Late in the night when the fires are out,/ Why does he gallop and gallop about?" ("Windy Nights," 3–6).

On the other hand, my title for this essay is *children* of the night, not *child*, because *Jekyll and Hyde* cannot be reduced to the life of Robert Louis Stevenson. He transforms biographical materials and emotions into a critical portrait of his times. He does so not by attempting a "realistic" fiction but by representing male anxiety itself. "Characters" are the *occasion* of this revelation. They act out patterns rather than express personal histories. They cannot be psychoanalyzed, but their actions can. My approach to the psyches of Stevenson's characters is basically through the insights of Stevenson's contemporary, Sigmund Freud.

Not only are Freud and Stevenson both products of late-nineteenth-century European culture; they share the more particular fact of personal concern with and anxiety about professionalism, fathers, and Fathers. Still more important, they envision the psyche, experience, and art as each multileveled and occlusive. "After all, what one wants to know is not what people did, but why they did it—or rather, why they *thought*

WILLIAM VEEDER

they did it." This fascination with the workings of the psyche is eminently characteristic of Freud, but the words here are Stevenson's (L1, 35). Equally Freudian is Stevenson's insistence that "everything is true; only the opposite is true too: *you must believe both equally or be damned*" (Furnas 412). This recognition of experience as self-contradictory attunes Stevenson to the self-deceptive workings of the psyche in others and in himself.

> You [Henley] were not quite sincere with yourself; you were seeking arguments to make me devote myself to plays, unbeknown, of course, to yourself. [L1, 304]

> [I am a person who is] a hater, indeed, of rudeness in others, but too often rude in all unconsciousness himself. . . . we [he and Fanny] had a dreadful over-hauling of my conduct as a son the other night; and my wife stripped me of my illusions and made me admit I had been a detestable bad one. [L2, 275, 295]

Stevenson sees art itself deriving from the same hidden sources of meaning and motive. *Jekyll and Hyde* "came out of a deep mine" (L2, 309). Stevenson's definition of art constitutes a Freudian challenge. "There is but one art—to omit" (L1, 173).

Jekyll and Hyde represents psychological experiences multilayered and repressed, and I will read it accordingly. As Dr. Jekyll hides beneath his distinguished professionalism the murderous Mr. Hyde, so the name "Jekyll" hides—as several critics have noted—the homicidal "je kyll."[9] Other names in the story work the same way. Dr. Lanyon, who dies because his professional judgment succumbs to his precipitate curiosity, is named "Hastie"; Utterson, despite his years of dour legalism, is the utter son in several senses, as I will show later. Names, in turn, are emblematic of the multilayered workings of virtually every feature of *Jekyll and Hyde*. In terms of plot: as we wonder what Hyde is doing on his late-night excursions, we wonder why Carew is mailing a letter (47) late at night in what may be an unsavory neighborhood down by the river (46). In terms of characterization: as we are unsatisfied by Jekyll's rationalization of his desire for the potion, we question whether Utterson's concern for Jekyll's safety accounts adequately for his obsession with Edward Hyde. In terms of setting: as we experience the horrific last hour of Jekyll/Hyde, we ask why the laboratory is presented as so benignly domestic. And, emblem of all these emblems, why is Jekyll's chemist named "Maw"?

In attempting to answer these and many other questions about the overdetermined narrative of *Jekyll and Hyde,* I make no claim that Robert Louis Stevenson is conscious of all their significances. Obviously he is not. What I do claim is that diverse elements coherently support

Stevenson's thoroughly conscious indictment of late-Victorian patriarchy. The overdetermined nature of this indictment requires a comparable intricacy of response from readers. I see male emotions ranging from friendship to rivalry to homoerotic desire to homicidal rage; individual characters enact various roles, with Jekyll, for example, functioning as model bourgeois and oedipal son and oedipal father and sibling rival and homosexual lover; scenes are shaped by diverse forces, from the biographical, to the contexts of Western patriarchy and its late-Victorian manifestations, to patterns of consciousness based on Freudian models which help illuminate both the traditional and the immediate dilemmas of patriarchal culture.

My historical interest is where I want to end this introduction, because such an interest helps emphasize a fact about *Jekyll and Hyde* that has remained largely unrecognized by critics. Stevenson's novella expresses the malaise of late-Victorian Britain. Stevenson shares the belief of his apparently more representative colleagues—Gissing, Moore, James, Hardy—that Mrs. Grundy and Mr. Mudie must be extirpated and that British fiction must become an adult representation of adult realities. (This revulsion at hypocrisy is part of what Stevenson's biographers have repeatedly pointed to—his participation in his generation's disaffiliation from organized religion and enthusiasm for Darwin and other secular thinkers.) What makes *Jekyll and Hyde* particularly late-Victorian becomes clear in light of the novella's most relevant High Victorian predecessors, the paradigm novels of oedipal conflict—*David Copperfield, Great Expectations,* and *The Ordeal of Richard Feverel.* Dickens and Meredith here focus on the son and present the professional characters as largely incidental. By focusing on patriarchy and professionalism, Stevenson is reflecting the widely recognized "autumnal" quality of late-Victorian life, the sense that something was the matter not simply at home but in society itself. Oedipal antagonism functions in Stevenson not as the private drama of Pip and Richard Feverel but as the latent cause of cultural decline.

I. Proper Distinctions and Illicit Elisions

My analysis of Stevenson's patriarchs is structured in terms of their traditional obligations. Studying "proper" distinctions and male ties will bring me to wedlock, and thus to the causes and the consequences of woman's exclusion from *Jekyll and Hyde.* Making distinctions presupposes recognizing similarities. "I see you feel as I do," Enfield's words to Utterson after Hyde's first outrage (32), echo Enfield's earlier empathy with the doctor at the scene of the outrage. "He was like the rest of us. . . . I knew what was in his mind" (31). Utterson is comparably bound to Poole during Hyde's subsequent atrocities. "I felt something of what you

WILLIAM VEEDER

describe" (68), the lawyer admits, after the two men have turned "both pale . . . [with] an answering horror in their eyes" (61) and before "the two men looked at each other with a scare" (71). Such ideal solidarity between patriarchs and servants and among patriarchs is the context for distinctions that damn outsiders. The chief object of exclusion is of course Edward Hyde, whose absolute disjunction is insisted on by terms drawn from religion ("Satan . . . devilish . . . child of Hell . . . Evil" [32, 36, 94, 68]), from zoology ("like a monkey . . . ape-like" [69, 101]), and from mythology ("Juggernaut . . . fiend . . . troglodytic" [31, 36, 40]). These exclusionary terms express the patriarchy's need to confirm Hyde as a usurper. Utterson's fear that Hyde would "step into the said Henry Jekyll's shoes" (35) seems allayed by Lanyon's description of Hyde's "laughable" appearance. "His clothes . . . although they were of rich and sober fabric, were enormously too large for him in every measurement" (77–78). Here is a patent pretender to a position that he literally cannot measure up to.

Or so the patriarchs want to believe. To establish that traditional distinctions are breaking down in late-Victorian society, *Jekyll and Hyde* dramatizes the thorough implication of patriarchy in Edward Hyde. A wonderful pun bonds Lanyon with Hyde when the doctor is called "hide-bound . . . hide-bound" (43). The cane that Hyde uses to kill Carew belongs ultimately to Utterson; the name that replaces Hyde's in the will of Jekyll is Utterson's own; and the expression that seems to confirm Hyde's alterity—"the other" (40)—is soon applied to Utterson (41). Enfield shares Hyde's propensity for night stalking and for bringing along a cane (in the context of Cain [29, 30]). Hyde's caning of Carew has no counterpart in Enfield's conduct, of course,[10] but in his role as narrator, Enfield reveals a complicity in Hyde's first act of night violence that colors the scene significantly and thus warrants our close attention.

Take, for example, the epithets which Enfield applies to the child trampler. "My gentleman . . . my gentleman . . . my prisoner . . . gentleman . . . my man" (31, 32, 33). Even allowing both for the slightly more formal British usage of "my" in such expressions and for a touch of irony in Enfield's tone, these phrases certainly involve him more personally with Hyde than judgmental phrases like "this monster . . . this demon . . . this blackguard . . . this beast" would have. Especially cued by "gentleman," we recognize in the outcome of the confrontation something closer to gentlemanly fellowship than we would expect. "So we all set off, the doctor and the child's father, and our friend and myself, and passed the rest of the night in my chambers; and next day, when we had breakfasted, went in a body to the bank" (32). How odd the interpolated—and thus ostensibly unnecessary—clause "when we had breakfasted." There is a civility, an instinct for form, that seems out of place if Hyde is really a fiend or troglodyte or ape. That "we all set off" is, moreover, inaccurate. All the women who partook so vigorously in the confrontation with Hyde are left behind. Of course, ladies could not enter a bachelor's flat at 4:00 A.M., but propriety is not the chief issue. Exclusion from Enfield's sentence and from the narrative's subsequent events occurs because "we" simply cannot mean "all." In Enfield's world, "we all" are all male. The old boys "in a body" exclude anybody else. Notice that the "all" includes the physician. Someone on this night was so ill that a doctor had to be called at 3:00 A.M., yet that doctor leaves the scene without ever seeing his patient. For the first of many times in *Jekyll and Hyde,* professionalism functions as a screen. The physician's night journey toward the patient has led to a very different goal—the presence of Hyde and the chambers of Enfield. "Chamber," which has already meant legal chambers in the novella (29), has its more private connotation here because the patriarchs will resolve this awkward matter privately. Even the law is an outsider when it does not foster the more absolute force of patriarchal will.

Exculpation of Hyde has marked Enfield's narration from the start. Though he expresses sincere outrage at Hyde behaving "like some damned Juggernaut" (31), Enfield makes our crucial first experience of Hyde quite benign. "I saw two figures; one a little man who was stumping along eastward at a good walk, and the other a girl of maybe eight or ten who was running as hard as she was able" (31). Note that "the other" here is not Hyde. "Little . . . stumping along. . . good walk" present him quite innocuously, whereas the other is the violent one running hard. We are then told that the two collided "naturally enough" (31). Why "naturally"? Since the streets have been established as absolutely quiet at 3:00 A.M., why didn't Hyde hear the furiously clattering feet of the girl and avoid her? Our suspicion is soon confirmed. "The rumour of the approach of any passenger preceded him by a long time. . . . the footfalls of a single person, while he is still a great way off, suddenly spring out distinct from the vast hum and clatter of the city" (38). Hyde's collision with the child is not inevitable, so why does an inveterate nightwalker like Enfield call it natural? At best, Hyde is socially insouciant if he is too preoccupied to hear the child's ringing footfall. At worst, Hyde did hear her coming, and collided with her intentionally. Either possibility is glossed over by Enfield's word "naturally."

Even with the aftermath of Hyde's outrage, Enfield reacts less wholeheartedly than his most indignant statements would warrant. He seems initially to respond like St. George when his fox-hunting expression "I gave a view halloa" (31) suggests he will run the malefactor to earth. Though he does indeed catch and collar Hyde, Enfield describes the

WILLIAM VEEDER

pursuit with the idiom "I . . . took to my heels" (31). He says, in other words, that he fled *from*, not *after*, Hyde. (The meaning "to flee from" is confirmed not only by the OED[11] but by Hyde himself, who apologizes to Lanyon with the words "my impatience has shown its heels to my politeness" [78]). An unconscious inclination to free Hyde, as well as the conscious determination to capture him, marks the patriarchy's uncomfortable implication in what it officially condemns. Enfield may call Hyde "a fellow that nobody would have to do with" (33), but he himself has already called Hyde "our friend" (32). The ironical edge to this expression in this context does not mitigate entirely the patriarchy's investment in the expression. Rather than nobody having anything to do with Hyde, everybody who counts has already had breakfast with him.

Hyde's stalking the London streets at 3:00 A.M. shows him up to no good, but Enfield is out at the same hour. What has *he* been doing? As a "well-known man about town" (29), Enfield explains himself with the glib "I was coming home from some place at the end of the world" (31). The name En(d)-field suggests that the patriarch is as much an extremist as the Juggernaut. I even find myself wondering about that other night-walker whom Hyde encounters, Sir Danvers Carew. What is he doing out? The official version is that he was "only inquiring his way. . . . he had been probably carrying [a letter] to the post" (46, 47). But I wonder. How could Carew not know his way to the mailbox if he were simply stepping out of his house to post a letter? Moreover, are we sure that Carew lives in this neighborhood? "Not far from the river" (46) could be a respectable place like Pimlico or Chelsea, but it could also be the rundown and dangerous docksides of Dickens, especially since a servant maid can apparently rent a whole house here (46).[12] And why does Carew carry no identification? Established men who leave their wallets behind but take their money and wander riverfront areas and engage young men in conversation—such men are recognizable types, particularly in light both of the prostitute who approaches Hyde at about the same hour (94) and of the verb "accosted" ("the old man bowed and accosted the other" [46]), which can mean "to solicit for immoral purposes." My point is not that Carew is such a man, but that Stevenson need not have set the situation up this way if he did not want to suggest the possibility of Carew's implication in Hyde. Stevenson need only establish unambiguously that Carew was mailing a letter at a postbox in his own square, that the servant maid was looking from her attic room in her master's own house, and that Hyde was trespassing into the neighborhood removed safely from Soho. The sheep would be distinct from the wolves. Instead, "man about town" is a term appropriate to Hyde and to Enfield and Carew. What all these men are "about" is unclear.

Distinctions blur so thoroughly that even an admirable servant of the patriarchy like Poole is implicated in Hyde. Poole speaks to Utterson "hoarsely" in a "broken" voice (62, 63), just as Hyde has addressed Utterson "hoarsely. . . . with a somewhat broken voice" (39, 40). What we take to be a sign of venality in Hyde—that he "did not look the lawyer in the face" (39) during their meeting in the bystreet—recurs with Poole who "had not once looked the lawyer in the face" (62) during their meeting in Utterson's home. Hyde's gesture of "stamping with his foot" (47) before Carew's murder is repeated by Poole who "stamped on the flags" (70) after Hyde's death. These associations of Poole with Hyde do not call seriously into question the servant's probity (context distinguishes each of his actions from Hyde's), but they do suggest that any male associated with patriarchy harbors a capacity for otherness.

Poole in this regard is aptly named. Watery depths belie the apparently taut surface of patriarchy. That Jekyll "is in deep waters" is recognized by Utterson (41), but the lawyer cannot see that the rest of the patriarchy is swamped, too. "The drowned city" of London (53) is their foggy common ground. Utterson and Poole entering "the deep well" of Jekyll's courtyard as "the scud had banked over the moon" (68) are in over their heads. They feel safer when they reach "the shelter of the theatre," but they cannot escape the depths simply by exchanging inside for outside. "Even in the houses the fog had begun to lie thickly" (51). Distinctions dissolve. Beneath the theater's "foggy cupola" (33), Utterson is particularly at risk because this realm that seems so ostensibly other is in fact close to home. The theater is called "gaunt" (51), the lawyer lives on "Gaunt Street" (39). Thus his home, which seemed safely apart from the scientific theater, is in fact associated with it. The reassuring distinctions and resolute differentiations essential to Utterson's repression of otherness are dissolved by the elision of inner and outer. All the world becomes a stage, as the drama of the unconscious is enacted in the "anatomical theatre" (88). Utterson, "though he enjoyed the theatre, had not crossed the doors of one for twenty years" (29). Nor does he realize that he has done so when he visits the anatomical theater for "the first time" (51). What Utterson has done is to bring together aspects of his life and personality carefully segregated and repressed. He has moved back through time, not only to his theater days but, since the anatomical theater is in effect a classroom, to his school days. What he will learn about now is body, the gross anatomy precluded by his celibate life. What he will be subjected to, what he will have an opportunity to learn (at last) about, is the animal in Jekyll and in all patriarchs, the Hyde in the doctor's laboratory. Whether Utterson—and Lanyon, who is "theatrical" (36)— will indeed learn from the opportunity is a question that cannot be answered until the end of Stevenson's novella.

What can be established now is that the blurring of distinctions

WILLIAM VEEDER

extends outward to involve professionalism itself. Medicine and pharmacology, which seem so oriented to the cerebral and rational, are in fact a springboard into humanity's common pool of the unconscious. "Watery green" (79) is the ultimate color of Jekyll's potion because a sea change rife and strange has occurred within him. The watery potion is his "sea of liberty" (86). When he enters this realm, "a current of disordered sensual images running like a millrace" in his fancy carries Jekyll to "freedom of the soul" (83). The resulting "solution of the bonds of obligation" (83) indicates how the unconscious threatens all distinctions. "Solution," especially in the rationalist context of lawyers and doctors, suggests conscious cerebration with its chains of logical thinking; but in the watery pool of the unconscious, "solution" means the opposite. It means dissolution, and indicates the dissolute.

The underwater realm beneath the theater's cupola is in effect this watery green potion of Jekyll. Everyone swims in the same fantasy, because everyone shares the same unconscious. Merging or dissolving of oppositions characterizes all of befogged London, where "nine in the morning" can resemble "twilight" (48), where "this mournful reinvasion of darkness" inverts our most basic categories so that daytime London becomes "some city in a nightmare." The dissolution of distinctions in the solution of the unconscious finds its ultimate emblem in the home of Henry Jekyll. Critics have noted how the very different faces of the house—patrician entrance hall and ratty back door—reflect Jekyll's two roles of patriarch and nightstalker. As these are the two roles of one man, however, Stevenson cannot allow even an architectural dichotomy to remain intact. Front and back, which seem so different, are also alike. The entrance hall and the laboratory each features oak presses (41, 70); the presses in the hall are called by the name applied to the lab, "cabinet" (41); and the flooring at both ends of the house is flagstone (41, 71).

The impossibility of keeping the laboratory's antisocial experiments distinct from the foyer's hospitable welcome is emphasized by another feature of Jekyll's house. The "anatomical theatre" (88) is also known as "old Dr. Denman's surgical theatre" (76). Denman is the primal father, the absent origin.[13] Henry Jekyll may not seem to derive from him, Jekyll's "tastes being rather chemical than anatomical" (51). But the very word that Jekyll applies to his laboratory, "cabinet," can mean "a den of a beast" (Jefford 69). That Jekyll's chemical tastes liberate Hyde's animality (beast as ape, den man as troglodyte) is revelatory not only of the doctor and the patriarchy but of late-Victorian society as well. In this period arise the sciences of anthropology and psychology. Darwin's tracing of human anatomy back to animal origins is complemented by anthropological and psychological attributions of social practices and emotional states to comparably archaic sources. The den is the origin of society.

Not only does patriarchal man derive from the den man, but patriarchy in its late-Victorian manifestation derives expressly from Denman. Dr. Jekyll inhabits the older doctor's house. Patrilineal succession—in keeping with Stevenson's view of the essentially bourgeois character of patriarchy in the nineteenth century—is not hereditary. It is professional. Jekyll effects succession through purchase rather than primogeniture, establishing a continuity of disciplines rather than of blood. As the professional son of Denman, Jekyll is the immediate heir to the primal den. Denman's "theatre" is also called "the dissecting rooms" (51) because what Stevenson dissects is the archaic nature of the life transferred from every father to every child, our residual savagery. The patricidal and fraternal rage that I will argue for in *Jekyll and Hyde* find their origin here. Freud posited the origin of civilization in the sons' slaughter of the father and their subsequent slaughter of themselves. Only then was the father exhumed as law and incorporated as conscience. And only *then* was patriarchy possible. Stevenson might subscribe to some such myth about the origins of society, but he would stress how inadequate conscience, patriarchal laws, and professional etiquette are in controlling the deepest antagonisms still raging in all us children of the night.

II. Male Ties and Members' Wars

The men of *Jekyll and Hyde* do not recognize the blurring of distinctions that implicates them in the other and that constitutes the general context of their lives. We readers are thus in a position of relative superiority to Jekyll's circle. What we see in particular is that the patriarchy's unconscious participation in Hyde threatens society itself because rage is directed not outward—through, say, imperialistic ventures—but back into communal life. In turn, communal safeguards, especially professionalism and friendship, function not to channel and contain but to screen and foster these destructive emotions. Males who should bond with fathers and brothers participate unconsciously in the oedipal anger and the sibling rivalry enacted by Edward Hyde. It is in light of the failure of male bonds that I will interpret the patriarchs' failure to marry—and thus the absence of women—in section 3.

Oedipal conflict and sibling rivalry are not obvious on the plot level of *Jekyll and Hyde,* where no fathers or brothers appear. Nor have scholars tended to see the novella in these terms.[14] Focusing first on the oedipal, I will begin with two passages that seem to me central to Stevenson's view of parent-child relations.

Today in Glasgow my father went off on some business, and my mother and I wandered about for two hours. We had lunch together, and were very merry over what people at the restaurant would think of us—mother and son they could not have supposed us to be. [L1, 76]

[Aboard a steamer] mine eye lighted on two girls, one of whom was sweet and pretty, talking to an old gentleman. . . . So I sidled up to the old gentleman, got into conversation with him and so with the damsel; and thereupon, having used the patriarch as a ladder, I kicked him down behind me. [L1, 30]

Louis is thus capable of seeing mother as object of desire, and of imagining himself dispatching a rival "patriarch." Desire proclaims itself in the Dedication to *A Child's Garden of Verses*, where Louis's beloved nurse, Cummy, is called "my second mother, my first wife." Rivalry with older men appears also in print, as Stevenson recounts (in the third person) his dream

of the son of a very rich and wicked man, the owner of broad acres and the most damnable temper. The dreamer (and that was the son) had lived much abroad, on purpose to avoid his parent; and when at length he returned to England, it was to find him married again to a young wife, who was supposed to have suffered cruelly and to loathe her yoke. . . . Meet they [father and son] did accordingly. . . . they quarrelled, and the son, stung by some intolerable insult, struck down the father dead. No suspicion was aroused; the dead man was found and buried, and the dreamer succeeding to the broad estates, and found himself installed under the same roof with the father's widow, for whom no provision had been made. ("A Chapter on Deams")

Homicidal antagonism cannot be contained within the dream world or the essay's pages. Louis and Thomas Stevenson depict hostility in shockingly lethal terms. Thomas, who informs Louis that "you have rendered my whole life a failure. . . . I would ten times sooner see you lying in your grave than that you should be shaking the faith of other young men" (Furnas 66; Calder 69), goes on to lament to Margaret, "I see nothing but destruction to himself as well as to us. . . . Is it fair that we should be half murdered by his conduct?" (Calder 134). Louis reciprocates. "I say, my dear friend [Fanny Sitwell], I am killing my father—he told me tonight (by the way) that I have alienated utterly my mother" (L1, 80). The last half of this sentence is as important as the first. Killing the father is counterproductive because the more the son fights for mother, the more she sides against him. Louis recognizes both the inevitability of father-son conflict ("a first child is a rival," he tells Gosse [L1, 277]) and the inevitable defeat of children of happy marriages. "The children of lovers are orphans," he says sadly enough (Calder 21).

What seems to me most telling about Louis's recognition of his inevitable defeat is that the recognition makes no difference—and that he knows this. Louis persists in the damned old war among the family members regardless of its outcome. Compulsion, the repeatedly repressed but inexorable recurrence of desire, is what oedipal conflict teaches him about the human psyche. Guilt and shame and resignation and love for the father whose love for him Louis never seriously doubted: all these forces cannot keep back an antagonism that surfaces in ways as diverse as the surfacings of oedipal rage in *Jekyll and Hyde*. For example, unable to appropriate Thomas's woman, Louis shifts to the professional level and takes what he can get. Editing his father's presidential address to the Royal Society of Edinburgh leaves Louis "feeling quite proud of the paper, as if it had been mine" (L2, 263). At other times, Louis uses the profession of writer to appropriate the father figure himself, turning the patriarch into the son whom Louis can then dominate. "When I have beaten Burns, I am driven at once, by my parental feelings, to console him with a sugar plum" (L1, 274).

To assume professionally the role of adult is more difficult for Stevenson in his fiction and poetry before *Jekyll and Hyde*. The patricidal protagonist of "Markheim" cannot escape sonship. And in the *Garden of Verses*, desire and antagonism are expressed through a persona perennially filial.

> We built a ship upon the stairs
> All made of back-bedroom chairs,
> And filled it full of sofa pillows
> To go a-sailing on the billows.
> . . . .
> We sailed along for days and days,
> And had the very best of plays;
>
> But Tom fell out and hurt his knee,
> So there was no one left but me.
> ["A Good Play" 1–4, 11–14][15]

The poet with the father named Tom can throw his rival out, but he knows that isolation, not mother, is the reward. Is she in the *front* bedroom, the master('s) bedroom, where the real father sails real billows on softer pillows?

> And my papa's a banker and as rich as he can be;
> But I, when I am stronger and can choose what I'm to do,
> O Leerie, I'll go round at night and light lamps with you!
> ["The Lamplighter" 6–8]

WILLIAM VEEDER

For though father denies it, I'm sure it [a stone] is gold.
But of all my treasures the last is the king.
There's very few children possess such a thing;
And that is a chisel, both handle and blade,
Which a man who is really a carpenter made.
["My Treasures" 12–16]

Wealth, the ultimate source of power in bourgeois patriarchy, is what the father as banker possesses and what the father as debunker of the stone denies to his son. In both cases the son rebels not by taking wealth directly from the father (such an emasculation would be too daunting) but by discovering alternative, superior values. "When I am stronger" means on the manifest level "stronger than I am now." but it suggests "stronger than father." Meanwhile, the son must be satisfied with Family Romance. Father is replaced by "real" men who *do* things rather than simply possess or debunk. The lamplighter illuminates for the boy the night where the father has hitherto held sway; the carpenter provides for the boy the tool to penetrate what has hitherto been barred. Reversed here is the usual pattern of the Family Romance where the child fantasizes moving up the social scale (my real parents are the King and Queen). Stevenson as upper-middle-class son envisions a move down to proletarian surrogates who (like D. H. Lawrence's gamekeepers) are capable of genuine puissance. The profession of the father is associated with impotence by the son who aspires to but obviously has not yet achieved professional status himself.

In both poems, the poet who is speaking through the boy has a wry distance that he shares with the adult reader. We know that the stone is not gold, that the boy will not become a lamplighter. This adult perspective could lead to what I defined in my introduction as essential to professional maturation for Stevenson: a comparable realization of the persistence and consequences of unresolved oedipal emotions in adult life. Wryness does not function this way in the *Garden*, however. Distancing effects proximity. As the verses are less about childhood than about an adult musing on childhood, so wryness acts to reinforce the fiction of our superiority to "childish" perceptions. Stevenson and we can then reexperience "childhood" realities. By indulging both in the desire/rage of oedipal emotions and in the guilt consequent on them, Stevenson allows himself and his readers to remain in thrall to the immaturity that we do not really want to escape.

Such regressiveness is not entirely harmful for Stevenson, however. His very sense that his regressive inclinations are shared by his adult readers means he has a critical perspective on adulthood as well as on childhood. He has defined the basic fact upon which Freud founded psychoanalysis—that adult difficulties derive from childhood traumas. Stevenson told William Archer: "The house [of life] is, indeed, a great thing, and should be rearranged on sanitary principles; but my heart and all my interest are with the dweller, that ancient of days and day-old infant man" (L2, 294). To dwell on this dweller is what Stevenson must do after the *Garden* and "Markheim." He must avoid self-defeating self-indulgence and must present the regressive desires of adulthood in terms of their deleterious consequences for society and self.

Oedipal rage seethes beneath the professional surface of *Jekyll and Hyde*. I will first discuss Henry Jekyll and the way Hyde expresses his pre- and postlatency rage against two "father"s—Carew and Lanyon. I will then show how Jekyll's anger is replicated throughout patriarchy, in the persons of Richard Enfield and Gabriel John Utterson.

When Henry Jekyll says of his first drinking of the potion, "that night I had come to the fatal crossroads" (85), he is saying more than that he had crossed the Rubicon. Readers who hear echoes of Oedipus's famous crossroads here can find confirmation throughout *Jekyll and Hyde*. "Hence the apelike tricks he [Hyde] would play on me . . . burning the letters and destroying the portrait of my father" (96). Like so many statements by patriarchs in the novella, this one implies a strong disjunction—*he* ruined *my* father's portrait. In fact, Hyde is expressing Jekyll. As a "child of Hell" (94), Hyde is not only hellish but childish.

> I was the first that could plod in the public eye with a load of genial respectability, and in a moment, like a schoolboy, strip off these lendings and spring headlong into the sea of liberty. [86]

Jekyll intends his metaphor to express liberation into a freer future, but "like a schoolboy" confirms the regressive nature of his transformation into Hyde. Hyde's physical littleness ("little" is the first adjective applied to him [30]) serves in part to indicate immaturity. His "little room in Soho" (87) suggests a nursery, especially in contrast with the "tall proportions" of Jekyll's "[bed]room in the square" (87). Hyde's ludicrous appearance in Jekyll's too-large suit suggests a little boy dressing up in daddy's clothes. And so, when we read that "Jekyll had more than a father's interest; Hyde had more than a son's indifference" (89), we can interpret the "more"s as Jekyll cannot. Hyde has more than a son's indifference because he has a son's rage; Jekyll has more than a father's interest because he has a son's interest. As oedipal conflict appears first in childhood and then reappears after latency, Jekyll's oedipal conflicts are dramatized in two successive events separated by an interval of quiescence. Regressive rage erupts when Hyde "in no more reasonable spirit than that in which a sick child may break a plaything" (90) kills Sir

Danvers Carew; this rage, recathected in postlatency terms of professionalism and friendship, then strikes down Dr. Lanyon.

Carew is, as we have seen, a model patriarch who radiates "an innocent and old-world kindness of disposition" (46). What fiend could kill so exemplary a gentleman? "There is of course no motive," Jefford maintains (70–71). Since every act is motivated, the apparent absence of provocation by Carew and the patent excessiveness of Hyde's reaction encourage us to look to the unconscious. What we see is a dramatization of the son's psyche, a playing out of oedipal, patricidal fantasy. Though "madman" and "ape-like" are applied to Hyde (47), these conventional explanations mask the true nature of a rage articulated initially by "stamping with his foot" (47). This is a gesture of petulant immaturity. In this context, Carew's exemplary nature marks him as the enemy whose slightest provocation will set Hyde off. And provocations do appear amid Carew's politenesses. Compare Stevenson's presentation of the men meeting—"the older man bowed and accosted the other" (46)—and an alternative version. "The older man bowed and greeted the small gentleman [this is Stevenson's epithet from the previous sentence]." My version is consistently benign. Stevenson's verb "accosted," which can mean to assault as well as to greet and to proposition, introduces the possibility of some aggressiveness from Sir Danvers. Stevenson's noun, "the other," suggests the alienation that would make Hyde hypersensitive to such aggressiveness. Or to condescension. "Something high too, as of a well-founded self content" (46) characterizes this man of "high position" (46) who towers above the "very small" Hyde (46). Does Carew seem high-handed to the embattled other?

> The older man bowed and accosted the other. . . . from his pointing, it sometimes appeared as if he were only inquiring his way; but the moon shone on his face as he spoke, and the girl was pleased to watch it. [46]

In his commentary on this scene, Jekyll exclaims, "I declare, at least, before God, no man morally sane could have been guilty of that crime . . ." So far, Jekyll seems singlemindedly orthodox, but his sentence is not over. ". . . guilty of that crime upon so pitiful a provocation" (90). For all his abhorrence of Hyde, Jekyll will not indict him unilaterally, will not absolve the fathers completely. "So pitiful a provocation" establishes that there was *some* provocation. The maid's narrative, with its "sometimes," "only," and "but," suggests that something more than "inquiring his way" must have occurred. For help in understanding what this is, we can look to the maid herself.

Why is the viewpoint in the murder scene female? Why is she positioned in the setting as she is? Why does she act (and not act) as she does? Answers in terms of mimesis do not account for the specifics of the scene as effectively as a reading in terms of fantasy projection. The viewpoint is female in part to assure the reader's sympathy for Carew through our empathetic response to her sympathy for him, but the maid's sympathy is complicated. Since woman's traditional association with sensitivity and pity would warrant her (and our) deeply emotional response to homicidal horrors, why does Stevenson go on and make this particular maid "romantic"? In addition to the answer that Peter K. Garrett has offered, another is suggested by the maid's positioning in the scene. With the woman up at the second floor window, the two men approach from opposite ends of the street and stop "within speech (just under the maid's eyes)" (46). The three figures form a triangle. The woman at the apex, the contending males squared off along the base: it is the classic oedipal configuration. Set in the place of the mother, the maid belongs to a patriarch, "her master" (46), and yet she is available to filial fantasy since she lives "alone" (46). Thus, although she is "romantically given" (46), she is not given to the patriarchy in any expressly sexual way that would preclude appropriation by the son. Positioning her "upon her box" (46) at the open window emphasizes her sexuality and availability.

Her actions and nonactions are, in turn, appropriate to her fantasy role. Why does she not cry out for help for Sir Danvers, and why does she faint for nearly *three hours* (47)? If she were positioned where Hyde could hurt her for crying out, fear would explain her silence and preclude any explanation in terms of oedipal fantasy. But situated safely above, the maid cannot be attacked by Hyde. We can therefore view her conduct in terms of the son's wish fulfillment. Silence implies consent. Mother does not cry out because she is captivated by the son's puissant attack on the weak father. Her fainting then functions as the next stage of the fantasy. Like the "little death" of orgasm, fainting attests to the son's adequacy as replacement for the father. Fainting also constitutes maternal complicity in the son's subversive assertion of himself, since she cannot call the police until Hyde has safely vanished from both the neighborhood and his Soho flat.

Since any situation of Hyde reflects an unconscious emotion of Jekyll's, we can suspect in the doctor an obsession with mother, too. With Jekyll, this link between the patricidal and the oedipal is more obliquely placed for several reasons, one of which is that he has on the conscious level repressed mother so completely that no female counterpart to the maid is possible. There is neither a picture of mother nor saved letters from her, as with father. There are, however, textual details that evoke questions. Why does Stevenson choose for Jekyll's chemist the bizarre name "Maw" (65)? Orality is stressed throughout the novel in the patriarchs' consumption of wine and in Jekyll's drinking of the potion.

Orality enters the murder scene at the moment of death. "Tasting delight in every blow," Jekyll/Hyde "mauled the unresisting body" (90). Especially in light of *"mauled,"* "Maw," which literally means mouth, suggests the ultimate source of oral satisfaction, Ma. The basically regressive nature of Jekyll's orality is expressed agonizingly in his cry, "find me some of the old" (66). Jekyll yearns to return to the old source of oral satisfaction. But he cannot. His biological mother is apparently dead, and, worse still, Jekyll is not dealing with *her* at Maw's. Men are in charge of Maw's, the "Messrs. Maw." Moreover, "the man at Maw's was main angry" (66). Why?

Jekyll has accused him of impurity. Jekyll's assumption that the new salt is "impure" (65) prompts him to demand "some of the old," purer substance. Later he realizes that it was the old which was tainted by some "unknown impurity" (96). This problem with the salt is of course essential to the eventual failure of Jekyll's pharmacological "experiment" as a scientific endeavor, but the psychological forces that impel him to experiment in the first place are also illuminated by the salt. On this level we have what Freud defines as characteristic of the son's response to parental sexuality (particularly primal scene fantasies).[16] Mother's possession by father is seen as violent and unclean. In *Jekyll and Hyde* what is presented in narrative terms—the man at Maws is very angry because he will not admit to impurity in his products—can be read in psychoanalytic terms as the father denying the son's interpretation of marital relations as impure. The angry father wants the son to both remove his interrupting presence and restrain his rival passion. The son must banish mother as an object of desire. Jekyll does this so absolutely that mother appears nowhere in the novella. Desire for her lingers, however, and reappears in Jekyll's initial desire for pure chemicals from the old times. "A return to the *old* days before I had made my discovery" is how Jekyll describes his reaction to his first public transformation into Hyde (92; my italics). Finally, however, Jekyll must accept the fact that desire is impure from the first. Does this acceptance, which every boy undergoes, lead in Jekyll's case to a sense that all subsequent relations with women are impure? Certainly the man who mentions no mother marries no wife.

Another death follows Sir Danvers's. To what extent is Lanyon a victim of murder? Critics have recognized an increasing violence in Hyde—ten years without incident, then the trampling of the girl, then the murder of Carew. Does Hyde's post-Carew career extend this trajectory of violence? Carew as a legislator, a lawmaker, can be seen as representing the Law to the son in the familial context. Like the Lacanian Absent Father, Carew represents interdiction to the son whose immaturity is manifest in the petulant rage with which he kills the father. Hyde takes the cane out with him on the night of father killing, as he did not on the night of the girl's trampling, because only now—with the Father—is the Phallus at stake. Lanyon, on the other hand, is not a legislator, but a professional peer. His association with the law comes through his role as articulator of the ethical standards appropriate to a profession in late-Victorian Britain. Hyde must, in turn, articulate antagonism in this postlatency situation in terms other than childish rage. To understand how murder is effected here, we should pause at the latency period between the two deaths.

Jekyll after Carew's death does not simply resume his former existence. He expressly returns to clinical medicine as opposed to the pharmacological "research" that has marked his career over the last dozen years and that has—crucially—alienated him from his friend Dr. Lanyon. As a clinician once more, Jekyll "laboured to relieve suffering . . . much was done for others" (92). Others are also served by Jekyll's return to his friends as "once more their familiar guest and entertainer" (56). We are told explicitly that at Jekyll's January 8 dinner "Lanyon had been there" along with Utterson and that "the face of the host had looked from one to the other as in the old days when the trio had been inseparable friends" (56). Returning to friendship and to clinical medicine constitutes a patching up of Jekyll's dual rupture with Lanyon. "The great Dr. Lanyon" is exclusively a clinician who "received his crowding patients" in his house on "Cavendish Square, that citadel of medicine" (36). Thus Lanyon—despite the fact that he is Jekyll's peer in age and distinction—stands forth as the patriarch when he speaks for medical orthodoxy in denouncing Jekyll's deviation into pharmacological experimentation.

> ". . . it's been more than ten years since Henry Jekyll became too fanciful for me. He began to go wrong, wrong in mind. . . . I have seen devilish little of the man. Such unscientific balderdash," added the doctor, flushing suddenly purple, "would have estranged Damon and Pythias." [36]

Jekyll's angry response to Lanyon's oft-expressed strictures can, in turn, be seen in terms of the professional disagreements which shaped the development of Robert Louis Stevenson and of all too many sons.

> "I never saw a man so distressed as you [Utterson] were about my will; unless it was that hide-bound pedant, Lanyon, at what he called my scientific heresies. O, I know he's a good fellow—you needn't frown—an excellent fellow, and I always mean to see more of him; but a hide-bound pedant for all that; an ignorant, blatant pedant. I was never more disappointed in any man than Lanyon." [43]

WILLIAM VEEDER

Jekyll's patching up of both his personal estrangement from Lanyon and his professional disengagement from orthodox medicine fares like most patch jobs. Pressure builds to the point of explosion.

> "Lanyon, you remember your vows: what follows is under the seal of our profession. And now, you who have so long been bound to the most narrow and material views, you who have denied the virtue of transcendental medicine, you who have derided your superiors—behold!" [80]

That the speaker here is not Jekyll but Hyde establishes powerfully the nonmimetic, fantasy quality of the scene. Hyde, we are told, "was indifferent to Jekyll" (89); Hyde is, moreover, not a doctor. Thus in terms of mimesis there is no "our" profession that binds Hyde with Lanyon, as there is no reason for Hyde to care about either Lanyon's "material views" or Jekyll's "transcendental medicine." The scene of Lanyon's death makes sense as fantasy, however. Hyde expresses that professional rebellion against repressive authority that is no more resolved within patriarchy than the earlier physical rage was. The "you who have derided your superiors" is the patriarch who in the son's eyes pretends to a professional adequacy he patently lacks. At issue is again, still, mastery. Hyde murders Lanyon, as he did Carew, by preying on the victim's weakness. As Carew had no defense against Hyde's cane, Lanyon is helpless before verbal assault.

> "And now," said he, "to settle what remains. Will you be wise? will you be guided? . . . Think before you answer, for it shall be done as you decide. . . . if you shall prefer to choose, a new province of knowledge and new avenues of fame and power shall be laid open to you . . . and your sight will be blasted by a prodigy to stagger the unbelief of Satan." [79]

In this rhetorical masterpiece, Hyde makes diverse appeals—to professional advancement ("new avenues to fame and power"), wonder ("a prodigy to stagger the unbelief of Satan"), free will ("if you prefer to choose")—which Lanyon cannot possibly resist. "I have gone too far in the way of inexplicable services to pause before I see the end" (80). By getting Lanyon to—in effect—commit suicide, to die in response to stimuli embraced rather than thrust on him, Jekyll/Hyde gets patriarchal professionalism to confirm its own inadequacy. Lanyon, so the son's logic goes, deserves to die because his own weakness is what does him in. "Your superiors" are thus both Jekyll as transcendental scientist and Jekyll as rhetorical son. More violent than the killing of Carew insofar as it exploits human weakness more fiendishly, the oedipal murder of Lanyon is linked directly with Carew by Lanyon's last words—"the murder of Carew" (80).

Mother for the postlatency Jekyll/Hyde is represented by Hyde's housekeeper. Her materialization after the Carew killing indicates how desire for mother is recathected and played out in the ongoing fantasy, the accelerating trajectory of violence. That the housekeeper functions primarily on the level of fantasy is emphasized by her relative superfluity on the level of narrative, where she does only two things—admit Utterson and Newcomen to Hyde's flat and announce Hyde's doings on the previous night. Utterson/Newcomen as the law could readily have gotten a search warrant to enter the flat; and its ransacked state testifies eloquently to Hyde's previous doings there. Moreover, nothing about either the housekeeper's actions in the narrative or her more general domestic chores requires the text's stress on her age as "old . . . old" (49). Seen in light of her first incarnation in the oedipal fantasy as the maid, mother as housekeeper has aged dramatically. Why? Mother's principal role in the postlatency son's fantasy is no longer expressly erotic. She must now believe in his adult adequacy in the face of patriarchal disapproval. Margaret Stevenson wounded Louis deeply by siding consistently with Thomas in the battles over profession and religion. As Louis put it, "you were persuaded [that I] was born to disgrace you" (L2, 193). Hyde's housekeeper has a similar conviction of filial failure.

> A flash of odious joy appeared on the woman's face. "Ah!" said she, "he is in trouble. What has he done?"
> Mr. Utterson and the inspector exchanged glances. "He don't seem a very popular character," observed the latter. "And now my good woman, just let me and this gentleman have a look about us." [49]

The housekeeper who initially presented "an evil face" (49) is now "my good woman" because she shows that her allegiance is ultimately with the law, with patriarchy. However intensely the son fantasizes his appropriation of mother and her approval of himself, he knows deep down that her heart belongs to daddy. The housekeeper's "smoothed" face (49) recalls the "smooth-faced man of fifty" who is the idol of patriarchy, Henry Jekyll (43); her "silvery hair" (49) resembles the "white hair" of both Lanyon and Carew (36, 46); and her "manners" are "excellent" (49) in accord with patriarchal practice and preference. As Jekyll's smooth professional surface is betrayed by "something of a slyish cast perhaps" (43), the housekeeper's face is smoothed "by hypocrisy" (49). Hypocritical mother has never really, the son knows, been part of his patricidal project, any more than that project can effect true emancipation from oedipal anxiety. Not only does patricide preclude the son's transition from mother to father, but anger at mother taints his continued tie to her. Misogyny, celibacy, and homosexuality are tangled in this tie to

132   WILLIAM VEEDER

mother, as we will soon see. First, however, I must establish that the oedipal dilemma itself is endemic to all of patriarchy, that Stevenson's indictment of oedipal regressiveness has full cultural force because Hyde enacts the anger and desire of not only Henry Jekyll but all men in Victorian society.

With Richard Enfield, oedipal antagonism surfaces suddenly in a sentence that begins innocuously enough. "I feel very strongly about putting questions; it partakes too much of the style of the day of judgment. You start a question and it's like . . ." (33). So far, Enfield has simply stated his dislike of prying. His point is clear, and sufficiently orthodox that nothing more need be said. When more is said, therefore, it speaks to another issue altogether.

> ". . . it's like starting a stone. You sit quietly on the top of a hill; and away the stone goes, starting others; and presently some bland old bird (the last you would have thought of) is knocked on the head in his own back garden and the family have to change their name. No sir . . ."

This eruption is as peculiar as the unconscious itself. Striking down the father here presages the Carew killing. Since there is no essential, inevitable link between prying and killing, Enfield's apparently irrelevant simile must be powerfully relevant to him. As Jekyll is safe from prosecution after the Carew murder because his dirty work against the old man is done by his other, so the agent in Enfield's simile is safely removed ("you sit quietly") from an act that destroys an "old bird" and that is done by "others." Enfield's simile thus achieves the same result as Jekyll's potion. "No sir." Father is extirpated.

Moreover, "the family have to change their name." Why? Preserving one's good name is an obsession in *Jekyll and Hyde*, but the only real threat to one's name is perpetration of or complicity in disgraceful acts. Since the family in Enfield's metaphor is patently victimized by a freak accident, why would their name be endangered? Where is their complicity? Enfield obliterates the family—renders it nameless and therefore nonexistant as a family—at the moment of the father's extirpation because the extinction of geneology itself is the ultimate aim of oedipal rage. The universality of this antidomestic anger is established by the "you." Enfield's interlocutor, his immediate "you," is Utterson, whose patricidal anger we will soon study, but the generalizing force of Enfield's simile extends "you" out to all of us complicitous children. The victimized father is "the last you would have thought of" because you cannot examine the simile closely enough to recognize whom you are in fact thinking of killing off. "You" is Enfield too, of course, any son as metaphor maker. "The day of judgment" is indeed at hand, and the son "on the top of a hill" is looking down like God the Father on the doomed father. The son is doubly safe—because he now is "high" and because the whole thing has been only a metaphor, a mere figure of speech.

The oedipal antagonism of Jekyll's fellow patriarchs is announced through Richard Enfield, but the ultimately maternal orientation of patriarchy requires for its presentation the ampler occasion of Gabriel John Utterson. He, unlike Enfield, is implicated directly—as opposed to metaphorically—in patricidal rage. Hyde, having killed Carew with the lawyer's stick (48), behaves bizarrely afterward in ways that confirm his link with Utterson. Why does Hyde not dispose of the obviously incriminating "other half" of the murder weapon, and why does he leave it specifically "behind the door" (49)? "The other," the phrase common to Hyde, Jekyll, and Utterson, appears here because Hyde as other has expressed the patricidal desire of the other owners of the cane, Jekyll *and* Utterson. The stick is not disposed of, is waiting for Utterson to find it, because it is (still) his stick, his weapon, the expression of his unconscious desires. The stick left "behind the door," rather than, say, flung into the fireplace with the checkbook, emphasizes Utterson's parallel with Jekyll who changes into Hyde—thus achieving the transformation that Utterson can only partake in projectively—behind the door of his laboratory.

Also like the regressive Jekyll, Utterson is characterized by orality. On the first page of the novel, we learn that Utterson is sociable "when the wine was to his taste" and that he drinks gin when "alone, to mortify his taste for vintages." Since Utterson does not drink to excess, why does mortification occur to him at all? His dour religiosity is an obvious answer, but I think there is a deeper reason, a tension reflected in Utterson's name. As the utter son, the devoted heir of patriarchy, he utters the truths of the fathers (as solicitor and as editor-narrator); but as udder son he remains regressively oriented to the breast.[17] His orality is a trait that Nabokov has stressed ("everything is very appetizingly put. Gabriel John Utterson mouths his words most roundly" [180]). Jefford rightly finds wine associated in the novel with domesticity and warmth, but whereas Jefford concludes that wine represents Stevenson's social ideal (52–54), I find this ideal undercut by the compensatory aspect of Utterson's drinking. For example, the Printer's Copy of *Jekyll and Hyde* offers the following revelatory moment:

> He [Utterson watching Jekyll's back door] made long stages on the pavement opposite, studying the bills of fare stuck on the sweating windows of the cookshop, reading the labels on various lotions or watching the bust of the proud lady swing stonily round upon him on her velvet pedestal at the perfumers;

WILLIAM VEEDER

but all the time still with one eye over his shoulder, spying at the door.

Utterson's unconscious is imaged forth here. That a son is barred from mother—thus creating feelings of oral deprivation—is represented by the window glass that bars Utterson's way to oral gratification. The "sweating . . . cookshop" associates warmth (and physicality) with food, while the "bill of fare" on the window indicates that Utterson cannot reach either. As a man literally out in the cold, he cannot get beyond the perceptual and verbal to the sensual and nutritious. "Bust," which of course means "statuette" on the manifest level, locates the maternal focus of Utterson's latent desires.

That preoedipal oral desire for mother coexists in the patriarchal psyche with oedipal anxieties about father is reflected in the two-directional nature of Utterson's gaze in the street scene. He is not only looking directly at the bust but also "spying" on Jekyll's door" with one eye over his shoulder." That Jekyll can be the oedipal father to Utterson as well as the oedipal son in his own fantasy life is facilitated by Stevenson's presentation of the doctor as the very embodiment of patriarchy— "M.D., D.C.L., LL.D., F.R.S. &c." (35). With professional degrees in law as well as medicine and with a Royal Society fellowship as well as a thriving practice, Jekyll as "a tall, fine build of a man" (66–67) stands forth impressively to speak for the fathers. "I was born . . . to a large fortune, endowed besides with excellent parts, inclined by nature to industry, fond of the respect of the wise and good among my fellow men" (81). Against so representative a patriarch Utterson directs the patricidal antagonism characteristic of the oedipal son. Though he can only spy furtively on the domestic door of Henry Jekyll the sleeping patriarch, Utterson can breach with impunity the professional door of Dr. Jekyll the errant scientist. What the breach reveals is what we have seen throughout *Jekyll and Hyde*—that the professional is a screen for the domestic.

> The candle was set upon the nearest table to light them [Utterson and Poole] to the attack; and they drew near with bated breath to where the patient foot was still going up and down, up and down in the quiet of the night.
> "Jekyll," cried Utterson, with a loud voice, "I demand to see you. . . . if not by fair means, then by foul—if not of your own consent, then by brute force!". . . . The besiegers, appalled by their own riot and the stillness that had succeeded, stood back a little and peered in. There lay the cabinet before their eyes in the quiet lamplight, a good fire glowing and chattering on the hearth, the kettle singing its thin strain, a drawer or two open, pages neatly set forth on the business table, and nearer the fire,

the things laid out for tea; the quietest room you would have said. . . . [69–70]

Of the many odd aspects of this scene, the one I want to begin with is its *domesticity*. Nothing about a professional laboratory requires the quiet lamp and good fire, the kettle and tea. What we have bodied forth here, as we did with the bust in the perfumer's window, is the subconscious of Gabriel John Utterson. For him, Jekyll/Hyde is father/mother in cozy domesticity. Only by seeing the break-in as a kind of parlor primal scene can I explain why Utterson is "appalled." The scene seems, morally speaking, a simple case of sheep versus goat; the forces of order bring into containment the force of disorder. Yet Stevenson reverses the polarities. Utterson is the "loud" one, Hyde the "patient." The echoed words "quiet . . . quietest" link Jekyll/Hyde's domestic harmony with nature's evening. Since right is apparently on Utterson's side, why is *he* the one associated with "riot"? An answer lies in Utterson's cry, "let our name be vengeance" (68). Ostensibly Utterson is responding with righteous indignation. "I believe poor Harry is killed, and I believe his murderer . . . is still lurking in his victim's room" (68). But the scene works more complicatedly than this. The very word "vengeance" in so allusive a novella evokes the biblical warning, "Vengeance is mine, saith the Lord" (Romans 12:15). Prohibitions against taking matters into one's own hands are, in this case, equally strong on the legal side. Utterson is justified in breaking down the door only if he is saving Jekyll's life. If poor Harry is dead already and Edward Hyde is still in the room, Utterson must call the police. Hyde cannot escape in the interim because the room's only windows are barred and its only doors are blocked by Poole, Utterson, Bradshaw, and the knifeboy. The riot that "appalled" Utterson is instigated by more than anger at Hyde killing Jekyll. Utterson through his surrogate Poole is directing against Jekyll the oedipal "vengeance" that Jekyll directed against Carew through Hyde. For Utterson, Jekyll is father at this moment.

> Poole swung the axe over his shoulder; the blow shook the building, and the red baize door leaped against the lock and hinges. A dismal screech, as of mere animal terror, rang from the cabinet. Up went the axe again, and again the panels crashed and the frame bounded; four times the blow fell; but the wood was tough and the fittings were of excellent workmanship; and it was not until the fifth, that the lock burst in sunder, and the wreck of the door fell inwards upon the carpet. [69]

This moment echoes the murder of Carew. As the murder weapon was of "tough and heavy wood" (47), the door's "wood was tough"; as

　　　　　　　　　　　　　　　　　　　　WILLIAM VEEDER

Carew's beaten "body jumped upon the roadway" (47), the beaten "frame bounded"; as Carew's "bones were audibly shattered," the "panels crashed." Utterson is acting out that oedipal rage which Stevenson in "The House of Eld" figured so graphically in terms of wood and axes. "Old is the tree and the fruit good; / Very old and thick the wood. / Woodman, is your courage stout? / Beware! the root is wrapped about / Your mother's heart, your father's bones; / And like the mandrake comes with groans."

To understand a second way in which traditional male bonds are sundered, in which regressive violence is directed within the patriarchy, we should consider Utterson's antagonism toward Jekyll's other self, Edward Hyde. Fratricidal, not patricidal, rage is at work here, as another of the sacred ties of patriarchy is snapped. Stevenson, though an only child, knew sibling rivalry as well as oedipal rage. His sentence to Gosse from which I excerpted earlier reads in full: "A first son is a rival [of the father], a second is a rival of the first." Sibling rivalry is hard for Stevenson to avoid because, as his biographers have detailed, he cannot avoid falling in love with older married women who have children. What I want to stress is the consequence of this tendency to make the beloved into mother and thus the lover into son: other sons become rivals. Having told Fanny Sitwell expressly that "you have another son" in himself (Calder 74), Louis goes on to establish his sonship in and through the extirpation of Fanny's own son, Bertie. "And now I think of you reading it [my letter] in bed behind the little curtain, and no Bertie there, I do not know what longing comes over me to go to you for two hours" (Calder 74). With Fanny Stevenson, matters are much the same, as she realizes. "I love . . . to see my two boys so happy" (Furnas 342). Louis and Lloyd were devoted to one another (even to the point of collaborating on fiction), but given Louis's insatiable demands for affection and attention, how could he not know moments of resentment at Fanny's devotion to the biological son who never ceased depending on her for financial as well as emotional support? "The war in the members" involves all family members.

Sibling rivalry characterizes patriarchal behavior in *Jekyll and Hyde* through what critics have never discussed—Stevenson's manifold allusions to Genesis. The biblical tales of Cain and Abel and of Esau and Jacob feature sons fighting for paternal approbation. Cain's desire to win the "respect" of God the Father (5:4) leads to the murder of Abel; Jacob's determination to win the "blessing" of Isaac (27:16) results in the disaffiliation of Esau. Alerted to fraternal rivalry on page 1 of *Jekyll and Hyde* when Utterson expresses approval of "Cain's heresy. . . . I let my brother go the devil in his own way," we soon encounter allusions to Esau and Jacob. (These rival brothers are expressly established by Stevenson as the prototypes of the sibling rivals in *The Master of Ballantrae*.) Jacob's famous dichotomy—"my brother is a hairy man, and I am a smooth man" (27:11)—is replicated in Jekyll and Hyde. Like smooth Jacob, Jekyll is "smooth-faced" (43). Like Esau, whose "hands were hairy" (27:23), Hyde's hands are "thickly shaded with a swart growth of hair" (88). Esau from birth is Hyde-like, since he comes forth "hairy all over like a hair-cloak" or hide (25:25). As Jacob appropriates this cloak (in effect) by putting animal hides onto his hands and neck (27:16), Jekyll can "assume, like a thick cloak, that [body] of Edward Hyde" (86). Jekyll's "red" potion (79), which transforms him into Hyde, recalls the "red pottage" (25:30) that achieves a comparable effect for Jacob, who is in effect transformed into Esau—by being made heir—once the elder brother consumes the red substance.

The very fact that Esau is the *elder* brother, however, indicates that Stevenson has dealt complexly with his source. He has reversed the whole biblical situation, insofar as the relative ages of his characters should require the pairing of Jekyll with Esau and Hyde with Jacob. And there are ways in which Jekyll *is* Esau and Hyde Jacob. Jekyll is linked to the hirsute Esau by his nickname "Harry" (68). Like Esau's "good raiment" (27:15) which is appropriated by Jacob, Jekyll's "rich and sober" suit bedecks Hyde. Finally the elder, homicidal Cain of the biblical story is paired in Stevenson's story not only with the younger Hyde who murders with a cane, but also with the elder doctor who owns the cane and is named "je kyll."

Complicating the parallels between fictional characters and their biblical counterparts enables *Jekyll and Hyde* to avoid the simple dichotomy of the biblical parables. Genesis's message of "two separate nations" (25:23)—Abel versus Cain, Jacob versus Esau—confirms that myth of the chosen people and thus that exclusion of the other, which is the basic myth of patriarchy. Stevenson insists that the other is the only nation. Patriarchs in *Jekyll and Hyde* harbor toward one another the same fraternal rivalry that we see in Genesis. Jekyll, for example, intends to express devotion to his lifelong friend Lanyon by saying, "there never was a day when . . . I would not have sacrificed . . . my left hand for you" (74). The idiom is "my right hand." Jekyll's compliment is left-handed because patriarchs, despite their ostensible unity, put self before brotherhood, make brother into other. Utterson is sincerely shocked at Carew's death and sincerely concerned for Jekyll's welfare, but on a deeper level his conduct reflects Cain's question, "Am I my brother's keeper?" (4:9). Utterson considers "the death of Sir Danvers . . . more than paid for by the disappearance of Mr. Hyde" (56). Utterson enacts

Cain's heresy and lets his brother Carew go to the devil (or to St. Peter) in his own way—provided that Hyde goes to hell, too.

Hyde, though considerably younger, is Utterson's sibling rival. As the younger brother Jacob appropriated Esau's birthright, Hyde poses a comparable threat to Utterson, who returns obsessively to the spectre of Hyde as "heir to a quarter-million pounds sterling" (48). Like Cain, who expresses his fear of disaffiliation in Hyde-like terms—"from Thy face shall I be hid" (4:14)—Utterson fears that he will be hidden by the younger man inheriting. ("Agents of obscure enterprises," as well as "shady lawyers" [40], are taking over Jekyll's neighborhood). Lawyer Utterson is thus not simply being his brother's keeper (or attorney) when he admonishes Jekyll about the will. Obsessed with the possibility that Hyde will inherit, Utterson uses professional concerns to screen his refusal to participate in disinheriting himself. The Printer's Copy indicates how friendship as well as professionalism screens his obsession. "He made up his mind to even strech friendship in so good a cause." The Notebook Draft emphasizes how emotional the discovery of the codicil is for the supposedly "cold, scanty" (29) lawyer.

> On the desk of the business table [in Jekyll's laboratory], among a neat array of papers, a very large envelope was uppermost, and bore, in Dr. Jekyll's hand, the name of Mr. Utterson. The lawyer tore it open and as his hands were shaking with emotion, the enclosures fell to the floor. The first was a will, . . .

That Utterson replaces Hyde in the codicil to the will (72) proves to be an expensive triumph. Jekyll, as well as Carew, must pay for the disappearance of Mr. Hyde.

III. Misogyny and Homosexuality

We have seen so far that patriarchs in *Jekyll and Hyde* fail to live up to their traditional obligations of maintaining proper distinctions and of effecting filial and fraternal bonds. Their third failure—to marry—involves a misogyny that derives, like the other patriarchal failures, from unresolved ambivalences toward mother. Here again Stevenson manages to transform materials from his own life into a critical portrait of his times.

Robert Louis Stevenson has been widely and quite properly acclaimed for his "chivalry" toward women—his tenderness to Cummy, his deference toward the fair sex generally and his defense of prostitutes in particular, his devotion to Fanny Sitwell as "Madonna," his concern for the reputation of the precariously poised Mrs. Fanny Vandegrift Osbourne. There are, however, darker emotions as well. Antagonism toward woman is particularly surprising in Stevenson when it strikes the much cooed over Cummy. Having assured her that "God will make good to you all the good you have done," Louis cannot end his sentence without adding, "and mercifully forgive you all the evil" (L1, 37). Resentment here, like oedipal rage, carries over into Stevenson's fiction. "*John Knox* goes on, and a horrible story of a nurse which I think almost too cruel to go on with: I wonder why my stories are always so nasty" (L1, 177). The two-pronged attack on the spiritual father of Scotland and the surrogate mother of Louis continues for more than a month. "I have been working hard at John Knox, and at the horrid story I have in hand, and walking in the rain. Do you know this story of mine is horrible; I only work at it by fits and starts, because I feel as if it were a sort of crime against humanity—it is so cruel" (L1, 178).

That the crime is not against "humanity" is probably what prompts Stevenson to eventually destroy the nurse story. Repression operates even more powerfully on anger at mother herself. When Thomas lashes Louis with having "utterly alienated" Margaret, the father is not only indicting the son for unnatural cruelty. He is also reconfirming his own conjugal bond with Margaret—and thus her "betrayal" of her son. Louis feels the pain of mother's preference no less than the power of father's possession.

> My Dear Mother,—I give my father up. I give him a parable. . . . And he takes it backside foremost, and shakes his head, and is gloomier than ever. Tell him that I give him up. I don't want such a parent. This is not the man for my money. . . . Here I am on the threshold of another year, when, according to all human foresight, I should long ago have been resolved into my elements; here am I, who you were persuaded was born to disgrace you—and, I will do you the justice to add, on no insufficient grounds—no very burning discredit when all is done. . . . There is he [Thomas], at his not first youth, able to take more exercise than I at thirty-three, and gaining a stone's weight, a thing of which I am incapable. There are you: has the man no gratitude? There is Smeoroch [the dog]: is he blind? Tell him for me that all this is
> NOT THE TRUE BLUE!   [L2, 193–94]

How symptomatic it is—Louis sincerely desiring to relieve paternal gloom, and then capitalizing on his failure in order to attack Thomas. But more is being expressed here than oedipal rage. Mother too is attacked. "You were persuaded [I] was born to disgrace you." The alienating force of maternal doubt (Margaret stuck by Thomas in all the battles with Louis) is compounded by Mother's status as father's possession. "There are you: has the man no gratitude? There is Smeoroch: is he blind?"

Especially highlighted by the syntactic parallelism, the equation of mother with dog reduces marriage to a master-pet and even to an animal relationship. Biological maternity is rejected outright when Louis tells his Madonna, Mrs. Sitwell, that "nobody loves a mere mother as much as I love you" (Calder 76).

The virtual exclusion of woman from Stevenson's pre-1890s fiction is at times explained away by him. *Treasure Island,* for example: "no women in the story, Lloyd's orders; and who so blithe to obey? It's awful fun boy's stories; you just indulge the pleasures of your heart, that's all" (L1, 61). This explanation opens itself to some nice objections, but there is a more direct line to take. When Lloyd Osbourne's peers are not the readership of a novel and yet the novelist continues to exclude women, there is obviously a continuity between the children's and the adult enterprises. The violence inherent in such exclusion of woman bursts forth in 1886 when Edward Hyde is roaming the night streets.

> Once a woman spoke to him, offering, I think, a box of lights. He smote her in the face, and she fled. [94]

Since Jekyll remembers all the other particulars of his day as Hyde (the hotel was in Portland Street, the letters were sent registered, etc.), why is he unsure what the woman offered Hyde? A woman who walks the streets late at night asking men if they need a light is offering quite another type of box.[18] And Jekyll (and Stevenson's readers) know it. Jekyll does not want to admit that the violence of Hyde's response is directed against female sexuality, for such an admission would confirm misogyny too starkly.

Hyde's first act of violence partakes of misogyny, since Stevenson makes the trampled child female. Though we know she is on the streets because she is on an errand of mercy, Hyde's violence to her presages his treatment of the streetwalker. Patriarchy is implicated in the girl's injury because Enfield's response to her and to her female partisans emphasizes the complicity of his narration in Hyde's violence. "Then [after the collision] came the horrible part of the thing; for the man trampled calmly over the child's body and left her screaming on the ground" (31). Is any reader of this sentence prepared for Enfield's next remark? "It sounds nothing to hear." That Enfield goes on to add "but it was hellish to see" does not unring the bell. Enfield's first sentence has been *horrible* to hear. Although modesty at his storytelling prowess is probably Enfield's rationale for the disclaimer "it sounds nothing to hear," he nowhere else apologizes for narrative skills that are obviously first rate. ". . . her screaming on the ground. It sounds nothing to hear. . . ." Enfield's sequence of words turns a deaf ear to the girl's screams. Downplaying her suffering mitigates Hyde's offense in the same way that

Enfield did earlier when he presented the girl as the violent "other" and made Hyde the one proceeding "at a good walk."
Adult females fare still worse in Enfield's subsequent narration.

> We told the man we could and would make such a scandal out of this. . . . And all the time, as we were pitching it in red hot, we were keeping the women off him as best we could, for they were wild as harpies. I never saw a circle of such hateful faces. [32]

No wonder the women were not invited to breakfast. What we do wonder is whether the women are actually more violent than the men. "Harpies" suggests a different order of virulence from "pitching it in red hot." Is Hyde actually more endangered by the women than by the men? Or are the men "keeping the women off" him in order to keep him to themselves in Enfield's chamber? "They were as wild as harpies. I never saw such a circle of hateful faces." Enfield might defend himself from charges of misogyny by insisting that the "circle" here is a sweeping indictment of red-hot men as well as women harpies. But Enfield's syntax prompts a more exclusive reading. "They . . . harpies . . . hateful faces." Our equation of women with hateful is particularly likely once Stevenson deletes from the Printer's Copy the next clause of the sentence: "I declare we looked like fiends."

Comparable doubts about Utterson's attitude toward women surface when another night woman appears. "It was a wild, cold, seasonable night of March, with a pale moon, lying on her back . . ." (63). Sexual innuendo would be precluded if Stevenson did here what he does in his letters—keep gender out of the description altogether. "There was a half-moon lying over on its back . . . a very inartistic moon that would have damned a picture" (L1, 194). Instead, the *Jekyll and Hyde* sentence emphasizes gender by associating "her" with clouds "of the most diaphanous and lawny texture" (63). The erotic evocation of diaphanous nightwear is complicated by the violence of describing clouds as a "flying wrack"—evoking the meaning of "wrack" as "wreck/destruction" and recalling the other violent night flights in the novella.

Whose description, whose perception, is all this? Since Utterson is the ostensible point of view in the chapter, is he the source of the bizarre image of the moon on her back? Certainly Utterson has already projected on reality a vision of commercialized sexuality.

> The inhabitants [of Jekyll's bystreet] were all doing well . . . laying out the surplus of their gains in *coquetry*, so that the shop fronts stood along that thoroughfare with *an air of invitation,* like rows of smiling *saleswomen.* Even on Sunday, when it *veiled its more florid charms* . . . the street shone out in contrast to its dingy neighbourhood, like a fire in a forest [30; my italics]

WILLIAM VEEDER

This description ends with the conventional, Chamber of Commerce notion that "with its freshly painted shutters, well-polished brasses, and general cleanliness and gaiety of note [the street] instantly caught and pleased the eye of the passenger." Why, then, does Stevenson introduce language so unconventional with chamber of commerce descriptions, so redolent of female sexuality and so suggestive of prostitution and rampant passion? Since Enfield and Utterson are walking down the street, are we to assume that the description of it reflects the tendency of men professional and misogynistic to associate commerce with whoring? Since this street is the site in the Notebook Draft of "the bust of the proud lady . . . at the perfumer's," does bust in the service of commerce show woman as whore? Lloyd Osbourne spoke for the patriarchy: no women.

That patriarchs in *Jekyll and Hyde* are too misogynistic to wed may explain why there are so few women in the novella, but it does not explain why patriarchs are misogynistic. To begin to answer this question, I must complicate things further. Men antagonistic to women are attracted to men. Jekyll and Hyde fit quite obviously into a long tradition of male doubles—from Caleb Williams and Falkland, Frankenstein and the Monster, and Robert Wringhim Cowan and Gil Martin, to Eugene Wrayburn and Bradley Headstone, and on to Dorian Gray and his picture. *Jekyll and Hyde* draws on this tradition for both structural and psychological components. Structurally, the interchange between a pair of men—as in the Cain/Abel and Damon/Pythias stories foreground by Stevenson—shapes the staging of or constitutes subject matter in every scene in the novella:

> Cain and Abel (29), Utterson and Enfield (29), Enfield and Hyde (31–32), Utterson and Lanyon (36), Damon and Pythias (36), Utterson and Hyde (37), Mr. Hyde and Mr. Seek (38), Utterson and Poole (41), Utterson and Jekyll (43), Hyde and Carew (46), Hyde and the servant Maid's master (46), Carew and Utterson (47), Utterson and Newcomen (49), Utterson and Jekyll (51), Utterson and Guest (53), Utterson and Enfield (60), Utterson and Poole (62–73), Utterson and Lanyon (74), Lanyon and Jekyll/Hyde (77–80).

In terms of psychology, the homoerotic element so prominent in the tradition of the male double recurs in *Jekyll and Hyde*. "There was something queer about that gentleman," Poole says of Hyde (68). Homosexual inclinations are as occluded as they are intense in *Jekyll and Hyde*, because patriarchs contribute to their culture's repressions of inversion, even as they incline toward it. "The more it looks like Queer Street, the less I ask," Enfield admits (33). But repression cannot thwart desire absolutely. What happens to language in Enfield's and Poole's sentences—the traditional Victorian connotation of "queer" as "odd" shading into its later connotation of "homoerotic"[19]—occurs also in the psyches of patriarchs and in the plot of the novella, as celibate men replace women with one another. Take, for example, the fact that Hyde is called Jekyll's "favorite" (48). Would Utterson be so worried about a blackmail threat to Jekyll, would the doctor be so vulnerable to disgrace, if his secret related only to women? Especially in light of other features— both the general context of public school friendships ("old *mates* at school and college") and the specific situation of Hyde entering Jekyll's domain from the rear, and from a "by-street"[20]—Nabokov's response to "favorite" is appropriate.

> Favorite . . . sounds almost like *minion*. The all-male patterns that Gwynne has mentioned may suggest by a twist of thought that Jekyll's secret adventures were homosexual practices so common in London behind the Victorian veil. Utterson's first supposition is that Hyde blackmails the good doctor—and it is hard to imagine what special grounds for blackmailing would there have been in a bachelor's consorting with ladies of light morals. Or do Utterson and Enfield suspect that Hyde is Jekyll's illegitimate son? . . . But the difference in age as implied by the difference in their appearance does not seem to be quite sufficient for Hyde to be Jekyll's son. Moreover, in his will Jekyll calls Hyde his "friend and benefactor," a curious choice of words perhaps bitterly ironic but hardly referring to a son. [194]

The point as I see it is not that patriarchs "really are" homosexual, as though this were one state, but that late-Victorian professional men feel emotions that they can neither express nor comprehend. An *aura* of homosexuality serves to signal both the homoerotic nature of many male bonds and the lethal consequences of them.

> He [Utterson] sat on one side of his own hearth, with Mr. Guest, his head clerk, upon the other, and midway between them, at a nicely calculated distance from the fire, a bottle of a particular old wine. . . . the room was gay with firelight. In the bottom the acids were long ago resolved; the imperial dye had softened with time, as the colour grows richer in stained windows; and the glow of hot autumn afternoons on hillside vineyards was ready to be set free and to disperse the fogs of London. Insensibly the lawyer melted. [53–54]

Granted that on one level a tender human friendship exists between these men: friendship cannot account for all the details, the agents of affect, that appear in the scene. Why, for example, in a scene that ostensibly is pure plot contrivance—a handwriting expert is brought in to examine Hyde's script and, with supreme convenience, is presented with Jekyll's as well—are there so many layers of literary materials? "The melting mood" is one of Victorian fiction's conventional expressions for emotional surrender, but I have never seen the expression applied to a man. Utterson melts in a scene almost parodic of conventional seduction—the irresistible male *guest,* the cozy warmth of the evening privacy, the lubricating bottle of wine. Senuousity in Utterson's scene is intensified by the infusion of Keats. As Utterson's bottle has "long dwelt unsunned in the foundations," Keats's wine in the "Ode to a Nightingale" "hath been/ Cooled a long age in the deep-delvéd earth" (11–12). Wine that radiates "the glow of hot autumn afternoons on hillside vineyards" in Utterson's passage tastes, in Keats's, of "the country green,/ . . . and sunburnt myrth!/ O for a beaker of the warm south" (13, 14–15). Keats wants to "drink, and leave the world unseen" (19) because a world so redolent of death makes mockery of the body's warm sensuality. Utterson too is "ready to be set free," but what shackles him is not mortality. "The room was gay." Homophobia is the shackle that his body's deep-buried sensuality seeks to slip.[21]

Mr. Guest is not Utterson's chief object of desire, however. "Familiar guest" is Utterson's term for Henry Jekyll (56). Utterson's scene with Guest has its counterpart with Jekyll "[who] now sat on the opposite side of the fire . . . you could see by his looks that he cherished for Mr. Utterson a sincere and warm affection" (43). Genuine friendship obtains between these men, as it did between Utterson and Guest. But as the word "gay" in the first fireside scene is echoed by "gaily" in the second (43), so professional concerns mask personal obsessions in the second scene as they did in the first. Then the relation of lawyer to clerk screened Utterson's attraction to this house guest; now the relation of lawyer to (quasi)client allows Utterson to discuss Jekyll's choice of Edward Hyde as his heir. Utterson here is not only dealing with his sense of Cain-like exclusion from the will but also exploring the reason for his exclusion— Jekyll's mysterious "intimacy" with Hyde. Help in defining this intimacy is provided by another scene where professionalism acts as a screen in Utterson's relationship with Jekyll. "The hand of Henry Jekyll (as you [Utterson] have often remarked) was professional in shape and size; it was large, firm, white and comely" (87–88). To descant on the beauty of the beloved's hands is conventional enough for a lover, but what heterosexual man speaks, let alone often, about the hands of a *man?* The Notebook Draft version sentence reads, "The hand of Henry Jekyll, as we have often jocularly said, was eminently professional in shape and size; it was large, firm, white and comely, the hand of a lady's doctor in a word." The revisions of the sentence focus attention on Utterson. He rather than "we" discussed the hand; no jocularity is admitted; and deletion of the dig at lady's doctors precludes any heterosexual link of Jekyll and ladies.

What we are left with is Utterson's sensual and obsessive attention to Jekyll, and the "professional" as a screen for the obsessional.

Jekyll's role in the psychology of the novella is thus as overdetermined as desire itself. The oedipal father and the regressive son is also the male lover.

> . . . [Utterson] would see a room in a rich house, where his friend lay asleep, dreaming and smiling at his dreams; and then the door of that room would be opened, the curtains of the bed plucked apart, the sleeper recalled, and, lo! There would stand by his side a figure to whom power was given, and even at that dead hour, he must rise and do its bidding. [37]

This scene, we should note immediately, is not happening, it is being imagined. We focus less upon the Jekyll-Hyde relationship than upon Utterson's relation to it. Although Utterson insists that his friend's *safety* is the issue, there is a deeper concern with his friend's bondage. The "power" of Hyde, more than the danger to Jekyll, obsesses Utterson here. This obsession has the force of duration. The will "had *long* been the lawyer's eyesore. . . . out of the shifting, insubstantial mists, that had so *long* baffled his eye, there leaped up the sudden, definite presentment of a fiend" (35–36; my italics). In making his will, Jekyll has lost his will.

Utterson's long obsession with Hyde's power is brought into violent focus on this particular night by the revelation of Hyde's key: ". . . whipped out a key, went in . . . 'You are sure he used a key?' . . . drew a key from his pocket like one approaching home . . . blowing in the key . . . 'Mr. Hyde has a key.' . . . 'he still had his key with him' " (32, 34, 39, 41, 67). Beyond the obviously erotic aspects of whipping out and going in, there is the possessiveness that these acts signify for Utterson. "His friend's strange preference or bondage (call it what you please)" (38). We can call it what we please because preference and bondage are interchangeable in light of Jekyll's will, or rather Hyde's. Identities merge. "As he [Utterson] lay and tossed in the gross darkness of the night and the curtained room" (37), he imagines "the curtains of the bed plucked apart." The connection between "curtained" and "curtains" links Utterson's bed with Jekyll's, and thus associates Utterson with Jekyll's intimacy with Hyde. "The figure . . . haunted the lawyer all night; and if at any time he dozed over, it was but to see it glide more stealthily through the sleeping houses" (37). The conversion of Jekyll's house into houses signals that Utterson is unconsciously imagining Hyde's entry into other night places. Is one of these the "gross darkness" of Utterson's own repressed desire? His reference to Jekyll's "strange preference or bondage" occurs *after* we learn that the lawyer's own "imagination . . . was engaged, or rather enslaved" (37).

Utterson is thus attracted to, as well as emulous of, Edward Hyde.

Once Hyde gets Jekyll's will, he becomes that will. He becomes in effect what has always attracted Utterson to Jekyll. That Hyde can be seen as the penis of Jekyll was proposed years ago by Dr. Mark Kanzer. Though I believe Kanzer is close to the mark, his argument—that Hyde is small and deformed—seems weak. Kanzer describes as anatomical what is symbolic.[22] Hyde is Jekyll's phallus. Or rather, Hyde represents two contradictory perceptions of patriarchy: the patriarchal claim to phallic presence, to power, control, will; and (as we will see in section 4) the opposite, the patriarchal sense of itself as absent, the reality of impotence and dysfunction. Hyde is the phallus insofar as Utterson sees him as "the figure to whom power is given." Hyde's possession of the key to Jekyll's place (in every sense) puts into his hands the perquisites of patriarchy—ownership, access, ultimately the power to reify the nonself. Status as Jekyll's heir in the legal will assures the lawyer that Hyde can exercise his will over the future as well as the present. Utterson fosters this power, for he preserves the will in "the inmost private part of his safe" (35). This detail is so odd that it warrants explanation. Since Utterson did not draw up the will, since Jekyll's inheritance is in fact the responsibility of some other attorney, why does the novella emphasize *Utterson's* role in preserving the document? He must have a symbolic, psychological relationship with it. However repressive Utterson's act of shutting away the will is, and however the document assures his disinheritance from Jekyll, Utterson's "private" is the receptacle that keeps "safe" the will/phallus of the next patriarch. Utterson has no comparable will of his own.

Why are there no women in *Jekyll and Hyde?* Because patriarchs seek men. Why, then, is there the aura of homosexuality and not the fact of genital intercourse? Because what patriarchs seek in men is mirroring. Professionalism allows relations to seem "mature" and yet to remain at a postlatency "adolescent" stage, which in turn replicates the preoedipal stage of mother-child mirroring. Why patriarchs crave such mirroring, why they fear truly mature relationships with peer-aged women, becomes clear when we see what Jekyll sees in his mirror. Edward Hyde. Experiencing "new life. . . the raging energies of life . . . all his energy of life" (84, 95), Jekyll testifies that Hyde's "love of life is wonderful" (96). Jekyll makes evident the most elemental desires of patriarchy—to thwart death and to effect immortality. "The bonds of obligation . . . the dryness of a life of study . . . plod[ding] in the public eye with a load of genial respectability . . . the self-denying toils of my professional life" (83, 85, 86, 91). Jekyll is indisputably bored with conventional probity and intensely alive to outré pleasures, but he cannot be explained in terms of any vulgar hedonism. A finer explanation offers itself if we take another of Jekyll's self-characterizations—"the elderly and discontented doctor" (90)—and provide the explanatory causality that Jekyll's coordinate syntax cannot acknowledge. "Discontented" *because* "elderly," Jekyll once again uses professionalism to screen his emotional state. This time what he is repressing is not oedipal rage and regressive desire but the fear of death that lies behind them both. By saying that he is tired of being a dutiful doctor, Jekyll expresses his anxiety about tiring, aging.

Jekyll is waging war against time itself. This war involves patriarchy not only in its specifically late-Victorian, professional manifestation, but also in its traditional form. Patriarchy presupposes time, constitutes an accommodation with mortality. Patrilineal succession envisions the endurance not of an individual but of the tradition. A son gets to become a father because he accepts the next stage: the handing on of his status to a younger successor and the going on to death. Jekyll in effect goes back on the bargain: ". . . that what was dead, and had no shape, should usurp the offices of life . . ." (95). Jekyll fears the inanimate taking over the animate, process being returned to stasis. "The restrictions of natural life" (91) are what obsess him. Since body allows for the fragmentation that leads to dissolution (as opposed to mere dissoluteness), what Jekyll seeks is wholeness. Hyde is the "idol in the glass" because he is the mirror reversal of life's very sequence, the integration sought by the "imperfect and divided" doctor (84). Thus "Hyde struggling after freedom" seeks the "liberty" (90) of timelessness.

That this "liberty" is called a "sea" links Jekyll's escape from mortality to the fluidity images that mark his transformation into Hyde—the "current of disordered sensual images" that runs "like a millrace" in his fancy (83)—and thus to his obsession with orality. The Jekyll who "swallowed the transforming draught" compared himself with a "drunkard" (90). In drink, as in "the sea of liberty," Jekyll seeks the ultimate oneness, amnoetic, maternal. To "spring headlong into the sea" (86) suggests reverse birth, as the "impenetrable mantle" of Hyde suggests the womb where Jekyll's "safety was complete." The "pangs of dissolution" (85) involve nothing less than the dissolution of identity itself as a way to dissolve time. In the mirror of mother is oneness.

Against the attraction of maternal security, woman as wife cannot prevail. Misogyny, Hyde's punching the face of the prostitute, is the inevitable response to peer-aged women whose desires draw the son on to adulthood and thus to death. The prostitute offers fire, and Jekyll seeks water. She offers light, and he desires darkness.

IV. Consequences and Conclusions

Immortality through regression is a doomed dream, and Jekyll knows it. Notice that he keeps saying "young*er*" (83, 84; my italics), not young. He speaks of Hyde's "comparative youth" (90) because he knows that you cannot unring a bell. "Lighter, happier in body. . . . more express and single . . ." (83, 84). Jekyll senses the comparative nature of any change in nature. However restrictive "natural life" is, the struggle against those restrictions is unnatural. And doomed. The consequences of regression are manifest in *Jekyll and Hyde* both immediately (as impotence and dysfunction) and more generally (as solipsism and nonbeing).

First, impotence. The murder of Carew leaves Hyde "trembling . . . and still hearkening in my wake for the steps of the avenger" (91). Any violent victory is chimerical. Killing Carew snaps "the stick . . . in the middle under the stress" (47). One half of the stick ending up in "the neighbouring gutter" (47) suggests that the self-hate which caused the son to assault the father has only increased, since murder confirms the filial impotence that prompted the assault in the first place. "Neighbouring" reaffirms the social nature of all human actions. Hyde may disregard the bonds of patriarchy and strike out self-aggrandizingly, but he remains in a neighborhood. There are neighbors to witness his crime; there is within himself the abiding sense of community, which guiltily directs his broken stick to the appropriate gutter.

The association of guilt with impotence persists as the homicidal narrative proceeds. Hyde's apprehensive state soon after the murder of Carew—"still harkening in my wake for the steps of the avenger" (91)—reappears months later as he encounters his next victim. Lanyon "bid him enter, [but] he did not obey me without a searching backward glance into the darkness of the square. There was a policeman not far off, advancing with his bull's eye open" (77). Here, as with Utterson, the son's basic anxieties are projected onto experience. The association of "bull" with the authoritative male—and with the law he embodies and enforces—confirms the son's belief in the father's phallic superiority. Castration cannot harm the father because his superiority neither resides in a specific organ nor abides in a particular man. Superior by virtue of the son's perception of his superiority, the father bull returns still more puissant when filial inadequacy is compounded by filial guilt.

Emasculation, in turn, characterizes Hyde himself. He ultimately represents less the phallus than patriarchal pretensions to it. Despite all his "masculine" traits of preternatural strength and animal agility, Hyde is prey to what the late nineteenth century associated particularly with women. "Wrestling against the approaches of hysteria" (78), Hyde resembles Jekyll's "hysterical whimpering" housemaid (64), just as Jekyll himself (who calls his fears "unmanning" [58]) is repeatedly characterized by the conventional feminine trait that marked the maid at the window—"faintness . . . half fainting . . . faint . . . faintness" (53, 80, 92). Hyde, the erstwhile phallic predator, is heard "weeping like a woman" (69). Effeminacy marks his "steps [that] fell lightly and oddly, with a certain swing . . . different indeed from the heavy creaking tread of Henry Jekyll" in his patriarchal role (69). How reminiscent of the moon "lying on her back" is Hyde's corpse as Utterson "turned it on its back" (70).

The other half of the shattered cane goes to Utterson because his association with the subconscious rage expressed through Hyde requires his association, too, with the guilty impotence of filial failure. Utterson, like Hyde (and like all "honest" men, the lawyer attests), feels "terror of the law" when police are near (48). The broken stick that he shares with Hyde indicates their common guilt and prepares us for Utterson's version of Hyde's impotence—patriarchal dysfunction. Utterson and his peers fail to assume the leadership that is the responsibility and the glory of patriarchy. In Jekyll's absence, his servants are "like a flock of sheep" (63). That they are looking to the patriarch as Good Shepherd is confirmed when a grateful servant cried out, "Bless God! it's Mr. Utterson" (64). Can Utterson fulfill this role? Attestations to his decisiveness in the break-in scene (" 'my shoulders are broad enough to bear the blame' . . . [he] lead the way" [68]) are undercut by moments almost comically indecisive. After announcing to Poole with a seriousness appropriate to his patriarchal station, "if you say that [Jekyll is murdered] . . . I shall consider it my duty to break in that door," and after receiving from Poole the apparently appropriate response of, "Ah, Mr. Utterson, that's talking," the lawyer goes on.

> "And now comes the second question. . . . Who is going to do it?" . . .
> "Why, you and me, sir," was the undaunted reply.
> "That's very well said," returned the lawyer. [67]

Who else would do the breaking in once Utterson announces it as his duty? "Undaunted" characterizes the servant rather than the lawyer because Utterson is daunted and daunting. "That's talking" becomes ironical in light of the subsequent exchange; Utterson is all talk, whereas Poole's words are genuinely "well said" because they bespeak action. Two pages later, Utterson seems at last galvanized to action and utters the cry, "let our name be vengeance," but his very next sentence is, "Call Bradshaw" (68). That the lawyer actually has a task for Bradshaw does not prevent us from feeling an immediate drop in intensity here. Even the act of reading is beyond Utterson. "He caught up the next paper; it was a note in the doctor's hand and dated at the top. 'O Poole,' the lawyer cried, 'he was alive and here this very day. He . . .'" (72). After listening to Utterson go on for seven more lines, Poole speaks for the reader when he

WILLIAM VEEDER

intervenes. "Why don't you read it, sir?" Utterson's answer—"Because I fear"—is quite moving as an admission of what all human beings feel at times. But we cannot be overly impressed with Utterson here because we recognize that he does not fight back determinedly against the fear that, unacknowledged, undermines most of what typifies the patriarchy.

Gentlemanly manners, for instance. Ostensibly one of patriarchy's principal tools for handling experience, manners function like professional etiquette in *Jekyll and Hyde,* less as a mode of action than as a screen for fears and rages. In the break-in scene, Poole provides Utterson with the crucial letter to Maw's: " 'This is a strange note,' said Mr. Utterson; and then sharply, 'How do you come to have it open?' " (66). At a moment of peril, the lawyer quibbles about etiquette—and with a servant of unimpeachable probity who subsequently answers Utterson's question resoundingly (the note was opened by the man at Maw's). What is not answered is why Utterson asked the question in the first place. He is afraid at every level, and uses manners and superior rank to turn aside from the crucial, threatening issues. Earlier in the scene when he confronted the servants huddled sheeplike,

"Are you all here?" said the lawyer peevishly. "Very irregular, very unseemly: your master would be far from pleased."
"They're all afraid," said Poole. [64]

The servants share Utterson's "fear," but rather than admit the common plight of them all, the lawyer focuses on decorum as a way of venting anxiety while maintaining superiority. "Peevishly" contrasts with "master" to stress both how trivial manners are at so dire a moment and how far Utterson is from the mastery appropriate to patriarchy. A still more invidious contrast establishes the moral issue involved in manners. Utterson makes a bargain with Hyde:

"How did you [Utterson] know me?" he [Hyde] asked.
"On your side," said Mr. Utterson, "will you do me a favour?"
"With pleasure," replied the other. "What shall it be?"
"Will you let me see your face?" asked the lawyer. [39]

After Hyde masters his disinclination to comply, he insists on the other half of the bargain.

"And now," said the other, "how did you know me?"
"By description," was the reply.
"Whose description?"
"We have common friends," said Mr. Utterson.
"Common friends!" echoed Mr. Hyde, a little hoarsely.
"Who are they?"

"Jekyll, for instance," said the lawyer.

"He never told you," cried Mr. Hyde, with a flush of anger. "I did not think you would have lied."

"Come," said Mr. Utterson, "that is not fitting language."

The other snarled aloud into a savage laugh. [39–40]

Hyde is three times called "the other" here, but the liar is Utterson. Hyde does the gentlemanly thing and keeps his bargain; Utterson not only fails to keep his part but resorts to manners when caught red-handed. "Fitting language" is what the liar insists on. No wonder Hyde laughs.

Utterson with the lie, like Enfield with the breakfast, shows that patriarchs will do whatever they wish, and then insist on a veneer of "proper" conduct. That such self-indulgence is not only inherently weak and morally wrong but potentially fatal is attested to by Lanyon during Hyde's midnight visit. Besides giving Hyde a lesson in manners—" 'You forget that I have not yet the pleasure of your acquaintance. Be seated.' And I showed him an example, and sat down in my customary seat" (78)—Lanyon seeks to control the situation by other traditional guarantors of order. "As I followed him into the bright light of the consulting room, I kept my hand ready on my weapon. Here, at last, I had a chance of clearly seeing him. I had never set eyes on him before" (77). Lanyon has never seen anything like Hyde, yet the doctor is relying on traditional defenses. "The bright light of the consulting room" represents the light of reason that this positivist clinician trusts in to illuminate life's mysteries. And if reason should fail, there is always force. Lanyon's weapon being "old" (77) suggests both that violence is an age-old patriarchal solution to problems and that this solution is old-fashioned, outmoded. "Self-defense" Lanyon indeed needs, but what he needs defense against is his self. Hyde is a threat only to the extent that Lanyon cannot resist his own curiosity. Though the doctor maintains his gentlemanly facade, "affecting coolness that I was far from truly possessing" (79), he has no more self-control than the rest of the patriarchs. "I have gone too far in the way of inexplicable services to pause before I see the end" (80). What he sees is Jekyll, and it ends him. Why?

Professionalism functions here to screen the same homoerotic attractions and ultimate impotence that characterize other patriarchs. "Under the seal of our profession" (80) occurs most unprofessional behavior because Lanyon's "curiosity" and "services" (80) go far beyond clinical medicine. As little Hyde grows into large Jekyll, Lanyon sees the transformation as expressly erectile: "there came, I thought, a change—he seemed to swell" (80). The aura of phallic presence here parodies the fact of patriarchal impotence. With his life "shaken to its roots" (80), Lanyon soon dies. Especially in light of Otto Rank's insight that the return of the double is the advent of death,[23] Lanyon seems doubly doomed because Jekyll and Hyde are both his doubles. Jekyll the patriarch/scientist is Lanyon's reflection in the cultural mirror, so that when Jekyll is also Hyde, Dr. Lanyon cannot accept his own alterity, cannot accept himself as Hyde too. When the man named "Hastie" (80) meets a man entering with "haste" (77), he is in effect confronting his mirror image. And it kills him. Hasty Lanyon is unable to resist the knowledge proffered by Hyde because that knowledge is already hidden in the doctor's unconscious. Characterized *before* the Hyde scene by "a shock of hair prematurely white" (36), Lanyon is already shocked by his unconscious sense of participation in Jekyll's other side (this is why Lanyon has inveighed so ferociously against Jekyll's transcendental medicine). But Lanyon has never advanced to the maturity of a self-control based on self-knowledge. Defended only by manners, bright lights, gun, and "the seal of our profession"—the old weapons of traditional responses—Lanyon, who has never had to face the Hyde hidden within us all, succumbs to the epiphany which is self-revelation.

Death does not eliminate all the patriarchs of Jekyll's circle, but the consequences of regressive desire do ultimately mark all of patriarchy with a kind of solipsistic nonbeing.

> Next, in the course of their [Utterson's and Poole's] review of the chamber, the searchers came to the cheval glass, into whose depths they looked with an involuntary horror. But it was so turned as to show them nothing but the rosy glow playing on the roof, the fire sparkling in a hundred repetitions along the glazed front of the presses, and their own pale and fearful countenances stooping to look in.
> "This glass has seen some strange things, sir," whispered Poole.
> "And surely none stranger than itself," echoed the lawyer, in the same tone. [71]

Both the staging and the style of this scene are revelatory. Why is the mirror turned up? How it might have become turned this way—Jekyll/Hyde hit it as he fell—does not mean that it *must* be so turned. The odds are better that a small man falling in a large room would not have hit the mirror. Once again, setting functions to reveal psyche. The upturned mirror cannot reflect the dead Hyde on the floor. Utterson and Poole are looking down, bent over staring into the mirror, but they do not see into "depths." They see upward—the "rosy" glow and "sparkling" light of domestic bliss. They are too frightened, too "pale and fearful," for their "involuntary" glance to recognize the reality they want to ignore.

Patriarchs who have wanted to overlook Hyde and death manage to overlook both at this moment of supposed "depth" perception.

The consequences of rejecting the other are reflected stylistically in Stevenson's passage. Compare

> But it was so turned as to show them nothing but the rosy glow . . .

and

> But it was so turned as to show them only the rosy glow . . .

Syntax in Stevenson's sentence makes us make a mistake. Providing a direct object to "show" completes a basic syntactic unit. We read: "it was so turned as to show them nothing." The construction "nothing but" then carries us on to the opposite meaning, to what the mirror does show, but the syntax of the sentence's initial ten words has given no hint that the "nothing but" construction will appear. What is the effect of the syntax making us assume that the mirror showed nothing when in fact it shows to the patriarchs their very faces?

The "strange things" that the mirror has seen are principally Jekyll and Hyde, who are each direct reflections and mirrored reversals of one another as doubles. The mirror is their solipsistic world. Utterson and his double, his reflecting Poole, are in that world in every sense. Their faces appear in the mirror because their lives are inseparable from the lives of Jekyll and Hyde, from the plot of *Jekyll and Hyde*. Diction emphasizes the reflected and self-reflexive relation of Utterson and Poole when the lawyer "echoed" the servant "in the same tone." Utterson as the uttering son who replicates the values of the fathers mirrors in his upright life the professional probity of Jekyll, Lanyon, and Carew; Utterson as the repressed son who cannot find utterance for anger and oral deprivation is reflected in the rages of Hyde, who dies by drinking poison.

The conjunction of orality and the cheval glass marks the men of *Jekyll and Hyde* as caught in the Lacanian mirror stage. The failure to resolve oedipal tensions and to unite with peer-aged women leaves patriarchs in diadic relations (Damon-Pythias, Utterson-Enfield, Utterson-Poole), which screen the persistence of the mother-child bond. The "imaginary" nature of homosocial harmony is reflected in the other intimation of Stevenson's syntactically ambiguous sentence—that there is nothing in the mirror. Utterson demonstrates—and indeed constitutes—himself as "nothing" by his very denial of the mirror. When Poole says, "this glass has seen some strange things," and the lawyer replies, "and surely none stranger than itself," Utterson singles out the mirror itself as odd. What he is saying on the literal level—that a cheval glass is unusual in a laboratory—is an evasion on the psychological level. At this dire moment, many things are stranger than the mirror. By not in effect accepting his image in the glass, Utterson can deny his membership in the Jekyll-Hyde group of mirror gazers, the solipsistic, narcissistic men who see in other men the workings of their own desires. Utterson's very verb "echoed" confirms him, however, as a rearticulation of others. His rejection of the self as other is the ultimate solipsism, the absolute mirror. As the diadic mirroring with the mother constitutes a denial of everything outside the relationship, including death, so Utterson's denial of his relationship with the mirror as external object confirms his own imaginary status, his essential nonbeing.

This brings me to one last, epitomizing—because mirroring and irreflective—quotation from Henry Jekyll. "He, I say—I cannot say, I" (94). Identity is doubly isolating because Jekyll can think of himself as other when he should not, and cannot think of himself as other when he should. He is not Hyde, thus Hyde must be a "he" rather than an "I." But Jekyll is also not really I "the elderly and discontented doctor" (90). Because Jekyll cannot bring together his two selves, his conscious and unconscious, he is neither self. Thus "I cannot say, I" means more than Jekyll's inability to call himself Hyde. Jekyll cannot call himself anything. A patriarchal system that sets out to assure self-definition by excluding undesirables ends up by excluding itself, through the exclusion of half of every self. If you cannot call the other "I," you cannot name yourself.

Stevenson would thus agree with Lacan and others that identity is mirrored alienation, though he would insist that alienation can become community if we can accept the alienated and alienating other as the self. The novella's patriarchs cannot do this, however. Jekyll, who imagines that he can banish Hyde "like the stain of a breath upon a mirror" (86), proves as transitory as his mirror image whose death coincides with his own. The images of Utterson and Poole are comparable stains on the cheval glass. They lack depth and permanence because they do not know themselves as absence. They suffer—on the level of narrative—the fate of Jekyll, who thinks that the potion which can distinguish him from Hyde means that "my troubles will roll away like a story that is told" (75). In the end, Jekyll realizes that his life coincides with his story, that he will die not twitching on the floor but putting down his pen. "This is the true hour of my death" (96). Utterson and Enfield do not realize even this. Utterson reads the narratives of Lanyon and Jekyll in the assumption that meaning and thus being will result, but what happens is that Utterson fades from the narration, becoming only a character in Jekyll's narrative. Enfield is not even named here. He has been absorbed in the novel's last word, "end." What could be conventional—and thus reassuring and patriarchal—if it were "the end," becomes an unsettling reassertion of continuity as "an end." This end is both final and one of many. Patriarchy remains a fiction that is over and is still going on.

NOTES

I would like to express my gratitude to colleagues who, as they have done so generously in the past, gave time and ideas to my work: Richard D. Altick, Lawrence Buell, Frederick Crews, Paul J. Emmett, Jr., Robert A. Ferguson, Susan M. Griffin, Gordon D. Hirsch, Lawrence Rothfield, Ronald Thomas, Mark Turner; particularly Lauren Berlant, Lisa Ruddick, Jeffrey Stern, and Richard Strier. I would also like to thank the seminar on literature and psychoanalysis at the Chicago Institute for Psychoanalysis for the help with a draft of this essay; and the students in my Anglo-American Gothic classes and seminars, especially Timothy Child, Douglas Jones, and Karen Rosenthal.

1. Though critics have not given detailed attention to any of Jekyll's peers, they have at times mentioned ambiguities of characters on which I will focus. Eigner, who calls Enfield "a sturdy young business man" (188), also lists him among "the 'down-going men'" (146). Hennelly, recognizing that Enfield blackmails Hyde as Enfield supposes Hyde is doing to Jekyll, says, "even Enfield . . . is symbolically returning from some Hyde-like, dark quest beyond civilization and consciousness" (13). See also Nabokov (189) and Saposnik (111). With Lanyon, the "hasty" aspect has been noted by Egan (31), the "hide-bound" by Hennelly (11) and Fraustino (236). Fraustino goes on to attribute Lanyon's dilemma to a "society [which] purposely cultivates self-deceit in obscuring from its Lanyons the truth about themselves" (236). Saposnik concentrates on Lanyon himself as one who "abandoned Jekyll because he was afraid of the temptation to which he finally succumbed" (111). Utterson has, expectably, generated the widest range of interpretation. Most complimentary are Block's crediting of Utterson with "the acquisition of knowledge through intense sympathy" (448), Saposnik's calling him "a partisan in the best sense of the term" (110), Hennelly's saying that "only Utterson seems to be finally 'free' within such a cultural straight-jacket [Victorian repressiveness]. . . . Only he achieves, in the tale's idiom, the 'balanced' ideal" (10, 11), and Heath's listing Utterson along with Enfield as a man with a "shaken but healthy identity" (104). Most critical are Miyoshi's contention that "there is something furtive and suppressed about him. . . . [his tolerance] looks suspiciously like the result not of charity but of indifference" (471); Egan's, that Utterson "remains to the end only the bewildered onlooker" (31); and Fraustino's, that Utterson fails because he "attempts to articulate reality by means of language" (237).

2. Besides Day and Miyoshi, see Eigner, Fraustino, Hennelly, Saposnik, and Welsch.

3. "Friend" and its derivatives occur on pages 29 (three times), 30, 32 (twice), 35, 36 (four times), 37, 38, 39 (three times), 40, 41, 51, 52 (twice), 53, 56 (three times), 57, 58 (four times), 59 (twice), 66, 72, 74, 75, and 90.

4. Among numerous discussions of patriarchy recently, those particularly helpful to me have been: Veronica Beechey, "On Patriarchy," *Feminist Review* 1

(1979): 66–82; Christine Delphy, "Patriarchy, Feminism, and Their Intellectuals," *Close to Home*, tr. and ed. by Diana Leonard (Amherst: University of Massachusetts Press, 1984), 138–53; George B. Forgie, *Patricide in the House Divided* (New York: W. W. Norton and Co., 1979); Annette Kuhn, "Structures of Patriarchy and Capital in the Family," in *Feminism and Materialism*, ed. Annette Kuhn and Ann Marie Wolpe (London: Routledge and Kegan Paul, 1978), 42–67; Gerda Lerner, *The Creation of Patriarchy* (New York: Oxford University Press, 1986); Catharine A. MacKinnon, "Feminism, Marxism, Method, and the State: An Agenda for Theory," *Signs* 7 (1982): 515–44; Roisin McDonough and Rachel Harrison, "Patriarchy and Relations of Production," in *Feminism and Materialism*, 11–41; Janice A. Radway, *Reading the Romance* (Chapel Hill: University of North Carolina Press, 1984); Michael Paul Rogin, *Subversive Genealogy* (Berkeley: University of California Press, 1983); Gayle Rubin, "The Traffic in Women: Notes on the 'Political Economy' of Sex," in *Toward an Anthropology of Women*, ed. Rayna R. Reiter (New York: Monthly Review Press, 1975), 157–210; and Eve Kosofsky Sedgwick, *Between Men* (New York: Columbia University Press, 1985).

5. Henry James a century ago noted the absence of women in Stevenson's work (Maixner 292). In 1939, Gwynn, calling Jekyll's circle "a community of monks" (130), concluded that "a sure instinct guided him [Stevenson]. Insistence on the sexual would have brought colours into the story alien to its pattern; what he desired was to convey the presence of evil wholly divorced from good" (131). Stevenson's "instinct" is defended by Saposnik with a different argument. "The Victorian era was male-centered; and a story so directed at the essence of its moral behavior is best seen from a male perspective. . . . [also] a peculiarly masculine breed of asceticism" pervades the tale (110). Even Nabokov says that "a certain amiable, jovial, and lighthearted strain running through the pleasures of a gayblade would then have been difficult to reconcile with the medieval rising as a black scarecrow against a livid sky in the guise of Hyde" (194). Day has much more usefully connected the "striking" absence of women with the sickness of Victorian relations as Stevenson sees them. "In their search for pleasure, Henry Jekyll and Dorian Gray throw off the feminine world of respectability and thus their pursuit takes on a purely masculine, sadistic form, finally transformed into the masochism of suicide" (92). Recently Heath has included the absence of women in his extensive discussion of sexuality in *Jekyll and Hyde*.

6. Harvie makes an excellent case for Stevenson's fundamental conservatism. First locating Stevenson in the general swing to the right that characterized the 1870s and 1880s, Harvie then concentrates on the man himself. Though "Stevenson, fundamentally always a Tory, did his bit for journalistic Unionism when in 1887 he dreamed up a crazy scheme of moving his whole family to Ireland. . . . Stevenson is much more logically conservative than we generally credit him with being. . . . Stevenson was, by birth, a Scottish Tory" (112–13). This group, however establishment-oriented, shared Louis's "hatred of pharasaism and humbug" (113). Retaining from his early socialist days "his religious belief, and an imaginative sympathy—not so much with the poor *per se*, as with their attitude to the rich," Stevenson fairly quickly "became a solidly anti-

Gladstonian Tory whose hostility to Liberalism while less rancid than, say, Rudyard Kipling's, far pre-dated the split of 1886" (115).

7. Magali Sarfatti Larson, *The Rise of Professionalism* (Berkeley: University of California Press, 1977), 4, 5.

8. Stevenson mentions these instances of "brown" in "A Chapter on Dreams"; Kanzer connects them in his interpretation of Stevenson's psychological life.

9. For critics who discuss "je kyll," see Egan (30), Miyoshi (473), Saposnik (note 11).

10. Violence also colors Enfield through his name. "Enfield" is both the Sussex site of the Royal Small Arms Factory founded in the eighteenth century and the weapons produced there. "Enfield riflemen" and "Enfield skirmishers" were important components of the British infantry. Stevenson's fascination with the military was lifelong and is well documented by his biographers (Furnas 22, 198, 201, 202, 208, 387; Calder 38, 41, 47, 120, 159). Ordnance, in particular, recurs often in Stevenson's correspondence up through 1886. "Grenades and torpedoes . . . artillery range . . . big short . . . minute guns . . . 'a red canonball' . . . platoon firing . . . fire a gun to leeward" (L1, 41, 227, 300; L2, 20, 28, 151). In addition, there is, of course, *Ben Gunn.* Enfield's genealogy is, therefore, long and violent; what is unique about him is his placement in the ostensibly genteel world of Victorian patriarchy.

11. From its first entry in 1547 to its most recent, the OED records as the meaning of "to take to one's heels" only "to run away."

12. The maid could be house-sitting for her master during his absence, but the month of October (46) seems too late for any seasonal vacation and the expression "living alone" seems inappropriate to house-sitting. The possibility of homosexual innuendo in the Carew/Hyde encounter is raised by Charyn in his "Afterword" to the Bantam edition of the novella (New York: 1981), 113.

13. For devolution in Stevenson, see Block and Lawler.

14. Kanzer and Fiedler examine oedipal features of Stevenson's personality and various works but do almost nothing with *Jekyll and Hyde.* Hennelly sees the link to Oedipus but discusses it only in terms of "self-actualizing choice. . . . [Jekyll] like Oedipus, chooses his own fate" (12). Calder is willing to recognize "oedipal jealousy" in Stevenson's "cry of exclusion 'my mother is my father's wife' " (75), but she resolutely denies Stevenson's "need for a mother figure" (70). Why? Because Stevenson desired Mrs. Sitwell sexually. Calder is unquestionably correct about the nature of Stevenson's desire for Fanny Sitwell, but Calder does not allow for the fact that sexual desire can indicate precisely an attraction *to* mother, if the son has indeed found a woman who evokes his lingering oedipal and pre-oedipal desires. Calling Mrs. Sitwell "mother" can both be "part of his later rationalization" after Fanny declined any sexual liaison (70) and still reveal the reality of Louis's initial oedipal/sexual desire for her.

15. In *A Child's Garden of Verses,* illustrated by Charles Robinson (Boulder, Colo.: Shambhala Publications, 1979). Subsequent poems are cited from this edition, with line references included in the text.

16. Freud's fullest description of the primal scene is in his analysis of the wolfman (from the *History of an Infantile Neurosis,* in *The Standard Edition of*

the Complete Psychological Works of Sigmund Freud, vol. 17, tr. James Strachey [London: Hogarth Press, 1964], particularly "The Dream and Primal Scene," 29–47). Among critics of Stevenson, Kanzer is by far the most perceptive about primal scene materials in Louis's life and work.

17. Critics who concentrate on the lawyer's first and second names draw understandably benign conclusions about his character. Hennelly discusses "Gabriel Utterson's prophetic narrative like that of his angel namesake" (12); Saposnik finds in him "a combination of justice and mercy (as his names Gabriel John suggest)" (10). In my reading of *Jekyll and Hyde*, the benign potential of Utterson's first names is undercut by the nature of his utterances. His story is prophetic in the ironic sense that his inability to see augers the decline of Victorian patriarchy; justice and mercy are just what he cannot articulate when the stakes are highest and the threats most immediate. No annunciation is voiced by this Gabriel who generates neither progeny nor ample insight; little light is divided from darkness by this John for whom the notion of "in the beginning was the word" signifies an ironic imprisonment of language.

18. In addition to the tradition that extends from Pandora's box to Portia's caskets, there is the slang association of "box" with the female genital, which Spears calls "widespread" by the 1900s.

19. "Queer" meaning "male homosexual" has entered "general slang" by the early 1900s, according to Spears; Partridge (8th edition) locates the same meaning "since ca. 1900."

20. "By-street" occurs repeatedly in the novella where "side street" or even "street" would have sufficed mimetically. The OED lists "bisexual" as early as 1824, when Coleridge uses it in *Aids to Reflection*.

21. Establishing that "no scholarly work has been done on the origins of 'gay' in the sense under discussion [meaning male homosexual], and an embarrassment of riches complicates its history," John Boswell locates "*gai*" meaning "a openly homosexual person" as early as fourteenth-century France (*Christianity, Social Tolerance, and Homosexuality* [Chicago: University of Chicago Press, 1983], 43). Stevenson's excellent knowledge of French and his presence in the artistic communities of Paris and Barbizon, make his knowledge of the French usage of *gai* probable. By "the early 20th century," Boswell adds, " 'gay' was common in the English homosexual subculture." Stevenson's acceptance into Bohemia and into the literary inner circle of Britain, where Pater and Wilde moved with their followers, where the *Yellow Book* group and other London aesthetes would flourish by the early 1890s, and where close friends like Gosse revealed homosexual inclinations, means that Stevenson's hearing by 1886 a password common a few years later is highly likely. Eve Kosofsky Sedgwick makes a forceful case for the homoerotic connotations of the words "gay" and "queer" in Henry James's turn-of-the-century story "The Beast in the Jungle" ("The Beast in the Closet: James and the Writing of Homosexual Panic" in *Sex, Politics, and Science*, Selected Papers for the English Institute, 1983–84, ed. Ruth Bernard Yeazell [Baltimore: Johns Hopkins University Press, 1984], 148–86). James was of course in close contact with *The Yellow Book* and Gosse, as well as with homosexual young men such as Jocelyn Perse. From my recent immersion in Anglo-American gothic fiction between 1885 and 1914, I have

little doubt that the use of "gay" and "queer" in the homoerotic sense was widespread in the years before 1900.

Furnas establishes quite properly that Stevenson's "times allowed *friend* a significant warmth greater than ours now permit. . . . in the 1870's, particularly in intellectual-aesthetic circles, 'friends' were gloatingly added up and acknowledged claims not dissimilar to, though less formal than, those of blood-brothers in preliterate cultures" (39). Furnas then goes on, "let no fool try to read perversion into the above. It is difficult to comprehend Louis's relations with Bob Stevenson or Henley or Henry James without understanding precisely what was meant or not meant by his ability frankly to write, 'I love you, Henley, from my soul'" (39–40). Furnas's defensiveness here highlights the questions that his rhetoric wants to repress. Calder is less anxious: "It is noticeable again and again, in men who may well have had no hidden homosexual tendencies (and also in men who did—Edmund Gosse, for instance) that the male appreciation of Stevenson was often intensely physical" (65). For me the issue is not whether Stevenson's friends were latently or actively homosexual but whether his sensibility and his experience allowed for perception of the homoerotic bonds that characterize the men of *Jekyll and Hyde*. Compare, for example, Stevenson's response to seeing Henley and Jekyll's response to becoming Hyde: "the look of his face was like wine to me" (Furnas 106); "the thought . . . delighted me like wine" (91). Henley's conflicts with Fanny quite obviously involve rivalry. "Henley was jealous of the love and time Louis gave to his wife. For it is clear that Henley was, in a sense, in love with him. . . . Henley's jealousy rivaled Fanny's. . . . like many others, Henley loved Louis" (Calder 95, 164). Among these others was Sidney Colvin. "[Fanny] believed Louis's love for Colvin to equal his love for her. Colvin himself was not above jealousy" (Calder 155). Triangles were complicated by Louis's penchant for role reversal. He often configured the maternal Fanny in startlingly masculine terms. Calling her "my dear fellow" and "My dearest little man," he sounds, as Furnas recognizes, an "unusual note . . . his letters to her sound almost like Damon writing to Pythias" (256, 257). In turn, personalities as strong as Fanny's and Henley's draw out the feminine side of Louis, which Henley stressed in the early version of his famous poem on Stevenson. "With a subtle trace / Of feminine force. . . . a streak of Puck, / More Cleopatra, of Hamlet most of all." That Henley later changed these lines to "With trace on trace / Of passion, impudence, and energy. . . . a streak of Puck, / Much Antony . . ." confirms in the very act of repression the "feminine" appeal that Louis exercised. Stevenson was conscious of this feminine component. He admits to giving Seraphina "a trait taken from myself" (L2, 338); he recognizes in Alexander's portrait of him "a mixture of aztec idol, a lion, an Indian Rajah, and a woman" (L2, 342–43). Stevenson's capacity to envision various roles for himself and others and to evoke and reciprocate strong emotions in persons of both sexes are for me marks of his exceptional interest as a human being and sources of his psychological penetration as a writer.

22. Kanzer uses the word *phallus* but clearly he means penis ("Hyde is small and possessed of some nameless deformity" [Geduld 122]).

23. Otto Rank, *The Double,* tr. and ed. Harry Tucker, Jr. (Chapel Hill: University of North Carolina Press, 1971).

The Struggle for a Dichotomy: Abjection in Jekyll and His Interpreters

JERROLD E. HOGLE

I. Some Remaining Questions

By now it should be apparent that, despite its claims, the "Full" confession at the end of Stevenson's *Strange Case of Dr Jekyll and Mr Hyde* does not explain all the mysteries left unsolved in the narratives preceding it. Henry Jekyll's "Statement of the Case" clearly raises as many questions as it answers about what the creation of "Edward Hyde" actually hides.[1] The doctor's rooting of his self-division in a basic "duplicity" inhabiting the very "womb of [human] consciousness" (81–82) turns out to be a cover for a different awareness, just as Peter Garrett has argued. To construct the core of human nature as a binary opposition, Jekyll admits, is to provide no more than a "point" beyond which the scientific "knowledge [of his day] does not"—or will not—"pass"; were human understanding to penetrate this screen, a man might really "be known for a mere polity of multifarious, incongruous, and independent denizens" irreducible to a good/evil split (82). Hyde, then, for Jekyll the main emblem of this split, is fashioned for the public eye, not simply to conceal the division in man (which he only succeeds in revealing) but to ensure that the notion of "two sides" keeps conscious Western thought (Jekyll's included) from sensing a deeper play of differences, a nonbinary polymorphism, at the "base" of human nature. Surely we must wonder, more than Jekyll does, why he feels impelled to follow this course and why he then insists on keeping to it in the face of its horrible consequences and the admitted insufficiency of his grounding assumptions.

Garrett's responses to these quandaries, I think, begin to help us with the problem of that "polity," especially when his best suggestions are supported or furthered by Ronald Thomas. Both writers correctly interpret the "Statement" as questioning the age-old tradition of identity as a self-contained unity of thesis and antithesis. These critics see how much Jekyll launches himself explicitly into the figurality of language, in part by just writing out a theory of his own being. The constitution of his nature is thereby thrown into the spacing and separateness of many "grammatical and narrative positions" (to quote Garrett), and the effect is to scatter the doctor's "I" across the multiplicity (and possible combinations) of words, the "independent denizens" of language. Suppositions of unity and self-containment are dissolved into "multifarious" figures and the displacement of each figure by others as the discourse of self-articulation develops. Such is the dispersion of coming into language, prior to "unity" and "self-containment," needed to compose these or any constructions of a man's foundations.

Hyde, we can even say, though produced in part to conceal the figural basis of the self from the self, is the supreme indicator that any representation of a person is like a written text—doubling, concealing, and standing in for its "original" the way an act of writing mirrors, hides, and supplants its author. Much as writers often have, Dr. Jekyll, Hyde's "underwriter" in many ways, has declared his sense of his own hidden nature by figuring and naming part of it in a substitute "countenance" or "stamp" (83) that defines its author publicly by being different from, removed beyond, and protective of his privacy. Jekyll even works out the different signature for Hyde that reangles and thereby obscures his own. In doing so, he inevitably makes this image for half of his "essence" always other than itself without an essence at its core. The Hyde-figure, like any word, keeps "hiding" its meaning by deferring to other signs (such as Jekyll's signature on a check), which then defer to other ones themselves (as when the check and the name "Hyde" lead Utterson to refer to Jekyll's will). That is why Hyde's various interpreters, confronted by his mysterious "deformity"—or de-formation in the direction of different forms—can only "describe him," write him out, without ever getting to the bottom of him (34). He is too much a form of writing *at* bottom to be "uncovered" by writings about him, too much a self-obscuring product of figural substitution prompting other figures to interpret his obscurity.

Garrett is also right when he shows, moreover, that the figural process of self-constitution, along with its "multifarious" ways of interrelating its "denizens," is violently suppressed in the "Statement" (and the tale) by established patterns of discourse that wrest this "polity" into dichotomous "simplifications" (Garrett's apt word).[2] I would even go a step further and say that this concealment of sheer figurality, always by a writing that depends on figural relations, is a choice deliberately made by Henry Jekyll. He composes all his symbolic stand-ins using a combination of rhetorical modes that will ensure his being "read" in a certain way. Willfully refusing any deeper awareness, the doctor configures his "nature" according to the "hard law" prescribed in the codes of his Protestant "religion" (81), codes very like the almost Calvinist schemes of the Covenanters forced on young Stevenson by his

JERROLD E. HOGLE

Scottish father and his nanny.[3] This styling of humanity sees the essence of fallen man as split, like the whole world after the Fall itself, between the God-seeking forces of constructive good and the destructive, Satanic forces of antisocial evil. This rhetoric can be reinforced, as Stevenson well knew,[4] by late-Victorian variants on the theory of evolution that picture modern man as struggling to separate the fully civilized from the still-primitive tendencies in himself. Having adopted this combination of vocabularies, the doctor must match the rigid dualism in such a blend of ideologies to keep its other supporters, whose approval he craves, from castigating him as one who blurs the distinction. He therefore contorts the "impatient gaeity" he feels in himself (81), the movement of energy that cannot be categorized as serenely "God-like" or "civilized," into a figure sufficiently Satanic and "troglodytic" (40) to separate this primitive "devil within" from the well-to-do scientist "fond of the respect of the [reputedly] wise and good among his fellow men" (81). He names that figure "Hyde," ostensibly because this "double," resembling those in previous gothic tales by Stevenson and other writers, conceals, "like a thick cloak" (86), Jekyll's connection with uncivilized lawlessness and his attempt to divorce his daylight awareness from the dark half of the duplicity that supposedly inhabits everyone. Hyde as finally created and made manifest, we find, restrains (and so hides) the figural mobility that could transfer a self-image into several different contexts of figures (not just one) or rearrange the figures that make it up into more than one order. Indeed, the violence with which Jekyll's binary discourse confines these (and his) possibilities forces his "other" to imitate that violence, to be predictably and fiendishly destructive, in order to take its place in the limited discourse system imposed on it and giving it its most visible form.

Yet even as they see or point us toward all this, Garrett and Thomas limit Jekyll's "Statement" themselves, though never so violently. They regard the "polity" and its repression mainly as the consequences of a person's entrance into written or spoken language. They only rarely note another vital point: the figural substitution stressed most in this tale is the metamorphosis of one person's physique. What makes Stevenson's best-known *doppelgänger* story such a "Strange Case" is not the reflection of part of the self in a different person (more conventional than "strange" in gothic fiction by 1886).[5] It is the fact that refiguration occurs in and across a single body. If Jekyll is a "polity" of differences where various relations can be formed among the "denizens," that is mainly because there is a polymorphic body language, what Jekyll calls a "trembling immateriality" or "mist-like transience," permeating "this seemingly so solid body in which we walk attired" (82). This basis of his "impatient gaiety," this amorphous interplay, composed of different droplets or elements (as in a mist) able to be drawn together or apart (like words), can produce many different arrangements of the "powers that ma[k]e up [the] spirit" (83). Each combination, in turn, can give off its own "aura and effulgence" (83), its own "countenance" and "stamp," that is just one of the figurations into which the body's visage can be transformed.

The "Statement" anticipates Freud's theory of what "libido" is before it is forced to become an aggressive and phallic resistance to the "super-ego" or Voice of Social Law. According to "On Narcissism: An Introduction,"[6] libido is first a sheer "differentiation" or tending outward of the "auto-erotic instincts" that extend the drives of the basic "germ-plasm," the play of elements that reforms itself in and within each human body. These instincts reach outward through the sensations of a person's "erotogenic zones," the signs of desire that Jekyll terms "secret pleasures" and "indescribable sensations" (90, 95), scattered yet interrelated, like elements of a language, across a person's unstable anatomy. Each different casting of desire toward the world therefore prompts a specific interplay among these zones that physiologically affects how the body feels and appears. If this potential becomes, say, phallic aggression and its corresponding "countenance," that is because the will, reacting to stimuli such as the superego's restrictions on what desire can pursue, urges the malleable "differentiation" to bring its zones or figural "denizens" into a particular set of relationships, thus producing a certain "aura and effulgence" visible to observers. On seeing these primordial possibilities, in spite of his governing code, Jekyll realizes that they threaten his two-sided self-image and yet can be used to establish it in his own body. Although body language is basically a "transient" play of differences not entirely subject to the will but rather inclined toward continual reorganization by an unwilled force, "even as a wind might toss the curtains of a pavilion" (82), this quasi-linguistic ability to substitute one visage for another can still be harnessed by binary thinking. A mixture of drugs that oscillates between opposite colors (variations on red and green) can be imbibed into the transience so as to guide the "wind" into moving between two contrasting erotogenic interplays and thus between only one "aura" of inner "powers" and "a second form" (83).

But what is the point, even so? Even if we add these further dimensions to what Garrett and Thomas have noted, we still do not grasp why a dichotomy is produced, either in the submission of verbal relations to one particular code or in the reconstitution of body language by an obedience to religious and cultural standards (one form of the superego). Our concerns are also complicated now by the double inclination we see in both body language and linguistic representation as they sometimes resist, yet also turn readily toward, the ways they can be dichotomized by means they provide themselves. We must wonder if it is resistance or submission that really gains the upper hand in the end. We must even wonder what drives body language toward spreading its own "transience" into the multiplicity of cultural rhetorics that finally describe the "indescribable" in binary ways.

To be sure, there are some other answers to our remaining quandaries offered, or at least broached, in William Veeder's blend of Freudian and Marxist explanations. His effort, for one thing, both modifies and brilliantly completes what the Anglo-American tradition of psychoanalytic criticism has long tried to say about Stevenson's characters. What Jekyll's personal "devil" conceals yet reveals, I must agree with Veeder, is not only the phallic aggression of the son against the father, much as such a drive does indeed motivate all the men in this world of relentless antagonism among would-be patriarchs.[7] The genesis of Hyde also shows that sheer libido can be channeled into an oedipal attitude of rivalry only because the superego is culturally constructed as the Voice of the Father. Veeder inclines more than he knows toward René Girard's revision of psychoanalytic theory,[8] in which the Oedipus and related complexes are based on "mimetic desire." This kind of longing makes each person want the state of being that seems most desirable to another figure, a figure who seems similar to the self but also superior to it in appearing to have greater access to the goal. Each man Stevenson depicts, as Girard might put it, fashions a sense of himself by setting up other males as possessors of a completeness of phallic power, which the self-fashioner wants and feels that he now lacks. No man actually embodies the desired completeness, so even supposed male exemplars (such as Jekyll) look outside themselves for it and become, like the others, envious of, submissive to, yet furiously angry at whichever "other" seems to have what they have not. With the desideratum located in no one man and yet in a Supreme Male that most men in a patriarchy seek to imitate or be in some way, an abstract Father's Dictum (with Phallus) is projected by the common desire, taking forms ranging from a single father figure to the Word of God and the Patriarch's Law. Particular men then direct their longings toward both satisfying and trying to overthrow this Standard so that they can seem to occupy a Throne that is actually only mythical and forever out of reach. Hyde incarnates this drive by being a scapegoat, supposedly the only location of such socially destructive urges, created in part to ensure that these passions do not seem to exist in the "respectable" men who really base their lives on them. The respectable facade of a "Dr. Jekyll," meanwhile, is the image crafted to deny the presence of this aggressive envy in the "wise and good" and to grant the possessor a semblance of the completeness that he keeps seeking in the constructed superego. Power has been culturally set up as a legitimized object of exclusively male desire, then men have been urged to pursue that end in conflict with virtually every other male, yet all this while they have been asked to adjust their self-images to hide the fact that this violent rivalry is the real foundation of the social order. An "outlaw" and "outside" nature has consequently been fabricated over against a "moral" insider's demeanor, even though the outcast drives are the ones most "inside" the men of late-Victorian Europe, as this novella presents them.

Veeder's reading of this process, in any case, starts to explain better than any previous view the much-discussed near-exclusion of women (and hence the feminine voice) from the "community of monks" in the tale (Gwynn 130). In fact, within Veeder's assumptions, his own argument on this point can be carried further than he takes it himself. When a young man, as Freud saw, desires the phallic power of whatever or whoever is set up as the powerful Father, the youth is at first seeking the father's bodily means of access to the mother's birth canal, that primal object of desire toward which the son is always drawn back to some extent.[9] But the desirous man soon finds that a union with the mother—and later with any women recalling her—could mean a loss of the phallic self-completion and conjunction with strictly male power that patriarchal logic urges men to seek. The mother, at least at the primal scene of conception, harbors the "unclean" immersion of the phallic in the nonphallic, where the primacy of one over the other cannot be decided. She and other women, in addition, linked to certain "nonmasculine" qualities by the artificial gender classifications of patriarchal discourse,[10] seem to harbor characteristics to which a presumed "man" must not link himself, even though he has some of them already. Mother is also the ejector and thus partial rejector of the self, having (it seems) chosen the father's phallus over the son's. Given that she brought the son forth to be different and distant from her, she is now like her substitutes in being an inadequate conduit unable to return the son to absolute maternal security. Moreover, she is the beginning as end, a locus of death, in that reabsorption by her would dissipate the seeker's male identity and deny him the immortality that the patriarchy claims he will gain by becoming a father and not the mother. Women, being clearly attached to such associations and constructions, must therefore be as exiled from masculinity as possible, while men change the object of their desire to the power, supposedly in other men, to subdue and silence women. The "feminine" must be marginalized entirely to the levels of children, servingwomen, or "unclean" streetwalkers if it is to be noticed or allowed to speak at all. And Hyde, incarnating this reactive misogyny (again so that it will not be as blatant in other men), must even respond to the "box of lights" offered by the streetwoman by smiting her in the face (94), just as Veeder has said. Women, after all, are the greatest threats to patriarchal assumptions, since they deny the supposedly self-sufficient

JERROLD E. HOGLE

power of men in the very fact that women are necessary for the existence and procreation of males.

Veeder, perhaps more than any other critic, thus shows why all the men in this tale are self-contradictory in myriad ways as they attempt to achieve masculine consistency with the fabrication of a male "double nature." They all desire to both overcome *and* obey the father, thus rebelling against any supreme patriarch with a phallic aggression modelled on the father's own violence. They all must long for women and the mother, yet they deny the equal value, independence, centrality, and primacy of the feminine,[11] replacing the attraction of this half-similar/half-different "human nature" with a power play against it hidden inside the demeanor of an unmixed (albeit two-sided) masculinity. In addition, as Veeder says in his Marxist moments, Stevenson's men are tossed between the postures and orientations of different classes at a time when especially middle-class men are allowed to move rapidly across the various strata. From Sir Danvers Carew to Jekyll himself, each man is partly aristocratic, partly bourgeois, and occasionally lower-class in his economic base, demeanor, orientation, dress, home, and pleasures. This confusion is only fitting in a world of male rivalry where each man models himself on others who seem to be higher-class and for that reason supposedly closer to complete phallic potency. In this context, of course, Hyde is once more the scapegoat, plainly embodying this incoherence so that the men around him do not seem to reveal their ravenous class consciousness. He strives in his wanderings from a base in low-life Soho to avoid "scenes" in the way a "gentleman" should (32), always in higher-class clothing manifestly too large for him and in expectation of money from an upper-middle-class doctor.

Jekyll and Hyde, we should remember, continues the English tradition of the gothic novel, and some able Marxist critics have recently shown how much that very kind of fiction is concerned with the quest for a coherent self-image amid the class conflicts of a widespread shift in economic patterns during the late eighteenth and nineteenth centuries.[12] Jekyll, withdrawing into a decayed anatomical theater in order to replace an old form of science with a new one, recalls many a gothic hero who hopes to construct a unified sense of self in an antiquated location apparently removed from the vagaries of rapid economic change. Such a hero must invariably find that he has taken into his retreat the very class conflicts that he would escape and is dominated by them enough to style himself according to incompatible rhetorics from different social levels. That is the way novels style themselves generally and Horace Walpole styled his fiction specifically in 1764 by launching the gothic mode, and thus the gothic hero, as a flagrant stitching of elements from the bourgeois comic "novel" into the fabric of aristocratic "romance" and tragedy.[13] Because of this multiplicity, Veeder rightly suggests, Jekyll and his observers have to become "polities" of "independent denizens," especially if they construct themselves according to a supposedly monolithic ideology that is actually based on a conflict of class-based attitudes, which the ideological attempt at unity cannot quite suppress.

Still, though I will henceforth use some of Veeder's conclusions (with my modifications) under the assumption that he has already substantiated them, I do find that some questions still demand answers, even if his work is read as expanding the traditions out of which his analysis comes. For me, Veeder places the psychology he articulates too much *between* the changeability of body language, on the one hand, and the turning of the sheer potentials in linguistic relations toward the constraints of organized verbal systems, on the other. He therefore fails to account for some references in the tale to both these levels of language and does not seen any connection between the submission to patriarchal thinking and what happens to body language in its passage toward the possibilities and restrictions of conventional discourse. He does not realize, to be more specific, how much body language includes even for Henry Jekyll. The doctor does not simply desire or fear a mother or woman located somewhere else. Jekyll speaks of a "womb of consciousness" in his own being that makes what is feminine a part of a man. Gender distinctions turn out to be blurred and really impossible at this preverbal, prelogical stage. Indeed, the first emergence of Hyde from Jekyll's body, as the doctor remembers it in the "Statement," can be thought of as the erection of an aggressive male phallus only at a late moment when patriarchal lenses have been imposed on that eruption. Initially this event is remembered as a giving birth complete with "pangs" and "nausea," not to mention the expulsion of a "younger, lighter," and "less developed" being—Hyde as infant (83–84). The male body is not just partly female but is able to retain visceral memories of the birth process (involving phallic and nonphallic elements) from which the male person once emerged.

On top of all this, such a recollection allows for the possibility of *reversible* birth. Hyde can be reincorporated into Jekyll again and again as readily as he can come forth from his "father" figure. This oscillation between emergence and reabsorption is even matched by a similar tug-of-war between birth and death. Death in this sort of body language is not, as it is in Freud or Veeder, a unified state before the differentiation of birth attainable (one secretly hopes) in a return to the mother.[14] It is a motion toward dissolution that is simultaneous with the instant of emergence. When Hyde turns back into Jekyll before a terrified Dr. Lanyon, the process inextricably combines reabsorption, multiple polymorphism, the birth of an infant from a womb, and a descent toward death (prompting Lanyon's demise very soon after). The changing figure "seemed to swell—his face became suddenly black [the color of death]—the features seemed to melt and alter" until they became a "pale and shaken" Jekyll "groping before him" as an infant would, yet also "like a man restored from death" (80). The inconsistencies in oedipal feelings are much later and even more coherent than the inseparable contraries at this primordial level: birth/death, female/male, infant/adult, inside/outside. Though a Jekyll-Hyde separation does try to conceal the masculine will to power, that repression is not possible until this earlier "polity" of incongruities has been repressed already. This one may be the most basic polity of all and is certainly the one that must be forgotten most often if a binary opposition is going to be imposed on a primal state where differences include their counterparts as aspects of themselves.

Meanwhile, there is the problem of how Jekyll/Hyde's "birth," as it emerges through several levels of verbal articulation, makes possible the distortion of an almost nongendered body language into the language of opposition, class distinction, gender dichotomies, and male supremacy (the order of discourse that fashions a Jekyll-Hyde split). This struggle, very like the struggle of a writer (as Stevenson must have seen), is the process leading to what Veeder exposes but the one he is most unable to point out or explain. He does not see how the emergence of a person into a maze of class conflicts is the spreading of that subject into the concatenation of different class languages, into the "heteroglossia" brought back to our awareness (as Thomas has shown) by the rediscovered work of Mikhail Bakhtin.[15] Worse yet for Veeder's oedipal scenario, he does not realize how much the Law of the Father enthroned and assumed in the thinking of Stevenson's characters comes from the need of the verbalized self for a *reader* of his coming-into-language. For Jekyll in his "Statement," the Voice of the Patriarch is that "respect of the wise and good among" the observers to whom the doctor feels he must look for a definition of himself. What determines their wisdom and goodness is their reputed adherence to and enforcement of a dichotomous code, as we have seen, so they form, as mythologized (with Jekyll's consent), a specific reading "public" demanding a divided "countenance" in order to grant a legitimate identity to anyone who values and appeals to their judgment (81).

Jekyll chooses to have his visible body language and modes of expression organized by this supposed perspective into what is legal or illegal, "respectable" or "outlawed," for a "proper upper-class man." Whatever he does or says, and certainly whatever he writes, is geared to that Master Reader's (and Father's) apparent standards and anticipated response. To confront that Reader with bodily or linguistic figural interplays that would circumvent or explode the restrictions on sign relations in the code would be to lose the selfhood pursued in this entire submission, to be in fact "indescribable" or unreadable and hence outside the hegemonic ideology so valued by Jekyll and his friends. Whatever might not be admissable under the Law (from the "woman" in the "man" to the "gaiety" of changeable relations among erotogenic sensations or verbal signs) must be cast into and hidden behind an "outlaw" countenance so as to acquire a readable status as what is "evil and forbidden" in the two-sided sense of man accepted by "the wise and good." The psychoanalytic tradition extended by Veeder cannot articulate this linguistic anamorphosis. The abasement to which Jekyll subjects himself is rendered more accurately by the French psycho-analysis of Jacques Lacan and others. They see the subject as impelled to fashion itself as an "other" (or self-image) using the Other of possible language combinations only to run up against a third other, the Fa-ther/Reader, who appears to decide what combinations are sanctioned or unsanctioned.[16]

There are, then, several problems that remain to be solved in Jekyll's "Statement" and Stevenson's tale, despite the number of useful revelations in the essays preceding mine. The solutions, moreover, can be found with the aid of interpretive vocabularies that my colleagues in most cases have only begun to use. Given what I have noted so far, five major questions, it seems to me, are still unanswered and in need of such additional approaches. The first one is the general, overriding question: (1) What is the process—and what is the succession in that process—that produces a "multifarious" body language in a Henry Jekyll and then carries that "polity" into language, where it both resists and submits to a binary discourse system encouraging a Jekyll-Hyde split? It is this process and what happens in it that the creation of Hyde represses (and dimly reveals) before that substitution of one visage for another represses or acts out what my colleagues have revealed about it. There are also four questions bound up with this principal one: (2) What exactly is the womanhood or birth process retained in what seems a "masculine" body language, and how and why are those "memories" so violently and repeatedly (but not completely) cast away in the attempt to establish a "maleness" obsessed with attaining the Father's phallic power? (3) What does it mean for a being with such a body language to be thrown into a social arena of multiple and conflicting languages, the distances between which the self must bridge to present the illusion of a unified nature? (4) Is the nondichotomous figural movement among myriad (but not strictly separated) differences, the "impatient gaiety" in body language and potential sign relations prior to a definite discourse, able to be entirely suppressed by the violence of binary rhetoric, considering that all self-articulations depend on these subliminal levels of language? and

JERROLD E. HOGLE

(5) What creates the apparent necessity for a restraining discourse system and fuels the drive to impose that patriarchal Law on all the bodies, thought patterns, class connections, and modes of self-expression in Stevenson's characters, making them all submit to a fatherly Master Reader? I want to propose some possible answers to all these queries, answers that solve at least some of the mysteries left to us by Jekyll's confession and its recent interpreters. I do not claim to depart radically from my colleagues in this effort; I want only to further what they have started. I want to expose the underlying figural movements in *Jekyll and Hyde* that make such conclusions about it possible, all in a way that reveals the dimensions of the struggle that the characters (and even the text) go through in striving to achieve a binary vision of man—and occasionally failing to do so.

II. Abjection and the Stages in its Process

To answer our main question and begin to deal with the others, we need a name for the basic dynamic that insists on the contradictions remaining in a person's body language but then works to repress them and submit them to a Law denying their primordial interconnection. The word must be contradictory in itself if it is to encompass stages ranging from acknowledgment to refusal to submission. Jekyll's "Statement," as it happens, provides a very appropriate term when he laments his enslavement to both Hyde's unrestrained "gaiety" and his own repressive sickness "at the mere thought of him." The doctor bemoans "the *abjection* [as well as the] passion of this attachment" (96, my italics). Though it does refer to Jekyll's sense that he is now a slave to his inclinations, "abjection" also has multiple meanings that point to what makes Hyde the concealment of a "polity." On the one hand, abjection most literally means an active "throwing away" or "casting off" of something.[17] That sense implies a knowledge of what is being cast away and a determination to throw it off because of what it is. Jekyll confirms this meaning when he briefly recognizes the "gaiety" of body language reerupting in Hyde (especially at the latter's "birth") and then consigns this play of differences to a "sickening" figure that he tries to cast away from his own proper nature as a disease needing to be thrown off. On the other hand, abjection has a passive meaning, also quite literal, that refers to the state of being "cast down" by or "thrown under" the force of some apparent authority. This abasement is what Jekyll accepts when he allows a particular rhetoric of self-construction to make him strictly dual, to propose a Satanic figure for hiding what the rhetoric would deny, and to enslave the doctor under the supposition that these constructions of his more multiple drives are absolutely necessary. Abjection, enacted in all its senses, is therefore what leads Jekyll from reimmersions in a body language reminiscent of birth to the suppression of that "multifarious" condition under the language of duplicity demanded by the Law.

A word with some revealing implications, though, is not enough by itself if we want to detail all the stages in the process it names and so discover, for example, how abjection begins and what in that beginning leads to later "castings off." Fortunately, a survey of these stages and what occurs in each one to prompt its successors appears in Julia Kristeva's *Powers of Horror: An Essay on Abjection*.[18] Many of the surprising images in *Jekyll and Hyde* that I have emphasized in questioning my colleagues start to make astonishing sense when the steps described by Kristeva are explained in their temporal order, even though she neither mentions Stevenson's best-known "horror" story nor presents these stages herself in chronological succession. Let me, then, specify these steps as she describes them, though not as she orders them, and return after that to Stevenson's text to analyze all it does with what she reveals.

For Kristeva, abjection begins at the tortuous moment of birth, before the separation of child from mother is even complete, at which point there is a "throwing off" of both beings by each other while the two are still intimately connected and closely in touch with their previous interrelation. Since later recollective rejections are partial reenactments of this one, "abjection [always] preserves [if dimly] what existed in the archaism of [this] pre-objectal relationship[:] the immemorial violence with which a body becomes separated from another body in order to be" (10). At that primordial instant, which the grown body still remembers in its erotogenic interplays, the emergent being is the "in-between, the ambiguous, the composite" of what are later taken to be opposed possibilities (4). He/she is inside/outside of the mother, the pleasure (of birth)/the pain (of separation), different from another/part of another, able to separate/able to be reabsorbed, distinct as a sexual being/bound up with mother's (indeed two others') sexuality, in a condition of want (facing a rupture from sustenance)/in a state of immediate satisfaction (from the womb and the placenta), and, if a male child, an incipient "masculine" being/still a "feminine" or ambisexual process in the mother's body. The emergent figure in this transitional confusion, and to some degree thereafter, is thus an open, heterogenous potentiality of diverse and (later) nonsensical sensation combinations. Some of these are associated with emergence and resistance to absorption, some with the satisfactions of being contained, and some with both at once. Hence they must come to seem "incongruous" and "independent" the more the differences in their relations with each other become conscious and

JERROLD E. HOGLE

articulated in adult interpretations of what we retain from the birth process.

This incongruity is most pronounced, Kristeva adds, when we later see it as an oscillation between life and death. Although the moment of birth may be the supreme redeclaration of life, it is also, as a dissolution of one bodily state, a launching into a movement toward another dissolution. Birth initiates a "drive which, propelled by an initial loss, does not cease wandering [over inadequate substitutes for the lost state], unsated, deceived, warped, until [this drive] finds its only stable object—death," another loss (23). If there is a death wish visible in acts of aggression (as Freud supposes and Hyde's suicide suggests), that is because the commit-ment to death is coincident with the separation process (and the consequent want) inaugurating existence.[19] Beginning life, "incon-gruously," means beginning death, just as the male emergence from a woman leads to a man longing for and possessing "feminine" qualities.

An individual life cannot come to be unless such supposed contra-dictions interact during its rising out of the primordial "germ-plasm." And yet that being cannot become genuinely individual—the process of casting off cannot continue—unless this cacophony is passed beyond (though it must be obscurely recalled) as the body leaves the birth process behind and strives to distinguish itself from it. Indeed, the greatest of psychological horrors may be the half-awareness that this non-difference/difference, this death-in-life or femininity-in-maleness, threatens our hard-won separate existence because of what our body language retains from the primal concatenation. For there to be a self that is neither half-contained by another nor committed to death as much as life, the inaugural "polity," under its own urging, must somehow be "thrown away" from a body and psyche where its sensations can still be felt.

Consequently, a method for casting it off, as well as retaining it, is also provided by the birth process. As the basic "differentiation" proceeds, the body language of partly self/partly mother must give way to the delivered body that is an external sign of an internal, hidden movement outward, much of which the body remembers but from which it is now removed. Right as birth happens, we could say, the emergent person acquires the qualities of a linguistic figure (what Hyde clearly is and so what Jekyll must be). As a reference, like a figure, to something elsewhere and receding, the person is an otherness-from-himself within himself, a difference from his possible "others" that is not a total divorce, a tendency to harken backward that is countered by a turning out and ahead to other substitute signs as referents for his desire, and a need for an interpretation by other beings that will recontextualize the uprooted self, picking up on the fact that part of him resists being reabsorbed into what has become an absence. A person's entrance into life to the point of being nameable and contextualized outside the mother's body, in other words, is simultaneously an entrance into verbal relations where figures defer to different figures. There, once-amalgamated tendencies of the body turn into referents or versions of separate (albeit relatable) terms. To become a distinguishable "I" in this complex of many visible differences, the figure must accept and exploit that separation. Being a term now constituted in part by its distance from other terms, he must divide the "self" even from that otherness-from-itself that carries the "I" toward other locations into which it might disappear.

To be sure, the incipient "I" after birth can dissipate into the Lacanian and Bakhtinian Other of many possible sign relations. The emergent person/figure, recalling both the spreading multiplicity of its body language and its nature as a sign, has at least an early inclination toward a number of different and even contradictory verbal/cultural contexts. But an "I" can exist in particular contexts or definite combinations of them only if a "primal repression" disallows some potential and contradictory relations (Kristeva 12). Some order of discourse must limit the subject's relational options and consign all excluded ones (including most erotogenic memories of the birth state) to an unnamable, taboo status. These castoffs, to seem completely "other," must be covered over by a symbol of what the "I" seems *not* to be (a "devil," for instance) that helps to declare the "I" a specific entity separate from that opposite. This basic division, the one making possible all the subsequent binary distinctions that establish the tendencies at birth as contradictory, is clearly what abjects the inaugural heterogeneity and then searches for further masks to conceal the primordial "polity" from conscious awareness. Such a separation/rejection, in fact, is so close to and indicative of the birth process it would obscure that it must itself be abjected in an additional cloaking of its own act of suppression (a "Hyde" concealing and reembodying the "devil within"). One is simply "not born" fully, not distanced enough from the nonidentity of the birth state, until this step has been attained. Only then can the self created as an interpretable "other" stand out from and within the Other that (like the mother) made it symbolically possible yet keeps threatening to dissolve its individuality.

There are, to be sure, many potential ways to achieve the double concealment demanded by this progression. Kristeva agrees, however, with Lacan—and particularly with Marxist/feminist revisions of him— that the self as fabricated "other" is read out of and according to configurations permitted by the Other only if there is that third other or reader who assumes or imposes certain limited configurations as the lexicons within which the terms of the "self" are defined. In Western and still-

JERROLD E. HOGLE

patriarchal societies, that reader is almost invariably the father figure locally and the Law of the Father culturally, a fact that the would-be self is usually willing to accept because the pull of the father's intervention helps to complete the separation from the mother. In order to gain socially acceptable limits, the self as sign must henceforth seek to be construed as the Father/reader needs to configure it, else that patriarch could not maintain his position as "the one that prohibits, separates, [and] prevents contact" with the birth process (Kristeva 59). The self regarded as an incomplete, outreaching figure, consequently, has to be read as best symbolized by the phallus. This is the mark of difference from the feminine (the father's own mark) that best casts off the ambisexuality, the woman-in-the-male, of the primal cacophony.[20]

Yet abjection cannot stop there. In reducing an interpretable subject to a sort of phallus, the Father/reader confronts the symbol of his own supremacy (the mask concealing the sheer power play establishing male dominance) as what it really is: the sign of that division from the feminine that constitutes an insufficient being, a figure in need of another and then many others. This figure, above all, is what the Father must not be if he is to be entirely distinguished from femininity and regarded as self-sufficient compared with those he interprets. The phallus as sign of power must, therefore, be concealed (to hide the power play further) but also distinguished (albeit fictively) from incomplete, lesser versions of it. Each variant, supposedly, has to locate the complete forms of itself *in* the Father-reader as what it would like to attain and imitate. The Father's hidden phallus must come to seem a locus of power, which "inferior" desire must rival and resent. The latter drive must then take the form of the angry "son" (one of Hyde's roles), because desire has construed itself phallically according to the Father's prescriptions. The result must be a phallic declaration of envy that *both* furthers the concealment of the primal intertextuality/intersexuality *and* judges itself as outlawed and punishable by the standards of the "reading" it seems to oppose.

In this way, double abjection can become almost entirely successful. The multiplicity of the self can be cast out of sight and mind by the "substitute stamp" restyling it as phallic libido; then that libido can be rendered outcast, fearful, and loathsome as well—the "abject" figure (the Hyde) incarnating all the abjected inclinations without overtly revealing the process that casts them down. The outcast can come to seem the antithesis that allows the thesis of an "I" to declare itself as sanctioned by the Father to hate and punish this other, even to destroy the self (as Jekyll finally does), if the other is felt within the self too often. As Kristeva notes (57–89), patriarchal religion, Catholic and Protestant Christianity included, is especially useful for symbolically deploying such a gerrymandered desire into this splitting and ranking of the self's possibilities. Then, too, within the Satanic outlaw level produced by such an ordering of thought, the "feminine," which recalls the mother-in-the male, can easily be made the most "radical evil" (70). Since woman may reveal the indistinctness in body language that man most wants to escape, phallic aggression can debase her into silence or marginality. Then male desire, with much of itself abjected, can devote itself to challenging the Law of the Father with distortion mirrors of the Father's own utterly "masculine" procedures. Yes, there is a certain wildly playful plea- sure/pain—or *jouissance* for Kristeva—in some such rebellions, since they can launch the self into disguised recollections of the primordial multiplicity. But the half-conscious, half-preconscious aim of rivalry within a patriarchal order is to reconstruct all these memory traces and their initial concealments as "sin" or "filth" in order to consign them to a deep, forbidden underworld far from what appears to be the social norm. Abjection achieves its trajectory most completely when its beginnings lead to this end and take the need for the emergent figure to be different from its coming forth to the point where that emergence has become what the "self" most fears and denies.

III. What Jekyll and His Observers "Cast Off" and How Their Attempts Both Succeed and Fail

Kristeva's description of this abjection process, I would maintain, is the best answer there is to our principal question and portions of the others, especially if we consider how much it explains about the body language and methods of repression that we have already noticed in *Jekyll and Hyde*. Now, if we look again at Stevenson's text and probe further into what happens when its main characters come into discourse, we can provide more complete answers to the other questions, too, aided, though not totally confined, by the perspective that Kristeva has sug- gested. Jekyll and his immediate interpreters (Utterson, Enfield, and Lanyon), it turns out, carry through—or are carried ahead by—all aspects of the abjection process, "throwing away" just what abjection does for many of the reasons mentioned in *Powers of Horror*. In addition, these characters complicate Kristeva's sense of some of the stages through which abjection proceeds. These men attempt psychological, social, and verbal "castings away" with such deliberate force that what is abjected returns from repression *in* the repressive thoughts, actions, or figural displays. This success-becoming-failure occurs during three endeavors involving three different stages: the rhetorical presentation or configuration of the self that tries, but cannot manage, to hide remnants of the birth process and the woman-in-the-man (the targets of our second question); the launching of the emergent figure into a cultural maze of many incompatible symbolic options (the subject of our third question);

and the effort to resist the fact that verbalizations of the self, particularly written ones, look back to a more primordial "writing," where the self is but a figure deferring to other figures (the focus of our fourth question). Thorough answers to at least three more of our remaining queries, we discover, can be found if we look at how these abjections undermine their aims in the very act of achieving them.

First of all, *Jekyll and Hyde* recounts several rejections of the birth process that end up recalling it. Most of these "throwings off" are attempted by Henry Jekyll when he is reconfigured as Edward Hyde. The Hyde-figure, we now can see, is the doctor's rhetorical attempt, using binary thinking, to conceal both his obsession with masculine rivalry (the Law's method of repressing the woman-in-the-man) and the birth process, which male-supremacist rhetoric casts away from men in order to establish them as "masculine." Hyde layers the stages of abjection in his very being, albeit with the aim of obscuring them, pressing down hard on the earliest ones with the logic of the later, patriarchal injunctions. As a result, since he is so obsessively bent on casting the deepest levels away from the doctor and other such gentlemen, Hyde's moments of emergence, reabsorption, or self-assertion bring out the birth stage he is formed to efface. His reverse transformation in Lanyon's consulting room blatantly recalls the forthcoming/reabsorbed, life-giving/death-announcing, formed/de-forming, and masculine/feminine states of the male fetus half-emerging from and half-remaining in the mother.[21] Jekyll's first anamorphosis into Hyde makes such a reversion possible, we must remember, by being itself "a grinding in the bones" suggesting "the hour of birth or death" all at once (83). Jekyll's body and psyche are so unable to forget the violent beginning (and the sense of an ending) that they want to leave behind that they have to regard all the later divisions of his being as emerging from an "*agonized* womb of consciousness," where multiple possibilities for the self are still "continually struggling" (82, my italics).

Furthermore, Hyde's emergence, like an infant's, from this retained potentiality reveals a postnatal drive in Jekyll to divide his coming forth into visible and concealed levels. A definite "form and countenance" *must* be "substituted" for the "mist-like transience" of the body that the "wind" in body language could keep driving from one "fleshing vestment" to another (83, 82). Substitution may be potentially continual, but the fact that Jekyll is a figure separate from this motion (albeit *because* of this motion) means that he is thrown forth into an emergence of "selfhood" out of a series of ruptures that try to leave past potentials behind again and again. A "self" seen as other than its beginnings must be a signifier removed from a sequestered signified. Then it must further its distance from those now cast-off depths in a second rupture by acting divided, usually by station, from figures like the self, some of whom might draw it back to what it would forget. Jekyll, long accustomed to thinking according to such separations by class, must take the more shifting otherness reappearing in himself (as "impatient gaiety" or potential *jouissance*) to be a threat to all the personal-social distinctions (the fabricated identity) that such ruptures are supposed to produce. He therefore takes advantage of figuration as a division of the figure from any possible "other" and thus (it would seem) from its own otherness-inside-itself. He attaches the "incongruity" he fears to an "other" of himself, a signified from which he wants to become utterly separate. He then covers that abjection more by making the other itself a figure with a class and meaning supposedly different from anything Jekyll might visibly reflect. The image thus thrown forth, naturally, responds in kind with an effort to divide itself from what is consigned to it by imitating, rivaling, and even redoubling the divisive/repressive violence of his "father"-figure.[22]

Hyde, in fact, points most strongly at what he is supposed to abject in the various acts of aggression he chooses to commit, even though they usually attempt to erase all signs of the threats in body language to a clear identity. One such act, of course, is his initial phallic rising from Jekyll as a rebellious son's reverse reflection of the Absolute Father's supposedly life-giving powers. The doctor wants that erection, once it has left birth's "deadly nausea" behind, to be the rebirth of a child only in one sense: the resurgence of an entirely separated, self-serving "love of life" that makes him "younger, lighter, happier in body" without any "bonds of obligation" to any other being (such as a mother) or to the death originally announced with the birth (83, 91). But the "smaller" being turns out to be dependent on another body for life and "less robust" as well as "less developed"; he is still a part of a different existence and "an imprint of deformity and decay" in the very leaping forth of his new energy (84). All this time, too, the more Hyde tries to seem phallically erupted away from infancy, the more he resembles the half-separated child prone to tantrums who comes forth from yet is still bound up with nonphallic woman. He consequently needs to make his first publicly noticed deed the "trampling" of a female child, and he must do that "calmly" without seeming to notice her sex, her youth, or her continuing existence (31). These traits in her are the very ones he would most like to ignore, as though he were entirely "above" them. Nevertheless, they are revealed as what he wants to crush most violently, as what most recalls the "polity" endangering his—and Jekyll's—claim to an adult male nature.

Indeed, the entire scene built around the trampling, though it does suggest the ironies that Veeder has found in it, also shows how Hyde serves the general need of Victorian men to beat down the child and the woman in themselves. Hyde's walking over the girl does violate Christian and secular laws, but this movement of a quasi-phallic "Juggernaut" (31), this dragging of an erected, masculine, once-hindu idol-figure over people (mainly women and children) whose enthrallment reveals its power,[23] is far less daunting to the men at the scene than the way the girl might remind them of what they retain in their body language. Hyde's violence allows them to say next to nothing to or about the child or her sex. It encourages them to marginalize her—to refer to her, as Enfield does, mainly in the words of the male "Sawbones" who arrives—and concentrate instead on her abuser, "the man in the middle" (31), the mediator between the men and the casting down they secretly want to perform. Compared with what the girl recalls, Hyde's potentially threatening "deformity" is more easily labeled "hellish" or "apocryphal" (31–32). It seems out of all sanctioned bounds, yet, unlike what the girl implies, it can be admitted to the purview of institutionally sanctioned concepts of evil. Meanwhile, albeit disguised by these labels, the Hyde/male alliance becomes increasingly visible. The faces of the men surrounding him soon appear as full of "sickness" and "hate" as Hyde's own visage. This male-supremacist crowd even turns into its own sort of Juggernaut, coming to Hyde's defense, as it sweeps aside those "wild" and angry "women" who hurtle toward him and rage like "harpies" against the violence done to a girl (31–32).

To be a Juggernaut, it turns out, is to challenge the Law of the Father with the behavior that the Law continually encourages yet tries to dissociate from its public declarations. In response, the power-seeking cruelty in that behavior starts to come out in the male observers. Yet when they see that their target has already beaten down what the myth of male supremacy must fend off to survive, the monstrousness of this nominally Christian group can be shunted off onto the seemingly pagan, Satanic Hyde (a scapegoat once again). At the same time the real aim of the men can be accomplished; the screams of the girl and the women, which try to announce the primordial suppression of the feminine, can be either silenced or degraded to the status of irrationalities uttered by powerless children or insane "harpies." Once this abjection has taken place, the situation can turn into a negotiation among men alone for funds that will go to neither the women nor the girl directly, whereupon the issue can become, at least for Enfield, the male source of the money (32–33).[24] For all these reasons (as well as the ones Veeder notes), the men involved do not call the police, who might arrest and incarcerate a very useful figure. Hyde, by exploiting his obscurity to divert his audience from the girl to himself to a transaction only between men, has reinforced the figural displacements of attention that make patriarchal dominance possible (and frequently unapparent). Just to make sure that this fact is made less visible, along with what is primally abjected, Enfield consigns Hyde verbally to all kinds of foreign, inhuman conditions, leaving most onlookers (from his fellow spectators to most commentators on Stevenson's tale) unable to see an entire abjection process that this one scene has placed horrifically before the eyes of every reader.

Even so, Jekyll's immediate observers, as all the men in this scene begin to show, do not really escape recollections of the birth process or the concomitant need to throw off any awareness of it. Utterson, the doctor's most persistent "reader" and the principal voice of the Father's Law (the "son" of "Utterance") in the text, tries to be so repressively "austere with himself" (29), to escape his connection with birth and woman so completely in "his bachelor house" (35), that he drinks "gin when . . . alone, to mortify a taste for vintages" (29). Otherwise he might be released into "fanciful" behavior outside "the sane and customary sides of life" that he clings to for safety (35).[25] Yet to remain secure "by the fire" at home to which he often retreats (35, 54, 62), Utterson must psychologically and figuratively cast off, into the outer darkness and "fog" of the conveniently "drowned city" (53), that "mist-like" and "wind"-driven "transience" of body language made so reminiscent of the birth process in Jekyll's "Statement of the Case." As a result, when Utterson even begins to indulge in wine (as he does with Guest), the narrator, so close here to the lawyer's point of view yet more aware of what it will not admit to itself, alludes to a "procession [out in] the town's life" that resembles the interrelational movements across a person's body. City life becomes, more than anything else, a transformative energy among the denizens "rolling through . . . great arteries with a sound as of a mighty wind" under the light of "lamps" that glimmer "like [a body's] carbuncles" (53–54). Worse yet, when Utterson rushes into this "procession" toward Jekyll's house on the "last night" (having just offered another glass of wine [62]), he must face what his transference outward has abjected most of all—that "pale moon, lying on her back as though the wind had tilted her," accompanied and partly concealed by "a flying wrack of the most diaphanous and lawny texture" (63).

It is no wonder that, "struggle as he might [at this point], there [is] borne in on his mind a crushing anticipation of calamity" (63). What the lawyer has "thrown away" reappears as a woman/mother reclining, possibly in the attitude of "pale" death, perhaps in the birth position, or conceivably in anticipation of the intercourse leading to birth *and* death (Diana, the virgin moon goddess, having been transformed into the Venus embodying both sexuality and the cycles of inseminated life). This figure, moreover, is driven to "her" posture by the "wind" that for Jekyll urges the body to transfigure itself. She is therefore covered by an

JERROLD E. HOGLE

erotic/erotogenic "texture" shifting its appearance from "diaphanous" to "lawny," from the features of a cloud goddess to those of a Mother Nature (or Venus Genetrix). This multileveled emergence even suggests, in the way "wrack" anticipates the "racking pangs" connected with the birth of Hyde, the emission of interwoven, polymorphous covers from an "agonized womb."

Utterson at this juncture epitomizes all the men in the novella. Despite deliberate attempts to elude it, he is plainly assaulted by a nearly conscious awareness of the birth stage and the woman-in-the-self that could destroy his masculine individuality and reveal the "incongruous" foundations of the Law. Were he, like Lanyon, to go so far as to consciously recognize Jekyll's birth/death/transformation, brought on by a draught of a winelike liquid ("first of a reddish hue"), his "lawyer's way" would surely be transfigured as rapidly as that potion shifts from its initial color to purple and green in multiple "metamorphoses" that transfigure all supposed identities (79). Utterson would either be drawn into Lanyon's accelerated drift toward death or be disorganized into the Dionysian "high pressure of spirits" (in multiple senses of "spirits") that he has consigned to the "Cains" of this world with his maxim "let my brother go to the devil in his own way" (29).[26] He therefore persists in seeing Jekyll and Hyde as separate beings (like Abel and Cain), even when physical evidence to the contrary is conclusive. Why else would Utterson avoid the obvious conclusion, given his very legalistic view of signatures (54–55), when he sees the "blasphemies" he connects with Satan/Hyde written in a "pious work" from Jekyll's library by the doctor's "own" undistorted "hand" (71)?

Once we have discovered all this, however, we must not assume that the terror we see is focused only on recollections of the *physical* process of birth. Jekyll/Hyde and his "readers" also encounter problems, at the very moments when they claim they do not, with what they retain from that other stage just after birth: the launching of the human figure into a "heteroglossia" of many different social/symbolic orders, all affiliated with particular class orientations or ideologies that compete with yet relate to one another. The basic problem here is that this spreading of body language into a further play of differences forces the resulting "self" to be *very* literally a "polity of multifarious, incongruous, and independent denizens"—and in two different meanings of the word "denizen." The nearly formless person in quest of some definite shapes, first of all, though only some ideological systems impinge on him initially, has to be an "inhabitant" of several orders from the start. He must be pulled back and forth between them (made different inhabitants of different locations), especially in a Victorian Britain striving to maintain class distinctions while also encouraging those "self-made" shifts among the classes.[27] At the same time, wherever this self feels placed at a given juncture, it must live "from within" that position out toward another or several others, as in both the Latin root of denizen (*de-intus*, "out from inside") and the British use of the term to describe someone acquiring rights of citizenship in a country not his own.[28] It is this dizzying transferability, an excessively possible shift among class roles *and* between the rhetorical stances or accoutrements appropriate to each, that both permits Jekyll to slide from high-bourgeois respectability to working-class Soho and frightens him enough to make him attempt a bisection of himself into two class postures, each with certain behaviors and styles that try not to drift too obviously from one cultural frame to another.

By displacing all that high-bourgeois codes might find unrespectable in him (including memories of the birth process) into a figure ensconced in a lower-class area, the doctor fancies he can form, albeit superficially, an old-style, clearly divided chain of separate social and moral ranks in himself. He imagines he can thereafter pursue that "imperious desire to carry my head high," which aristocratic ideology, linked to his inheritance of "a large fortune," has urged on him (81). At the same time, he can covertly enact the war against that supremacy toward which he feels driven because he is really *sub*aristocratic. He can use his beating of Sir Danvers Carew (ignoring the latter's own bourgeois base) and his bequest to Hyde in a new will as steps in an assault by a lower-class being on the station and inheritance proper to a higher-class person. Indeed, Jekyll can even conceal how bourgeois this second drive is, how an unrespectable rivalry really lies at the heart of Victorian "respectability." He makes such aims inhabit a figure from much poorer, criminal contexts whose attempt to wear fine clothes too big for him prompts Utterson to see him as only the illegitimate son of a high-bourgeois man temporarily dragged downward into the sins "of his youth" (33).

All the while, too, Jekyll strives to borrow even stronger means of suppression from the rhetorical model for his hierarchy, the Great Chain of Being, so as to complete the hyde-ing of what Fredric Jameson would call his "political unconscious."[29] Since the Great Chain is supposed to emanate or fall away from a Divine and Rational Judge who comprehends all levels while insisting on their differences,[30] Jekyll unifies and cloaks the class and gender struggle within his thinking by accepting a "religious" Voice of the Father as his own rhetoric for judging his "nature." That vocabulary then contrives, as much as it can, to incorporate all potential rivals, such as bourgeois theories of "progressive" evolution, into its rhetorical style. It attempts to turn heteroglossia into a monological utterance, in which dichotomizing phrases are but signs that one primordial Fall is being repeated. "I [writes Jekyll] was slowly losing hold of my original self, and becoming slowly incorporated with my second and worse" (89).

But cultural/rhetorical heterogeneity, like its counterpart in body language, cannot be successfully abjected in the end. That the partly high-bourgeois Jekyll must live *out* of himself toward aristocratic, poor, and criminal possibilities—which must, in turn, live toward counterparts themselves—means that one or more of these class positions must be living *within* a different one (as aliens, really, to which each situation must also refer while it articulates itself). The doctor's house (a revealing indicator, as several have seen)[31] tries to seem undivided in a setting of divisions where locations associated with one class are becoming inhabited by other classes. Jekyll's mansion presents itself as unlike surrounding buildings in being "occupied entire" and manifestly "wealth[y]" in front (40), yet it lies in an area of different and changing, though generally middle-class, establishments ranging from the "shop fronts" of *very* bourgeois proprietors "all emulously hoping to do better still" (30) to homes of once "high estate" now leased as "flats and chambers" to "map-engravers, architects, [and] lawyers" (40). Consequently, each portion of the house repeats the turning-elsewhere that permeates its surroundings. The "hall" is "furnished with costly cabinets" and "warmed" by an "open fire" that ("emulously") reach "after the fashion of an [aristocratic] country house" (41). The floor here is "paved," however, with the same flagstones that cover the ground just outside the back door (71). Near this point is a rear "court" (hardly a royal one) that suffers from "sordid negligence," a kind of Soho in small where "tramps [have] slouched into the recess and struck matches on the panels" (30). The parts of the house as one moves among them shift from class level to class level, spatially reenacting the temporal history of the district. Each realm contains portions of a supposedly distant one—the floor of the interior at front repeats the ground outside at the back—as differences bleed over into each other while still remaining somewhat distinct.

Moreover, if Jekyll imagines that these differences can be driven apart by a portion of him becoming Hyde and taking rooms in Soho itself, he only redoubles the paradox he would escape by making this attempt. He furnishes some of the rooms "with the luxury and good taste" of his grander house (49), so this lower-class residence is external to itself at the very heart of itself, just as his mansion is. The dress and manner of Hyde then echo that discordance in all the intermixed ways we noted earlier. He even carries the cacophony with him in the full name Jekyll has chosen for him, "Edward Hyde," since it repeats the given name of the most famous Earl of Clarendon in the seventeenth century, whose *History of the Rebellion* articulated reasons and methods for both resisting and supporting the power of the ruling classes.[32] In whatever location Jekyll places himself/himselves, he is immersed in conflicting styles of being that parody ways of life outside the location, then parody each other in carnivalesque mockery. His identity ends up being a parody of the very notion "identity" (literally a "sameness" throughout one being or entity). Before he tries to become at one with himself in a figural assertion, there is the "struggle" of bodily contradictions in what is retained from the "womb," and the assertion itself only reworks that conflict with some differences in being "a struggle among socio-linguistic points of view."[33]

The doctor cannot even abject this centrifugal dispersion in what he takes to be his ultimate recourse: his centripetal rhetoric. He writes his confession in his "theater"/"laboratory"/"dissecting-rooms," amid labels that have been used "indifferently" to describe the same building yet that still point to the very different states (and even additions) through which the building has passed (51). Partly as a result, Jekyll exposes similar differences among the groups of terms in the vocabularies that he now tries to baste seamlessly (and religiously) together. His Covenanter's language, of course, assumes an ordained constancy in fallen human nature. The "terms of [the inner] debate are as old and commonplace as man," he writes, so "it fell out with me, as it falls with so vast a majority of my fellows, that I [tried to choose] the better part [of me] and was found wanting in the strength to keep to it" (89). The doctor's evolutionary rhetoric works differently, however. Although this kind of discourse has become more dualistic (in its popular form) since Darwin's *Origin of Species*,[34] Jekyll still depends on its progressive sense of how bodily and mental faculties develop, even when "the [troglodytic] animal within me [seems to be] licking the chops of memory" (92). If Hyde is to be a resurgence of primitive tendencies, he must clearly be a regression to what presently survives only in vestigial memories, not a shift to a depraved interplay of "powers" that has always been a part of human nature in the same unchanging way. Without a development beyond a barely remembered state, there cannot be the progression in human science on which Jekyll relies for so much that he says, does, and leaves to future beings. A jarring distance between "socio-linguistic points of view" becomes increasingly apparent the more we watch them trying to become identical in the doctor's "Statement of the Case."

Moreover, once that gap becomes glaringly obvious as Jekyll's efforts to bridge it turn increasingly frantic, it has to reveal his suppressed reasons for choosing and combining incompatible schemes. The doctor wants verbally to sever any link between the stable/univocal "I" he wishes to be and his ability to "leap almost without transition," without

JERROLD E. HOGLE

chemical assistance (so it turns out), into different states of "fancy" with which other states really do not cohere, except perhaps in "death" (95). The assignment of this latter motion to a "hellish" level "caged in his flesh" simply does not provide enough distance on its own. The "horror" can too easily "struggle to be born" over and over (as Hyde does), revealing what it has been employed to repress and calling attention to a fearful otherness in the present structure of the body (95). To make what is "hellish" resemble the primordial "amorphous dust" beginning to "gesticulate" (the doctor's last desperate gesture toward evolution) is to displace self-transformation back from personal being to the dawn of all being, as though the basic "energy of life" were far away in historical time as well as deep down in bodily space (95). No one rhetoric can create that illusion by itself, since the nature of any figural creation is to seek its completion outside its own frame of reference. Two symbolic orders playing off of one another can seem to satisfy this incompletion in both, especially if the second provides an external location for the otherness-from-itself in the first. The only hitch is that the two orders must be different enough to defer to each other. The two must somehow announce the distance between themselves, as Jekyll's rhetorics certainly do, thereby questioning the certainty of the unified order that they have tried to project together.

Every character in the novella attempts such an interplay and so must encounter the disappointments that ensue. Each feels compelled to propose such a unification at the start, to demonstrate its impossibility in the end, and finally to reveal that the reasons for the proposal and its failure are bound up with the nature of social/symbolic relations. Lanyon, as Jekyll/Hyde points out just prior to changing appearances before him, tries to draw all seemingly "transcendental" speculation into the positivistic sphere of "material" experimentation (80). All thought that cannot be so assimilated he dismisses as "fanciful" and thus outside reasonable discourse (36), just about where Utterson would place it. But after seeing the transformation, Lanyon mixes his usual, detailed, empirical description of "muscular activity" with incongruous leaps into half-suppositions about "cause[s that] lie much deeper in the nature of man" (77). He must even remember that he has exclaimed "O God!" repeatedly in disconnected appeals to an invisible level that we have never heard him desire before this moment (80). His effort to probe scientifically to "the very essence of the creature that faced me" (78) has led him to a figure's simultaneous turning out from itself toward another appearance and retreating into itself behind that appearance, both of which are the basic gestures of verbal symbols making them cry out for analogues and responses. Indeed, Lanyon has seen the most radical form of the figural posture in beholding the outside/inside birth state at the point where it announces the "otherness" inside itself: the eventual death of what it now seems to signify. Faced with the "essence" of a symbolic form that makes symbolic orders defer outside themselves as individual figures must, the interpreter has to refer rapidly from one order to another, if only to match that very movement in the observed figure as it seeks context after context—or class after class—in the hope of re-placing a lost or fading significance.

Not surprisingly, Lanyon hopes to make the center of one order the place of final refuge. And when the resulting call to God is not answered, he chooses the death revealed to him as lying behind *and* ahead of any figure's quest outside itself. It seems that one destination unites all symbolic orders at last. Still, he dies leaving a double-sealed manuscript for Utterson to read. Lanyon thereby acknowledges, at least tacitly, that all self-representations are figural concealments of other figural concealments. He also ends his life by launching the signs of his death into another interpreter's negotiation between different rhetorics. It makes no difference that Lanyon's text cannot be read until the "death or disappearance" of that figurality (Jekyll/Hyde) that he most wants to cast out of awareness (58). The figural movement toward different contexts will continue. Utterson will be left to wonder why he has now seen "Jekyll" and "disappearance" mentioned together in two different types of writing (59), one a will drafted prior to its author's death and the other an envelope concealing an epistle to be read after its subject's death.

Jekyll and Hyde has, by now, shifted its focus to that third level of abjection, the one where readable writing (or sanctioned discourse) is used to suppress a prewriting, which naturally resists suppression because it is so bound up with what tries to deny it. This level of the text may, in some ways, be the most ironic and threatening to readers. It calls attention to the sheer figurality in the very ciphers that we now read, the words that we, like Jekyll, often try to take back to a stable truth supposedly beyond all figuration. Inscription throughout Stevenson's novella is supposed to offer the illusion that such a referent exists. Letters, checks, and wills cover over or "cover for" the sheer movement of figural substitution that allows certain body languages in Jekyll to reappear (under cover) as Edward Hyde. Writing, in fact, tries to abject as many aspects of figurality as possible: its referring of erotogenic signs to other such signs or feelings in the bodies and psyches of people; its half-intimating/half-forgetting of the different point (the birthplace) from which a figure erupts; its displacing of itself in substitutes in order to "be itself"; its holding to the difference and distance between "independent" figures that interrelate nevertheless; and its encouraging of its forms to drift across several symbolic systems in a search for significance that will only turn outward again the moment any particular context grants a function to a figure.

But every text trying to suppress these movements must still reveal its dependence on all of them. Lanyon can turn to a metaphysical vocabulary when an empirical one proves inadequate only if the shifting figure he wants to define (Jekyll/Hyde) can be transferred from context to context. The transfer can balance this differentiation with some maintenance of the figure's identity, moreover, only if the figure is what it is by becoming a different substitute looking back reflexively to a previous version of itself. In the meantime, the figure cannot tend toward this progressive/regressive existence unless it is already a coming forth from another place to which it half-returns and from which it keeps departing. All of this points squarely at the birth process, too, in which the figure is an interaction among its different possible inclinations and appearances. The reader looking for an object at one with itself behind or beyond what Lanyon sees must confront instead the "terror" of primordial figural "change" and all its incongruities (80). The object turns out to be constituted and projected by the swerve back-and-forth between figures that permits even the very act of reading, let alone the production of this and all other narratives.

Any establishment of a distinctive "I," we have to admit, depends on setting up a subject over against an "other" with only one of the two being regarded as a figure. If only so that such claims may seem possible, the revelations of Lanyon's account are quite deliberately avoided by every other character's acts of self-inscription. Perhaps most of all, writing in this tale works to distance its succession of figures from the *body* seen as a figure in motion, as able to be different from itself within itself by inclining toward various different shapes from a variety of contexts. The desire to conceal this possibility is one reason Hyde covers his abjection of woman/child with that check supposedly signed by a person from a different class and why Jekyll creates a will that transfers property to a "friend and benefactor" able to inherit only if the doctor is completely removed from the scene (35). Such maneuvers make effective use of the way readable sentence patterns and notes of exchange turn reversible figural play into seemingly one-way transactions from the subject through the verb (the check and will, in this case) to the object. These constructions allow the crossing from figure to figure already *in* a figure to become a passage of exchangeable elements (such as money or property) between separated differences, one "here" and one "over there." This is the relationship between the inscribed "I" and the body sought by all texts throughout *Jekyll and Hyde*. If this assumption holds, the body can be either the nonfigural object to which the written subject refers from a distance (in the tradition of Cartesian dualism) or the author at one with himself to whom the text seems to look back when it becomes the object of a reader's attention. Certainly such binary options available when someone comes into discourse are what allow and encourage Jekyll to de-scribe himself as having two distinct natures living in separate locations. Edward Hyde can now be the figural being in which the doctor can conceal the figural nature of *all* being—making everyone fearful of "writing him out" completely. Henry Jekyll, in turn, can be the "true subject," as the removed reference point, of the substitute form that conceals him just as writing conceals its writer.

Yet this attempt, though encouraged by the grammar and spacing of conventional written discourse (as well as its separateness from writer and reader), points to ironies even more primal than those revealed by Lanyon. After Jekyll is forced to cover for Hyde with a check under-written by the doctor's own signature—a tactical error that threatens to reveal how easily styles of writing can be transferred from one figuration of the self to another—he tries to hide this plurality-in-apparent-unity "by sloping [his] own hand backwards" to give Hyde the distinct way of signing his name that I have mentioned already (87). The doctor thereby leaves a further clue to what he is really doing (as Mr. Guest begins to see) instead of successfully dissociating the Hyde figure from the Jekyll "original." Writing, Jekyll reminds us, is one of the extensions of the body. It is a kind of birth process in which an emission from the body repositions a portion of the body outside the already amorphous boundaries of the self. A signature identifying a body or "self" *as* itself is another indication that the self is constituted by its otherness or figurality, its relentless transfiguration into a display of signs (its sign-nature) that is read by others into one or more contexts where a univocal self is thoroughly dispersed.[35] To differentiate a signature by distorting one, the "original" being itself a distortion and differentiation of the identity it establishes, is to reenact (or double) in visible writing the primal anamorphic (doubling) movement, the writing-before-writing, that inscription tries to obscure. Writing is reconnected to the life of the body from which textualization works so hard to remove itself. That fact escapes immediate detection by the various interpreters in this tale only because Utterson and the Law that he enforces must keep the connection abjected. Otherwise they will have to admit the nonidentical foundation of all the legal writs that assume the signature to be the principal sign of distinct identities.

In this novella, writing cannot even leave behind the one occurrence—death—from which a readable text really does seem divorced. Above all, writing appears to exist here as what should survive and transcend the dissolution to which birth commits us. Jekyll's will, especially when rewritten to substitute Utterson for Hyde as beneficiary, is intended to and does survive the "dead malefactor stretched upon the carpet" at the end (72). Lanyon's narrative, too, exists to outlast and explain two deaths, or at least its author's demise and its main subject's "disappearance." The bodies moulder, it would seem, while their epitaphs live on for readers to reanimate with significance. Nevertheless, the separation is again superficial, far more a hope than a fact. Jekyll's revised will confronts Utterson as one document among three other pieces of writing that lie (when the lawyer drops them) on "the floor" with the body (72). This series of papers offers a fanned-out figural interpretation of a stretched-out figure of death. Such epitaphs or glosses help construct a sort of inscribed crypt where the body also lies in figural obscurity.[36] The papers share the cadaver's status as sign, aided by the fact that the body retains the features of a figure incarnating figural substitution. All the signs together then defer to one another for interpretation and so force Utterson to dart his eyes between the "papers" and "the dead" (72). The principal quality of the body, its death, we have to say, thus spreads to the nearby signifiers that are so like the body in being indicators of what is irretrievably gone.

Death is always the leaving of an interpretable image, either a body or some sign of a disappearance, which looks to other such signs for its meaning, since it cannot contain any meaning itself. Those signs, in their ways, look back to it. They move beyond death only to return, for they themselves resemble its initial inscription of an absence.[37] This movement is manifestly similar to the one that we have seen generating any figure or relationship of figures. All these motions share the two-directional process that inscription depends on yet denies with its ability to say "it is absent." Hence the disappearance/death/writing connection that Utterson repeatedly confronts. A cipher, like a death, is a silent reminder that some activity (such as the physical act of writing) has partly vanished *and* has altered its appearance. A death, like a cipher, is the lasting mark of a loss and often of a previous significance now distorted and shrouded in mystery. The death mark, therefore, looks toward other inscriptions to solve the mystery, yet only as they refuse to give it definite roots and instead rework its own dis-appearance of the disappearing past. Since conventional discourse cannot bear that these rootless anamorphoses really underlie it, we should not be surprised that Utterson finally refuses to face the implications of the "crypt" he beholds. As he sees his name placed in Hyde's position in the will to become (as Hyde was) a substitute image for what now lies dead (a sign of death himself), Utterson finds his feelings "indescribable" (72), just as unable to be fully written out as the Hyde for whom he now substitutes. The figural position that the lawyer here assumes is that of the sign of an absence that can never be made completely present. He has become, like any sign, dependent on texts and contexts that cannot entirely manifest what they claim to comprehend. To dodge this awareness, Utterson decides to read the documents and the body as evidence that Jekyll has only "fled" (72). That way they can seem to be indicators of a single, definite presence, however distant, which can be recovered at some point and will not leave Utterson facing the grounds of his own existence as figural substitutions that look back to no ground.

Lanyon, of course, cannot take that way out. In addition to all the other aspects of figurality that he must acknowledge against his will, he must face up to additional aspects of death-as-figure/figure-as-death that do not enter into Utterson's reactions to the "last night." As he observes Jekyll/Hyde's primordial "change" moving *into* death's blackness while also recalling a death from which it seems to emerge, Lanyon must realize that figuration is a simultaneous coming out from and drive toward death. The ever-emerging figure inevitably supplants its previous body language and leaves the latter to recede into death as the mother's body has or will. At the same time, the figure instantly moves, as though it were indeed a cipher being written on a page, toward being what Jekyll has called Hyde: the black "*imprint* of deformity and decay." Its future at its birth is deformation into a mere (and erasable) epitaph of forgotten or decayed meaning. It becomes, at most, a trace that must turn for significance to other marks of loss. To behold this dying in two directions as the very "essence" of both the human figure and its forms of refiguration is to see that the self is always looking back and ahead to the disappearance of part or all of its being. Because Lanyon cannot escape this awareness, he must take himself to be an inscription of death even as he also becomes its inscriber on paper.

Consequently, when Utterson last sees him, Lanyon is not just dying; he has "his death-warrant written legibly upon his face" (57). Following the lead of his Christian name, "Hastie," he has rushed the truth about his figural nature toward its eventual conclusion and back to its foundations. He refuses to see that death's turning toward other signs can also mean revived life as well as the spreading of death from figure to figure. He hopes that in death there will be a deferral of his own figure to God's transcendence of human decay, as he indicates by repeating "God's name" to Utterson (57) after calling to Him in the face of Jekyll/Hyde's transformation. To the end, in other words, Lanyon, like Utterson and even Jekyll, wants to see primal figurality as "abnormal and misbegotten" (78), something that can be divorced from fallen human being by a final restoration of man to his birthright (creation in God's image). Even so, by trying to force this judgment on an embodiment of man's "multifarious" figural nature, Lanyon succeeds only in finding

JERROLD E. HOGLE

that nature to be his actual birthright. The movements of figuration turn out to be the "facts of life" most basic to himself and to his "scientific" discourse.

The more abjection succeeds, we must conclude, the more it fails in this *Strange Case of Dr Jekyll and Mr Hyde*. The characters try to cast off a great deal: the birth process with its ambisexuality, the launching of human figures into ideological conflicts, the relation of linear discourse to multidirectional figuration, or the dependence of self-description on the self as a figural distortion announcing its own disappearance. Yet every deliberate avoidance of these subliminal realities only states their existence in concealments of them—the only way they can be stated, since they all inherently strive to obfuscate themselves. This result has been inevitable because each uprooted "grounding" can negate itself only by contorting itself into one or more of the others. All of them, in addition, turn out to be underwritten by what they would efface, by a reversible, irrational passage of figures from form to form to form that makes every supposed "center" of existence a decentering of itself inside itself (a turning outward from within, as in the moment of birth). Just when an "essence" has been specified, then, by being set over against a supposedly nonessential derivative or extension, the precondition that permits any relation (including this opposition) between one position and another redeclares itself—returns from repression—as the involuntary shift of any figure towards other possible manifestations and links with additional figures. The most extreme attempts at abjection, since they are especially conscious of "casting off," prompt a regression, albeit unsought, into what really sets abjection in motion.

This unexpected return at the moment when it seems most interdicted applies equally to Jekyll/Hyde, his various observers, the texture of a body trying to remain a unity, and the body of a discourse proposing to articulate a definite truth. When Jekyll believes he has most completely achieved the separation of his "true" and aberrant natures—at that moment when he renounces the Soho life as though "Hyde [were] henceforth impossible" (91)—that is the time when his form starts altering itself against his will. The primary cause is not a fallen sinner's lust for evil (Jekyll's later explanation), nor even the doctor's desire to disguise his connection with abjected levels, but a commonplace movement where one figure simply sees himself (or itself) and is seen in terms of others. The first unwilled "shuddering" leading to the change is brought on when Jekyll "compar[es himself] to other men" as he sits "on a bench" in Regent's Park (92). Here he defers to half-different/half-similar figures as aids to self-definition in a turning out from himself (a birth process) that has to relocate the placement of his "nature" and so reconstitute him in some other form. Yes, the doctor becomes Mr. Hyde again, but he finds that, before he does, he has thought of the sheer displacement of his being toward other possible versions of it, the formation of a context in which an "I" can be established as similar to and different from other ones. That process, of course, is the transfer between positions into which every person is launched on becoming a term in a system of language.

Utterson finds that his own ruminations are based on a similar foundation when he finally sees Hyde and fancies himself now able to pinpoint the source of the "loathing" that all observers feel in the "dwarfish" man's presence:

> There *is* something more, if I could find a name for it. God bless me, the man seems hardly human! Something troglodytic, shall we say? or can it be the old story of Dr. Fell? or is it the mere radiance of a foul soul that thus transpires through, and trans-figures, its clay continent? The last, I think; for, O my poor old Henry Jekyll, if ever I read Satan's signature upon a face, it is upon that of your new friend! [40]

Just as Jekyll falls into bodily transformation by trying to define a person using figures different from the first one he mentions (himself), so Utterson's attempt "to get to the bottom" of someone here produces a dancing play in his language that leaps across alternative definitions of Hyde before the lawyer is aware of how "fanciful" he is being. Again like Jekyll, and very much in the manner of Lanyon, Utterson is assaulted by the transferability of a figure, its perpetual drive to reorient itself, and the lawyer finds this energy to be what underlies the rhetoric that he uses to fix on one definition of the figure he observes. This "semiotic hetero-geneity" (to quote Kristeva again[38]) both hurls thinking across wildly different frames of reference and sweeps every analogue into a driving rhythm of shifts. The result is an onslaught of anaphoras and apostrophes with almost a life of its own that threatens a loss of the logical sense on which the lawyer has come to rely.[39] All Utterson can do to recover his abjecting equilibrium is choose the one among the ana-logues that most seems to provide the central cause he seeks. He therefore fixes on the old Platonic and Christian notion of a "foul soul" emanating its nature toward and into its bodily enclosure. He can then try using this option to subsume all the others and deny the implications of his performative play among figures. Yet, as he does so, he calls attention to figural motion more explicitly than anyone else in the tale. The centrality of a spiritual evil is too clearly made possible by a double drive: the "transpiration" of tendencies across zones in the body and the "transfiguration" of that movement into the figural restructuring of the body across different interplays of words. Both these tendencies, in fact,

JERROLD E. HOGLE

must be inscribed on the body in order for it to be read as having any sort of center. If Hyde's face is to reflect a Satanic "signature," it must first be written on with indicators interpretable under one or more lexicons. In order for abjection, then, to suppress these prerequisites for its own occurrence, the "writing" itself must be presented as the location of evil and the main threat to the desired "core" of meaning—even though there can be no such Original Sin leaving signs of itself until there is the figuration that demands and resists abjection.

IV. Why Stevenson's Characters "Cast Down"—and Why He Has Written This Narrative the Way That He Has

Now we have some revealing answers, I believe, to four of the basic questions posed earlier. There is a very definite movement leading from the body language of the birth stage to the suppression of that "incongruity" under one-half of a culturally fashioned dichotomy. That process is the abjection sequence, which progressively "throws off" the "incongruous" memories of emergence to make Jekyll seem an "individual" separate from them. Eventually, this drive doubly conceals his multiplicity in the "evil" figure of a "son" who seeks the "Father's" phallic supremacy in a world of rivals for masculine power. Women are cast off from this effort of a man to "make sense" of himself according to a social "Law" because basic "feminine" qualities from the birth stage are retained in the visceral memory, much of which has to be thrown away from consciousness if a clearly bounded and socially viable "maleness" is to be constructed. An equal threat to this repressive "identity" is the way birth ejects an individual into different class-based ways for styling a "self." The fabrication of a double male nature is a way to arrange that cacophony into an order of ranks, especially if the language used to craft this creation seems to blend conflicting rhetorics into a homogeneity entitled to propose hierarchies from a "unified" position. The trouble is that the homogeneity falls apart on close scrutiny. Orders of language, even the one articulating the Law of the Father, turn out to be contests between rival systems just as much as the Law is really based on the rivalry of men in different cultural and familial positions. A "self" trying to put such differences together, even in a neatly divided self-image, must be exposed as crisscrossed by the class interplays that monological (albeit dichotomous) rhetorics try to deny. After all, the emergence of the self into language, even body language, generally is the casting of a subject into the interplays of figural difference where one position is always defined in relation to some other—and the other is not always an exact antithesis. The sheer deferral of figures to figures (even male to female or class pattern to class pattern) at this primal level of "readable" existence must be the most abjected process of all if a strictly antithetical reading is to be imposed on the male self by the Law of the Father. Yet this level is the most impossible to cast off because it underlies the very rhetoric in which any "throwing over there" is attempted. To make this latter effort too aggressively in the styling of a body or a confessional text is to highlight the figurality at the base of the struggle, bringing back all that has been repressed alongside it. The result is the unsought return throughout *Jekyll and Hyde* of body language, the woman-in-the-man, class conflict within the self, and figural play—all that has been abjected by the discourse trying to dominate Jekyll/Hyde and his interpreters.

But then there is that fifth question, which has been approached but has not yet been fully answered. Particularly when we are faced with repeated failures in the rhetoric of male dualities and such vivid intimations of what it has striven to abject, we still must wonder why Jekyll and his observers persist in their repressions as consistently and violently as Garrett has shown them to do. The rigidly judgmental "casting down" that enforces abjection, quite as much as what abjection "casts off," is strikingly apparent in every character or speaker who tries to explain the manifestations of male self-division. This novella, after all, appears fairly late in the history of gothic fiction. Not surprisingly (given the increased need for urban police methods as the nineteenth century wore on), the tale is right in line with what Thomas and others see at this stage of the gothic tradition: a turning away from the early encounters with dissolving identities at the hearts of decaying crypts to detective stories in which the most desirable point of view is that of "a character [or characters] who can explain and organize [the dissolution] into a meaningful pattern" (Day, 52). Stevenson grants several figures such a perspective in this *Strange Case,* particularly Enfield, Lanyon, and Utterson (the self-appointed "Mr. Seek" determined to get to the bottom of "Mr. Hyde"), and they all pursue the kind of total explanation that demands singular causes with precise theses and antitheses.

These men are not only cast down by the Law of the Father to the point of casting off what we have seen them abject; in the patriarchal society of this time and place, they are the Law's agents and enforcers, who are clearly everywhere (not just among the police), wresting the objects of their scrutiny into the divided shapes the Law demands. The omniscient narrator even seems part of this detective squad in search of targets for dichotomous reconstruction, as when he reads the "symbols of [Utterson's] after-dinner face" and finds such duplicities as a love for "the theater" hidden behind the lawyer's refusal to go to a play "for twenty years" (29). No wonder Jekyll concludes the novella with the sort of confession he offers. The procedure of his interpreters leading up to that point, the code of the "wise and good" that he himself seeks to imitate, insists that he write out his past as he does in a way that can be deciphered by *all* the father/readers obeying the dictates of the Law. Jekyll/Hyde is set up to be a detective or analyst's "case," even for himself, because that way of probing people to draw them out is the sociolinguistic "world situation" into which the human "war among the members" is always launched and by which it is laid out (like a strangled body) for articulation. Why is that situation so pervasive? Why is an interpreting scheme that "casts [tendencies] down" or "throws [them] under" its scrutiny so readily accepted by those completing the abjection process? Why, too, is Stevenson's tale structured in a way that emphasizes this building pressure on Jekyll to confess as he does at the end? And why is the very style of the whole work, like the rhetoric of Jekyll's "Statement," able to convey this pressing down on multiplicity yet equally able to intimate what is abjected by such power plays?

I want to close by offering two answers to these closely related questions. One answer draws us back to the ungrounded abjection sequence that we have discovered grounding this tale. There we find a stage that I have not yet thoroughly described, one that comes between the newborn's first emergence into language and the later choice of a Father/Reader. During this intervening time, as Lacan and Kristeva have shown, the emergent figure, though tending in multiple directions, reaches out for some sort of dictionary to provide some fairly consistent terms and analogues for the self. The confused and diffuse subject-in-language starts feeling a need to *know* itself in discourse as a "self" separate from other selves, albeit in relation to them, and from the welter that could reabsorb it if it did not become distinct. What the culture most consistently offers as a "reader"—along with the particular order of terms and significations dominating his discourse (even though it is but one order, or combination of orders, among competitors)—is thereby granted the role of "knower" able to organize the relationships of figures in which the new one will find some contexts for self-understanding and be able to "cast off" the earlier multiplicity. At the same time, the chosen readers and discourse systems naturally want to use the role they have been granted to achieve a dominance that suppresses their own similar foundations. To seek "knowledge" of the "self," just as Jean-Paul Sartre and Michel Foucault have revealed in different ways, is thus to give the self and its nature up to a "gaze of the Other," an interpretive discourse seeking power over those who look to it for their significance.[40] Such a discourse system casts human possibility down—and some of it out—to produce what Foucault calls a "grid of intelligibility" working to limit "mobile relations" within a supposed "rationality."

This grid, falsely claiming absolute validity while it actually contends with the other possible systems it keeps trying to subsume, becomes obsessed with the "will to knowledge" that seems to have granted it authority over the subject. It henceforth works through its agents, who control it far less than it controls them, to define and draw out "an area of investigation" ("sexuality," "indiscretion," "crime," "evil") in the now-enthralled subject. Such a pulling forth arranges or "deploys" that subject, to use Foucault's key term, into a schema of knowledge dividing the subject's "nature" into sanctioned and unsanctioned elements. All elements that might challenge the limits on figural relationship in the hegemonic discourse are, of course, consigned to unsanctioned levels. The worst threats become virtually unspeakable, except through half-sanctioned figures that hide such outcast potentials from view. This division comes to permeate the subject, however, only if he is made to confess all his tendencies in an official verbal arrangement of them according to patterns dictated by the Master Reader (or Father Confessor). There can really be no consciousness or ordering of "self" unless the subject finds himself deployed and divided up in such a fashion from the start. Even the discovery that the self is more multiple and figural than the domineering system allows can only be proposed *within* a discourse of power that works to debase it. There it must be consigned either to what the will-to-knowledge cannot encompass or to what can be taken as a simple resistance to sanctioned power. It must act out its challenge to authority in terms that the master discourse is able to grasp—and thus to *apprehend* in the way that serves the continuing power of the Law.

Once revealed, this part of the abjection struggle, particularly when it is exemplified in Stevenson's characters, makes quite plain the means (and the ease) by which this kind of subjection can come to rule large segments of a society. Certainly we now see why Henry Jekyll so readily accedes to such a "deployment" of him. It is not just that he apes the patriarchal/religious language of "the wise and good" who seem to speak the Voice of the Father. He believes, given his desire to know himself in language, that he cannot articulate himself intelligibly at all unless he conscripts himself in such a system that then divides him up into "excellent parts" and "faults" (81). Even for himself, he is always already an object of knowledge within this grid's continual attempt to assert its control over all its conscripts and all figural movements resistant to such confinement. This is why Jekyll chooses to conceal his own resistant tendencies in a Satanic "troglodyte" and criminal whom the hegemonic discourse can hunt down as such. Once he finds he can resist the master rhetoric only from within it, he "hydes" the resistances in a composite of all the "faults" that the system ascribes to him. He then presents that composite to the attention of "readers" conscripted into the system. He counts on the fact that their—or rather *our*—incomplete understanding (our tendency to read only through the hegemonic grid)

JERROLD E. HOGLE

will make us construe what we see as simple evil dissociated from the "excellent parts" that he presents to the world at other times according to the system's prescriptions. This gambit works quite well to situate Hyde as a separate object of knowledge for unreflective agents of the now-ascendent grid. Even if such readers begin to see deeper levels in the "troglodyte," that figure imitates their will-to-dominance so blatantly that they—or is it "we" again?—refuse to recognize Hyde as a portion of what is coded as "respectable." This fabrication begins to unravel in the story only when observers of it using the grid sense a dim threat harbored by the indescribable "deformation" of the proffered figure. In that vague shifting from one figural state toward another, the "knowing" (that is, abjecting) reader senses a drive that must be kept suppressed by the system if the system's power is not to be put in question.

Indeed, nearly every interpretive decision made by Jekyll/Hyde's observers in the tale is designed to "cast down" or rule out this challenge whenever it rears its head. When Enfield and then Utterson first confront Hyde as in some way connected with Jekyll, the possibility of his being one refiguration of Jekyll's body (and thus an indicator of any man's anamorphic body language) is certainly in the offing. Both interpreters see enough of a bodily resemblance to grab at the possibility of Jekyll having an illegitimate son. But they immediately steer away from any further figural/physical connections by falling back explicitly on a grid of intelligibility that disallows that option. Enfield, facing the figural link in Jekyll's signature on the check, rules "the whole business" out of his system, labeling it "apocryphal" or "Queer" (32–33). Utterson, on confronting Hyde's attempt to elude precise "description" by any other person (39–40), asserts that this deviation from expected rhetorical decorum "is not fitting language," not consonant with signifiers properly suited to already-coded signifieds (40). Later, Hyde's ability to reappear anyway in what the standard grid is able to observe forces such readers into wild inaccuracies just to *make* him fit what the system can organize. The established legal scrutiny of upper-bourgeois men, after all, can conceive of an error of youth (allowed to higher-class males) leading to blackmail and even a new heir. In addition, when such conclusions seem too superficial, a "reader" can construct the connection on the model of the Supremacy ceded to an all-powerful Male, the notion maintained at the very heart of the grid as the basis of the grid's domination. Utterson can fancy Jekyll submitting to a male "figure to whom power was given" and whose "bidding" the doctor must therefore "rise and do" (37). Then, finally, if an outcast body language or relationship starts being suggested at such moments—in, say, Jekyll's receptive feminine position or the homosexual connotations (two men becoming one) in this last image, as Veeder has argued—these observers can defer apparent meanings to later points at which a more "intelligible" truth *will* emerge and find a place in the system. Enfield and Utterson can agree not to judge too hastily after their first impressions because that stance "partakes too much of the style of the day of judgment," which is off in the future but must eventually arrive to expose everything to the Gaze of the Father (33). The tale is therefore structured as a series of deferrals or unsolved mysteries apparently resolved in Jekyll's religious judgment on his primally fallen nature (the *exact* sort of confession sought by the grid), and, in case there are any lingering implications of other possibilities, the doctor defers to the future (us) for a still more final judgment.

Admittedly, as I have tried to show, this phallic zeal for "penetrating to the bottom" is so insistent on the most primal level that it uncovers what it has tried to deny. The ultimate deferral in the "Statement," as we saw at the outset, reveals the "incongruous multiplicity" of basic figuration that the abjecting discourse has striven to resist all along. Even Jekyll/Hyde's final attempt to root out the cause of the involuntary transformations leads him, not to impurities in the recent salts he has used (his first theory), but, as Garrett sees, to an "unknown impurity" in the very "first supply" (96), an interaction of incongruities within the supposedly consistent "primal essence." All the same, there is no denying how much the structure of this narrative and the process insisting on that arrangement drive all the articulate characters more and more toward intoning the most official rhetorics of Victorian England. At most, we can say that the "ending" of this narrative—where Jekyll's life-ending conclusiveness is somewhat compromised by the silence of Utterson, whom we know to be reading this "Statement" in search of some satisfying facts—leaves the reader oscillating across a continuum between the two poles set up by abjection. We are made, on the one hand, especially in reading backward from the end, to see myriad intimations of what abjection "throws away." We come to sense, as I have shown by proceeding in this reverse manner myself, the ambisexual polymorphism of the centrifugal birth state as figurality sweeps it into the play of social postures and possibilities. On the other hand, we clearly perceive the centripetal, counting force of the repressive "grid of intelligibility" that "casts down" emergent longings to make them reappear (at their own request) in the guise of binary divisions and restricted possibilities. *Jekyll and Hyde* renders these extremes and their interplay with such a force, indeed with a subtlety too rarely ascribed to Robert Louis Stevenson, that both thrusts are made to seem as unavoidable as the nature of the biological/social existence they help to form. That is why the style of nearly every sentence both drives toward a repressive, conclusive judgment and opens up again, as signs must, toward digressive movements of suggestion that discourse can claim to master only later.

This fact suggests my second answer to our concluding set of questions: the inclinations of this novella's author. Stevenson writes his tale in this manner because such a double-edged style for him, quite simply, *is* the art of writing. His many essays on the style and sources of fiction are unequivocal about this equivocal aim. In "A Humble Remonstrance," that now-famous rejoinder to Henry James's "The Art of Fiction," the artist's principal achievement "is to half-shut his eyes against the dazzle and confusion of reality," against the "welter of impressions" (body language) combining observations, sensations, and even preconscious memories as they reappear in dreams. As James puts the matter, the writer should follow the possible filiations of empirical perceptions as they interrelate across the "huge spider-web" of the "threads" in "consciousness."[41] For Stevenson such an effort would force awareness to immerse itself in the "monstrous, infinite, illogical, [and] abrupt." Consciousness would dissolve and lose all sense of identity in a Nietzschean "brute energy" that is completely "inarticulate." Articulation should instead be a delivery from this "inexhaustible" multiplicity, however much such a "welter" provides the materials of all discourse (including the cacophony of possible language formations). Once that emergence occurs, the welter can give way to "the emphasis and the suppressions" of human "speech." Verbal art, which "imitates" that incipient "pattern" instead of Dionysian "life," can then further the delivery by increasing the consistency of both emphasis and suppression. It can render "impressions" as a thoroughly "artificial . . . series . . . all eloquent of the same idea" to a point where the "well-written" work "echoes and re-echoes . . . one creative and controlling thought," such as the permanently double nature of man. No wonder Jekyll feels he must take his body language "in one direction only" (82) by way of a socially recognized rhetoric that suppresses any other option. He must articulate himself by accepting the coming-into-discourse that his author must accept to articulate him.

This obedience is the only way, if we believe Stevenson's testimony in "A Chapter on Dreams," by which an author who has begun with dreamt fragments and vague associations (the main "sources" of this novella, according to the "Chapter") can claim any readable cohesion in the work or any identity for himself in the act of creation, any right to say—as Stevenson does of *Jekyll and Hyde*—"the meaning of this tale is therefore mine." There can be no speech, work, self, or meaning (in the usual sense of this last term) if the primal cacophony is not made "marketable," another key word in the "Chapter."[42] Body language and sheer figuration must become a language interpretable by readers who will validate the construct of the moment, who will grant it "meaning" and its author "authority," by finding some conventional order they understand in the discourse submitted to them. Stevenson, as the "Chapter" says, writes this and other tales as much to find buyers (for most of whom he must repress what he senses) as he does to explore the problem of multiple being (the return of the repressed). He and the main character he creates are consequently alienated, whatever their modes of self-presentation, into a marketplace of shopping readers where the sellers, to "make a sale," must appeal to a hegemonic discourse that controls them (a common currency) even in their acts of trying to manipulate it. They must, to "utter" anything, submit to a "grid of intelligibility" imposing a unity where there was none and demanding an "object of knowledge" at the heart of the readable surface to which readers are encouraged to probe.[43] If that is the inescapable situation of the multiple self and the writer all at once, why not construct a narrative that makes such a world order explicit? Why not submit thoroughly to the patriarchal power plays making utterance possible, to such an extent that discerning readers cannot miss what happens to human multiplicity as it enters the arena of human symbolization? Why not do so especially if the author is acutely conscious of the "infinite, illogical, [and] inarticulate thunder" from which identity and speech emerge?

At the time time, Stevenson also says in "A Humble Remonstrance," the best artistic quests for pattern do not silence that "thunder" entirely, even though much of their task is indeed to abject its continuous movement. The artist must only "*half*-shut his eyes to it" and so must find ways to turn back toward it in the very verbal patterning that suppresses the "confusion." Writing "On Some Technical Elements of Style in Literature," Stevenson decides that truly "literary" style is so "dense" with "two or more ways of viewing the subject at hand," even as it seems to craft a cohesive unity between the best-known meanings of its words, that it "unobtrusively" replaces the "shallow statements of the [mere] chronicler" with the "highest degree of elegant and pregnant implication" in a whole work or a single passage (such as "the agonized womb of consciousness"). The supposedly masculine imposition of a penetrating "grid" that wants to see resistance to it as strictly phallic, as the merest version of its own drive, must be countered in the greatest writing by a feminine opening toward multiple interrelations with which a figure is always impregnated.[44] A "treasure trove" of style, in the words of "A Gossip on Romance," is a womb-like synecdoche concealing yet delivering "whole vistas of secondary stories . . . radiated forth from [the reader's] discovery [of a figure], as they radiate from a striking particular in [cacophonous] life." To compress the "illogical" Jamesian web into figures striving to reflect a single center (the sort of figure Jekyll tries to create with Hyde) is only to have each figure fan out behind its "thick cloak" toward an ambisexual play among different "threads," the multiplicity of which is emphasized all the more *because* the figure attempts to conflate so many "independent beings" at once. The drive to accept the grid, in other words, if sought with a zeal for figuration so excessive as to expose the drive's forgotten impetus, must indicate, in its suppression *conscious* of suppression, the figural drift among supposed incompatibilities, and hence the birth process ("life"), from which the discourse of "identity" and narrative come. While Stevenson speaks of the dreams leading to *Jekyll and Hyde* as struggling to work out "a central idea" even before composition begins (in "A Chapter on Dreams"), he must simultaneously remember the struggle as one among numerous, separate "Brownies" in his psyche or body language laboring toward a seemingly univocal meaning in frantic efforts to relate their differences "piece by piece."

If Stevenson on paper, then, is the combination of conventionalist and rebel that biographers have shown us for so many years, he is so only as he resembles his own assessment of William Dean Howells in "A Humble Remonstrance": "For while [this writer apparently] holds all the little orthodoxies of the day . . . the living quality of much that he has done is of a contrary, I had almost said of a heretical, complexion." Stevenson is a heretic within the frame of orthodox discourse confirming and challenging that order's power with the nonidentities that both originate and question any intelligible "grid." The *Strange Case of Dr Jekyll and Mr Hyde,* in turn, because it carries through this conflicted endeavor as forcefully as anything its author ever wrote, is a striking example of literature ranging all the way between the disordering and ordering drives that bring the most suggestive writing into being. It is literature's special function, surely, to be the space where every cacophonous forelanguage seeks coherant verbalization and where sanctioned verbal orders are drawn back toward that figural mobility, even in concerted attempts to resist it. Since we all are being driven, at birth and after, back and forth between these drives in the act of reaching for and yet resisting the more systematic of the two, literature renders what we beings-in-language have been, are, refuse to be, can become, and must do to attain or overreach an inscribable identity. Hence, by concentrating on a "casting down" that only exposes what grounds and undermines it, *Jekyll and Hyde* depicts, more blatantly than most works, the primordial struggle of human life that literature exists to shape and configure as an extension or verbal enactment of this very struggle. In the last one hundred years, this tale has been placed on the margins of that effort by genre classifications, popularizations, repressive adaptations, and even limited scholarly frames of interpretation. Now, a century after its appearance, as it continues to be both standard and heretical in any careful reading of it, this riveting novella can take its place among all the great works that announce the nature and function of literature. It "improperly" presses literature to its proper limits, the ones that unsettle our concepts of human being by showing us the "incongruous" losses and gains in the process that brings any "identity" to birth.

NOTES

My work on this piece has been aided immeasurably by my Arizona colleagues Susan Hardy Aiken, Lynda Zwinger, and Patrick O'Donnell. I am particularly influenced here by Professor O'Donnell's "Becoming Discourse: Eudora Welty's 'Petrified Man,' " in *Changing Our Minds,* ed. Aiken et al. (Albany: State University of New York Press, in press). I am also grateful for discussions with several students—Karen Brennan, Eduardo Cadava, Michael Magoolaghan, Andrew Morrill, and Perrie Ridley—and for the many helpful suggestions offered by William Veeder in his capacity as coeditor of this volume. I dedicate the essay to Edgar Dryden, Professor of English and outgoing head of the department at the University of Arizona, in appreciation of his unflagging support for this and other projects.

1. I am, of course, indebted here and elsewhere to such previous analyses of the name "Hyde" as those in Egan (70), Miyoshi (472–73), Twitchell (236), and Saposnik ("The Anatomy," 731, n. 12).

2. Silverman is therefore correct as well, in reading this tale according to the "codes" specified in Roland Barthes's *S/Z,* to claim that the narrative "reflects the dominant symbolic oppositions of the [hegemonic] cultural code" and the "semic activity" that such a code demands (Silverman 276). Even so, like Garrett, I write to dispute the claim made later in the same study that Stevenson's novella "enables us to scrutinize the symbolic order to which it belongs, but not to dislocate it from that order" (278). Such a repression of what the text really shows repeats the assumption of too long a standing that Stevenson "impaled his moral imagination on a Calvinistic simplification that he had already rejected as belief" (Girling 75). Although the mistake is quite natural, most critics, I think, have been excessively inclined to interpret Jekyll simply as the doctor interprets himself.

3. See Daiches (6–12) and Calder (32–36).

4. Block has reminded us that Stevenson wrote *Jekyll and Hyde* right about the time of his most frequent talks with the evolutionary psychologist James Sully. See the helpful account of what Stevenson draws from Sully's rhetoric in Block, esp. 445–58. I think, though, that Stevenson's disagreements with Sully, also noted by Block, go further than Block suggests. More than Sully, Stevenson saw evolutionary thought as an increasingly popular *style,* which a progressive scientist, notwithstanding the incompatibilities, would probably try to blend with the rhetoric of a dualistic religion.

5. See Guerard and, especially, Tymms (15–90).

JERROLD E. HOGLE

6. Cited from Freud's *Collected Papers*, tr. Joan Riviere et al., 2d ed. (London: Hogarth Press, 1934), 4:30–59.

7. Indeed, I think Veeder gives less importance than he should to suggestions in the tale that Hyde is an embodiment of the son's phallus trying to gain the power of the father's, as Kanzer argues (esp. 429–32).

8. In René Girard, *Violence and the Sacred*, tr. Patrick Gregory (Baltimore: Johns Hopkins University Press, 1977), 169–92.

9. For the psychoanalytic sense of the mother, see, for example, Sigmund Freud, "Some Psychological Consequences of the Anatomical Distinction between the Sexes" and "Fetishism," *Collected Papers*, 5:186–204; Marie Bonaparte, *The Life and Works of Edgar Allen Poe: A Psycho-analytic Interpretation*, tr. John Rodker (London: Hogarth Press, 1949); and Jane Gallop, "The Phallic Mother: Freudian Analysis," *The Daughter's Seduction: Feminism and Psychoanalysis* (Ithaca, N.Y.: Cornell University Press, 1982), 113–31.

10. "Gender," we need to remind ourselves, is not identical to "sex" but is rather a linguistic-rhetorical-ideological shaping or construct ("man" or "woman") attached by social convention *with the aid* of sex to any person being born into any society. This "socially divided portraiture" is "no more 'natural' and inevitable than an occupational role," yet it too often operates as an "anchoring of activity," a grounding of a person's potential in a limited set of qualities or permitted actions. I quote the words of Erving Goffman, *Frame Analysis: An Essay on the Organization of Experience* (Cambridge, Mass.: Harvard University Press, 1974), 285.

11. Stevenson was quite sensitive to the blatant power plays in such denials, despite the lapses into patriarchal thinking that Veeder rightly attributes to him. He was outspoken on the unfairness of gender restrictions, as well as the victimization of women in marriage and prostitution. See Calder (54–56, 90–92).

12. See especially Punter (402–27) and Day (13–50). Oddly enough, Punter does little with his Marxist claims in his reading of *Jekyll and Hyde* (240–45), and Day does only a little more in his section devoted to that novella (89–92). Punter is most useful in his general theory of the gothic mode, while Day is especially helpful on the gender conflict in Jekyll. Stevenson, in any case, encourages such readings of his work by writing with some understanding of (and, for a while, some affinity with) Marxist revelations. On March 12, 1885, for example, not long before he starts *Jekyll and Hyde*, he writes to Edmund Gosse just prior to moving into the house at Bournemouth, "I am now a beastly householder, but have not yet entered on my domain. When I do, the social revolution will probably cast me back on my dung heap" (L2, 271).

13. See Horace Walpole's preface to the second edition of *The Castle of Otranto*, in *Three Gothic Novels*, ed. Peter Fairclough (Harmondsworth, England: Penguin Books, 1968), 43–48.

14. See *Beyond the Pleasure Principle*, in *The Standard Edition of the Complete Psychological Works of Sigmund Freud*, tr. James Strachey et al. (London: Hogarth Press, 1953–66), 17:7–64.

15. Bakhtin's Marxist base is best revealed in one of his books published under the name of V. N. Volosinov, *Marxism and the Philosophy of Language*, tr. Ladislav Matejka and I. R. Titunik (New York: Seminar Press, 1973). His best

definition of *heteroglossia*, though, is in "Discourse in the Novel," *The Dialogic Imagination: Four Essays*, ed. Michael Holquist, tr. Caryl Emerson and Holquist (Austin: University of Texas Press, 1981), 259–422.

16. See Jacques Lacan, "The Function of Language in Psychoanalysis," *The Language of the Self*, ed. and tr. Anthony Wilden (New York: Dell Publications, 1986), esp. 9–51.

17. My etymologies are all drawn from *The American Heritage Dictionary of the English Language*.

18. Julia Kristeva, *Powers of Horror: An Essay on Abjection*, tr. Leon S. Roudiez (New York: Columbia University Press, 1982), the text to which I refer in all my quotations from Kristeva unless I annotate them differently. *Abjection*, by the way, is the word in her original French text.

19. This Freudian sense of being-towards-death is helpfully extended for the study of narrative, in ways that assist me here and later, by Peter Brooks, "Freud's Masterplot," *Yale French Studies* 55–56 (1977), 280–300, revised and extended in Brooks's *Reading for the Plot: Design and Intention in Narrative* (New York: Alfred A. Knopf, 1984), esp. 90–142, 238–63. At the same time, I draw on this critic's notions only as I combine them with Kristeva's presentation of death as a concomitant of birth.

20. See the critiques of Lacan *using* Lacan's privileging of the phallus in Gallop (n. 10, above), 15–32, and in a collection of Lacan's essays with two editorial prefaces, *Feminine Sexuality: Jacques Lacan and the École Freudienne*, ed. Juliet Mitchell and Jacqueline Rose, tr. Rose (New York: Pantheon Books and W. W. Norton and Co., 1982). In this latter volume, in fact (138–61), we can also see how much the concept of "body language" as I use it here is influenced by Lacan's *lalangue* and primal *"jouissance* of the body." Other influences on the notion include the "semiotic activity" of Kristeva and the "forelanguage" proposed by Hélène Cixous. See Kristeva's "From One Identity to an Other," *Desire in Language: A Semiotic Approach to Litertaure and Art*, ed. Leon S. Roudiez, tr. Thomas Gora, Alice Jardine, and Roudiez (New York: Columbia University Press, 1980), 124–47, and Cixous's "The Laugh of the Medusa," tr. Keith and Paula Cohen, *New French Feminisms*, ed. Elaine Marks and Isabelle de Courtivron (Amherst: University of Massachusetts Press, 1980), 245–64.

21. It is in partially recalling this that Hyde is a version of the Freudian "uncanny." See Freud's "The Uncanny,'" in *Collected Papers*, 4:368–407, where the unfamiliar/familiar phantasm is often "a transformation of another phantasy . . . the phantasy, I mean, of intra-uterine existence" (397).

22. This making of a figure that then mimes and rivals the "father"-creator at a distance from him shows how much Stevenson was indebted to Mary Shelley's *Frankenstein*, though not in the way suggested by the most extensive account of the relationship between the two works (Eigner 161–64). For studies of the figurality in *Frankenstein* that Stevenson reworks (in my view), see Peter Brooks, "'Godlike Science'/'Unhallowed Arts': Language, Nature, and Monstrosity," *The Endurance of Frankenstein: Essays on Mary Shelley's Novel*, ed. George Levine and U. C. Knopfelmacher (Berkeley: University of California Press, 1979), 205–20, and Jerrold E. Hogle, "Otherness in *Frankenstein:* The

Confinement/Autonomy of Fabrication," *Structuralist Review* 2 (1980): 20–48.

23. See Calder's note on "Juggernaut" in her edition of *Jekyll and Hyde* (302, n. 1).

24. For more on women as objects or means by which men seek and establish relationships between themselves—often in gothic novels that influenced Stevenson—see Eve Kosofsky Sedgwick, *Between Men: English Literature and Male Homosocial Desire* (New York: Columbia University Press, 1985), 21–27 and 83–117.

25. See the exploration of the "wine theme" by Nabokov (130) and Jefford (51–55), as well as the revealing discussion of orality in Veeder's "Children of the Night" essay, in this volume.

26. This possibility, especially since it equates the "Dionysian" with the continual (though repressed) process of death and metamorphosis, opens Stevenson's tale to a Nietzschean reading, though not just the one that Garrett has suggested. Another one could be based on *The Birth of Tragedy,* tr. Clifton Fadiman, in *Philosophies of Art and Beauty,* ed. Albert Hofstadter and Richard Kuhns (Chicago: University of Chicago Press, 1964), esp. 498–510. It is not that Jekyll is "the Apollonian" and Hyde "the Dionysian," but that Hyde is an Apollonian veil fashioned to both conceal and render the Dionysian "terror."

27. For a helpful sense of the decade urging Stevenson toward such an awareness (the 1880s, at least in Britain), see the chapter "The Old Order Changes" in Stone (9–35).

28. This meaning could hardly have escaped Stevenson. In "A Chapter on Dreams," he writes of his conscious "I" as a "denizen of the pineal gland" who finds himself in the foreign domain of "the Brownies," almost entirely under their control, whenever he slips into the dreams that generate his stories and novels. Stevenson, we should recall, was a frequent expatriate, gaining a number of privileges in countries where he was not a native, and even lived out of himself when he wrote in his native Scotland, visiting "Foreign Lands" from his usual residence—a sick-bed, "The Land of Counterpane" (as in the poems bearing those titles in his *Child's Garden of Verses.*).

29. See Fredric Jameson, *The Political Unconscious: Narrative as a Socially Symbolic Act* (Ithaca, N.Y.: Cornell University Press, 1981), esp. 74–102.

30. I defer here, naturally, to Arthur O. Lovejoy, *The Great Chain of Being: A Study of the History of an Idea* (1936; reprint, New York: Harper and Row Publishers, 1960), 58–66.

31. See Egan (28–29), Saposnik, "The Anatomy" (725–26), Nabokov (184–88), Jefford (56–57), and, of course, Veeder in the essay just preceding mine.

32. See Edward Hyde, Earl of Clarendon, *The History of the Great Rebellion,* ed. Roger Lockyer (London: Oxford University Press, 1967).

33. Bakhtin, "Discourse in the Novel" 273.

34. See Block (443–52).

35. On this inevitability, see Jacques Derrida, "Signature Event Context," tr. Samuel Weber and Jeffrey Mehlman, *Glyph 1: Johns Hopkins Textual*

Studies, ed. Weber and Henry Sussman (Baltimore: Johns Hopkins University Press, 1977), 172–97. On the writing-before-writing that signatures reveal, see Derrida's *Of Grammatology,* tr. Gayatri Chakravorty Spivak (Baltimore: Johns Hopkins University Press, 1976), esp. 27–73.

36. This is a common process in English gothic novels, and I discuss what it usually reveals in "The Restless Labyrinth: Cryptonymy in the Gothic Novel," *Arizona Quarterly* 36 (1980): 330–58. For more on the gothic psyche and body moving toward death only to become figural conversions to forms of writing, see Eve Kosofsky Sedgwick, *The Coherance of Gothic Conventions* (New York: Arno, 1980), and "Character in the Veil: Imagery of the Surface in the Gothic Novel," *PMLA* 96 (1981): 255–71.

37. Here and in the next paragraph, I am indebted to Maurice Blanchot, "The Work and Death's Space," *The Space of Literature,* tr. Ann Smock (Lincoln: University of Nebraska Press, 1982), 85–159.

38. Kristeva, "From One Identity to an Other" 133.

39. Another suggestive point made by Nabokov (193) and expanded on by Jefford (59–60), though only Jefford begins to offer an impetus for the mobility in Utterson's words when he says (albeit vaguely) that "Hyde's realm is essentially that of the signifier" and of the "free movement" in the signifer that some define as "*evil*" (62).

40. See Jean-Paul Sartre, *Being and Nothingness: An Essay on Phenomenological Ontology,* trans. Hazel Barnes (New York: Philosophical Library, 1956), 221–302, and Michel Foucault in *The History of Sexuality,* tr. Robert Hurley (New York: Pantheon Books, 1978), 1:17–35 and 1:77–114.

41. "The Art of Fiction," *The House of Fiction: Essays on the Novel by Henry James,* ed. Leon Edel (1957; reprint, Westport, Conn.: Greenwood Press, 1973), 31.

42. See the Brantlinger and Boyle essay in this volume and Stevenson's sense of his audience the very month that his *Jekyll and Hyde* appeared (L2, 312–13, 2 January 1886).

43. Stevenson bowed to this necessity with *Jekyll and Hyde* when he gave an early draft over to his wife, Fanny, the way he had done in other cases. As Balfour tells us (L2, 12–14) on the testimony of Fanny's son Lloyd Osbourne, she "wrote [a] detailed criticism of the story," submitting the initial dreams to a still more coherent and centered discourse. In that critique, she urged her husband to make the tale the moral "allegory" she felt it was trying (and ought) to be, a piece with a veiled but underlying truth that both the narrative and the reader could target as the story developed. Moreover, even if Stevenson had not had this kind of "editor," he would probably have been driven somewhat toward a tale in which a confessional narrative is couched within more public and sanctioned "grids." After all, one of the tale's most often noted sources is a novel with that kind of structure: James Hogg's *Private Memoirs and Confessions of a Justified Sinner,* that great Scottish "shocker" published in 1824.

44. Stevenson must have been well attuned to this ambisexuality both in his acts of writing and in his own body language. First of all, if the imposition of coherence is a supposedly "masculine" act, he places himself in the "feminine" position when he submits his story to his wife's allegorization, thereby position-

ing her as the fatherly "grid of intelligibility." Then, too, he sends his text out toward the market from a sickbed where he continually bleeds from within, almost in a menstrual fashion, even as he tries to impose conventional patterns of discourse on the various suggestions of a body language out of control. The multiplicity and not strictly gendered movement of the birth process recalled in Hyde and in "pregnant" moments of style has to reflect Stevenson's own very personal sense of a body always becoming different from itself, flowing out of itself toward discourse, and thus being quite female within its masculinity. Here is a biographical basis for *Jekyll and Hyde* (and so much else) that manifestly cries out for further scholarly exploration.

STAGE AND SCREEN
PORTRAYALS

Richard Mansfield as Jekyll/Hyde in his 1887–88 stage adaptation of *Dr. Jekyll and Mr. Hyde*. Photo, Library of Congress.

Husband and Wife

Mrs. Jekyll : "Last night I lay awake longing for your return. At last I heard a step in the passage that leads into the laboratory. I crept down and called you. There was no answer, but I felt something steal past me in the dark, and as it passed the air seemed suddenly to freeze my blood. It must have been Mr. Hyde."

Dr. Jekyll : "And if it were?"

Mrs. Jekyll : "I want you to promise me he shall never come to the house while you are away. The terrible murder of last night has frightened me. I could not sleep if I thought in your absence that man was free to come and go in the house. I daresay I am foolish—but I want your promise."

Dr. Jekyll : "......I swear to God that in this world I will never set eyes on Mr. Hyde again......never again ......you shall hold me to my bond."

MISS DOROTHEA BAIRD and MR. H. B. IRVING

H. B. Irving and Dorothea Baird as Dr. and Mrs. Henry Jekyll in the Queen's Theatre production of *Dr. Jekyll and Mr. Hyde,* London, 1910. Photo, BBC Hulton Picture Library.

James Cruze and Harry Behnam as Jekyll and Hyde in the Thanhouser film of *Dr. Jekyll and Mr. Hyde*, 1912.

John Barrymore as Hyde in the Famous Players–Lasky film of *Dr. Jekyll and Mr. Hyde*, 1920. Photo, Museum of Modern Art/Film Stills Archive.

Arthur Phillips as Hyde in the Savoy Theatre production of *Dr. Jekyll and Mr. Hyde,* London, 1931. Photo, BBC Hulton Picture Library.

Group scene from the Savoy production. Photo, BBC Hulton Picture Library.

Fredric March in experimental makeup for Edward Hyde, for the Paramount
film of *Dr. Jekyll and Mr. Hyde,* 1932. Photo by Jack Shalitt, Paramount Studio;
from the collection of the American Museum of the Moving Image.

Fredric March as Jekyll contemplating himself as Hyde, composite press still.
Photo, Wisconsin Center for Film and Theater Research.

Spencer Tracy as Hyde in the MGM film of *Dr. Jekyll and Mr. Hyde,* 1941.
Photo, National Film Archive, London.

Ralph Bates and Martine Brunswick as Dr. Jekyll and Sister Hyde in the Hammer film of *Dr. Jekyll and Sister Hyde,* 1971. Photo, Museum of Modern Art/Film Stills Archive.

I V

QUESTIONS OF GENRE

SEVEN

Frankenstein, Detective Fiction, and *Jekyll and Hyde*

GORDON HIRSCH

I. In the Surgery of Victor Frankenstein

Located at the intersection of several genres, Stevenson's *Strange Case of Dr Jekyll and Mr Hyde* shares some features with the gothic novel, the detective story, and Victorian realistic fiction—with this last, for example, in its descriptions of the ambience of London. This essay explores the book's strong connection with its most important gothic predecessor, Mary Shelley's *Frankenstein,* as well as its relation to the emergent nineteenth-century genre of detective fiction, to which it belongs, but which it also deconstructs. Tracing the descent of *Jekyll and Hyde* from *Frankenstein,* seeing it as a book formed in the surgery of Victor Frankenstein, underscores its indebtedness to its gothic heritage, particularly with respect to the way the monstrous double, Mr. Hyde, is presented, like Frankenstein's monster, as a gothic signifier of repressed desire. There are other links between the two novels, however, that require attention first.[1]

Both books explore the theme of the double, as well as the protagonist's use of science to achieve a position apart from his fellows. Jekyll notes that his "scientific studies . . . led wholly towards the mystic and the transcendental" (81), were a kind of "transcendental medicine" (80), just as Victor Frankenstein declares that "my inquiries were directed to the metaphysical . . . secrets of the world," to learn "the hidden laws of nature."[2] Both novels consider the dangers that lie in wait when humans tamper with the unknown, intimating that scientific research beyond certain limits may be a terrible mistake. Stevenson suggests a connection between the two books when he notes that Dr. Jekyll "had bought [his] house from the heirs of a celebrated surgeon; . . . his own tastes being rather chemical than anatomical." Jekyll's chemical laboratory had once housed the "dissecting-rooms" of the surgeon: "The [surgical] theatre, once crowded with eager students . . . now [lies] gaunt and silent, the tables laden with chemical apparatus" (51). Victor Frankenstein's monster is, of course, an anatomical assemblage: "I collected bones from charnel houses and disturbed, with profane fingers, the tremendous secrets of the human frame. . . . The dissecting room and the slaughterhouse furnished many of my materials" (53). Although Stevenson gives Jekyll's surgical predecessor a name, "old Dr. Denman" (76), the recurrent, essentially gratuitous allusions to the fact that this part of the house was once a surgery imply that this motif is a subtle tribute—what would be called an *hommage* if it occurred in a French film—to *Frankenstein*.[3]

Jekyll's relationship with his double, Hyde, resembles Victor's with the monster. "Creatures," in the literal sense, they both come back to haunt their scientist-creators. Specific moments in the two texts, such as those involving each creature's (real or imagined) confrontation with his double, are quite similar. For example, Gabriel Utterson, Henry Jekyll's lawyer and friend, tossing fitfully in bed, imagines this scene:

> He would see a room in a rich house, where his friend [Jekyll] lay asleep, dreaming and smiling at his dreams; and then the door of that room would be opened, the curtains of the bed plucked apart, the sleeper recalled, and, lo! there would stand by his side a figure to whom power was given, and even at that dead hour, he must rise and do its bidding. [37]

Compare this with the moment when Victor Frankenstein is suddenly awakened from sleep by his newly animated monster:

> I started up from my sleep with horror. . . . I beheld the wretch, the miserable monster whom I had created. He held up the curtain of the bed; and his eyes, if eyes they may be called, were fixed on me. His jaws opened, and he muttered some inarticulate sounds while a grin wrinkled his cheeks. . . . One hand was stretched out, seemingly to detain me, but I escaped and rushed downstairs. [57]

This scene of being awakened by the double as he parts the bed curtains becomes a powerful image in both of the novels. Stevenson's writing acquires a special resonance here by virtue of Mary Shelley's claim that her own dream about this particular scene provided the essential germ for her novel.[4]

Each of the scientist-protagonists is fascinated and horrified by his alter ego, and in each case the relationship evolves toward virulent hatred and overwhelming despair. When Jekyll says of himself, "If I am the chief of sinners, I am the chief of sufferers also" (58), or claims that "no one has ever suffered such torments" (96), he could as well be speaking for Victor Frankenstein, who frequently decries *his* promethean overreaching and proclaims *his* anguish: "I had begun life with benevolent intentions. . . .

GORDON HIRSCH

Now all was blasted; . . . I was seized by remorse and the sense of guilt, which hurried me away to a hell of intense tortures such as no language can describe" (86). Both protagonists decline to reveal too much in the way of scientific detail (*Frankenstein* 199; *Jekyll and Hyde* 83); each seems at least at times to intend his narrative as monitory for his friend. Jekyll writes to Utterson, "I mean but to point out the warnings and the successive steps with which my chastisement approached" (87); Frankenstein hopes that "the relation of my disasters will be useful to" his auditor, Walton (28). Both protagonists find themselves increasingly isolated from the friends who might offer them succor, and Jekyll's eventual self-imprisonment in his "house of voluntary bondage" (59) is very like the literal or figural immuring of Victor Frankenstein and many another gothic hero.

Most important to the present discussion, however, is the similarity in the representation, or description, or, perhaps more aptly, in the reluctance to emphasize the physical appearance of the antisocial double in both books. Frankenstein's monster is envisaged by Victor and by his society as violent, bestial, and less than human, just as Hyde is "troglodytic" (40), possessed of an "ape-like fury" (47), moving "like a monkey" (68) or "cry[ing] out like a rat" (66). It is significant that the only detailed and specific physical description of Frankenstein's monster occurs before he has been animated (56); thereafter the specifics of his appearance (except for his size) go unmentioned. In Stevenson's novel, the reader is told that Hyde looks dwarfish in Jekyll's too-large clothing, and Hyde's hand is described more than once—for example, as "lean, corded, knuckly, of a dusky pallor and thickly shaded with a swart growth of hair" (88). But there is no other detailed description of the rest of Hyde's appearance, despite the fact that the book's central intelligence, Utterson, is for a time obsessed with the desire to get a look at Hyde's face.

The double in each book is repulsive, revolting; but in each book it is the *impression* that counts rather than any particularized physical description. Other characters respond instinctively to the appearance of the double: Frankenstein's monster details the reactions of others to what it describes in general terms as "a figure hideously deformed and loathsome" (115), or "the unnatural hideousness of my person" (126); while those who meet Mr. Hyde in the later book speak of "something abnormal and misbegotten in the very essence of the creature" (78), arousing a visceral recoil that one character, Dr. Lanyon, attributes to a kind of instinctive revulsion from evil (77). Hyde gives "a strong feeling of deformity," "an impression of deformity without any namable malformation" (34, 40). When he temporarily disappears from the book, the point that Hyde's deformity, like that of Frankenstein's monster, is most importantly a general effect is again driven home:

> He had never been photographed; and the few who could describe him differed widely, as common observers will. Only on one point were they agreed; and that was the haunting sense of *unexpressed* deformity with which the fugitive *impressed* his beholders. [50; my italics]

The horror in both books, then, resides in a kind of absence or gap, very well expressed in the play between the two related words used here— "unexpressed" but somehow capable of "impress[ing]" beholders. The appearance of the double is not to be concretely visualized, but its effects on those who behold it are deeply felt. Presumably this is so because Hyde's form and countenance "were the expression, and bore the stamp of lower elements in [Jekyll's] soul" (83). But the key point is that the monstrous in both books by its very nature resists detailed description. Because it is absent, it is both called forth in an act of desire and viewed as monstrous when it appears. It is impressive because not fully expressed.[5]

There are, of course, differences between Frankenstein's monster and Jekyll's Hyde that must also be recognized. On the most literal level, the former is "gigantic" (123) whereas the latter is small. (Is this inversion of size, indeed, another indication of relation?) The monster, unlike Hyde, comes into the world as a blank slate, not as morally evil, and he does not share the same physical body with his creator. Finally, the monster *is* deformed whereas Hyde is not, having only the "impression of deformity without any namable malformation" (40). Yet in both cases the cause of the popular reaction, the double's physical appearance, is deemphasized because the impression is what matters. It stands for something that cannot be explicitly named; it represents what is taboo, on the margins of social discourse. The difference between the two books is marked by Stevenson's relatively greater willingness to ignore physical detail altogether, because what is finally at stake, he recognizes, is an ethical and social horror, not a physical one.

What, then, can be said of this unexpressable evil and deformity in Stevenson's book? How is Mr. Hyde to be read? The text of *Jekyll and Hyde* offers some interesting interpretive clues, which also turn out to be relevant for *Frankenstein* and probably for Western culture as a whole. The "pleasures" that Dr. Jekyll has had to conceal while leading his eminently respectable life, before the creation of Hyde, seem to be of the ordinary, sensual sort: "Many a man would have even blazoned such irregularities as I was guilty of" (81)—many a Victorian male might brag about his sexual exploits, for example. And Jekyll begins by allowing Hyde to engage in these simple peccadilloes on his behalf: "The pleasures which I made haste to seek in my disguise [as Hyde] were, as I have said, undignified; I would scarce use a harder term. But in the hands of Edward Hyde, they soon began to turn toward the *monstrous*" (86; my italics point to another indication that *Frankenstein* is in the back of Stevenson's mind). Specifically, they rapidly turn toward the sadistic:[6] "His every act and thought centered on self; drinking pleasure with bestial avidity from any degree of torture to another; relentless like a man of stone" (86). Consider this description of the murderous assault on Sir Danvers Carew: "With a transport of glee, I mauled the unresisting body, tasting delight from every blow. . . . [I] fled from the scene of these excesses, at once glorying and trembling, my lust of evil gratified and stimulated, and my love of life screwed to the topmost peg" (90–91). Before Utterson ever sees Hyde, he construes him, on the basis of Enfield's story about the Juggernaut, to be "without bowels of mercy" (38). And at another point, Jekyll describes Hyde as "shaken with inordinate anger, strung to the pitch of murder, lusting to inflict pain" (93). If one thinks, as well, about the acts of Hyde that *are* specifically described—the attack on Carew, the calm and indifferent trampling of the little girl in the street, and Hyde's striking the face of the woman offering the box of lights—they are all unprovoked acts of sadism, and they are all directed at people (an old man, a child eight or ten years old, and a poor woman) representing a cross-section of the most vulnerable members of this society.

The weight of evidence argues that the monstrousness that is "absent" and unexpressed in Hyde—we do not know, really, what he looks like and we are not told in much detail what it is he does—is suppressed because it is in fact violent and sadistic, while Jekyll's secret "pleasures," in his life prior to the time of the story, probably are not. Whatever other erotic components Hyde's acts may have, sadism seems to be the transcendent sin, appropriating to itself all other forms of desire. Perhaps this is the gothic novel's insight into how our culture construes repressed desire, as sadism or even murder.

Victor Frankenstein's monster, too, murders. Whereas Hyde's violence is unprovoked, the monster's is fundamentally reactive, a response to his rejection and persecution. He murders because he cannot obtain his desires—affection, a mate. He is a gothic figure essentially because his repressed eroticism becomes terrifying and violent, a threat to society and social values. From the point of view of the conventional social world in which both the monster and Hyde are situated, they are similar: they impress ordinary folk as horrible, monstrous, and murderous because they manifest aspects of the self—monstrous passions—that are ordinarily suppressed. Familiar yet repellent, they produce an uncanny effect on those they encounter. They are identified with the inexplicable, the unarticulable—passion, violence, the irrational, the taboo. In this way they are quintessential expressions of the gothic genre, representing the return of repressed desire in a partly illegibile, sadistic form.

II. *Jekyll and Hyde* and Detective Fiction

One way of gauging the importance of the Shelleyan gothic to *Jekyll and Hyde* is to examine the relationship of the book to a second genre, that of detective fiction. Vladimir Nabokov enjoined his Cornell students, "Please completely forget, disremember, obliterate, unlearn, consign to oblivion any notion you may have had that 'Jekyll and Hyde' is some kind of mystery story, a detective story, or movie" (179).[7] But the context of mystery and detective fiction is crucial to the novel, as its full title, *Strange Case of Dr Jekyll and Mr Hyde*, signals. It must be understood, however, that the most important popularizer of the detective story is just about to publish at the time Stevenson is writing *Jekyll and Hyde* in 1885. Conan Doyle's first Sherlock Holmes book, *A Study in Scarlet*, was published in 1887, and his classic series of Sherlockian tales began to appear in the *Strand* in 1891. Though the form of detective fiction did not spring fully developed from Doyle's head, without antecedents, there are risks in speaking of it before it had, in effect, been codified by Doyle. Indeed, Jacques Barzun and Wendell Hertig Taylor, in trying to define the genre, declare that "detection is a game that must be played according to Doyle."[8] Ian Ousby, a recent historian of detective fiction, suggests, however, that two of Stevenson's early works, *The New Arabian Nights* (1881) and *The Dynamiter* (1885)—because of their interest in crime and detection, their whimsical and lightheartedly fantastic tone, and their development of a genteel, Holmes-like detective, Prince Florizel— were important influences on Doyle.[9] *The Dynamiter*, indeed, contains this paean to the detective:

> Chance will continually drag before our careless eyes a thousand eloquent clues, not to this mystery only, but to the countless mysteries by which we live surrounded. Then comes the part of the man of the world, of the detective born and bred. This clue, which the whole town beholds without comprehension, swift as a cat, he leaps upon it, and makes it his, follows it with craft and passion, and from one trifling circumstance divines a world.[10]

Before Stevenson and Doyle, of course, there are many precursors of modern detective fiction. In English, the list would include Godwin's *Caleb Williams*, Poe's Dupon stories ("The Murders in the Rue Morgue," "The Mystery of Marie Roget," and "The Purloined Letter"), Dickens's *Bleak House* and *The Mystery of Edwin Drood*, Collins's *The*

Woman in White and *The Moonstone,* and lesser works such as the *Recollections of a Detective Police-Officer* (1856) by "Thomas Waters" (William Russell) and the "sensation novels" of the 1860s and 1870s. John Cawelti has shown how mystery and detective fiction descends from the gothic tale, how Poe's Dupon stories are a kind of "benevolent inversion" of his more gothic "The Fall of the House of Usher": "the "demonic but benevolent" detective "performs an act of transcendent reason" to penetrate the dark secrets of the mysterious (gothic) room (or psyche) and exorcise the disruptive forces contained within it.[11]

Jekyll and Hyde is very close formally to the classic novel of mystery and detection. Cawelti stresses three elements as making up the formula for the detective story: (1) there is a mystery—certain key facts are concealed; (2) the story is structured around an inquiry into this mystery, usually with the aid of an inquirer-protagonist; and (3) the concealed facts are made known at the end (132). Though Cawelti quite reasonably insists that not everything that fits the formula ought to be considered a detective story, these elements are worth thinking about in relation to *Jekyll and Hyde,* for the sake of what they illuminate.

The text of *Jekyll and Hyde* itself alludes at least twice to the need for clearing up its various mysteries (38, 73). The fundamental mystery, introduced early on, involves the question of what precisely Hyde's relation to Jekyll is. Speculations on this subject are prompted initially by the strange clause in Jekyll's will declaring that Hyde shall inherit in the event of Jekyll's "disappearance or unexplained absence" (35), which implies that Jekyll might be made off with in some way. Furthermore, what is Hyde's hold over Jekyll? Enfield proposes an answer, one that is quite traditional in detective fiction, only to dismiss it right away: "Black mail, I suppose. . . . Though even that, you know, is far from explaining all" (33). Enfield also wonders why Hyde's appearance is so disturbing. And when Utterson tracks Hyde down and confronts him, other questions develop: Why does Hyde hesitate before showing Utterson his face? How does Hyde know with such certainty that Utterson is lying when he alludes to Jekyll as one of their "common friends" who might have described Hyde to Utterson (39)?

After the murder of Sir Danvers Carew, new mysteries arise. Why did this apparently unprovoked attack take place? How has Hyde managed to disappear so completely? How can the resemblances between Hyde's handwriting in his letter of farewell and Jekyll's own script be explained? Why does Jekyll isolate himself again after a couple of months of active engagement with his friends? Why does Jekyll slam his window shut and retreat to his cabinet with "an expression of such abject terror and despair" (61)? What has Hastie Lanyon seen that will bring on his death? What is in his sealed letter to Utterson? Who or what is in Jekyll's cabinet?

Has Hyde returned at last and murdered Jekyll? Quite in the best tradition of the mystery story, Poole says, "I think there's been foul play" (62): "That thing in the mask was never Dr. Jekyll . . . ; and it is the belief of my heart that there was murder done" (67). Practically each encounter with Jekyll or Hyde, each incident, raises further questions and provokes speculative answers. Detective fiction is quintessentially the genre of mystery, impedence, delay, supposition, and false supposition, and these elements structure Stevenson's book.

Cawelti's formula for classic detective fiction also includes the notion of an investigator, an inquirer-protagonist. Already in Stevenson's time, the tradition of the ratiocinative detective, the detective who uses his great powers of reason to catch the criminal, has come into play, although this will be further developed and emphasized by Doyle. Poe's archetypal detective Dupin insists on the importance of reason (to be coupled with great imaginative powers as well: in "The Purloined Letter" Poe makes clear that the detective ought to be a poet as well as a mathematician). And Dickens's Inspector Bucket in *Bleak House* proves to be masterful not only in the exercise of social power (exemplified by his omnipresent thrusting forefinger) but also in his rational skills: when everyone else is taken in by the ruse Lady Dedlock uses to throw off all pursuit, Bucket grasps that she and the working-class Jenny have exchanged garments. He also sees through the deceptions of Hortense, Lady Dedlock's maid and the real murderer. Dickens extols Bucket, imagining him as "he mounts a high tower in his mind, and looks out far and wide" to penetrate the mysteries about him.[12]

At the center of *Jekyll and Hyde* there is in fact a violent crime—the murder of Sir Danvers Carew and the apparent escape of the murderer—and in this context an Inspector Newcomen of Scotland Yard is introduced into the book.[13] Like many another police detective in fiction before and since, he is remarkable for his power over others—manifested in this case by his ability to gain entry to the rooms of the suspect, Hyde. The opposition of Hyde's housekeeper to Utterson's bid to inspect the flat melts away when the police inspector is identified. In Hyde's rooms, Newcomen discovers half of Dr. Jekyll's walking stick, the weapon used in the attack on Carew, and when he recovers Hyde's partially burned checkbook from the ashes of Hyde's burned papers, he expresses his confidence that it will be only a matter of time before he has his man:

> You may depend upon it, sir. . . . I have him in my hand. He must have lost his head, or he never would have . . . burned the cheque book. Why, money's life to the man. We have nothing to do but wait for him at the bank, and get out the handbills. [49–50]

He *sounds* the part, but his optimism is unfounded and the conclusions he draws quite erroneous. Newcomen proves to be like the bumbling official (or provincial) policeman of the detective story—Poe's prefect of police, Collins's Superintendent Seegrave, or Doyle's Lestrade. And there is no private, consulting detective here to exhibit a contrasting brilliance. Instead, we get as the story's principal investigator, Jekyll's lawyer and old friend, Gabriel Utterson.[14]

Throughout the book, it is really Utterson who strives to penetrate the mystery represented by Mr. Hyde. At first, Utterson displays some of the acumen of the detective-hero. In the book's first chapter, he pounces on Enfield's story with a confidence in his powers of observation and deduction, and with a one-upmanship worthy of Cuff or Dupin, declaring that he does not need to be told the name of the signatory of the check Hyde presented, "because I know it already," and admonishing his kinsman, "If you have been inexact in any point, you had better correct it" (34). Soon thereafter, he begins his "search for Mr. Hyde," uttering his most frequently cited line, "If he be Mr. Hyde, . . . I shall be Mr. Seek" (28). Seeking to learn who Mr. Hyde is and precisely what hold he has over the respectable Dr. Jekyll, Utterson, like many another ratiocinative detective, thinks that the suspicious and odd things he has been looking into must have a simple explanation:

> If he could but once set eyes on [Hyde], he thought the mystery would lighten, and perhaps roll altogether away, as was the habit of mysterious things when well examined. [38]

Unfortunately, however, a meeting with Hyde in the street does little to clarify matters for Utterson. But it also fails to slake his appetite for rational explanation. Throughout the novel, Utterson offers dozens of guesses aimed at explaining the book's various mysteries. He at first believes, for example, that Hyde must be blackmailing Jekyll, or that Hyde has dictated the terms of Jekyll's will and plans to murder him in order to inherit. After Jekyll has presented Hyde's "parting" letter to Utterson, Utterson is informed by Poole that the letter was *not* handed in at the front door, despite Jekyll's assertions to the contrary. His deduction is, "Plainly the letter had come by the laboratory door" (53). His faith in the explanatory power of the letter—that it will "put that mystery [of Jekyll's friendship with Hyde] to rights" (54)—must remain unshaken. When Guest compares the handwriting of Dr. Jekyll and Mr. Hyde and declares them virtually identical, Utterson leaps to the conclusion that Henry Jekyll has "forge[d] for a murderer" (55). Later, Poole comes to him to suggest that Hyde has murdered Jekyll and is ensconced in Jekyll's laboratory building, but Utterson dismisses the idea: "What could induce the murderer to stay? That won't hold water; it doesn't commend itself to reason" (65). Perhaps the finest example of Utterson's ability to rationalize and deny at the same time that he is "seeking" answers comes as he and Poole are poised to break down the door to Jekyll's locked apartment, after Poole has seen a strange figure who seems to be wearing a "mask upon his face . . . cry out like a rat and run from" him when discovered (66). Here is Utterson's response:

> These are all very strange circumstances, . . . but I think I begin to see daylight. Your master, Poole, is plainly seized with one of those maladies that both torture and deform the sufferer; hence the mask and the avoidance of friends; . . . hence his eagerness to find this drug, by means of which the poor soul retains some hope of ultimate recovery. . . . There is my explanation; it is sad enough, Poole, ay, and appalling to consider; but it is plain and natural, hangs well together and delivers us from all exorbitant alarms. [66]

A "plain and natural" explanation, certainly, my dear Utterson, but, as it turns out, quite a mistaken one. When Poole and Utterson discover the body of Hyde in Jekyll's cabinet, the lawyer concludes that they must now search for Henry Jekyll's body. When no body can be found, but a note from Jekyll dated that very day is discovered near Hyde's corpse, Utterson, in one of the book's more bitterly ironic turns, is led to suspect that Jekyll has murdered Hyde (72)!

Why do Utterson's rationalist inquiries seem to fall short so consistently? The explanation is to be found partly in Utterson's character, partly in the nature of his society, and partly in Stevenson's resistance to the rationalist assumptions of the emergent detective genre.

First, consider Stevenson's characterization of Utterson. Like many another fictional detective, Utterson turns out to be something of a psychological eccentric. Although Utterson is presented as the calm, rational investigator, Stevenson also makes it clear that he is as deeply divided as Dr. Jekyll, or as any person. Masao Miyoshi notes that Utterson's association with such people as his kinsman Richard Enfield, "the well-known man about town" who can be found "coming home from some place at the end of the world, about three o'clock of a black winter morning" (29, 31), "looks suspiciously [like] . . . vicarious pleasure" (Miyoshi, *Divided Self,* 296). Both Peter Garrett and William Veeder, in this volume, write of Utterson's obsession and identification with Hyde. Although the narrator describes Utterson as "a lover of the sane and customary sides of life, to whom the fanciful was the immodest" (35), he is from the very start of his "search for Mr. Hyde" immersed in a world of nightmare and prevarication, experiencing "a nausea and distaste of life" (41).

The novel's chief investigator and rational guide, in other words, has his own buried life. He shares more than he knows with Jekyll/Hyde. It is just that Utterson's division will not be owned by himself in this text. As the central consciousness for much of the narrative, and as the reader's stand-in while information and understanding are being sought, this detective figure is manifestly as divided as Henry Jekyll, but his contradictions can only be glimpsed behind and beneath layers of repression. If Henry Jekyll's mode of dealing with his division is to *project* aspects of himself onto another (Hyde), Utterson employs voyeuristic fantasies to participate vicariously in "the lives of downgoing men" (29). He is an inquiring detective who really does not want to know, a Mr. Seek who does not in fact wish to find.

Stevenson is making a point, too, about the way his society places its faith in rationality, in the rational solution of mysteries, at the same time that it keeps so much suppressed that it refuses to acknowledge. William Veeder discusses the bourgeois "professionalism" of Utterson's circle and sees it as the expression of a patriarchal social order in his essay "Children of the Night," in this volume. The interests of this class are also manifested by its absolute reliance on the rationalism of nineteenth-century science and its image in fiction, the scientific gathering of clues. Both Lanyon and Utterson are satirized for this naive faith. Lanyon's dismissal of Jekyll's "fanciful" research and "unscientific balderdash" (36) is made to sound very like Utterson's dismissal of Poole's theory that Hyde has returned to Jekyll's cabinet: "That won't hold water; it doesn't commend itself to reason" (65). Lanyon is, after all, "the great Dr. Lanyon," and his house on Cavendish Square is "that citadel of medicine" (36). When Jekyll requests that Lanyon go to Jekyll's house and bring away some of his chemicals, the request seems so odd to Lanyon as to persuade him of Jekyll's insanity—an absolute kind of dismissal (75). The rational and scientific are identified in this way with the respectable and with the *self-satisfaction* that accompanies respectability. Stevenson insists that Utterson and Lanyon are "thorough respectors of themselves and each other" (36), just as Sir Danvers Carew has a look of "well-founded self-content" (46). It is no accident that Jekyll's most frightening transformation into Hyde occurs on the park bench in a moment of "vainglorious thought," when he is full of the sense of his being "safe of all men's respect, wealthy, beloved" (92, 93). It is part of the respectability of these men and, finally, part of their "self-content" to insist on the value of science and rational explanation—the kind of rational account, closure, and formal structure that a detective story characteristically provides. It is also part of their vulnerability, however. There is no such thing as a disinterested rationalism, Stevenson insists; these men have an interest in seeing their kind of rationality triumphant, an interest that is intimated by their feelings of "self-content."

Utterson, in particular, is not at all averse to managing and suppressing the information he gathers if by doing so he can protect those in his social circle. Although he is by no means alone in his pleas for silence and suppression, it is a recurrent topic with him throughout the book, whether addressed to his clerk ("I shouldn't speak of this note, you know," [55]), or offered in support of his cousin's renewed resolve to censor his speech:

> "Here is another lesson to say nothing," said [Enfield]. "I am ashamed of my long tongue. Let us make a bargain never to refer to this again."
> "With all my heart," said the lawyer. [34]

Utterson expresses the hope that Hyde will *not* be brought to trial for Carew's murder for the sake of his friend and client, Henry Jekyll; after all, "if it came to a trial, your name might appear" (52). And he tells Poole to say nothing of Jekyll's "Full Statement," so that "if your master has fled or is dead, we may at least save his credit" (73). Above all, the reputations of those in one's social class must be protected.

One last reason the ratiocinative methods of detective fiction fall so woefully short can be attributed to this novel's fundamental ambivalence toward the genre itself. Utterson cannot reasonably deduce anything, and his logic consistently fails him in a nearly laughable way because the mystery he seeks to solve is at its core a supernatural one, a gothic one—namely, that Dr. Jekyll has divided himself by means of a chemical potion, that Hyde *is* Jekyll, transmogrified. Ordinarily, in detective stories the supernatural mode of the gothic has no place. What looks to be supernatural isn't. A classic instance of this is the mysteriously glowing hound in Conan Doyle's "The Hound of the Baskervilles" (1901–2), which turns out to be an ordinary, though savage, dog treated with phosphorescent paint. *Jekyll and Hyde,* however, has an irreducibly gothic premise. Most of the mysteries of the novel would be solved if Utterson knew that Jekyll and Hyde were not two but one. Utterson is, in a sense, in the wrong book, or at least in a book of the wrong genre. This narrative employs the ratiocinative methods and formal structure of the detective story, but also offers a satiric critique of those devices,[15] just as it supplies an ironic commentary on the self-contented, repressive modes favored by this society.

One should add that the rationalist assumptions of the detective genre had in fact been under fire from the genre's inception. The psychoanalyst,

GORDON HIRSCH

Jacques Lacan, near the end of his "Seminar on 'The Purloined Letter,' " makes the significant observation that even Dupin, who has been the story's exemplar of ratiocination, is implicated in a "rage," in passion and irrationality, once the letter is in his possession.[16] For Sherlock Holmes—in spite of his somewhat decadent indulgence in tobacco, morphine, and cocaine—cool reason reigns supreme; but in the explorative detective fictions of writers such as Poe and Stevenson, gothic attitudes and aesthetics intrude, and the passionate, irrational, and supernatural may undermine what Cawelti calls the detective's "act of transcendent reason."

III. Detection, Text, and Identity

The third element in Cawelti's formula for the classic detective novel—a feature as old as Edgar Allan Poe's stories, though, again, Doyle's use of this device is critical—is the way that the story moves toward a final narrative that will explain the mysteries. Detective fiction characteristically ends with a retelling of its story—from a more informed point of view.

The book's final chapter, "Henry Jekyll's Full Statement of the Case," is such a retelling. It is Jekyll's posthumous "confession" (72, 97); up to this point relatively little has been heard from him, and that little has hardly been candid or forthcoming.[17] One *does* read here about Jekyll's sense of his divided existence, about his use of chemicals to effect the "tranformation" into Hyde, and about the ascendancy of Hyde. An important shortcoming, however, of this "full statement of the case" is that it is presented from Henry Jekyll's point of view.[18] As readers move through it, they are likely to grow increasingly aware that they still lack Edward Hyde's account, *his* full statement of the case, even though Henry Jekyll, who after all shares "some of the phenomena of consciousness" with Hyde (95), will occasionally report something of what Hyde is feeling. Readers have, for example, been curious to know what, specifically, has motivated Hyde to commit the most heinous of his crimes, the murder of the conspicuously innocent and benevolent-looking "aged beautiful gentleman with white hair" (46), Sir Danvers Carew.[19] And Dr. Jekyll refrains from describing the "undignified" and "monstrous" pleasures that Hyde has pursued (86), a reticence that Hyde presumably would not share.

Despite Jekyll's statement, other mysteries remain as well, particularly about his last moments. How can it be *Hyde's* voice that seems, so uncharacteristically, to plead with Utterson before the lawyer breaks down the door: "Utterson, . . . for God's sake, have mercy!" (69)? How does Jekyll's manuscript survive when the doctor so fears that "Hyde will tear it in pieces" (97) if he becomes aware of it?

Finally, who commits suicide, Jekyll or Hyde? The book invites this question as it dissolves in puns and puzzles:

> Will Hyde die upon the scaffold? or will he find courage to release himself at the last moment? God knows; I am careless; this is the true hour of my death, and what is to follow concerns another than myself. Here, then, as I lay down the pen, and proceed to seal up my confession, I bring the life of that unhappy Henry Jekyll to an end. [97]

The "life" being brought to an end is Henry Jekyll's "life-span" ("This is the true hour of my death, and what is to follow concerns another . . ."). But it is also the end of a "life" in the sense that in laying down the pen Jekyll ends his "confession," the narrative of his life. Finally, is the reader also to take Jekyll's remark about bringing his life to an end as a suicide threat? A scant page earlier, Jekyll has spoken of Hyde's "fear of death" and his fear of Jekyll's "power to cut him off by suicide" (96). Readers often wonder whether Jekyll or Hyde has committed suicide. Probably the short answer is Hyde. Many pages earlier, Utterson, coming upon a corpse that is definitely Hyde's, knows that he is "looking on the body of a self-destroyer" (70). But it is important that the ambiguities, puns, lack of clear personal boundaries, and mysteries in the concluding section not be overlooked, in this book where identity is itself so insistently fluid.

Certainly much is clarified by Jekyll's statement, but questions remain. The book seems to back away from its detective fiction premise that a detective's masterly exposition of the true story of the crime, or a series of narratives from different perspectives fitting together like a jigsaw puzzle, or the culprit's "confession" at the end, will enable the reader to feel mastery over the book's mysteries and permit the reader to work back to some absolute truth, presence, or sense of closure. The book's emphasis throughout on the problematics of both textuality and identity ought to give pause to the reader.

Consider first the book's attitude toward texts. *Jekyll and Hyde* centers on writings of various sorts, beyond the narratives that constitute its last chapters. The novel records a large number of letters, for example—both Lanyon's narrative chapter and Jekyll's full statement are letters—letters enclosed within letters. But there are many other letters back and forth throughout the book—ranging from dinner invitations, through polite requests to do one thing or another, to impassioned cries for help.[20] The detective plot is even generated from a written document, a will, "the startling clauses" (38) of which initially persuade Utterson that he must play "Mr. Seek" to Mr. Hyde. The story begins, in other words, with an odd, unfathomable document and never retreats from its focus on reading and interpreting.

Utterson is prompted to become a reader not only of wills and written texts but also of faces: "And still the figure had no face by which he might know it. . . . There sprang up and grew apace in the lawyer's mind a singularly strong, almost an inordinate, curiosity to behold the features of the real Mr. Hyde" (38–39). When he encounters Hyde, Utterson's question is, "Will you let me see your face?" (39), and he concludes that he has "read Satan's signature" there (40). Later, when he visits Dr. Lanyon, he finds the latter's "death-warrant written legibly upon his face" (57). Dr. Jekyll, too, peruses his two faces in the cheval glass: "Even as good shone upon the countenance of [Jekyll], evil was written broadly and plainly on the face of [Hyde]" (84). Indeed, the very first sentences in the book force the reader to try to read Utterson's face: "At friendly meetings, and when the wine was to his taste, something eminently human beaconed from his eye; something indeed which never found its way into his talk, but which spoke . . . in these silent symbols of the after-dinner face" (29).

Voices, too, must be "read" in the novel.[21] Poole brings Utterson to the door of Jekyll's cabinet to listen for "my master's voice" (64), and when they conclude they have heard Hyde, not Jekyll, they break down the door. Similarly, Hyde's "odd light footstep" is at various times the object of attention and interpretation (38, 69).

Even buildings participate in this hermeneutic. The entrances to the dwellings of Jekyll/Hyde—one wearing "a great air of wealth and comfort" (40), the other squalid and degenerate—obviously are inscribed with the divided personality of the inhabitant(s).[22] Hyde's dwelling is read as if it were a face encountered on the streets of Blake's "London," bearing "Marks of weakness, marks of woe":

> A certain sinister block of building . . . showed no window, nothing but a door on the lower storey and a blind *forehead* of discoloured wall on the upper; and bore in every *feature,* the marks of prolonged and sordid negligence. [30; my italics]

Reading goes on everywhere in the book, then, as a fundamental activity of life. Yet despite the search for voice, identity, explanation, and presence in these various kinds of inscription, the book insists on a kind of plasticity, absence, deferral, *différance.*[23]

An interesting example of this kind of play with language may be found in the book's fascination with the various meanings of the significant word, "double," in the concluding chapter. Jekyll writes of supplying "my double" with a signature (87) and reflects "on the issues and possibilities of my double existence" (88). But later in this same paragraph he speaks of increasing his dosage of the transforming drug "to double, and once . . . to treble the amount" (89). A few pages later he again alludes to the "double dose" he requires (95). He also calls himself a "double-dealer" (81), and later (as Hyde) describes himself as one who takes pains "to make assurance doubly sure" (91). In this chapter, the language of doubleness turns back on itself again and again, as if to signal the duplicity even of this key term.

The clearest indication of the refusal of words to be unambiguous, however, and the one most relevant to the genre of detective fiction, comes in the one link between Jekyll and Hyde in their different personalities, their handwriting. Jekyll invents a handwriting for his double "by sloping my own hand backwards" (87), so that Hyde can have his own checking account. The hands, in other words, both are and are not distinctly different. Utterson's clerk, Guest, quickly notices the resemblance between the two: "The two hands are in many points identical; only differently sloped" (55).[24] Stevenson stresses, however, that Jekyll and Hyde can write in either hand (93). Thus Hyde can write a note in Jekyll's hand to Lanyon, begging his assistance in obtaining more of the transforming chemical, or sign a check with Jekyll's signature, or annotate "a copy of a pious work, for which Jekyll had several times expressed a great esteem, . . . in his [Jekyll's] own hand, with startling blasphemies" (71). In this last instance, Hyde clearly becomes a mocking, demonic voice within Jekyll. Utterson frequently worries about handwriting in the text in order to draw a distinction between Jekyll and Hyde, but it turns out to be a distinction without a difference:

> "This is unquestionably the doctor's hand, do you know?" resumed the lawyer.
> "I thought it looked like it," said the servant [Poole]. . . .
> "But what matters hand of write? . . . I've seen him [i.e., Hyde]." [66]

Writing lacks the univocality and authority that an Utterson would wish. In an age before fingerprints, handwriting ought to be distinctive, unique, proof of identity, but in this book it isn't. Enfield's great concern, too, about the validity of Jekyll's signature on the check offered by Hyde is misplaced. It is counterfeit only in the sense that all signatures are "counterfeit," as Derrida has argued. That is, they presuppose the absence of the signer, the irrecoverable nature of his or her intentions, and a resistance to any constraints of meaning that the context may seem to impose.[25] The fact that the name of the signatory on the check is "very well known and often printed" (32) ought to give Enfield pause rather than reassure him, in a book that explores the equivocal nature of writing.

A revealing sense of the irrepressibly multivocal quality of texts emerges from the letter that Hyde prepares for the chemist in Jekyll's handwriting:

> "Dr. Jekyll presents his compliments to Messrs. Maw. He assures them that their last sample is impure and quite useless for his present purpose. In the year 18—, Dr. J. purchased a somewhat large quantity from Messrs. M. He now begs them to search with most sedulous care, and should any of the same quality be left, to forward it to him at once. Expense is no consideration. The importance of this to Dr. J. can hardly be exaggerated." So far the letter had run composedly enough; but here with a sudden splutter of the pen, the writer's emotion had broken loose. "For God's sake," he added, "find me some of the old." [66]

The "sudden splutter of the pen," where the writer's emotion erupts from the civilized veneer of Jekyll's style, is reminiscent of "Exterminate all the brutes!"—the terrible postscript of Kurtz's report to the Society for the Suppression of Savage Customs in Conrad's *Heart of Darkness,* an addendum that effectively undermines all the high-minded rhetoric that has preceded it. Writing, speech, language have this deconstructive power in *Jekyll and Hyde* as well. Jekyll's piety prompts Hyde's blasphemous commentary in the margin; handwriting slanted one way implies the possibility of the same words in the same hand slanted another way. Signatures, wills, letters, texts—or, for that matter, faces, houses, footsteps, and voices—ask to be read and invite interpretation, but they may equivocate. Like Jekyll's white salt, they tend to be mixed in nature and impure. Similarly, the detective fiction form of *Jekyll and Hyde,* with its concluding statements coming in nested series of envelopes, offering "two narratives in which this mystery was now to be explained" (73), promises more than it can deliver.

Personal identity, too, may be more equivocal than one is accustomed to finding in classic mystery and detective fiction. In the early development of that genre, it is not unusual to find a bifurcation of the whole personality in which good and evil are intermingled so that pure evil may emerge as dominant under certain circumstances. The presumptive drug-induced murderousness of John Jasper in *The Mystery of Edwin Drood* serves as an example of this.

Although Stevenson's story seems to start from similar, bipolar assumptions, with Henry Jekyll writing of the "thorough and primitive duality of man" (82), he soon makes clear that the implications of his project extend far beyond this:

With every day, and from both sides of my intelligence, the moral and the intellectual, I thus drew steadily nearer to that truth, by whose partial discovery I have been doomed to such a dreadful shipwreck: that man is not truly one, but truly two. I say two, because the state of my knowledge does not pass beyond that point. Others will follow, others will outstrip me on the same lines; and I hazard the guess that man will be ultimately known for a mere polity of multifarious, incongruous and independent denizens. [82]

Here is the ultimate threat posed in *Jekyll and Hyde,* not that one person is actually two, but that he is many—thus really not one person at all but lacking a coherent self or identity.

Both Peter Garrett and Ronald Thomas explore this topic of self-division in their essays in this volume and discuss the instability of the use of nouns and pronouns in Jekyll's "Full Statement"—how Jekyll/Hyde's "I" shifts to "he" [i.e., *not* "me"] or "Hyde" or "Jekyll" to enact, textually, this sense that the self is a "polity" of competing and irreconcilable voices. Both Garrett and Thomas also cite favorite examples of this confusion in "naming" the self. I will quote one more instance, to show how difficult it is to assign responsibility for culpable behavior to any single entity, how difficult it is to identify the criminal in this mystery story:

Into the details of the infamy at which I [Jekyll] thus connived (for even now I can scarce grant that I committed it) I have no design of entering; I mean but to point out the warnings and the successive steps with which my chastisement approached. I met with one accident which, as it brought no consequence, I shall no more than mention. An act of cruelty to a child aroused against me [Hyde] the anger of a passerby, whom I [Jekyll; cf. 60] recognised the other day in the person of your kinsman [Enfield]; the doctor and the child's family joined him; there were moments when I [Hyde?] feared for my life; and, at last, in order to pacify their too just resentment, Edward Hyde had to bring them to the door, and pay them in a cheque drawn in the name of Henry Jekyll. [87]

There is more than one way to account for the shifting references of the nouns and pronouns in a passage like this. Jekyll and Hyde are not absolutely distinct characters; they are two who are also one. Furthermore, perhaps the exigencies of writing a clear narrative prompt the strategies Stevenson employs here, to enable the reader to follow and understand who did what to whom. Yet these shifts seem also to express something of the book's fundamental attitudes toward responsibility, agency, and guilt. Hyde, Jekyll, and—in the sense of the "contamination" that Garrett writes about, as Hyde's behavior spreads to others—Enfield, the doctor, the child's family, and the reader are all implicated in this violence and rage, and there is no single, isolable malefactor to be named. Moreover, what is the standing, finally, of the voice that can allude to the "too just resentment" of those who confront Hyde? What possible position of moral authority remains?

The novel's terror comes, then, from the fear of losing control over the parts of the self, from losing any sense of a coherent personal identity, and we are here very much in the gothic tradition of Mary Shelley, Hogg, and Brockden Brown, rather than in the more orderly realm of the detective novel.[26] There is a sense that the terrifying, inexplicable violence within the person and within society will break out once again, that conventional restraints will shatter, and that the belief in personal continuity and identity will prove unsustainable. There is a sense, in other words, of the corrosive presence of gothic passion in a narrative that might look to be organized as detective fiction. The gothic core becomes, like Hyde, "the slime of the pit [that seems] to utter cries and voices" (95).

Another image in the book that expresses something of the ambivalent attitudes toward the subversive, gothic elements it incorporates may be found in Utterson's perception of the lifting and resettling of the fog that shrouds Hyde's Soho environment:

> As the cab drew up before the address indicated, the fog lifted a little and showed him a dingy street, a gin palace, a low French eating-house, a shop for the retail of penny numbers and two-penny salads, many ragged children huddled in the doorways, and many women of many different nationalities passing out, key in hand, to have a morning glass; and the next moment the fog settled down again upon that part, as brown as umber, and cut [Utterson] off from his blackguardly surroundings. [48]

Like Henry Jekyll writing, "He, I say—I cannot say, I" (94), Utterson might *will* this cutting off of the blackguardly from his own respectability, but the novel itself refuses to permit a walling off of gothic passion and violence from reason, order, structure. Rather, it inhabits the foggy space between its gothic premise and its detective fiction structure, permitting its volatile, gothic elements to question the too-easy reassurances of detection.

Stevenson's novel, then, explodes the genre of detective fiction just at that point when, with Doyle, it is about to develop its essential form. The rationalist, bourgeois assumptions of the genre are challenged by the Romantic gothic attitudes that are inscribed in its origins. The psychological focus and epistemological skepticism of the gothic deconstructs the detective genre as Stevenson explores it. For one thing, personality is so riddled and divided that the detective himself is prey to his own repressions and contradictions. He is implicated in the "crimes" and mysteries he is investigating, though he has no awareness of this. As a result he becomes an object of some sport to the third-person narrator—a "Mr. Utterson," who can be treated formally, distantly, ironically. Because there is no disinterested, objective, rational ground on which the detective might stand, there is no possibility of a response to Dr. Jekyll's "confession"; there is no return to the presumed recipient of that statement, Utterson, for an evaluation of it. He vanishes from the end of the book in an unexpected and inexplicable way, just as he presumably attempts to grasp the significance of his investigations.

Furthermore, there is no criminal. His character is absolute multiplicity, to such a degree that even his narrative voice fractures into competing and incoherent selves. A number of the facts of the case cannot be established. *Some*one—whether Jekyll or Hyde—commits suicide. *Some*body is left behind dead on the floor. *Some*one wrote the last chapter, but the sense of decentering is expressed by the drift of the nouns and pronouns in the narration. The I-narrator here is less a person, a personality, an identity than a consciousness, a memory, an observer of the various constituents of the self. The "I" of this chapter is largely a narrative consciousness, neither Jekyll nor Hyde, a consciousness apart from any personality or identity. To the extent that the book has closure, it derives from the appended "confession" of an author who is dead, who has stage-managed his own "disappearance or unexplained absence" (35). The last chapter retells the story, in the manner of detective fiction, but it finally ends in puns and ambiguities—its mysteries (dis)solved. Sherlock Holmes, the rationalist detective, and all he stands for, are put under a kind of Derridean erasure at the very moment of origin by Stevenson's story; the figure of the detective is present, yet also strangely cancelled through. If the criminal is fragmented and the detective implicated in his crimes, and if reason itself, the essential tool of the detective, is tainted through its alliance with a particular class and distorted by the prism of individual psychology through which it must pass in order to be applied, then the gothic epistemology of Stevenson's book threatens the very method of detection and puts in question the effectiveness of the new, idealized type of ratiocinative detective who will debut in 1887, one year after *Jekyll and Hyde*.

NOTES

I wish to thank Michael Hanchor, Elizabeth Hirsch, Marty Roth, and William Veeder for their helpful criticism of the drafts of this essay.

1. There are some noteworthy biographical ties between Stevenson and Mary Shelley as well. Stevenson moved to Bournemouth in August 1884, about a

year before he began to write *Jekyll and Hyde,* and there he met and developed a close relationship with Shelley's son and daughter-in-law, Sir Percy and Lady Shelley. He dedicated *The Master of Ballantrae* (1889) to these friends, after having left England for the South Seas. Given this friendship, Stevenson must also have known that Mary Shelley was buried in the graveyard at St. Peter's Church, Bournemouth, after her death in 1851. See Furnas, *Voyage to Windward,* 237; Calder 206; and also L2, 210, 284–85, 325–26.

2. Mary Shelley, *Frankenstein; or, The Modern Prometheus,* ed. Harold Bloom (New York: New American Library, 1965), 37 and 36.

3. Edwin Eigner (161–64) is the only previous critic to discuss in detail the links between *Jekyll and Hyde* and *Frankenstein.* He considers such items as the motif of the double, but emphasizes the excessive self-righteousness of the protagonist and his inability to accept his own mixed nature. In fact, Eigner uses *Frankenstein* as a device to read *Jekyll and Hyde* as the "story of a creature turned diabolic in response to the hatred and rejection afforded him by society and by the man to whom he owes his life," a reading that advances his idea that Hyde "could have been a useful part" of Jekyll's character—"not when we first meet him . . . but earlier, in the days before Jekyll began to live his double life"— essentially outside the time frame of the novel, in other words.

4. Shelley recounts her dream in her 1831 "Author's Introduction": "The pale student of unhallowed arts . . . sleeps, but he is awakened; he opens his eyes; behold, the horrid thing stands at his bedside, opening his curtains and looking on him with yellow, watery, but speculative eyes." This causes Shelley to open *her* eyes in terror and to make "a transcript of the grim terrors of my waking dream" (x–xi), which becomes the start of her book. Stevenson describes the influence of *his* dreams on the genesis of *Jekyll and Hyde* in "A Chapter on Dreams"; see also Kanzer for commentary. Utterson's dreams are the only ones recounted in *Jekyll and Hyde,* but they are, as one might expect, striking and revealing as regards his obsession with Hyde. Curiously, a few pages after the dream passage cited in the text, he alludes to it as if it described an actual moment in Jekyll's life: "It turns me quite cold to think of this creature stealing like a thief to Harry's bedside; poor Harry, what an awakening!" (42).

5. Andrew Jefford (in Noble 60–63) makes a similar point about the "indeterminacy" of Hyde. He argues that this use of such an undefined signifier is more effective than any more specific image of "evil" could be. My view is similar, though I see Hyde less as a general signifier of "evil" than as a specifically gothic device, identified with violence and sadism, beyond the pale of precise description and outside the social order.

6. Vladimir Nabokov notes without amplification that "the only thing we do guess about Hyde's pleasures is that they are sadistic—he enjoys the infliction of pain" (196). He is typical of a number of critics who in a general way allude to, but choose not to confront, Hyde's sadism.

7. The rationale for this move is that "today's mystery story is the very negation of style, being, at the best, conventional literature," and Nabokov's intent is to praise *Jekyll and Hyde* as "a phenomenon of style" (179–80).

8. Jacques Barzun and Wendell Hertig Taylor, *A Catalogue of Crime* (New York: Harper, 1971), 5.

9. Ian Ousby, *Bloodhounds of Heaven: The Detective in English Fiction from Godwin to Doyle* (Cambridge, Mass.: Harvard University Press, 1976), 145–46.

10. *The Works of Robert Louis Stevenson,* South Seas Edition (New York: Scribner's, 1925), 8:10.

11. John Cawelti, *Adventure, Mystery, and Romance: Formula Stories as Art and Popular Culture* (Chicago: University of Chicago Press, 1976), 100–1. Poe was a particular favorite with Stevenson, who had already adapted elements from Poe's stories in *Treasure Island* (published 1883) and "Markheim" (written 1884–85). In the 2 January 1875 issue of *The Academy,* Stevenson published a review of an edition of Poe's *Works* in which he especially recommended "the three stories about C. August Dupin, the philosophical detective," to prospective readers (*Works of Stevenson,* 5:329).

12. Charles Dickens, *Bleak House,* ed. Norman Page (Harmondsworth: Penguin Books, 1981), 824.

13. Stevenson seems at his most Dickensian during the morning cab ride that Utterson and the police inspector take into the fog-shrouded quarter of Soho where Hyde lives, describing "its muddy ways, and slatternly passengers, and its lamps, which had never been extinguished or had been kindled afresh to combat this mournful reinvasion of darkness"; its twilight glow of "a rich, lurid brown, like the light of some strange conflagration"; and the momentary intrusions of "a haggard shaft of daylight" (48). There are a number of echoes of *Bleak House* here, ranging from Krook's spontaneous combustion (certainly, a "strange conflagration") to the mud, the "slipping and sliding" foot passengers, the expression of doubt whether "this day ever broke," and the "haggard and unwilling look" of the gas lamps "lighted two hours before their time"—all of which may be found in the opening three paragraphs of Dickens's novel. The motif of the police detective's penetration of one of London's less reputable districts may have prompted this virtuoso Dickensian performance by Stevenson.

14. William Patrick Day briefly notes that Utterson is a kind of detective, but dismisses the idea because he is unsuccessful and baffled (58). The point is a helpful one, though, and worth the fuller discussion here.

15. A. E. Murch shows how Stevenson, in subsequent books such as *The Wrong Box* (1888) and *The Wrecker* (1892), alludes to, and employs some of the devices of, detective fiction, but Murch argues that Stevenson's attitudes toward that genre remain divided (*The Development of the Detective Novel* [New York: Philosophical Library, 1958], 142–44). In *The Wrecker,* Stevenson describes "the police novel or mystery story" as "enthralling, but insignificant, like a game of chess, not a work of human art" (*Works of Stevenson* [n. 10, above], 21:422)—expressing some of the same ambivalence he felt generally toward literature written for mass audiences. This ambivalence toward popular fiction is the subject of the essay by Brantlinger and Boyle in this volume.

16. Jacques Lacan, "Seminar on 'The Purloined Letter,'" *Yale French Studies* 48 (1973): 71–72.

17. Stevenson has Jekyll characteristically adopt the rhetoric of concealment and evasion in his earlier exchanges with his friends. Notice the emphasis on

goodness and amity, the formality of the constructions, the exaggerated expressions of politeness and deference, and the repetitive circularity of these two examples of Jekyll's conversation:

> My good Utterson, . . . this is very good of you, this is downright good of you, and I cannot find words to thank you in. I believe you fully; I would trust you before any man alive, ay, before myself, if I could make the choice; but indeed it isn't what you fancy; it is not so bad as that; and just to put your good heart at rest, I will tell you one thing: the moment I choose, I can be rid of Mr. Hyde. I give you my hand upon that; and I thank you again and again; and I will just add one little word, Utterson, that I'm sure you'll take in good part: this is a private matter, and I beg of you to let it sleep. [44]

> You are very good. . . . I should like to [take a quick turn with you] very much; but no, no, no, it is quite impossible; I dare not. But indeed, Utterson, I am very glad to see you; this is really a great pleasure. I would ask you and Mr. Enfield up, but the place is really not fit. [60–61]

18. In keeping with the punning manner of this book, Jekyll's statement of the "case" is truly an argument made from a specific point of view, as well as an exposition of a matter requiring an investigation by the police, and even the record of a medical case history. The novel uses the word "case" variously throughout, as in the chapter title, "The Carew Murder Case," the book's full title (*Strange Case . . .*), and Dr. Lanyon's belief that with Jekyll he is "dealing with a case of cerebral disease" (77).

19. This question has prompted Jerome Charyn, in his afterward to *Dr. Jekyll and Mr. Hyde* (New York: Bantam Books, 1981) to indulge in two pages of speculation. One explanation he offers is this: "Isn't it possible that the kind old man is attempting to 'proposition' Hyde, and that Hyde trampled him out of rage?" As Charyn acknowledges, "We'll never know" (113).

20. One of the more curious of these letters is the one addressed to Utterson that Sir Danvers Carew is said to be out to mail when he is murdered. Its purpose and contents remain a mystery, even at the book's close.

21. Likewise voices must frequently be "read" in detective fiction. In "The Murders in the Rue Morgue," a key to the solution of the crime is Dupin's ability to interpret the difference between the gruff voice of the French sailor and the shrill voice of the "foreigner," who turns out to be the orangutan-murderer.

22. For a full discussion of Jekyll's divided house, see Nabokov 184–88.

23. See Jacques Derrida, "Différance," *Margins of Philosophy,* tr. Alan Bass (Chicago: University of Chicago Press, 1982), 1–27.

24. It is interesting that this identification is made by one who himself belongs and yet does not belong, whose name, Guest, itself suggests a primal kind of alienation and "différance."

25. See Jacques Derrida, "Signature Event Context," *Margins,* 307–30.

26. One of the most striking earlier expressions (1824) of this sense of self-fragmentation comes from Robert Wringhim in *The Private Memoirs and Confessions of a Justified Sinner,* by Stevenson's Scots predecessor, James Hogg: "I generally conceived myself to be two people. . . . [However,] the most

perverse part of it was that I rarely conceived *myself* to be any of the two persons. I thought for the most part that my companion [Gil-Martin] was one of them and my brother the other; and I found that, to be obliged to speak and answer in the character of another man, was a most awkward business at the long run" ([New York: W. W. Norton and Co., 1970], 139–40). On the evidence of a passage like this, it would seem that the history of the modern "schizo-text," which Ronald Thomas traces from Stevenson to Beckett in his essay in this volume, extends well back into Romantic gothic as well.

GORDON HIRSCH

Reframing *Jekyll and Hyde:* Robert Louis Stevenson and the Strange Case of Gothic Science Fiction

DONALD LAWLER

In this essay, I propose reading *Strange Case of Dr Jekyll and Mr Hyde* from the perspective of science fiction. Few SF critics have shown much interest in *Jekyll and Hyde,* perhaps because of its more prominent fantastic and gothic features; and yet this novel appears to occupy an important if unappreciated transitional position in the history of SF.[1] As we reframe *Jekyll and Hyde* by reading it (however marginally) as a gothic SF novel, hidden sources of its literary power are discovered in mythic transformations of ideas from the gothic fantastic and science, performed early in the development of both modern science and gothic SF.

Mary Shelley was the first writer to apply the transforming power of the gothic fantastic to the emerging techne of science and discover in the latter an active, mythic core. *Frankenstein* was the first gothic SF novel and, along with later works such as *Jekyll and Hyde,* foreshadowed disturbing intellectual and social aspects of scientific thinking and predicted that the coming struggle between the competing imperatives of the empirical and the humane in science would be a definitive one for the mind of the future. This struggle is one in which the present generation remains deeply involved.

New sources of literary power were derived later in the century from the speculations of physicists, especially in thermodynamics, and from Darwinist psychology and biology. Ideas from these and other new sciences were to become resources of symbolic expression for the emerging traditions of gothic SF. The complex interaction of the gothic fantastic with SF can only be suggested in the following pages, however, by looking to the early development of gothic SF from *Frankenstein* to *The Island of Dr. Moreau;* to some of the formal or *genre* results of conjugating SF in the gothic mode; and to the literary, scientific, and psychological forces that influenced the shaping of *Jekyll and Hyde* as a gothic SF novel.

Critics of science fiction seem agreed that modern SF begins with Mary Shelley's *Frankenstein*. As such, the new genre begins not with a celebration of science but instead by undercutting its subject matter with powerful, freshly minted stereotypes such as the mad scientist and his self-made alter ego, the monster. Mary Shelley's bogeys were the means of mythologizing science and producing the archetypal cautionary tale for a new, scientific era that was beginning. The conjunction of gothic, fantastic, and SF, therefore, starts with *Frankenstein*, which not only mythologized but also gothicized science, thereby inventing a symbolic mode for expressing the impact that science was beginning to produce on the human imagination.

It is true that there is little enough science in *Frankenstein*, but little was needed for Mary Shelley to discover in her modern Prometheus the mythic potential of science and its applied technology. Hers was a hero prepared to steal fire from heaven in the form of electric current and bring forth the new man. If science had not yet become a dominant cultural force, Mary Shelley's smattering of anatomy and biology, supplemented by rumors of Galvani's experimental animation of severed frogs' legs by means of electric fluxion, was all the science she required to storm the popular imagination. She gave the world a new image of itself in the destructive innocence of the man-made monster, produced in a laboratory, possessing neither soul nor name, left to rage against the constraints of the society that rejected him. In the relation between the Frankensteins, Shelley confronted the scientist with the obligations of his own science, both for that and future ages.

Mary Shelley invented SF by combining wild surmises about science with the dynamic psychological potentials of the gothic fantastic. It was the impact of the gothic fantastic on a nascent SF that accounts for much of the macabre symbolism of gothic SF and the curious, prophetic resonances found in later works shaped by its traditions, including *Jekyll and Hyde*.

The second of the early contributors to the gothic SF features of *Jekyll and Hyde* was Edgar Allan Poe. In addition to horror-adventure tales such as "Descent into the Maelstrom" and "The Narrative of A. Gordon Pym," there were stories such as "The Facts in the Case of M. Valdemar" and "Mesmeric Revelation," which further develop Shelleyan gothic SF, marking advances in the artistic management of both science and the gothic. Other tales and poems touching on variations of scientific themes ("Mellonta Tauta" and "The Conversation of Eiros and Charmion") are complemented by hoax tales with important SF elements, such as "Von Kempelen and His Discovery," "Maelzel's Chess Player," "The

DONALD LAWLER

Unparalleled Adventures of One Hans Pfaall," "The Balloon Hoax," and "Some Words with a Mummy." In these tales, the hoaxing appears to be played more on the characters than on the reader (or at least on Poe's more competent, Whiggish reader). In one way or another, these stories develop the premise of the deceptive nature of appearances and the inherent credulity of the scientifically minded.

These two variants of gothic and fantastic SF, emphasizing the horrific and hoaxing potentials of science, were to have their impact later in the century on Stevenson's *Jekyll and Hyde* and on subsequent writers from Wells to Vonnegut.[2]

II

The formal or genre traditions of gothic SF that help shape *Jekyll and Hyde,* therefore, arise from the gothic fantastic and from SF. The gothic contributes a psychosexual force generated by forbidden, repressed desire, which operates on both the structural and the psychological levels. Structurally, it accounts for the fragmented point of view, the multiple narrators, the themes of the self-created other self, the repressed narcissism of the hero that transforms him into an antihero, and the horrifying, symbolic qualities of the monster. In works like *Frankenstein* and *Jekyll and Hyde,* an autobiographical or confessional impulse is also active behind the symbolic encapsulation of repressed childhood desires. Freud could well have used either novel to supplement his remarks on *Oedipus the King* as an illustration of repressed infant sexuality and its consequences.

These points of genre are important because they contribute materially to the complex, artistic relationship between the emerging hybrid form of gothic SF and the allegorically driven, thematic design of *Jekyll and Hyde.* There is a tension and energy in the traditions of gothic SF to match the allegorical and psychological intentions of the narrative. Stevenson understood that these genre features resonated with other elements of the narrative. Varying the angles of critical inquiry reveals, for example, how psychology in *Jekyll and Hyde* serves the moral allegory, dramatizing the anti-Victorian lesson that Hyde is evil and repulsive because repressed and denied. As Hyde is the extension of Jekyll, gothic SF is an extension of science. In Stevenson's novel, this analogy, although central, has been overlooked and its implications all but lost. By this token, the gothic relationship between Jekyll and Hyde is more complicated than the Stevensons themselves could have guessed without knowing the twentieth century.

Implications of gothicized science are substantially advanced in the relationship between Jekyll and Hyde, attaining the status of a mythic revelation of hidden, perhaps even repressed, recognition that the technical application of new scientific thinking is a flawed and perhaps fatal enterprise.[3]

Supplementing the enthralled desire of gothic,[4] the fantastic contributes its own source of aesthetic power through its law of dynamic transformation: anything can become anything else. It is the idea of magic that lies at the heart of imagined, alternative realities, and it underlies the transformations apparent to everyone in *Jekyll and Hyde*.

Let us note that Stevenson's emphasis is not on scientific process but rather on those effects of transformation more fantastic than experimental. Possibly, this should be attributed to the effects of the allegory at work, or perhaps the traditional practice of gothic SF obliged Stevenson to defer formal introduction of scientific issues. Instead of stressing experimental process, Stevenson begins by emphasizing Hyde's absurdly, almost comically phallic manner—a condition that may account for both Enfield's and Utterson's instant aversion to Hyde's appearance and their inability to describe what they find so offensive in his appearance except in language that is heavily expurgated and censored. The force that overbalances a threatened outbreak of the comic is the sense of terror—a horror that comes from within the narrators and shares the universal condition of a common, corruptible nature. In these terms, gothicism is the psychodramatic representation of sin and its consequences without a redeeming theology and consequently without its sense of hope. The gothic and fantastic modes secularize the religious content of their archetypes.

The third genre in terms of which we are reading Stevenson's novel is SF, a modern genre in process of formation during the nineteenth century. Each of the major writers who mythologized the ideas of science made a contribution toward determining genre process. Even though in *Jekyll and Hyde* Stevenson does not try to explain or even theorize about how Jekyll is metamorphosed into Hyde, he makes it clear that the trick is done with chemicals. It may seem more like alchemy than pharmacology or chemistry, just as Frankenstein appears more practiced in hermetic arts rather than in anatomy or biology. Nevertheless, Stevenson's choice of chemicals rather than spells was critical because the substances remove the logic of the story from the realm of the fantastic into the scientific. The probabilities change.

One effect of Stevenson's placing *Jekyll and Hyde* within the tradition of gothic SF was to affirm, along with Shelley, Poe, and Hawthorne, that psychosexual forces are active at the conjunction of empirical reason with that portion of the creative imagination supplying the metaphors of science. The very idea that science uses figuration to give birth and expression to its most basic ideas would have been considered nonsense by Victorian scientists, and yet the dependence of science on figuration

　　　　　　　　　　　　　　　　　　DONALD LAWLER

and even myth has currently gained wide acceptance. It has become almost a commonplace of discourse among those probing the relationship between science and literature since the Victorian period.⁵ One of the forms taken by the mythic extension of scientific thinking has been SF, which may be described as thinking mythically about science.

III

Although there is little more science in *Jekyll and Hyde* than *Frankenstein*, what there is has a potential impact far greater than the casual reader may think, both in its own terms and in those of the gothic fantastic elements we have been examining. When Mary Shelley "gave her intended 'ghost story' a scientific context, she linked the gothic concept of the double with technology,"⁶ a union in which the hidden sources of psychic energy underlying scientific enterprise, especially what Louis Mumford calls "technics," are given forceful symbolic expression.⁷

The consequences of that conjunction are significant. For one thing, because gothic is essentially parodic,⁸ the mode undercuts heroic control, serving up instead parodies of the conventions of SF and, as Gordon Hirsch discusses, the detective story, and transforming the hero from one who, as Sherlock Holmes says, creates narrative through the scientific use of imagination, into an overreaching and ultimately ineffective antihero. Nor is the reader permitted the heroic exercise of solution and resolution, as in some fantastic SF forms (such as space opera) because, typically, gothic SF narratives are incomplete, unfinished, or unresolved. In a gothic story, to organize, complete, or resolve the narrative is, aesthetically, to escape the nightmare of the gothic world (as in *Dracula*). More commonly, the gothic tale ends with the victory of those unspeakable powers of enthralled desire.

Genre features help to identify Jekyll as a gothic antihero. Some parodic vectors of the gothic are revealed in the futility of Jekyll's philosophy, in his failed science, and in his amateurish use of impure chemicals. Failure in place of prior self-assurance and anticipated success is a feature of gothicized science discovered in Mary Shelley and, in a more sprightly manner, in Poe. *Frankenstein*'s prophetic vision of the moral, psychic, and physical flaws of the scientist are expressed in failed science, parodied in Poe's Von Kampelen and Count Allamistakeo, and implicated in Jekyll's self-experiments and their outcomes. Historically, SF has been, above all else, a cultural critique of science; but gothic SF goes further still.

We have seen that the first great invention of gothic SF was a gothicized science, which subverts rational science by allowing direct access to the unconscious or preconscious self. This was a new way of expressing science as a human force—that is, as the extension of physically charged inner states, marked by conflicts of dominance and repression. If Jekyll's experiments are evaluated within the framework of gothic SF, two things become clear about them. First, the story represents a case study of degeneration—one of the important scientific topics of the day, then understood as a corollary of recessive Darwinism. And second, there are important differences in the attitudes expressed by Robert Louis Stevenson and Mary Shelley toward science in their benchmark, gothic SF novels.

There may be in Jekyll's experiment a veiled social reference to Hyde's behavior as the urban equivalent of "going native,"[9] although Hyde may be closer to Wells's Morlocks than to Conrad's Kurtz. Still, there is no doubt that Hyde represents pre-evolved man in his atavistic, degenerated physical and psychological state. Jekyll himself goes even further:

> This was the shocking thing; that the slime of the pit seemed to utter cries and voices; that the amorphous dust gesticulated and sinned; that what was dead, and had no shape, should usurp the offices of life. [95]

Hyde appears to Jekyll so primitive as to be primordial, a lost link between the preanimate and animate life of the mind. Perhaps the most shocking thing is the overt, macabre gothicism of death claiming the offices of life. Equally strange seems Jekyll's tolerance of Hyde—no doubt the result of the doubled self; but we are surprised that the parodic imp of gothic SF should have transformed Jekyll from the familiar scientist as quest-hero into the seriocomic scientist-as-bungler. Although we may go back to the self-deluded Frankenstein for a model of malpractice, or later to Poe's Von Kempelen for the scientist as eccentric, or later still to Hawthorne's Aylmer for the scientist as puritan, Stevenson had an instructive predecessor of his own even closer to hand in a work he had completed only weeks before beginning *Jekyll and Hyde*.

It will be worth our while to focus briefly on this potboiler novel that Robert produced with Fanny Stevenson titled *More New Arabian Nights: The Dynamiter*, because it anticipates and therefore emphasizes certain key themes of the subsequent *Jekyll and Hyde,* and it helps establish the active influences at work in the author's imagination at that time. *The Dynamiter* represents London as a coney-catching playground for inquisitive youth, filled with deceiving people, especially one young woman of multiple identities. The story seems a fit preparation for the gothicized London of *Jekyll and Hyde.* Setting the tone for hoaxing the naive, inexperienced young adventurers is Stevenson's vision of "chance, the blind Madonna of the Pagan [that] rules this terrestrial bustle."[10] This phrase echoes a more pointed description in "A Humble Remonstrance": "Life is monstrous, infinite, illogical, abrupt and poignant: a

DONALD LAWLER

work of art, in comparison, is neat, finite, self-contained, rational, flowing and emasculate."

Illustrating chance and mischance in the scientific and mechanical order in this story is Dr. Grierson, known as "The Destroying Angel" (a sort of nineteenth-century Morman anticipation of Josef Mengele). In addition to getting rid of enemies of the "unsleeping eye" of the Morman church by means of explosive or corrosive agents, Grierson has been working for years on a formula for the elixir of life. Recapturing youth will be his own way of escaping the eye. But there are difficulties that lead to a series of spectacular failures: "A difficulty unforeseen—the impossibility of obtaining a drug in its full purity" (69). Grierson becomes convinced, as Jekyll later realizes, that "the singularly unstable equilibrium of the elixir . . . is due rather to the impurity than to the nature of the ingredients . . ." (74).

How are we to interpret such problems? Are Grierson and Jekyll inept pharmacologists, the reach of whose ambition has exceeded the grasp of their skills; or are they the exasperated victims of commercial preparations misrepresented as pure? Either way, they approach the ridiculous, hoaxed state of Poe's inventors and adventurers. Ironically, Grierson confides that he had come to London because nowhere else could he be certain of getting the pure stuff. Perhaps he, too, was a deceived patron of Messrs. Maw, where Jekyll bought the original ingredients for his formula. And yet for such a research scientist as Jekyll, a test for the purity of his chemicals should have been the very first step. Could he have been so distracted that he simply rushed headlong toward his encounter with Hyde by the shortest route? Or is the reader being duped by a Stevenson hoax?

Given the history of gothic SF, the potential for hoaxing cannot be ignored, but we should also remember that the gothic predicts failure of the hero at the very moment when success is both indispensable and anticipated. And that is precisely what happens to Jekyll. Another possible answer to the riddle of Jekyll's failure suggests itself in the very framework of its incongruity. Jekyll's reputation as well as the reader's presumptions may be casualties of the pattern of incongruity or randomness that the new scientific thinking was finding almost everywhere it looked at this time. In other words, for Stevenson the incongruity was intentional.

Another, related theme of *Jekyll and Hyde* seems to have been anticipated in the character of the dynamiter himself, a fellow bearing the burlesque code name "Zero." Speaking to his jittery landlord, the terrorist Zero complains (184), "When you speak of ease . . . in this age of scientific studies, you fill me with surprise. Are you not aware that chemicals are proverbially as fickle as woman and clockwork [the which he uses for his time bombs] as capricious as the very devil?" Zero and Jekyll learn the hard way the lesson that using chemicals is a throw of the dice and that nature (as metaphorically represented by the chemicals) is not to be depended on any more than the work of men (as represented by clocks). The fate of Zero is as melancholy if not as pathetic as Jekyll's: all Zero's bombs fail or misfire, except for the last, which finally blows him up. As his fate presages, there is a reciprocal level of risk in the use of science and technics. The more they are depended on, the less dependable they prove.

Stevenson's seriocomic treatment of contemporary terrorism is supported by his representation of Nature as flawed, fickle, and undependable for the unfortunate Zero. In turn, this view of nature rests on the conclusions of several contemporary scientists, whose contributions to formulating the second law of thermodynamics as statistically probable rather than certain were having a broad impact on late-nineteenth-century culture.[11] Rudolf Clausius and Lord Kelvin began their separate studies of the mechanical transfer of heat energy in the late 1840s. By the mid-sixties, Clausius had presented his vision of entropy while Lord Kelvin had published his conclusions on the continuous degradation of energy. By the mid-seventies, with contributions by Fechner and Helmholtz, the concept "of a final state of the universe that would result from the dissipation of all useful energy by transformation into heat at a uniform temperature" had been presented (Brush 65). As the new physics saw it, therefore, the "heat death" of the universe was the scientific vision of that goal toward which the whole creation moved. Elegant Jeremiahs indeed! Reinforcing this gloomy vision of the future were the Darwinist psychologists, whose ideas of devolution and degeneration as corollaries of evolution inspired Cesare Lombroso's controversial theory of recapitulation in criminal anthropology: "*adults* and *inferior* groups must be like *children* of superior groups, for the child represents a primitive adult ancestor."[12]

Although we may well find a theoretical basis in recapitulation for the appearance of Hyde, the degeneration of the overreacher Jekyll has still subtler applications.

> According to Boltzmann's interpretation of entropy, the message of the second law of thermodynamics becomes: there is a universal tendency for things to get more and more disordered. The molecular explanation of this tendency is simply that the overwhelming majority of all possible states are disordered, and thus if you start out from an ordered state the likelihood that you will reach some disordered state after any finite period of time is very high. [Brush 67]

This extension of the second law of thermodynamics was known as the theory of "molecular disorder," and it implied an underlying randomness in nature at the molecular level. These theories and their applications in related fields have a direct relevance for *Jekyll and Hyde* as a work of gothic SF. Chance and miscalculation occurring in Jekyll's experiments should have been considered neither unprecedented nor unexpected. Indeed, quite the reverse. And their function as agents of entropy precisely parallels the increasing disorder of Jekyll's moral life. Our encounters with Jekyll's misjudgment and professional incompetence provide more than an instructive contrast to the confident, progressive positivism of Jekyll before Hyde. Implied is the larger context of social and universal disorder as related forms of entropy that undercut the intentions of the characters in *Jekyll and Hyde*, mocking their attempts at leading orderly, coherent lives, let alone controlling experiments or solving mysteries of identity.

We cannot avoid the conclusion that the related theories of recessive Darwinism, molecular randomness, and entropy made important contributions to the current fund of ideas on which Stevenson drew. At a time when contemporary SF was dominated by Verne's engineering optimism, Stevenson anticipated Wells in preferring the more speculative and darker symbolism of entropy.[13]

Stevenson's attitudes toward science and nature differed considerably from Mary Shelley's. For one thing, this difference reflects their historical distance from one another, and the similarities of their stories and of their heroes only emphasize the authors' differences in outlook. To Mary Shelley, the universe remains morally sane, however fragile its laws. Aberrations were possible, they had been always possible, as classical mythology testified; but they were the results of old chaos or of Promethean overreaching. In the end, as in mythology, balance was restorable, even if restoration required intervention of the fates or furies. In *Frankenstein*, the narrator, Walton, is our test case. Hearing Frankenstein's story, he abandons his own obsessive quest and publishes (or causes his sister to publish) a tale that is at least in part a parable against intellectual pride and self-destroying obsessive egoism. As for Walton, he hears the voice of both reason and need in the petitions and threats of his crew, abandoning his own quest of greatness before a blood debt must be paid. As Frankenstein ends his story, he consoles himself with the same hope as the later Jekyll: that another may succeed where he has failed, presumably one who has learned the lesson of his narrative. Mary Shelley implies that a rational science may succeed where a science contaminated by superstition and driven by the ambition of a morally immature scientist has failed.

For the parallel scene in *Jekyll and Hyde*, we turn to the final chapter, Jekyll's "Full and Final Statement of the Case," which, as several contributors to our volume have noted, is in typically gothic style neither full nor final. "Others will follow, others will outstrip me on the same lines; and I hazard the guess that man will be ultimately known for a mere polity of multifarious, incongruous and independent denizens" (82). Such a world has become not only irrational but morally insane.[14] Behind appearances there were the forces of entropy and molecular randomness, bringing about that cosmic desiderata, that state of natural balance and equilibrium revealed by science and described in anthropomorphic terms as the heat death of the universe.[15] Biologically, this philosophy expresses itself, as we have seen already, in theories of devolution and degeneration—the coming down of what once went up. Both Hyde and Jekyll should be evaluated in these terms. In Hyde it is easy to see both degeneration and devolution. We must look more closely to discover that Jekyll the scientist is foiled not through simple incompetence or even errors made in haste or under unusual stress. His undoing is the result of the convergence of several factors, including the psychic fragmentation that is the destiny of the gothic SF hero, played against the randomness and entropy of nature.

No doubt there is a great deal of symbolic weight in the fact that Jekyll's materials were impure to begin with, making it impossible for pure materials to have the same effect. But let us remember that even the original formula did not work uniformly—how could it?—suggesting, among other things, both molecular randomness, on the one hand, and the psychodynamics of the relationship between Jekyll and Hyde on the other. It seems, therefore, that only in chaos and uncertainty is the creative energy of life to be found. In such a world, are we to expect stability and uniformity?

Stevenson's novel appears to reinforce the paradox that order is unnatural and not productive of life and perhaps that we are even deluded to expect otherwise. If we look at the more typically upright Victorian men of the novel, Utterson and Enfield seem not merely anomalous in their sanity but rigidly isolated, self-contained, and sterile. Despite the horrible fates reserved for Jekyll and Hyde, neither Utterson nor Enfield, considered as foils, wins our sympathetic admiration. They are little more than requirements of storytelling. Their reward for respectability is to have no family, nothing to leave behind, and nothing of themselves to write about. At least Jekyll produced Hyde. Even Dr. Lanyon's death expressed a more sympathetic understanding of his friend, Jekyll, than all the snooping of Utterson. We may surmise that Lanyon abandoned the moral superiority of his class out of both sympathy for Jekyll and a common shame. For him, the emblematic meaning

DONALD LAWLER

of the Hyde-into-Jekyll transformation was a shocked recognition of the repressed avatar hidden in his own nature.

Unlike Frankenstein, Jekyll hardly raises the possibility of restored balance or an integrating vision of life. Rather than the classical assumption of reason satisfied if not triumphant, Jekyll's intuition is the more modern one of a world disintegrated, precariously balanced between a human subjective delusion of order and the uncertainties of nature's principles. In the mid-seventies, Lord Kelvin concluded that not even entropy itself was certain! Is it to be wondered that these ideas as well as the attitudes engendered by them found expression in SF?

In gothic SF the additional transformative impulses of the fantastic were carried into the heart of SF from the start, producing a madly prophetic symbolism of serious disorder in the philosophy of science and its growing hegemony over the modern mind. In the persistence of gothic SF, we behold not anachronism but rather a progressive vehicle of expression for humanizing, however erratically and grotesquely, the unrepresented in nature, as implied in scientific concepts of devolution, randomness, indeterminacy, and the rest of the new ideas that enthralled the nineteenth-century mind to powerful metaphors of despair.

Therein lies the catch to which gothic SF and *Jekyll and Hyde* gave symbolic form long before it arose to challenge the minds of the great modern, natural philosophers: Einstein, Heisenberg, Bohr, Gödel, and Shannon. In the gothic world, this catch finds its voice: if science begins at the underside of consciousness, it is predestined to create monstrous self-projections. Since gothic science does, indeed, begin in the imagination, it must participate the unconscious at the intuitive, creative level in its attempt to save the appearances of coherent nature. Nor can science, modeled on its real-world practice, avoid metaphors and myth in shaping its paradigm narratives. Even if gothicized science could avoid drawing on the same primitive forces that energize the psychic and erotic symbols of the gothic fantastic, gothic science expresses those limitations inherent in reason uncorrected by moral values, on the one hand, yet checked by nature's indeterminacy, on the other.

Put another way, gothic SF, when viewed as a critique of science and its method, predicts that discovery resulting from what Einstein called the free invention of the imagination leads to the creation of the gothic world by the production of monstrous aberrations, whatever the scientist's intention. It also predicts, although this corollary forms no part of the present study, that a purely rational science despiritualizes, dehumanizes, and mechanizes the world and its people. Nor can nature be conceived as neutral in this gothic vision of the world. To a man like Stevenson, suffering from a lingering, terminal illness, nature could hardly be thought otherwise than fickle, uncertain, and unreliable. And

Stevenson had plenty of scientific testimony to support his personal experience of nature as the betrayer of a man's hope.

This theme and its representation in *Jekyll and Hyde* is Stevenson's signal contribution to gothic SF. Nature responds to the uses that the antiheroes of *More New Arabian Nights: The Dynamiter* and *Jekyll and Hyde* make of it. The more nature is relied on, the more critical become its imperfections. Its fickleness is proverbial. Its elements, organization, and process come from the recesses of another mind—one that is both mysterious and radically different from our own. One of the symbolic systems SF has employed for that estrangement from and attraction to that other mind is the gothic.

This process began when Mary Shelley gothicized science in *Frankenstein,* producing the form of a new aesthetic response to science and beginning a tradition that continues into the present. Gothicized science projected an inner, psychic world, fractured and unbalanced by the stresses of an enthralled, forbidden desire, onto an outer world interpreted and manipulated with increasing confidence by science and technics. Gothicized science as an invention of the gothic mind became the subjective correlative (if Eliot's famous formula may be reversed) for the controlling analogy of nightmare that reintegrates the world of technics. When the two worlds of gothic SF are thus joined, they express the distorting but humanizing power of the protean unconscious that has escaped the control of an integrated personality. Stevenson's contribution to this tradition, heretofore overlooked, was to introduce into the gothic SF tradition the new scientific ideas, which, in challenging the commonsense paradigms of the human experience of its world, made all the more phantasmagorical those displacements of gothicized science.

Our inquiry has led us, first, to discover what energizing forces were contributed by gothic fantasy to the gothic SF tradition appropriated by Stevenson and reflected in the argument of *Jekyll and Hyde* and, second, to examine how these components of the genre combined synergistically with new mythic paradigms out of science to reset the course of gothic SF. The random uncertainties, discontinuities, and relativism of later gothic SF may be traced to beginnings in Stevenson's *Strange Case of Dr. Jekyll and Mr. Hyde.* When unpacked this way, the scientific aspect of the case becomes richer, perhaps stranger, and potentially more terrifying than once supposed.

Gothic SF symbolizes for us those repressed psychic powers that energize not only the secondary mythologies of science in fiction but perhaps some of the primary ones as well. There is in the character of Western, experimental science something that answers to the name "gothic science," something below the surface of everything done in the name of science. The linkage between gothicized science and a real-world

DONALD LAWLER

gothic science should be of special concern in an age of acid rains and mechanical hearts.

One day perhaps Stevenson will be honored as a writer who contributed to the tradition of those who brought ideas, attitudes, and the mythologies of science into the experience of the general culture of the mind in ways to make them unforgettable. By placing *Jekyll and Hyde* in the tradition of gothic SF, we do not limit its potential meanings but rather enhance them.

NOTES

1. Occasional references to *Jekyll and Hyde* as SF are made by SF critics, usually in passing. Peter Nicholls, in *The Science Fiction Encyclopedia* (Garden City, N.Y.: Doubleday, 1979), mentions it as an example of gothic SF. Katherine Morsperger's treatment of the novel, in Magill's *Survey of Science Fiction Literature,* does little more than identify the novel as SF, while emphasizing its allegorical and fantastic features. Darko Suvin, in *Victorian Science Fiction in the U.K.: The Discourses of Knowledge and of Power* (Boston: G. K. Hall and Co., 1983), identifies the novel as a "limiting case of considerable importance" (94), but argues that it should not be regarded as SF at all. Although we are breaking some new ground here, a much fuller study is needed to establish a theoretical basis for explaining the emergence of modern gothic SF, let alone the rest of the SF genre.

2. The more gothic tales, such as "Valdemar," seem to have left an impression on the imagination of Hawthorne and through him on Stevenson. The hoax tales may have had an influence on Melville's *The Confidence Man,* in which the theme of fraudulent science as a confidence game is introduced. The next step in the subversion of the mystique of science through hoaxing characters or readers seems to have been taken by Mark Twain in *A Connecticut Yankee in King Arthur's Court.*

3. Fear of science and its technology is also heard earlier, in stories by Hawthorne ("The Birthmark," "Rappaccini's Daughter"), and later, in novels by Wells (*The Island of Dr. Moreau*), within the gothic SF tradition. In addition, other types of SF arose in the twentieth century to find new directions for the Frankenstein or Jekyll archetypes in anti-utopias and dystopias, in cautionary tales of social SF, and in post-holocaust stories. In these latter-day stories, however, emphasis is placed more obviously on the effects of science and technology misapplied or run amok. Gothic SF remains the species of choice for probing the psychological and philosophical issues implied in the perception of a fundamental wrongness in the very enterprise of science itself.

4. This telling phrase, explaining a source of the power of the gothic fantastic, was introduced in William Patrick Day, *In the Circles of Fear and Desire* (Chicago: University of Chicago Press, 1985).

5. Until Einstein, Bohr, Heisenberg, Schrödinger, and Gödel, the ruling paradigms were Newtonian in their orientation and positivist in attitude. It was not really until after World War II that scientists themselves (Heisenberg,

Gamow, Hoyle, Chardin, and Jastrow, for example) and scholars such as Thomas Kuhn in *The Structure of Scientific Revolutions* (Chicago: University of Chicago Press, 1962/1970) began saying what soon became obvious. To many, such as Todorov and Suvin, such notions would be inadmissible, despite historic evidence that metaphor and myth are necessary extensions of scientific language. Indeed, one may go so far as to claim that metaphor and myth are among the materials of scientific thinking, even though the uses to which they are put are quite different from those of the artist. George Levine's essay "Darwin and the Evolution of Fiction" in the *New York Times Book Review* (5 October 1986, 1, 60–61) is an effective, recent, short treatment of the conversion of scientific ideas into myths of modern culture, and there are numerous longer works across the spectrum from quantum physics to Zen Buddhism.

6. Martin Troop, *Mary Shelley's Monster* (Boston: Houghton-Mifflin, 1976), 25.

7. The hidden linkage is that found in the psychological makeup of Drs. Frankenstein and Jekyll as typical overreachers, whose quest for knowledge is understood to be the quest for power, dominance, and control over both life and spirit. The parallels between the two and their stories are many. Both are Prometheans, using science to attain forbidden ends. The knowledge becomes psychoactive in the persons of their self-created doubles. But their act of self-creation is transformed by the gothic world into the opposite of what the protagonists expected. In denying the feminine principle of procreation, the scientists first fragment and later destroy the self, thereby creating new myths for the scientific age. Both heroes play at self-disclosure in their doubles, just as each author plays similar games of psychic disclosure. In each story there is an allegorical linkage between the monster made by science and science itself. Thus, questions are raised of the relationship of humans to their science, science to technics, and science to nature. Moreover, the psychosexual dimensions of gothic transformation examined above in the text also bear heavily on this linkage and its consequences for gothic SF and whatever it has been saying about science in its special idiom.

8. William Day stresses, I believe rightly, both the parodic and the unfinished nature of the gothic fantastic; these functions of the form certainly extend themselves into gothic SF. If we think only of such works as *The Island of Dr. Moreau, A Voyage to Arcturus, The Stars My Destination,* and the four-volume *Book of the New Sun,* we can see the outline of a continuing and ever-mutating tradition.

9. Punter (24) raises the issue of imperial gothic, a theme that was treated earlier and at greater length by Judith Wilt, "The Imperial Mouth: Imperialism, the Gothic and Science Fiction," *Journal of Popular Culture* 14 (1981): 618–28.

10. Fanny Van de Grift Stevenson and Robert Louis Stevenson, *More New Arabian Nights. The Dynamiter* (New York: Scribner's, 1898), 10. (Originally published London: Longmans, 1885; a Dover reprint is forthcoming.)

11. The conclusions drawn here suggest an earlier date for the influence of "the physical principle of dissipation of energy" on nineteenth-century writers than suggested by Stephen G. Brush, *The Temperature of History,* (New York: B. Franklin, 1978), 61: "There was remarkable little impact on European thought

DONALD LAWLER

until the end of the nineteenth century. It is only around 1900 that we find an increasing number of references to the second law of thermodynamics, and attempt to connect it with general historical tendencies." Yet one can think of numerous English writers, such as Tennyson and Hardy, who were directly influenced by reading scientists and philosophers whose work was derived from that of Clausius, Lord Kelvin, Boltzmann, and Maxwell and from related developments in Darwinism as it was applied to a spectrum of fields from psychology and biology to sociology and economics. A point that should be emphasized is how well established was this nineteenth-century habit of mind that at the same time desired and discounted principles that would apply not only to all science but to all culture as well. Certainly the relationship between fin de siècle ennui, pessimism, and a sense of exhaustion, on the one hand, and the implications of mid-century physics and biology, on the other hand, is both specific and profound.

At the very least, *Jekyll and Hyde* reveals an earlier literary influence, although perhaps not entirely conscious, than has been generally thought.

12. Stephen Jay Gould, *The Mismeasure of Man* (New York: W. W. Norton and Co., 1981), 115.

13. Perhaps there is a lesson for critics and historians of SF to be learned in this case. Historically, referential SF has lagged behind fantastic or intuitive SF in finding expression for the impact of new scientific paradigms. It has been the rare author, such as Wells, Stapeldon, Niven, or Benford, who combines the gift of mythopoesis with an ability to represent scientific thinking and ways that scientific reframing changes perception and experience of secondary realities. It is surprising but accurate to place Stevenson in that company by virtue of this novel.

14. See especially *Jekyll and Hyde,* 90–91, where Stevenson uses the phrase "morally sane." In fact, Victorians had a category of human psychology, now lost, treating moral insanity and its symptoms. For a discussion of literary applications to Conrad, see Barbara Gates, "Kurtz's Moral Insanity," *Victorians Institute Journal* 11 (1982–83): 53–59.

15. Since the "heat death" hypothesis depends on a steady-state model, it has been exploded, so to speak, by the theory of the expanding universe, which sounds more agreeably optimistic. However, just when it appeared safe once more to live in our galaxy, physicists have begun to speak of a hypothetical black hole, expanding at the heart of the galactic core, that is busily gobbling up all surrounding matter. For some SF transformations of this latest doomsday prophecy, see Larry Niven's "Known Space" series, especially "At the Core," *Ringworld,* and *Protector.* If cultural history repeats itself, we had better prepare for future waves of saturnine speculation.

V
QUESTIONS OF CONTEXT

NINE

The Education of Edward Hyde:
Stevenson's "Gothic Gnome" and the Mass Readership of Late-Victorian England

PATRICK BRANTLINGER
AND RICHARD BOYLE

On 25 January 1886, *The Times of London* reviewed a "sparsely-printed little shilling volume" entitled *Strange Case of Dr Jekyll and Mr Hyde.* According to Charles Longman, this review initiated the story's immense popularity, although the tale was packaged from the start to be a best-seller (Maixner 205). Dr. Thomas Scott recalled Stevenson's annunciation one morning that "I've got my shilling shocker." This, said Scott, was "the period of the shilling shockers," and at a time before Stevenson's "success was ensured, when he was in financial difficulties," his publishers had been "urging him, much against his inclination, to write such a book."[1] Yet Stevenson had been quite willing to publish earlier stories in popular formats. "The Body Snatcher" had appeared in the 1884 Christmas extra of *The Pall Mall Gazette,* which "advertised it in the streets in a way as horrible as the story itself" (Hammerton 318).

For Longman's part, *Jekyll and Hyde* was deliberately formatted as a "shilling shocker" aimed at the 1885 Christmas market, though because completed too late it was withheld from the booksellers until the new year (Swearingen 99). For his part, because of "financial fluctuations," Stevenson had been "racking my brain for a plot of any sort" ("A Chapter on Dreams"). Despite being able to fall back on his father, Stevenson desperately wanted to earn his living as a writer. Producing a "shilling shocker" for Longmans might disagree with his sense of the higher aims of literature, but it agreed with his desire for financial independence and popularity.

"The wheels of Byles the Butcher drive exceedingly swiftly," Stevenson wrote apologetically to F. W. H. Myers. Therefore, "*Jekyll* was conceived, written, re-written, re-re-written, and printed inside ten weeks" (L2, 294). What Stevenson meant by "Byles the Butcher" was perhaps his "initial monetary impulse" (Swearingen 99). The "white-hot haste" with which he produced the story, Stevenson hoped, would help to excuse some of the solecisms Myers detected in it. Paradoxically it could perhaps also explain or excuse its astonishing popular success.

Other stories that he labored over and considered more serious might never be bestsellers; but popularity and seriousness seemed antithetical. Despite lavish praise by Myers and others, Stevenson's own statements about the story tend to be defensively ironic. Instead of a masterpiece that would win the unconditional approval of the most discriminating readers, he had produced a "Gothic gnome," a "fine bogey tale." Through the revision prompted by Fanny, he had converted this tale into a "moral allegory," but the revision had perhaps only given it another source of appeal to the mass readership who, both he and Longmans believed, were the real arbiters of the late-Victorian literary marketplace.

In part because of his deep-rooted ambivalence toward that marketplace, Stevenson responded ambivalently to *Jekyll and Hyde,* at times referring to it as if it were a despised double, or at least the unwanted spawn of the weaker, Hyde-like side of himself, as in the Byles-the-Butcher letter, or in his account of its genesis in "A Chapter on Dreams," according to which his "Brownies" invented Hyde while his waking or rational self supplied the "morality." Such ambivalence suggests that *Jekyll and Hyde* can be read, in part, as a kind of gothic version of George Gissing's *New Grub Street.* It has always been read as an "allegory" about good and evil, about "the war in the members" and the "double nature" of human nature. We intend here to read it also as an unconscious "allegory" about the commercialization of literature and the emergence of a mass consumer society in the late-Victorian period.

I

The various accounts of the genesis of the "fine bogey tale," including Stevenson's, are all marked by an ambivalence or doubleness that stems from the fundamental contradiction between the sense of literature as a high calling and the desire for popular fame and fortune. According to Stevenson,

> I had long been trying to write a story on [the] strong sense of man's double being. . . . Then came one of those financial fluctuations. . . . For two days I went about racking my brains for a plot of any sort; and on the second night I dreamed the scene at the window, and a scene afterwards split in two, in which Hyde, pursued for some crime, took the powder. . . . All the rest was made awake, and consciously, although I think I can trace in much of it the manner of my Brownies. The meaning of the tale is therefore mine, and had long pre-existed. . . . Mine, too, is the setting, mine the characters. All that was given me was the matter of three scenes, and the central idea of a voluntary change becoming involuntary. ["A Chapter on Dreams"]

This division of labor, between his waking self who supplied the "meaning" and his "Brownies" who supplied, through dream, the central "scenes" and "manner" of the story, itself points to "man's double being." Stevenson's account applies the chief message of *Jekyll and Hyde* to the history of its production. As personifications of the mind's dreamlife, the Brownies are Stevenson's doubles, creatures hidden inside the waking personality who beg comparison with the "dwarfish" or "gnomelike" Mr. Hyde. Stevenson says that, in the division of labor that produced the tale, he took care "of the morality, worse luck!" because "my Brownies have not a rudiment of what we call a conscience" ("A Chapter on Dreams").

A similar division of labor is evident in the accounts by Fanny Stevenson and Lloyd Osbourne, except that in these Fanny plays the part of "conscience" or supplier of "meaning." They both indicate that the first draft, itself written in "white-hot haste," was tossed into the fire because of Fanny's reaction to it. Stevenson had apparently written a mere "crawler" or tale of terror, without any more serious intention than to entertain, but Fanny thought that "it was really an allegory."

> The morning after her husband had the dream . . . he came with a radiant countenance to show his work to his wife, saying it was the best thing he had ever done. She read it and thought it the worst. . . . At last . . . she put her objections to it . . . in writing, complaining that he had treated it simply as a story, whereas it was in reality an allegory. After . . . seeing the justice of her criticism, with characteristic impulsiveness he immediately burned his first draft and rewrote it from a different point of view. . . . [Sanchez 118]

It is not altogether apparent what "allegory" and "story" mean, but Osbourne added, "In the first draft Jekyll's nature was bad all through, and the Hyde change was worked only for the sake of a disguise" (65). In other words, the sharp moral antithesis—the struggle between the mostly good, outward self (Jekyll) and the evil, hidden self (Hyde)—was not a feature of the first draft. The "allegorization" that Fanny demanded apparently changed a horror story *tout simple* into one about the warfare between good and evil, giving it a religious or philosophical gloss. Whether or not this transformation has made *Jekyll and Hyde* a better work of art, it probably did make it seem more serious and respectable and may therefore also have helped to attract a broader spectrum of readers than a mere shilling shocker would have. Instead of just a crawler, it became, so to speak, a crawler with a purpose.

If this interpretation is correct, then Stevenson's own explanation of why he burned the first draft acquires an intriguing ambiguity. According to Osbourne, both he and Fanny "cried out at the folly of destroying the manuscript," but Stevenson "justified himself vehemently. 'It was all wrong,' he said. 'In trying to save some of it I should have got hopelessly off the track. *The only way was to put temptation beyond my reach'*" (65; our italics). What was the "temptation" that led to the burning of the first draft? The simplest reading is that it was merely to make life easier for the writer by relying on a botched job. But *"it was all wrong."* Perhaps there was a further temptation to produce a story in which the evil side of human nature would go unchallenged by the good—a story lacking "conscience" that would cater to the most sensational and therefore also "popular" tastes of readers. But the allegorization of *Jekyll and Hyde* may also have helped make it a popular success, by rendering it just as respectable as it was "wrong" or criminal.

The Jekyll/Hyde split between "allegory" and mere "story" is similar to the other, more familiar dichotomies of Stevenson's life and work. There are, for example, the conflicts between bourgeois respectability and bohemianism, engineering and art, and Calvinism and free thought that marked Stevenson's troubled relations with his family. As for his art, his letters and essays reveal his vacillations between "realism" and "romance." In each case, Stevenson affirms the creative energy or vitality of what he simultaneously regards as the less serious or less moral half of the antithesis. Stevenson defines most of his fiction in terms of romance or "the novel of adventure," and therefore criticizes the various realisms as both drab and pseudoscientific. But his defenses of romance often lack conviction. He is aware "English people of the present day are apt . . . to look somewhat down on incident [in fiction], and reserve their admiration for the clink of teaspoons and the accents of the curate" ("A Gossip on Romance"). But he associates romance or the fiction of "incident" with daydream, escape, and childhood rather than with visionary qualities that both transcend and see more deeply into reality than the rational mind. At the end of "A Humble Remonstrance," for example, he calls Scott both "a great romantic" and "an idle child," as if these phrases were synonymous. Perhaps the universal, timeless appeal of "romance" seemed unconsciously problematic to him because of its kinship to that contemporary popular or mass appeal, which he believed he should resist.

What Andrew Noble describes as "Stevenson's ambivalent relationship to his audience and to money" (21) shows up throughout his letters and essays. When some of his well-wishers looked askance at the publication of *Treasure Island* in *Young Folks*, Stevenson wrote angrily to Henley,

> To those who ask me . . . to do nothing but refined, high-toned, bejay-bedamned masterpieces, I will offer the following bar-

gain: I agree to their proposal if they give me £1000 . . . and at the same time effect such a change in my nature that I shall be content to take it from them instead of earning it. If they cannot manage these trifling matters, by God, I'll trouble them to hold their tongues, by God. . . . Let them write their damn masterpieces for themselves. . . . [Calder 172]

This is the sort of difficulty expressed by the struggling writers in *New Grub Street*, whose efforts to write what they consider serious literature are not marketable, although other, less serious forms of writing—the kinds of "journalism," for example, that Jasper Milvain cynically masters and markets—achieve high levels of popular success.

For Stevenson and Gissing alike, the choice was not between being read and going completely unread but between producing popular or unpopular kinds of writing. Earlier writers and publishers had necessarily aimed their works at smaller, more uniform, more clearly middle- or upper-class readerships. But by the 1880s there had emerged a growing "massification" and yet also diversification of the literary marketplace, rooted in the development of mass literacy from about the 1830s forward. New techniques of mass production, such as the high-speed Hoe press, coupled with the abolition of the last "taxes on knowledge" by 1855, led to "a new and remarkable phase of general expansion" for popular journalism between mid-century and the 1890s.[2] Together with increasing numbers of readers and leisure for reading, these developments had by the 1880s created the conditions in which "the sale of sensational novels in serial form [might exceed] two million copies a week, with individual titles selling from ten to sixty thousand each."[3]

Late-Victorian critics did much moralizing about the sad state of popular taste, though given the massive increase in reading material of all sorts and in reading as an activity, the complaints sound weak or contradictory. In his 1880 essay "Copyright," Matthew Arnold lamented the development of "a cheap literature, hideous and ignoble of aspect, like the tawdry novels which flare in the book-shelves of our railway stations, and which seem designed . . . for people with a low standard of life."[4] Perhaps the remarkable fact, however, was not that "tawdry novels" existed, but that there were for the first time in history large numbers of people who, though their "standard of life" might be beneath Arnold's, were able and willing to read them. But the fear of mass literacy was powerful in late-Victorian England. In an 1887 *Edinburgh Review* article on "the literature of the streets," B. G. Johns asserted that it was "a disgrace to our boasted civilisation" that "a nation like England, which spends millions on the education of her children, and boasts of teaching every poor boy and girl to read, should provide for them no fiction but of an infamously worthless kind."[5] Johns ranked Stevenson among the writers of "healthful" fiction, but went on to say, "The worst of modern novels are too often among the most popular." The "garbage of the 'Penny Dreadfuls'" was, he believed, especially "poisonous" to the newly literate masses. Such "depraved" literature was criminal, Johns thought, both because it dealt with crime and because it directly stimulated "foul aims" and "vicious" behavior.

Framed by these mass cultural trends and anxieties, Stevenson's resuscitation of older "romance" forms of story telling can be understood as an effort to mediate between an ideal of literature as high art and a desire for mass-market success. The same effort is evident in the work of the other late-Victorian "romancers" such as H. Rider Haggard and H. G. Wells. According to Fredric Jameson:

> It is in the context of the gradual reification of realism in late capitalism that romance once again comes to be felt as the place of narrative heterogeneity and of freedom from that reality principle to which a now oppressive realistic representation is the hostage. Romance now again seems to offer the possibility of sensing other historical rhythms, and of demonic or Utopian transformations of a real now unshakably set in place. . . .[6]

As Jameson also notes, however, the late-Victorian romance that emerged between the breakdown of realism and the rise of modernism tended toward "popular . . . or mass culture," sharing "the commercialized cultural discourse of what, in late capitalism, is often described as a media society" (206). Jameson diagnoses Conrad's *Lord Jim* as "schizophrenic" because of its unresolved tension between mass cultural "romance" and high cultural "modernism," and a similar diagnosis, though in terms of "romance" and "realism," applies to much of Stevenson's fiction.

The "utopian" search for a "salvational future" is less evident than "demonic . . . transformations" in late Victorian writing, because "romance" from the outset seemed both highly mannered—a recasting of obsolete forms—and itself "hostage" to the new, seemingly progressive, industrialized mass market. What Stevenson specifically resurrected in *Jekyll and Hyde* was the old gothic message about the evil within, given a scientific emphasis by the "powders," as a mass cultural entertainment or "shilling shocker." By reviving the devalued, mass cultural conventions of "romance," Stevenson could cater to the new mass readership while also seeking to satisfy his own ideal of a serious literature that would have universal appeal. But Hyde—the evil within Jekyll—surfaces within the Stevenson romance as an oblique, unconscious condemnation of the same fictional stratagems that sensationalize and commodify art in order to gain mass market success. Stevenson's discovery of Hyde first within himself as dream, alter ego, and literary invention involved the author/creator in a subtle form of cultural damnation.

On numerous occasions, Stevenson defended romances on the grounds of their universality, but without explicitly equating such universality with mass market appeal. "The great creative writer shows us . . . the apotheosis of the day-dreams of common men," particularly in the form of the "romance" or "adventure novel" ("A Gossip on Romance"). But if Stevenson could view the "day-dreams of common men" positively, he could also treat the "gross mass of mankind" with Arnoldian contempt, an attitude that frequently caused him to disparage his own work because of its popularity. Thus he considered *The Black Arrow* mere "tushery" and *St. Ives* a mere "tissue of adventures," with "no philosophic pith under the yarn" (Eigner 5). *Treasure Island* might be better than these potboilers (which had no great popular success anyway), but it was also no more than an "elementary novel of adventure," written for the boy readers of *Young Folks*. "The truth is I am pretty nearly useless at literature," he declared late in his career. "My skill . . . was a very little dose of inspiration, and a pretty little trick of style . . . improved by the most heroic industry. So far, I have managed to please the journalists. But I am a fictitious article and have long known it" (L4, 327).

Stevenson was indeed a "fictitious article"—the storyteller-hero whose stories formed key episodes in a picaresque career. His "heroic industry" in the face of disease and death, his fabled bohemianism, his South Seas adventures—these also were chapters of the Stevenson romance, the general story that can be read between the lines of such clearly "fictitious" or perhaps even factitious stories as *Jekyll and Hyde*. By the late nineteenth century, the writer as "personality" or "celebrity" had also become an important commodity that publishers and critics sought to market.[7] From the outset of his career, Stevenson was taken up by such fellow writers as Leslie Stephen, Sidney Colvin, and Andrew Lang, for whom, as Jenni Calder notes, "literature . . . had grown demoralised, and needed to be rescued" (87). Stevenson appeared to them as a potential rescuer, though his mass cultural ventures threatened to demoralize them further. But for his critics and admirers, even those stories and essays most removed from autobiography arranged themselves as episodes in a version of that quite typical modern genre—the Carlylean saga of "The Hero as Man of Letters." *Jekyll and Hyde* can thus be read as a palimpsest between or beneath whose lines the knowing reader will discern the well-advertised originary dream, the incineration of the first draft, and the subsequent allegorization of the story at Fanny's behest.

Stevenson's "Gothic gnome," in other words, mirrors the story of an exemplary struggling artist, torn between the desire to produce "master-pieces" and the knowledge that popular success lay in the contrary directions of "shilling shocker" and "moral allegory." For the supposedly undiscriminating mass readership, there was the "crawler" plain and simple, though this was also a palimpsest in which the form of the gothic thriller, as Hirsch and Lawler have shown, was overwritten by the patterns of the detective story and science fiction. For a supposedly more sophisticated sort of reader, there was the moral allegory about good and evil; *Jekyll and Hyde* served as the subject, we are told, for numerous late-Victorian sermons. But for the discriminating elite such as Henry James and Edmund Gosse, there would also be the heroic and self-pitying story of its writer's struggle against adversity, which included the adversity of having to cater to the cultural mass market of the late-Victorian age.

II

Stevenson's ambivalence toward his "audience and money" shows up dramatically in a letter he wrote to Gosse in 1886:

> What the public likes is work (of any kind) a little loosely executed. . . . I know that good work sometimes hits; but, with my hand on my heart, I think it is by an accident. And I know also that good work must succeed at last; but that is not the doing of the public; they are only shamed into silence or affectation. I do not write for the public; I do write for money, a nobler deity; and most of all for myself, not perhaps any more noble, but both more intelligent and nearer home.
>
> Let us tell each other sad stories of the bestiality of the beast whom we feed. What he likes is the newspaper; and to me the press is the mouth of a sewer, where lying is professed as from an university chair, and everything prurient, and ignoble, and essentially dull, finds its abode and pulpit. I do not like mankind; but men, and not all of these—and fewer women. As for respecting the race, and, above all, that fatuous rabble of burgesses called 'the public,' God save me from such irreligion! —that way lies disgrace and dishonour. *There must be something wrong in me, or I would not be popular.* [L2, 281; our italics]

The contempt that Stevenson here expresses toward "the public" and his own popularity is similar to that expressed by Gissing in *New Grub Street*. Both believed that the commercial exploitation of a new, qualitatively inferior mass readership with "a low standard of life" was undermining serious literature. For both, an ideal of high culture was opposed to a social reality dominated by "journalism" or "the press" and by the transformation of art into a mere "trade."

Stevenson's ambivalence toward his own popular success implies that there must be "something wrong in" any story successful with "the public." Obviously there is "something wrong in" *Jekyll and Hyde* and that is Hyde himself, whose physique and criminal propensities make him virtually a stereotype of "the populace," if not of "that fatuous rabble of burgesses called 'the public.' " Though not straight from "the mouth of a sewer," Hyde belongs to the slums of "darkest London." When not at home with or within Jekyll, he lives in the "blackguardly surroundings" of Soho (48), where Utterson travels with Inspector Newcomen as through "a district of some city in a nightmare":

> As the cab drew up before the address indicated, the fog lifted a little and showed him a dingy street, a gin palace, a low French eating-house, a shop for the retail of penny numbers and two-penny salads, many ragged children huddled in the doorways, and many women of many different nationalities passing out, key in hand, to have a morning glass. . . . [48]

The literature of Soho is even cheaper than its food. But this "dismal quarter" with its "muddy ways, and slatternly passengers" (48) is not illiterate; it is as appropriate a haunt for "penny numbers" as for Hyde, and also for other members of the "dangerous classes," who fifty years earlier would probably not have been readers.

Though such biased class language does not occur in the story, the idea that there were "dangerous" or "criminal classes" was a powerful one from the mid-Victorian period forward.[8] Universal education and literacy were not eradicating crime, as some early reformers had hoped. In 1876, Cesare Lombroso had published his influential study of the hereditary nature of crime and "moral insanity," arguing that much criminal activity could be explained in terms of physical and mental "atavism." Lombroso also argued that, "contrary to general belief, the influence of education on crime is very slight."[9] His chief work was not translated into English until 1911, but Lombroso's basic ideas had gained currency by the 1880s through social scientists and evolutionary psychologists such as Stevenson's friend James Sully (Block 463).

Hyde himself is, of course, an atavistic creature, whose "dwarfish . . . ape-like" appearance reflects the stereotype of the Irish hooligan. As Perry Curtis describes the stereotype, "Paddy" was "childish, emotionally unstable, ignorant . . . primitive . . . dirty, vengeful, and violent."[10] He was also allegedly "ape-like" and often stunted in growth or "dwarfish." Curtis quotes a letter by Charles Kingsley describing "white chimpanzees" in Ireland, and in 1845 James Anthony Froude found much of that country's population "more like tribes of squalid apes than human beings" (Curtis 84, 85). The threat of Fenianism and the Irish Home Rule controversy, which was to split the Liberal party in 1886, form the political background of *The Dynamiter* (1884) and help to explain Hyde's stereotypic traits. Though originally belonging to Utterson, the "heavy cane" with which Hyde "clubs" Sir Danvers Carew might easily have been a shillelagh, and the brutal murder of an M.P. must have caused many readers to recall the 1882 Phoenix Park murders in Dublin. The theme of the increasingly dangerous "Irish Franken-stein," often employed by English caricaturists, has both Celtic and gothic overtones, which Stevenson's depiction of Hyde also mirrors (see figs. 9.1–9.3).[11]

Nevertheless, *Jekyll and Hyde* is totally lacking in explicit political themes. The allegorization prompted by Fanny apparently did not lead to any elaboration of its social content. Hyde is an emanation of Jekyll's "transcendental medicine" or of Stevenson's nightmare, rather than of either a social class system that spawned criminality or an imperial domination that had shackled Ireland for centuries. Whatever the "moral" of the story—and at first there was none—it has to do with good versus evil in the abstract, not with the politics or even the police of late-Victorian society. The novella's anachronistic style and ahistoricism help it to seem timeless and universal, while also obscuring the literary sleight of hand that sneaks Hyde into the heart of the respectable bour-geoisie. Jekyll's metamorphosis is a matter of certain unbelievable "powders," not of politics nor even of science. But the mass cultural format of the first edition promised topical reality enough to the "popu-lace"—the same readers who would have responded to the newsboys whom Utterson hears "crying themselves hoarse along the footways: 'Special edition. Shocking murder of an M.P.' " (53).

Stevenson as popular author shares in the criminal "popularity" or populace-like nature of Hyde. "There must be something wrong in me, or I would not be popular." The statement is, in a sense, the formula of *Jekyll and Hyde* itself. There is "something wrong in" the story—that is, Hyde—and this accounts for its popularity. Further, the story was "wrong" not only because Hyde was "in" it but because the germ of it was still the "crawler" that perhaps did nothing more than pander to the low tastes of "that fatuous rabble . . . the public," whereas Fanny told him it was "wrong"; it needed to be rendered morally acceptable, even though allegorization did not necessarily move it closer to the sort of masterpiece by which Stevenson longed to gain recognition. It was "wrong" also because it was immediately and immensely popular; more than anything else he had written, *Jekyll and Hyde* brought Stevenson

THE IRISH FRANKENSTEIN.

Fɪɢ. 9.1. "The Irish Frankenstein," *Punch*, 4 November 1843

FIG. 9.2. Fenianism as Irish Frankenstein, *The Tomahawk*, 18 December 1869

PATRICK BRANTLINGER AND RICHARD BOYLE

THE IRISH FRANKENSTEIN.

"The baneful and blood-stained Monster * * * yet was it not my Master to the very extent that it was my Creature? * * * Ha! I had breathed into it my own spirit?" * * * (*Extract from the Works of* C. S. P—RN—LL, M.P.

FIG. 9.3. "The Irish Frankenstein," *Punch*, 20 May 1882

fame and fortune. Hyde was thus both a chief cause of his creator's popular success and an ironic, albeit unconscious image of that popularity—the "ape-like," atavistic image of "the people."

Despite his degenerate nature, Hyde retains one of Jekyll's upper-class traits. Though his hands are smaller, more gnarled, yet stronger than Jekyll's, Hyde's handwriting is identical to Jekyll's; it must therefore be disguised by slanting it differently. "When, by sloping my own hand backwards, I had supplied my double with a signature," says Jekyll, "I thought I sat beyond the reach of fate" (87). One might say that this is the only education Hyde needs, because despite his "ape-like," "deformed" physique and personality, he is completely literate. When Jekyll transforms into Hyde while dozing on a bench in Regent's Park, Hyde's ability to write in Jekyll's hand is what rescues him from discovery and capture by the police. "Then I remembered that of my original character, one part remained to me: *I could write my own hand;* and once I had conceived that kindling spark, the way that I must follow became lighted up from end to end" (93; our italics). The passage strongly suggests that the *only* thing that does not change through Jekyll's metamorphosis is the ability to write in Jekyll's hand, though *what* gets written changes dramatically.

Hyde's slanted handwriting proves a poor disguise. Utterson shows the "murderer's autograph" to his head clerk, Guest, who compares it with Jekyll's handwriting and declares, "There's a rather singular resemblance; the two hands are in many points identical; only differently sloped" (55). Further, more often than not the disguise is dropped, as in the Regent's Park episode or in the privacy of Jekyll's laboratory. On these occasions, Hyde writes like Jekyll. And he also makes use of Jekyll's library. In Jekyll's quarters, Hyde apparently entertains himself by reading whatever is available. Given Jekyll's sober, upper-class tastes, however, such reading material is far removed from penny numbers or shilling shockers. "There were several books on a shelf; one lay beside the tea things open, and Utterson was amazed to find it a copy of a pious work for which Jekyll had several times expressed a great esteem, annotated, *in his own hand,* with startling blasphemies" (71; our italics). In his narrative, Jekyll speaks of "the ape-like tricks that [Hyde] would play me, scrawling *in my own hand* blasphemies on the pages of my books" (96; our italics).

Works of theology are an odd sort of reading for a mad scientist, let alone for his demonic double. Within the terms of the Stevenson romance, however, they perhaps correspond to "moral allegory" as the obverse of "crawler." In any case, we are also told that Utterson was in the habit of sitting down by the fire after his solitary, abstemious dinners with "a volume of some dry divinity on his reading-desk" (35). In the chapter where this is mentioned, however, Utterson neglects such "dry,"

PATRICK BRANTLINGER AND RICHARD BOYLE

pious reading for a more intriguing although distressing sort—the "holograph" will which Jekyll has drawn up and entrusted to the lawyer. Or did Hyde draw up the will? In his narration, Jekyll says, "I next drew up that will to which you [Utterson] so much objected" (86), but the "I" is ambiguous in this context. Because they share the same handwriting, it is impossible to know whether Jekyll or Hyde authored the will. Utterson cannot know, since he "had refused to lend the least assistance in the making of it." Similarly, Utterson can't tell whether Jekyll and Hyde wrote the check for ninety pounds to recompense the trampled girl and her family, though no doubt Hyde was its author because he obtains it so quickly. Enfield thought it might prove to be "a forgery," but on the contrary "the cheque was genuine" (32). The ambiguous, perhaps double authorship of several pieces of writing within the text mirror its double nature as "story" and "allegory," shilling shocker and tale with a "conscience," at once criminal and morally improving.

Among the many recommendations by which Myers hoped to help Stevenson turn a near-masterpiece into the genuine article, one concerned the improbability of Hyde's retention of Jekyll's handwriting. "I think you miss a point for want of familiarity with recent psycho-physical discussions," Myers told Stevenson. "Handwriting in cases of double personality . . . *is not* and *cannot be* the same in the two personalities. Hyde's writing might look like Jekyll's done *with the left hand,* or done when partly drunk, or ill: that is the kind of resemblance there might be. Your imagination can make a good point of this" (Maixner, 215). But through the motif of identical calligraphy, Stevenson makes a deeper, much more complex point about cultural authority. Though their values are several worlds or at least social classes apart, Jekyll and Hyde share the same ability to express those values, and they do so even in the same "hand" or with the same "signature." Though Jekyll, like all mad scientists, menaces society through his overcultivated, overambitious intellect, Hyde menaces society not just by his criminal violence but by his ability to write checks and letters, draw up wills, and pen blasphemies in books of theology. Further, though he does not write his confessions (he leaves that up to Jekyll), let alone a culturally blasphemous "shilling shocker," Hyde is nevertheless the hero or antihero of such a "shocker" —one that was, perhaps, purely "evil" until "allegorized." And this "shilling shocker," bearing "Satan's signature" (40) as its central image (Utterson reads that "signature" in Hyde's face), helped to establish Stevenson's literary celebrity and success story. As the Brownies (Stevenson claimed) were the authors of the originary nightmare, so the uncannily literate Edward Hyde was in an important way the author of the Stevenson romance.

When Utterson and Inspector Newcomen enter Hyde's Soho

residence, they discover something quite different from its "blackguardly surroundings." The rooms Hyde uses are "furnished with luxury and good taste." They are evidently the rooms of an epicure, who takes pleasure in art. "A closet was filled with wine; the plate was of silver, the napery elegant; a good picture hung upon the walls, a gift (as Utterson supposed) from Henry Jekyll, who was much of a connoisseur; and the carpets were of many plies and agreeable in colour" (49). Perhaps Hyde retains more of Jekyll's traits than just his handwriting. Or is the evidence of epicureanism pure Hyde, whereas Jekyll, like Utterson, adheres to a routine of abstinence and "dry divinity"? Whatever the case, the Soho flat is not some Fagin's roost in the underworld slums but a setting implying sensual enjoyment, perhaps libertinism, of an apparently upper-class sort. Further, there is more evidence of Hyde's reading in the apartment—unless it is Jekyll's reading—or perhaps it is evidence of his/his writing. The rooms, says Utterson, appeared to have been "recently and hurriedly ransacked," while on "the hearth there lay a pile of grey ashes, as though many papers had been burned" (49).

What "papers" would Hyde, or perhaps Jekyll, need to burn? The scientific texts and records of their transformations appear to have been left in Jekyll's laboratory. There would be no occasion to bring works of theology to Soho, unless Hyde so enjoyed writing blasphemies on their pages that he couldn't resist bringing some along. Perhaps the papers are business or legal documents such as the will; the only item that can be rescued from the ashes is "the butt end of a green cheque book" (49). Or perhaps the papers represent some confession of Jekyll's—a first draft of his final narrative, which, as Jekyll writes it, is in imminent danger of destruction. "If my narrative has hitherto escaped destruction, it has been by a combination of great prudence and great good luck. Should the throes of change take me in the act of writing it, Hyde will tear it in pieces" (97).

Whatever the burned papers may represent within the context of the story, within the context of the Stevenson romance the associations between art and the furnishings of the Soho apartment and between Hyde's destruction of manuscripts and Stevenson's incineration of his unallegorized first draft point to the buried theme of cultural authority. If Hyde shares Jekyll's handwriting, he also shares Stevenson's. He is the shadowy, demonic double of the artist, bent on complete bohemian or artistic license and also on the desecration of art, for whom the ultimate "temptation" is to write or to live stories all "wrong"— "blasphemies," "forgeries," stories of and about pure evil, though perhaps "allegorized" to make them seem respectable—calculated only to thrill the ignorant masses into granting them a meretricious "popularity." Such stories could be purchased as penny numbers in Soho, or from newsboys hawking papers on the streets, or from Longmans as shilling shockers, or perhaps even transmuted into sermons about the duality of human nature. Their heroes and readers alike might be Edward Hydes, and so might their authors, who would write and sign themselves with "Satan's signature." "This was the shocking thing," Jekyll declares, "that the slime of the pit seemed to utter cries and voices" (95). His distress echoes Stevenson's in regard to "the bestiality of the beast whom we feed. What he likes is the newspaper; and to me the press is the mouth of a sewer, where lying is professed as from a university chair" (L2, 281).

Hyde's writing produces lies or half-lies, forged checks that are genuine, and "blasphemies" in Jekyll's "own hand," scrawled in revered texts. Within the larger context of the Stevenson romance, Hyde lurks in a shadowy borderland between a criminal literature of the slums—penny numbers, shilling shockers—and the moral allegory that Fanny urged her husband to write, while the authentic "masterpiece" that Stevenson dreamed of writing hovered outside his range like a mirage. What renders Hyde especially menacing in these cultural terms, however, has perhaps less to do with the Stevenson romance than with the politics of literacy. Hyde's ability to write in Jekyll's "hand" when all of Jekyll's other virtuous, upper-class attributes have vanished renders him dangerous in a more insidious way than his violence. "We must educate our masters," Robert Lowe had declared at the time of the Second Reform Bill. The third bill had passed in 1884, but the idea that mass literacy would hold back the barbarous vandalism that the upper classes feared the "lower orders" would visit on them seemed, perhaps, even less realistic than it had in 1867 or 1832. Hyde's ability to write is a nightmare version of the writing on the wall for "civilized," "respectable" Victorian Britain. When Jekyll discovers that he can no longer control the transformations and that Hyde is taking control of him, he declares, "This reversal of my previous experience, seemed, like the Babylonian finger on the wall, to be spelling out the letters of my judgement" (88).

In an early, somewhat perplexed review, James Noble wrote,

> "The Strange Case of Dr. Jekyll and Mr. Hyde" is not an orthodox three-volume novel; it is not even a one-volume novel of the ordinary type; it is simply a paper-covered shilling story, belonging, so far as external appearance goes, to a class of literature familiarity with which has bred in the minds of most readers a certain measure of contempt. [Maixner 203]

But though the original story had deserved to burn, this particular "shilling shocker" had been plucked out of the fires of its imaginary damnation by "allegorization," and it was, many of its reviewers believed, as near to being a "masterpiece" as anything its author had yet written.

NOTES

1. Rosaline Masson, ed., *I Can Remember Robert Louis Stevenson* (New York: Frederick A. Stokes, 1923), 269.

2. Raymond Williams, *The Long Revolution* (Harmondsworth: Penguin Books, 1965), 215.

3. Richard D. Altick, *The English Common Reader: A Social History of the Mass Reading Public, 1800–1900* (Chicago: University of Chicago Press, 1963), 308.

4. Matthew Arnold, "Copyright," *English Literature and Irish Politics,* ed. R. H. Super (Ann Arbor: University of Michigan Press, 1973), 126.

5. [B. G. Johns,] "The Literature of the Streets," *Edinburgh Review* 165 (1887): 61.

6. Fredric Jameson, *The Political Unconscious: Narrative as a Socially Symbolic Act* (Ithaca, N.Y.: Cornell University Press, 1982), 104.

7. Rachel Bowlby, *Just Looking: Consumer Culture in Dreiser, Gissing and Zola* (New York: Methuen, 1985), 29.

8. Honoré Fregier may have been the first person to use the phrase *dangerous classes;* his *Des classes dangereuses de la population dans les grandes villes* appeared in 1840. The phrase was current in English by the 1850s, along with *criminal classes, predatory classes,* and some others. See Gertrude Himmelfarb, *The Idea of Poverty: England in the Early Industrial Age* (New York: Vintage Books, 1985), 371–400.

9. Cesare Lombroso, *Criminal Man* (Montclair, N.J.: Patterson Smith, 1972), 149.

10. L. P. Curtis, *Anglo-Saxons and Celts: A Study of Anti-Irish Prejudice in Victorian England* (Bridgeport, Conn.: Bridgeport University Press, 1968), 53.

11. For the impact of Fenianism on late-Victorian fiction, see Barbara Melchiori, *Terrorism in the Late Victorian Novel* (London: Croom Helm, 1985).

Horrors of the Body:
Hollywood's Discourse
on Beauty and Rouben Mamoulian's
Dr. Jekyll and Mr. Hyde

VIRGINIA WRIGHT WEXMAN

Let us not picture the bourgeoisie symbolically castrating itself the better to refuse others the right to have a sex and make use of it as they please. This class must be seen rather as being occupied from the mid-eighteenth century on with creating its own sexuality and forming a specific body based on it, a "class" body with its health, hygiene, descent, and race: the autosexualization of its body, the incarnation of sex in its body, the endogamy of sex and the body.

Michel Foucault, *The History of Sexuality*

Robert Louis Stevenson's *Strange Case of Dr Jekyll and Mr Hyde* has been the basis for at least sixty-nine films, some by directors as distinguished as F. W. Murnau and Jean Renoir.[1] A major reason for its enduring popularity as a subject for cinematic adaptation is its focus on the human body. The story's central revelation is constructed as a scene of bodily transformation. In addition—and here I disagree with Gordon Hirsch—Stevenson has gone out of his way to punctuate the narrative with sustained descriptions of his characters' physical characteristics. Mainstream narrative cinema is well adapted to elaborate on this motif, and the dual role of Jekyll and Hyde has attracted actors from John Barrymore to Jerry Lewis as a challenge to their talents.

Of all the cinematic versions of Stevenson's tale, Rouben Mamoulian's, released in January 1932, is usually regarded as the most accomplished.[2] This evaluation is based on the film's stylistic bravado as well as on the Academy Award–winning performance of Fredric March in the title role. Mamoulian emphasizes the representation of the human form even more than other directors do, both by March's suggestive portrayal and by stylistic devices, many of which—including mirrors, shadows, statuary, split-screen techniques, and lap dissolves—multiply images of the body.

The centrality of the film's representation of the body was recognized by most of its early reviewers. The critic for *The New Yorker* responded to a portrayal of Hyde "as athletic and exuberant as might have been that of Douglas Fairbanks, Senior."[3] *The New York Times* commented that, in the depiction of Hyde, "virtually every imaginable possibility is taken advantage of to make this creature 'reflecting the lower elements of Dr. Jekyll's soul' thoroughly hideous."[4] The *Time* reviewer notes "[t]he fascinating problem of how to change from the sleek and handsome Dr. Jekyll into the menacing and ugly Mr. Hyde," and he goes on to point out, "The face of the handsome young British sawbones becomes by barely perceptible degrees of trick photography the visage of a sabre-toothed baboon with pig eyes and a tassel of primeval hair."[5]

By contrast, subsequent commentary on Mamoulian's *Jekyll and Hyde* has not probed the full implications of the film's focus on the body. Some studies have concentrated instead on Mamoulian's use of cinematic devices that set the film apart from the original novel.[6] To compare the narrative tropes of the novel and film in order to distinguish the formal properties of the two media, however, bypasses the issue of *what* is being expressed in each representation. Critics who have considered *Jekyll and Hyde* as an example of the horror genre, by contrast, treat more substantive questions relating to the body and its sexuality, but because they generally limit their attention to issues of sexuality and gender difference, the sociological, historical, and anthropological aspects of its representation of the body have been overlooked.[7] A consideration of these broader aspects, however, deepens our understanding of the film's portrayal of gender and sexuality by placing these issues in a new context.

Recent arguments about the politics of the body, most notably those raised by Michel Foucault, have emphasized the crucial role played by discourses on the human form in regulating private life. In the cinema, the star system is often seen as having such a function.[8] In particular, Hollywood is often considered to have played a major role in the process of channeling sexual desire in part through idealized depictions of romantic attachment between "suitable" partners—"suitable" largely by virtue of standards of physical beauty.[9] Hollywood's discourse on beauty is pervasive and complex, constructing sexual preference both within individual films and more generally by means of its promotion of stars.[10] In the process of becoming part of this discourse, Stevenson's story has, in all of its major cinematic incarnations, been altered in various ways to present the body as the focus of sexual attraction. Most obviously, women, though conspicuously absent from Stevenson's story (as a number of essays in the present volume point out), move to center stage in all of the film versions, providing a focal point for the movies' emphasis on "love interest." And in Mamoulian's *Jekyll and Hyde,* Fredric March, most widely known at the time for his roles in romantic comedy, presents a particularly handsome Jekyll to anchor the newly central love plot.

VIRGINIA WRIGHT WEXMAN

Hyde's ugliness, by contrast, provides the focal point for the story's horrific dimension, thereby signaling its position as the center around which the historical contradiction that motivates the film is elaborated, the contradiction between new business interests and new utopian aspirations held by previously disenfranchized groups. Fredric Jameson has suggested that historical contradiction is typically figured in a text through "imagery of libidinal revolution and of bodily transforma-tion."[11] In Jameson's view, the contradiction buried beneath the text's discourse on the body can be considered in terms of three horizons: historical events, class conflicts, and changing modes of production. Each of these horizons is characterized by competition between con-flicting interests. In Mamoulian's *Jekyll and Hyde,* the three levels described by Jameson are figured respectively in the film's narrative structure, its characterization, and its style. At each level, the ideological contradiction is displaced onto a drama centered on the individuated body and is aestheticized through reified conceptions of beauty and ugliness. The film's moments of violence occur when the underlying historical contradiction threatens to disrupt the smooth flow of this idealized discourse on beauty.

I. Historical Events and Structure

At the level of historical events, the early 1930s was notably a time in which the United States was preparing for a change in leadership style. With the Depression almost at its nadir and New Deal politics on the horizon, the country was entering an uncertain era. Hollywood re-sponded to these changing conditions by supplying the public with socially conscious melodramas such as *Wild Boys of the Road* and *I Was a Fugitive from a Chain Gang* and with escapist musicals such as the Gold Diggers series and *Forty-Second Street.* Conflicts generated in films that reflected the historical moment more subtly can also be read as analogues of contradictions being played out on the American po-litical scene.

The major political conflict of the day was the opposition between Hoover and Roosevelt, whose campaigns were at their height when *Jekyll and Hyde* was released. If Hoover's impersonal rigidity had much in common with General Carew's tradition-bound militarism, Roose-velt's widely known concern for the underprivileged immigrant popu-lation was reflected in Dr. Jekyll's solicitude for his patient Mrs. Luca (a name more readily identified with 1930s America than with Victorian England).[12] In the film's structure this opposition is figured as a clash of cultures.

Initially, the plot of *Jekyll and Hyde* delineates two societies: the lecture hall, with Dr. Jekyll at its center; and the drawing room, dominated by Jekyll's father-in-law-to-be General Carew. Each society represents contrasting values. In the lecture hall are individual style, intellectual daring, optimism, and spontaneity; in the drawing room, ritual, pomp, and impersonal, inflexible rules. Anthropologist Mary Douglas describes these contrasting values as they are expressed by attitudes towards the body in different cultures. A society dominated by ritual like that of the General may give rise to an alternate culture devoted to individual style in the guise of millennialism, the utopian vision of a new, freer social order. In millennialism,

> The religious style is spontaneity, enthusiasm and effervescence. Bodily dissociation in trance, induced by dance or drugs, is valued along with other symbols of non-differentiation. Distinguishing social categories are devalued, but the individual is exalted. The self is presented without inhibition or shyness. There is little or no self-consciousness about sexual or other bodily orifices and functions. As to intellectual style, there is little concern with differentiated units of time, respect for past, or programme for the future. The dead are forgotten. Intellectual discriminations are not useful or valued.[13]

Dr. Jekyll's mission, with its attendent rhetoric of ecstacy, bodily dissociation, drugs, disdain for temporality, and exaltation of the individual, exemplifies this pattern. Yet Jekyll's millennialist aspirations ultimately fail. His world is overpowered by that of the General, from whose perspective his experiments appear at first nonsensical and eventually immoral.

The figure who bridges these two worlds is Dr. Lanyon, subordinate and skeptical at the lecture, compliant and orthodox at the Carews'. Jekyll is never comfortable in the General's drawing room and abandons it at the first opportunity to speak to Muriel in the garden. Lanyon, however, is entirely at home there. Though Muriel loves Jekyll, the General himself favors Lanyon, who shares his own values. Whereas the old man's exchanges with Jekyll are characterized by friction, he is "delighted" to welcome Lanyon. "Punctual for dinner, punctual in everything, eh," is his greeting. After the first scene, the millennialist culture of the lecture hall with its enthralled students disappears, and Jekyll becomes an isolated figure. His rivalry with Lanyon develops in the traditional, tightly bounded society of the General. Here the question becomes, Who will inherit the mantle of leadership possessed by the impressively titled "General Sir Danvers Carew"? After the General's murder, Lanyon is the one who ultimately triumphs, acting as Jekyll's judge and overseeing his execution. The violence that marks his victory, however, suggests the film's forceful repression of the progressive values represented by Jekyll.

In the case of an ambiguous line of succession such as this, Douglas claims "accusations of witchcraft are used to denigrate rivals and pull them down in the competition for leadership" (112). The identification of Hyde, Jekyll's alter ego, with witchcraft, is thoroughgoing. In Douglas's description, the witch

> is associated symbolically with the reverse of the way that a normal human lives, with night instead of day. His powers are abnormal, he can fly, be in two places at once, change his shape. Above all, he is a deceiver, someone whose external appearance does not automatically betray his interior nature. . . . The loyalty of the witch, instead of being committed firmly to his group, flies out loose. He goes alone to contend with alien personifications of lust and power. The witch himself has no firm anchorage in the social structure. [113]

Though he is never actually labeled as a witch, Hyde is characterized as diabolical, nocturnal, and preternaturally agile.[14] He can even be conjured up by the appearance of a cat. His position as a witch is most conspicuously suggested by his extreme ugliness, an ugliness that makes his ultimate demise aesthetically as well as morally satisfying to the film's audience.

The plot's development from an opening that affirms the progressive ideals represented by Jekyll to a conclusion that features a witchhunt is consistent with the conflicting historical forces at work when the film was made. General Carew's conservative position was related not only to the popular image of Hoover but more generally to the interests of the business community at large, whereas Jekyll's utopian project spoke to the aspirations of the underprivileged toward greater freedom and equality on the eve of the New Deal era.

Though the film's pessimistic ending did not foreshadow Roosevelt's coming triumph, the story's outcome is in keeping with the fears of Wall Street bankers—on whom Hollywood was increasingly dependent—that the New Deal would usher in social anarchy. At Paramount, where *Jekyll and Hyde* was produced, Adolph Zukor, in collaboration with Wall Street associates, was in the process of pushing out his partner Jesse Lasky. Lasky, a creatively oriented entrepreneur, had hired *Jekyll and Hyde*'s director Rouben Mamoulian away from a career in opera to help Paramount meet the new technical challenge of sound. Whether Lasky's flagging fortunes would affect protégés such as Mamoulian was at that point unclear.[15] In these circumstances one can see why Mamoulian, who conceived the *Jekyll and Hyde* project, might have felt an affinity for the story of a creative innovator crushed by an impersonal, tradition-bound society.

II. Class Conflict and Characterization

Such historical events took place against a background of larger conflicts involving newly unstable class structures. If big business feared that the New Dealers' concern with the disadvantaged could lead to social anarchy, their apprehensions focused on two groups—woman and blacks. At the level of characterization, *Jekyll and Hyde*'s figuration of the body addresses itself specifically to these groups, each of which posed its own threat to the established social system. Women were being repositioned within the home after the relative freedom available to them during the previous decade; blacks were undergoing a new process of segregation from the rest of the population so that their position as an underclass could be maintained following their "Great Migration" to the north in search of jobs in the late 1920s. *Jekyll and Hyde* displaces these tensions by constructing a discourse on the body that centers on sexuality rather than economics. At the level of its deep structure, however, this discourse speaks to the economic conflict between these two disenfranchised groups and the business community.

Of all the critics of Mamoulian's *Jekyll and Hyde,* only William Everson has noted the racial overtones in Mr. Hyde's dark skin, thick lips, and broad, flat nose.[16] This representation builds on a racial-Darwinian undercurrent in Stevenson's story, which is explicated in this volume by Lawler and by Brantlinger and Boyle. This aspect of Mamoulian's film sets it apart from other cinematic versions of the Jekyll and Hyde story produced at different historical moments.[17] By contrast, Spencer Tracy created a Hyde who looked very similar to Jekyll, and in John Robertson's 1920 film, John Barrymore played Hyde as a gigantic spider. Even without the conspicuous physical markers provided by Fredric March's makeup, racial overtones are inescapable in Mamoulian's conception of Hyde as a primitive man. In reconstructing the prevailing ideology of the period, Harvard Sitkoff points out that white supremacy was justified by a rationale of racial superiority that "asserted a unilinear vertical progression of the races with Negroes biologically the most inferior and Caucasians the most exalted."[18] The universality of this mode of discrimination is attested to by Frantz Fanon, who observes that, in all colonialist situations, "when the settler seeks to describe the native fully in exact terms, he constantly refers to the bestiary."[19] To justify this hierarchy, biologists from the Victorian era onward propagated "notions of the inadequate cranial capacity of Negroes, their ape-like physical characteristics, and the horrors resulting from race crossing or intermixture," notions that were reproduced in encyclopedias and textbooks.[20]

This "horror" of racial intermixture was defined as a cinematic taboo in the Motion Picture Production Code of 1930, which specified, "MIS-CEGENATION (sex relationship between the white and black races) is forbidden."[21] The horror of miscegenation had earlier been depicted in the figure of the black rapist in the 1914 film *Birth of a Nation,* which provoked a vehement protest by civil rights activists. Griffith's epic was followed by more disguised representations of the abhorrent nature of interracial coupling.[22] The most famous of these was undoubtedly Cooper and Schoedsack's *King Kong,* released in 1933 to great popular acclaim. Though *King Kong* took a somewhat sympathetic view of the fate of the "primitive" in modern industrialized society, it played up the threat represented by the beast's attraction to the "golden woman."[23] Similarly, in *Jekyll and Hyde* it is the monster's determination to appropriate the sexuality of white womanhood that defines his malevolence. After sadistically tormenting one white woman, Hyde ravishes her when she faints from terror. On being thwarted in his attempt to rape another white woman, he murders her protector.

Angela Davis has suggested that the image of the black rapist plays an important role as myth in American culture and cites its function as a justification for lynching. Davis points out that lynchings have run in cycles that can be related to the need to suppress blacks during periods when they are threatening to gain economic or political power. She further observes that, though less than half of all lynchings are provoked by alleged rapes of white women, popular conceptions of lynching have always focused on this crime; "The myth of the Black rapist has been methodically conjured up whenever recurrent waves of violence and terror against the Black community have required convincing justification."[24] *Jekyll and Hyde* concludes with a sequence that bears a sinister resemblance to a lynching, complete with an angry mob and the shooting of a monstrous criminal who is suspended in the air, as though hanging from a tree (fig. 10.1). This allusion to lynching appeared shortly after the Scottsboro case, a sensational, racially charged rape trial widely reported in the media in 1931; and it foreshadowed the revived activity of the Ku Klux Klan during the 1930s.[25]

The abomination represented by Hyde's sexual appetite is made palpable by his hideousness. While Jekyll's handsome demeanor is often enhanced by backlighting and is set off by the grace of his carriage, the coarse, typically underlit features of Hyde are complemented by stealthy, apelike movements. Thus, the racial overtones inherent in the representation of Hyde are intimately associated with his physical repulsiveness. In a study of the representation of blacks in the nineteenth century,

Fig. 10.1

Sander S. Gilman shows that "[t]he antithesis of European sexual mores and beauty is embodied in the black."[26] The sexuality of blacks is thereby constructed as repugnant. Ivy, the prostitute whom Hyde takes as his mistress, tells him as much on their first meeting. "You ain't no beauty," she says. By contrast, she responds to her first look at Jekyll by associating his attractive demeanor with his privileged class status, commenting, "Anybody can see now that you're a real gent, you are."

In this film, as in the culture at large, to be beautiful is to be white. On first encountering Ivy, Hyde praises her beauty, noting especially her "yellow hair" and "pale face." The idealized erotic paintings and statuary associated with the film's sexual encounters are conspicuously white, as are the heroic representations of human figures associated with Jekyll's grand aspirations. By contrast, the statue beside the mirror in which Jekyll first sees himself as Hyde is of a black demon, and it is Hyde's swarthy appearance that defines the nature of his travesty of the accepted ideals of romantic love.

The myth of the black rapist employs the discourse of sexual desire to suppress women as well as blacks. Showing that the projection of sexual desire onto blacks has, in the past, allowed white males to affirm their control over their own sexuality, Gilman goes on to assert that such a projection of sexual desire may be further displaced onto a certain kind of woman.

The "white *man's* burden" thus becomes his sexuality and its control, and it is this which is transferred into the need to control the other, the other as sexualized female. The colonial mentality which sees "natives" as needing control is easily transferred to "woman"—but woman as exemplified by the caste of prostitute. [237]

In *Jekyll and Hyde* it is Ivy's position as a prostitute that makes her vulnerable. Alone on the streets or in the music hall, she can be readily accosted by casual customers or long-term lovers. As she says to her landlady, "Who cares what becomes of the likes of me?" Thus the independent flapper, whose sexuality was glamorized in movies of the 1920s, is transformed in this 1932 film into the prostitute whose sexual assertiveness marks her for destruction.[27] By contrast, the General's daughter Muriel scarcely ventures outside of his drawing room. When she defies her father's wishes by agreeing to receive her errant fiancé, Jekyll, she triggers the anarchic ravages of Hyde's lust. In the case of both women, their assertiveness is what provokes the violence against them—violence that the film codes as the result of sexually perverse desire rather than economic frustration.

The authority by which the film justifies the repression of woman's will is suggested by Jekyll's profession. Foucault and others have noted that physicians intervene in modern family life through their alliance with women and their authority over matters pertaining to the body.[28] Foucault has postulated a panoptic system of "policing" bodies through a process of confession. Authority is vested in the doctor-confessor, who assumes the role formerly held by the priest. Near the opening of *Jekyll and Hyde,* the scene between Dr. Jekyll and Mrs. Luca emphasizes the woman's dependence on her doctor and the doctor's ability to elicit a "confession of the body." As he touches her, Jekyll asks, "It hurts, doesn't it?" Mrs. Luca replies, "Yes, yes sir." "Sometimes a doctor must hurt you to make you well," Jekyll explains. The underlying dynamic of sexual control inherent in this confessional relationship between doctor and patient is made explicit in a subsequent scene, when Ivy, erotically aroused by the doctor's touch, appropriates this touch by placing her hand over his (fig. 10.2). By effecting this reversal, Ivy declares her ability to seize the sexual power implicit in the doctor's authority over the body.

That Jekyll should be susceptible to such an appropriation of his authority is a function of his attitude toward his own sexuality. Sexual desire is what spurs his millennialist mission. His lack of sexual control is what endangers his marriage to the General's daughter, a marriage within his own group, which is designed to ensure monopolization of

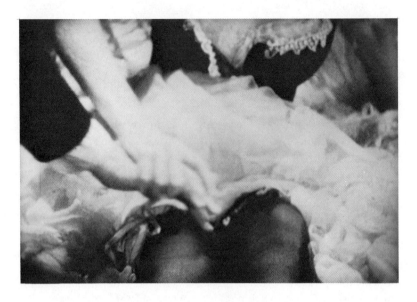

FIG. 10.2

social rewards by that group. The danger of relinquishing this monopolization through sexual commitments that cross class and racial lines is what must be contained. Following his feverish attempts to sublimate this sexual energy by dedicating himself to his scientific experiments, Jekyll, in the guise of his alter ego, Hyde, resorts to the instant sexual gratification offered by the lower-class Ivy. From this perspective, it appears that Jekyll's willingness to involve himself in interclass sexuality with Ivy calls up the "horror" of interracial sexuality, a horror represented by the image of the black rapist.

The regressive nature of this horror is suggested by the film's shifting representations of morality. At first, Jekyll speaks of his mission in terms of a specialized medical discourse centered on hygiene; he wants to be "clean in my innermost thoughts and desires." His modern medical perspective sees sin in terms of disease, specifically disease associated with promiscuous sexuality. His vision is soon overwhelmed, however, by a discourse characteristic of more primitive cultures in which disease, crime, and religion are not distinguished from one another.[29] When Ivy confronts Jekyll a second time with a more abject confession of the body, showing him the whip marks on her back, the doctor's attempt to medicalize the situation by prescribing a lotion is rebuffed. "A lotion won't do the trick, sir," Ivy assures him. "No sir. It's more than that, sir." What is "more than that" is the evil represented by Hyde, an evil that, during the same interview, causes Jekyll to abandon his medical persona

VIRGINIA WRIGHT WEXMAN

and exclaim, "Horrible, horrible!" This same cry of "Horrible!" is uttered by Lanyon in response to the confession offered up by the spectacle of Jekyll's own body as it transforms itself before his eyes. This last "confession" scene occurs in Lanyon's study, where a prominent portrait of Queen Victoria and a candlestick in the shape of a cross provide Jekyll's subsequent verbal confession with overtones that are more legal and religious than medical (fig. 10.3). Earlier, Jekyll had accused his colleague of having "no interest in science at all," a charge that speaks to the regressive nature of Lanyon's authority.

If Lanyon's ultimate triumph over Jekyll represents a rejection of science as an instrument of human liberation, it also affirms the power of science as a tool of oppression. Because Jekyll's alter ego, Hyde, is made so thoroughly despicable, a monstrous defiler of both white womanhood and civilized patriarchal authority, Lanyon's suppression of him is legitimated. However, the violent means Lanyon must use to effect this suppression suggest the nature of the power through which the underlying struggle between competing class interests will be resolved. This is a power that uses science as weaponry.

Both Jekyll and Lanyon deploy phallic objects that symbolize their authority. For Jekyll, this object is his cane, the cane that he uses to skewer Ivy's garter and that Hyde employs to subdue people who get in his way. To express his joy about his approaching marriage, Jekyll brandishes this cane aloft; but by this point in the action his values have been so dis-

Fig. 10.3

Fig. 10.4

Fig. 10.5

VIRGINIA WRIGHT WEXMAN

credited by what has transpired that his own tiny figure is dwarfed by the vast space of his entry hall with its single upright candelstick, a reminder of the sexual energy that has motivated him, and which now threatens to overpower him (fig. 10.4). By contrast, Lanyon possesses a more modern symbol of patriarchal oppression: a gun. Unlike Stevenson's deployment of an "old" gun to establish, as Veeder notes, the inadequacy of Lanyon's old-fashioned, patriarchal response to new dangers, Mamoulian presents the gun as a way for Lanyon to transcend the limitations of his body, enabling him to dominate even the brutal Hyde, whose cane lies useless in the foreground of the frame during his visit to Lanyon's study (fig. 10.5). The gun's power as an instrument of oppression is attested to by the film's final scene, in which Lanyon leads a police detective to Jekyll's laboratory in order to accuse him of General Carew's murder. Informed that Hyde has a knife, the detective shoots him. The unlikeliness of a British police officer carrying a gun is here overlooked in the interests of demonstrating the power of superior technology in the struggle for class dominance.

III. Modes of Production and Style

The struggle for dominance was an issue during the early 1930s, not only within the United States itself but also internationally. In this arena, the contradiction between big business and a newly aspiring underclass was represented in the clash between capitalism and communism.

Hollywood's answer to the threat of foreign rivalry had always been to appropriate the world's most talented filmmakers and assimilate their innovative styles into its own "classical" codes. As David Bordwell has shown, "Hollywood has perpetually renewed itself by assimilating techniques from experimental movements."[30] This process of assimilation took place in the context of conflicting American class interests. The utopian ideals of the nascent groups were expressed in Hollywood's "international" stylistic practices, an internationalism that expressed the American aspiration to be perceived as an amalgam of cultures in which different voices blended into a harmonious whole. At the same time, this process of stylistic assimilation served the hegemonic interests of American business by making it possible for American perspectives to be expressed in "international" terms.

In 1930, Paramount had attempted to carry out this strategy of assimilation by hiring the great Soviet director Sergei Eisenstein. But Eisenstein's methods of working were too antithetical to the American system to be readily assimilated, and his presence on the American scene was disturbing to the federal government. His contract was soon cancelled. However, the movie industry did not remain unaffected by the innovations represented in films such as *Potemkin* and *October*, both of which were distributed in the United States during the late 1920s. This influence appears conspicuously in *Dr. Jekyll and Mr. Hyde,* a Paramount production mounted by a Russian director who had left his country during the Revolution.

Mamoulian, with his cosmopolitan background, has traditionally been praised for an innovative, rhythmical style that seems to raise his films above politics into a realm of ineffable feeling akin to that of music. As Tom Milne commented in his book on the director, "One is almost tempted to say that every Mamoulian film is a musical."[31] Yet even style may have ideological implications. Mamoulian embellished *Jekyll and Hyde* with arresting stylistic features derived from a variety of foreign sources—including Soviet montage—which gave the film an attractive aura of sophisticated internationalism. As a director working within the constraints of the Hollywood mode of production, however, he incorporated these stylistic innovations into a context very different from Eisenstein's. Neither *Potemkin* nor *October* features individuated heroes; the nobility of people working as a group is what is celebrated. Mamoulian, by contrast, uses style, including dramatic point-of-view shots, dissolves, mirror shots, and striking sound effects, to draw the spectator into the world of a single protagonist.

Mamoulian's pervasive use of statues in *Jekyll and Hyde* as an ironic commentary on the action is indebted to films such as *Potemkin* and *October*. More strikingly, Eisensteinian aesthetics motivate the Mamoulian montage sequence that occurs as Jekyll plays the organ following the General's acquiescence to his early marriage. This montage is composed of five elements: a candelabrum (fig. 10.6), a bronze statue of an athlete holding aloft a wreath of victory (fig. 10.7), a marble bust (fig. 10.8), Jekyll's butler Poole (fig. 10.9), and a fire blazing in the fireplace (fig. 10.10). Unlike most montage sequences in Hollywood films, this group of images does not perform a clearly defined narrative function, such as collapsing time, increasing suspense through parallel editing, or providing a soliloquy-like insight into the protagonist's consciousness. Instead, these images articulate an idea.

To grasp this idea, we must first understand the relationship between Mamoulian's stylistic innovations and those of Eisenstein. Eisenstein's ideology is utopian, centered on a vision of communal action and social equality. In *October,* for example, montages of statues suggest the aristocracy's false pretentions to unshakable authority while the "ordinary" living people who stand beside them are dignified by contrast. For Mamoulian, however, utopia is represented solely in terms of an individual and is associated with an ideal of physical beauty represented by the body and its sexuality. This vision of utopia is what the montage in *Jekyll and Hyde* articulates. In this scheme, it is not the vitality of the

VIRGINIA WRIGHT WEXMAN

FIG. 10.6

FIG. 10.7

HOLLYWOOD, BEAUTY, AND ROUBEN MAMOULIAN   297

Fig. 10.8

Fig. 10.9

Fig. 10.10

Fig. 10.11

social system that is expressed but rather the fate of a single person within it.

Jekyll aspires to a state in which the body enjoys eternal rapture and eternal youth. His romantic yearnings are expressed as childlike physical exuberance: "I could sing or dance or roll a hoop." Mamoulian contrasts this exuberance with imagery of aging and death. The Arcadian setting of Jekyll's love scene with Muriel is complemented by the skeleton in the doctor's laboratory, a skeleton that is more than once shown in conjunction with Jekyll's aging butler, Poole (fig. 10.11).[32] The "memento mori" suggested by the skeleton finds its counterpart in the second incarnation of Hyde. This second Hyde, who first appears in the park while Jekyll is on his way to the General's, is made horrible not by features suggesting racial difference but by signs of age: grizzled hair and wrinkles. In contrast to the earlier transformation scene, this one occurs in nature and is triggered spontaneously by the revelation of nature's own brutal laws. In a scene missing from most prints of the film now in distribution, Jekyll catches sight of a cat eating a bird. The same law of nature that decrees that the bird must serve as the cat's prey also dictates that all living creatures must succumb to the process of aging and death. If the horror of racial and sexual difference grows out of the social order, the horror of aging arises as an inevitable consequence of humanity's place as a part of the natural world.

Hollywood's equation of beauty and youth is evident during the love scene in the garden, when the entrance of the Carews' butler, Hudson, interrupts the lovers' embrace. Panning along the ground in anticipation of this interruption, the camera reveals an androgynous putto, two water lilies floating on a pond, and then the shadow of the butler. Thus the idealized figure of the statue is followed by the more evanescent beauty of the water lilies. And the shadow of what is to come is cast by the presence of a member of another class, a figure unthreatening in this context but presaging the film's subsequent class-related complications. The camera repeats a similar panning motion later, after Jekyll swallows the potion. Now, however, the imagery is more overtly sinister, for the camera moves from the fireplace with its leaping flames to the skeleton to the black demon beside the mirror.

The montage sequence during Jekyll's organ scene states this inevitability more emphatically. The first and last images of fire suggest the control of powerful elements and, especially seen in relation to the fire in Jekyll's laboratory, connote the hellfire awaiting those who fail to achieve this control.[33] The two pieces of statuary suggest the idealized nature of Jekyll's aspirations, though the second, being whiter and more androgynous than the first, offers a racially and sexually revised version of this ideal. The wrinkled countenance of Poole here serves as a reminder

VIRGINIA WRIGHT WEXMAN

that, even in a society unblemished by racial and sexual difference, death must still exist.

Ultimately, these images come together in the last scene. As Poole confronts Jekyll in his laboratory, the latter is flanked on one side by the skeleton and on the other by a blazing fire, which threatens to consume him (fig. 10.12). Locked into a single frame, these images will soon be conjoined in the narrative as well. Thus, by juxtaposing this imagery and by focusing it on a single individual, Mamoulian has placed the transgression of the *social* laws of racial and sexual difference on a level with the transgression of the *natural* laws of mortality. Jekyll's belief that he can disregard the laws of class and gender is an error as tragic as his conviction that he can overcome the laws of mortality. In the absence of a utopian vision of community such as that posed by Eisenstein's cinema, Mamoulian's cosmopolitan style is ultimately bound to the ideology of Hollywood, presenting its individualized utopia as an evanescent arcadia, shadowed by the absolute laws of death and difference. Mamoulian finds in nature a reflection of the cultural impasse he confronted. Thus, at its deepest level his brilliant technique can only express his despair in the face of this impasse, a despair figured in the film as an implacable fate.

Writing in the nineteenth century, Robert Louis Stevenson had no way of knowing what his story of human metamorphosis would come to signify in the body-centered consumer culture of the twentieth. Nonethe-

FIG. 10.12

less, his awareness of the tension between patriarchy, with its standards of aesthetic taste and connoisseurship, and the devolutionary features of Hyde and the human psyche was readily adaptable to the dark vision of Mamoulian in Hollywood. In Mamoulian's *Dr. Jekyll and Mr. Hyde* the beauty of statues may be timeless, but the beauty of the human body is not. The film portrays death as an absolute limit to the idealizations of physical beauty promoted by art—and by Hollywood. Lacking a common utopian ideal that is social rather than individual, Hollywood substitutes representations of physical beauty for a vision of social harmony. Such representations are based not only on youth and sexuality but also on variables such as class, race, and gender; these, in turn, are inflected by the historical moment. Some of the most recent adaptations of the *Jekyll and Hyde* story, including Jerry Lewis's *The Nutty Professor* (1963), Terence Fisher's *The Two Faces of Dr. Jekyll* (1960), and Charles B. Griffith's *Dr. Heckell and Mr. Hype* (1984), present Hyde as handsomer than Jekyll, suggesting that the cinema is becoming more self-conscious about its role as a purveyor of standards of physical appearance. But in today's culture these standards still constitute the measure by which human "perfection" is judged. Considered in the context of this culture, Fredric March's transformation from a handsome matinee idol into a hideous monster constitutes more than an actor's gimmick. In the Hollywood Arcadia, as in the modern world at large, the body beautiful is a complicated construction.

APPENDIX

The following plot summary of the 1932 *Dr. Jekyll and Mr. Hyde* covers sequences that are missing from the 16mm copies of the film currently circulating in the United States but that were included in the original release print. The descriptions of the missing sequences are marked off by square brackets. The version currently circulating is reproduced in the form of frame enlargements in *Rouben Mamoulian's Dr. Jekyll and Mr. Hyde*, ed. Richard J. Anobile (New York: Universe Books, 1975).

[As Dr. Jekyll plays Bach's "Prelude and Fugue in D Minor" on the organ in his house, he is interrupted by Poole, his butler, who informs him that it is time for his lecture.] Jekyll is driven to the lecture hall by his coachman. There he speaks to a packed house about the two halves of the human soul. Afterward, he visits patients in the free ward of the hospital, rejecting his friend Dr. Lanyon's suggestion that he pay a house call to the Duchess Densmores instead.

Having resolved to operate on a woman patient in the free ward, Jekyll declines the opportunity to accompany Lanyon to General Carew's dinner party, telling his friend that he will arrive after dinner "for the dancing." Later, at the Carews', he apologizes for his lateness and takes the General's daughter Muriel, his fiancée, into the garden. There he urges her to set an earlier date for their wedding. Though she is agreeable, her father refuses to allow this change of plans.

While on his way home from the General's with Lanyon, Jekyll rescues a young woman named Ivy Pierson from a man who is abusing her. Up in her room, he determines that she is not seriously injured, but, before he can leave, she [disrobes and] kisses him. Lanyon, who intrudes at this moment, disapproves of Jekyll's conduct. During their subsequent discussion, Jekyll defends his sexual desires and vows to embark on experiments to "separate the two natures in us."

After long hours in his laboratory, Jekyll perfects a formula that can transform him into the libidinous Hyde. Once Jekyll is transformed, his alter ego immediately sets off in search of Ivy. On discovering her in a music hall, Hyde intimidates her into cooperating with his desires and establishes her in an elaborate apartment. There he visits her regularly, using her sexually, beating her, and sadistically taunting her about her fear and hatred of him.

The news that Muriel and her father are returning to the city after an absence leads Jekyll to resolve that he will give up his dangerous experiments. He throws away the key to the back door of his laboratory, sends Ivy fifty pounds, and goes to visit the Carews. After apologizing to Muriel and the General for not having kept in touch with them, he succeeds in persuading them both to move up the date of the wedding. Returning home in a state of jubilation, he begins to play the organ, but is interrupted by the arrival of Ivy, who has come to thank him for his gift and to beg him to save her from Hyde. He promises her that he will see that Hyde never bothers her again.

A few days later Jekyll leaves his house to attend a dinner at the Carews, where his marriage is to be announced. On the way, he stops in the park to listen to a bird. [He begins to recite Keats's "Ode to a Nightingale," but stops when he notices a cat stalking the bird. After witnessing the cat devour the bird,] he feels himself involuntarily changing into Hyde. Once the transformation is complete, Hyde hurries off to Ivy's while Muriel waits in vain for Jekyll to arrive at their dinner.

Furious with Ivy for soliciting Jekyll's help, Hyde strangles her. Though her cries rouse the neighbors, he manages to escape. However, he no longer has the key to Jekyll's laboratory. Hastily, he writes Lanyon a note in Jeykll's hand, begging him to fetch the necessary chemicals and give them to "a man" who will call for them. When Hyde appears at Lanyon's to collect the chemicals, however, Lanyon refuses to relinquish them without being "assured of Dr. Jekyll's safety." Hyde then mixes and drinks the potion in Lanyton's presence, transforming himself back into Jekyll. After hearing Jekyll's confession, Lanyon extracts from him a promise that he will "never mix that drug again" and that he will give up Muriel.

The next evening, Jekyll visits Muriel to release her from their engagement. After their interview, as he watches her from the terrace, he is again involuntarily transformed into Hyde. After creeping into the Carews' drawing room, Hyde attempts to rape the young woman and, when her father rushes in to defend her, he kills the old man with his cane. With the police and a crowd of citizenry in pursuit, Hyde escapes back into Jekyll's laboratory and quickly mixes the formula that will change him back into the "innocent" Dr. Jekyll. Lanyon, however, discovers Jekyll's broken cane on the Carews' terrace and rushes to Jekyll's laboratory to accuse him of the crime. Before his incredulous pursuers, Jekyll is transformed back into Hyde for the last time. After brandishing a knife, he is shot by a police detective. In death, his body resumes its original configuration as Dr. Jekyll.

NOTES

I am grateful to Linda Williams, John Huntington, Robert Sklar, and the members of the Columbia Seminar on Film and Related Arts for their comments on earlier drafts of this essay.

1. For a history of the stage and screen adaptations of the novel, see Harry M. Geduld, *The Definitive Dr. Jekyll and Mr. Hyde Companion* (New York: Garland Publishers, 1983).

2. MGM purchased the rights to the Mamoulian version and withdrew it from circulation for many years to ensure the preeminence of its own *Jekyll and Hyde* starring Spencer Tracy (directed by Victor Fleming). For this reason, Mamoulian's film was long unavailable for study and even now is not as widely known as the Tracy remake, despite its high reputation. Readers unfamiliar with the 1932 *Jekyll and Hyde* may consult the plot summary in the appendix.

3. J. C. M., "The Current Cinema," *New Yorker,* 9 January 1932, 75.

4. Mordaunt Hall, "The Screen," *New York Times,* 2 January 1932, 14.

5. "Cinema," *Time,* 11 January 1932, 25.

6. See Peter Lehman and William Luhr, "Narrative Comparison," in Peter Lehman and William Luhr, *Authorship and Narrative in Cinema* (New York: G. P. Putnam's Sons, 1977), 199–282; and S. S. Prawer, "Book into Film. I: Mamoulian's *Dr. Jekyll and Mr. Hyde,*" in S. S. Prawer, *Caligari's Children: The Film as a Tale of Terror* (New York: Oxford University Press, 1981), 86–107. An essay by Jorge Luis Borges entitled "Dr. Jekyll and Edward Hyde, Verwandelt" (*Filmkritik* 24 [September 1980]: 413–14) criticizes both the Mamoulian and the Fleming adaptations for simplifying the original novel.

7. See, for example, James B. Twitchell, *Dreadful Pleasures* (New York: Oxford University Press, 1985).

8. See Edgar Morin, *The Stars,* trans. Richard Howard (New York: Grove

Press, 1960); Richard Dyer, *Stars* (London: British Film Institute, 1982); and Richard de Cordova, "The Emergence of the Star System in America," *Wide Angle* 6, no. 4 (1985): 4–14.

9. For discussions of the centrality of the couple in mainstream cinema, see Janet Bergstrom, "Alternation, Segmentation, Hypnosis: Interview with Raymond Bellour," *Camera Obscura,* nos. 3–4 (n.d.): 71–103; and Robin Wood, "An Introduction to the American Horror Film," in *Movies and Methods,* ed. Bill Nichols (Berkeley: University of California Press, 1985), 195–220.

10. Though the concept of physical beauty has traditionally been regarded as an abstract ideal, it has more recently been the focus of examination as a social construct. For an example of the former approach, see John Ligget, "Beauty," *The Human Face* (New York: Stein and Day, 1974); and Kenneth Clark, *Feminine Beauty* (New York: Rizzoli International Publishers, 1980). The latter approach has been taken by Susan Sontag ("Beauty: How Will It Change Next?," *Vogue,* May 1975, 116–17); and Lois Banner, (*American Beauty* [New York: Alfred A. Knopf, 1983]), among others.

11. Fredric Jameson, *The Political Unconscious: Narrative as a Socially Symbolic Act* (Ithaca, N.Y.: Cornell University Press, 1981), 74.

12. See Robert S. McElvaine, *The Great Depression: America 1929–1941* (New York: New York Times Book Company, 1984); David Burner, *Herbert Hoover* (New York: Knopf, 1979); Richard Norton Smith, *An Uncommon Man: The Triumph of Herbert Hoover* (New York: Simon and Schuster, 1984); Elliot A. Rosen, *Hoover, Roosevelt, and the Brains Trust: From Depression to New Deal* (New York: Columbia University Press, 1977); and Albert U. Romasco, *The Politics of Recovery: Roosevelt's New Deal* (New York: Oxford University Press, 1983).

13. Mary Douglas, *Natural Symbols: Explorations in Cosmology* (New York: Pantheon Books, 1982), 149.

14. For a more extended discussion of Hyde's identification with the devil, see Janice R. Welsch, "The Horrific and the Tragic," in *The English Novel and the Movies,* ed. Michael Klein and Gillian Parker (New York: Ungar Publishing Co., 1981), 165–79.

15. See J. G. Edmonds and Reiko Mimura, *Paramount Pictures and the People Who Made Them* (New York: A. S. Barnes, 1980); Jesse H. Lasky with Don Weldon, *I Blow My Own Horn* (Garden City, N.Y.: Doubleday and Co., 1957); and Adolph Zukor with Dale Kramer, *The Public Is Never Wrong* (New York: G. P. Putnam's Sons, 1953).

16. William H. Everson, *Classics of the Horror Film* (Secaucus, N.J.: Citadel Press, 1974), 74. In general, studies of blacks in film have confined their attention to images overtly presented in terms of racial difference and have not attempted to generate textual readings. See, for example, Donald Bogle, *Toms, Coons, Mulattoes, Mammies, and Bucks: An Interpretive History of Blacks in American Film* (New York: Viking Press, 1973); James P. Murray, *To Find an Image: Black Films from Uncle Tom to Superfly* (New York: Bobbs-Merrill, 1973); Daniel J. Leab, *From Sambo to Superspade: The Black Experience in Motion Pictures* (Boston: Houghton-Mifflin, 1975); Jim Pines, *Blacks in Films: A Survey of Racial Themes and Images* (London: Studio Vista, 1975); Thomas Cripps, *Slow*

Fade to Black (Bloomington: Indiana University Press, 1976); and James R. Nesteby, *Black Images in American Films, 1896–1934* (Washington, D.C.: University Press of America, 1982). More recently, in an essay entitled "Colonialism, Racism and Representation" (in Nichols [n. 9, above], 632–49), Robert Stam and Louise Spense have begun the project of using newly developed strategies of textual reading to deconstruct cinematic representations of racial difference.

17. Mamoulian's previous experience as director of the stage version of George Gershwin's folk opera *Porgy and Bess* may have influenced the racially linked primitivism of his Hyde.

18. Harvard Sitkoff, *A New Deal for Blacks: The Emergence of Civil Rights as a National Issue.* Volume 1: *The Depression Decade* (New York: Oxford University Press, 1978), 6.

19. Frantz Fanon, *The Wretched of the Earth,* Constance Farrington (New York: Grove Press, 1963), 42.

20. Sitkoff, 29.

21. "The Motion Picture Production Code of 1930," in *The Movies in Our Midst: Documents in the Cultural History of Film in America,* ed. Gerald Mast (Chicago: University of Chicago Press, 1982), 333.

22. For a discussion of the figure of the black rapist in *Birth of a Nation,* see Michael Rogin, " 'The Sword Became a Flashing Vision': D. W. Griffith's *Birth of a Nation,*" *Representations,* 9 (Winter 1985): 150–95.

23. For a discussion of *King Kong*'s use of the concept of the primitive man, see Noel Carroll, "*King Kong:* Ape and Essence," in *Planks of Reason: Essays on the Horror Film,* ed. Barry Grant (Metuchen, N.J.: Scarecrow Press, 1984), 215–44.

24. Angela Davis, "The Myth of the Black Rapist," in *Women, Race, and Class* (New York: Vintage, 1983), 173. See also Jacquelin Dowd Hall, " 'The Mind that Burns in Each Body': Women, Rape, and Racial Violence," in *Powers of Desire: The Politics of Sexuality,* ed. Ann Snitow, Christine Stansell, and Sharon Thompson (New York: Monthly Review Press, 1983), 328–49; and Hazel V. Carby, " 'On the Threshold of Woman's Era': Lynching, Empire, and Sexuality in Black Feminist Theory," *Critical Inquiry* 12, no. 1 (Special Issue on "Race," Writing, and Difference), ed. Henry Louis Gates, Jr. (Autumn 1985): 262–77.

Davis cites statistics showing that 405 out of the 455 men executed in the United States for rape between 1930 and 1967 have been black, while the number of blacks accused in reported rapes has only been 47 percent (172, 179). Presumably, the percentage of blacks responsible for unreported rapes is even lower, since assailants of higher social standing are less likely to incur formal charges.

25. For a more extensive discussion of these issues, see John B. Kirby, *Black Americans in the Roosevelt Era* (Knoxville: University of Tennessee Press, 1980).

26. Sander S. Gilman, "Black Bodies, White Bodies: Toward an Iconography of Female Sexuality in Late Nineteenth Century Art," *Critical Inquiry* 12, no. 1 (Special Issue on "Race," Writing and Difference), ed. Henry Louis Gates, Jr. (Autumn 1985): 212.

VIRGINIA WRIGHT WEXMAN

27. For a discussion of the connection between female sexuality and the figure of the monster in horror films, see Linda Williams, "When the Woman Looks," in *Re-Vision: Essays in Feminist Film Criticism*, ed. Mary Ann Doane, Patricia Mellencamp, and Linda Williams (Frederick, Md.: University Publications of America, 1984), 83–99.

28. See Michel Foucault, *The Birth of the Clinic*, trans. A. M. Sheridan Smith (New York: Vintage Books, 1975); Jacques Donzelot, *The Policing of Families*, tr. Robert Hurley (New York: Pantheon Books, 1979); and Bryan S. Turner, *The Body and Society* (New York: Basil Blackwell, 1984).

29. See Turner, 212.

30. David Bordwell, "The Bounds of Difference," in David Bordwell, Janet Staiger, and Kristin Thompson, *The Classical Hollywood Cinema: Film Style and Mode of Production to 1960* (New York: Columbia University Press, 1985), 72.

31. Tom Milne, *Rouben Mamoulian* (Bloomington and London: Indiana University Press, 1969), 13. This claim is certainly valid as far as it goes. In particular, the term *operatic*, which is often applied to the style of *Jekyll and Hyde*, seems an appropriate one and points to the influence of Mamoulian's earlier work in opera on his cinematic technique. Other discussions of Mamoulian's stylistic innovations in *Jekyll and Hyde* can be found in Ivan Butler, "Three Early Sound Horror Classics," in his *The Horror Film* (New York: A. S. Barnes, 1967), 45–59; and Michael Stevastakis, "Mamoulian's *Dr. Jekyll and Mr. Hyde*," *Journal of Film and Video* 37, no. 4 (Fall 1985): 15–26.

32. For a more extensive discussion of the relationship between these images, see Erwin Panofsky's classic essay, "Et in Arcadia Ego," in his *Meaning in the Visual Arts* (Garden City, N.Y.: Doubleday and Co.–Anchor Books, 1957), 295–320.

33. In view of Mamoulian's extensive background in opera, it seems likely that the motif of hellfire as a punishment for lack of sexual discipline, as well as other motifs such as Ivy's "Champagne Aria," were inspired by Mozart's *Don Giovanni*.

Bibliography

This bibliography lists texts pertaining specifically to *Jekyll and Hyde* and various other texts that either provide basic information about Stevenson's life or mark important moments in the development of his reputation.

Ashe, Matthew. "Stevenson after Fifty Years." *Catholic World* 160 (1944): 241–45.

Aring, Charles D. "The Case Becomes Less Strange." *American Scholar* 30 (1960–61): 67–78.

Balfour, Graham. *The Life of Robert Louis Stevenson.* 2 vols. New York: Charles Scribner's Sons, 1901.

Berman, Barbara L. "*The Strange Case of Dr Jekyll & Mr Hyde.*" In *Survey of Modern Literature*, edited by Frank N. Magill, 4:1834–39. Englewood Cliffs N.J.: Salem Press, 1983.

Block, Ed, Jr. "James Sully, Evolutionist Psychology, and Late Victorian Gothic Fiction." *Victorian Studies* 25 (1982): 443–67.

Brooks, Peter. *The Melodramatic Imagination.* New Haven, Conn.: Yale University Press, 1976.

Calder, Jenni. *Robert Louis Stevenson: A Life Study.* New York: Oxford University Press, 1980.

Chesterton, G. K. *Robert Louis Stevenson.* New York: Dodd, Mead, & Co., 1928.

Daiches, David. *Robert Louis Stevenson.* Norfolk, Conn.: New Directions, 1947.

Daleski, H. M. *The Divided Heroine*, 20–24. New York: Holmes and Meier, 1984.

Day, William Patrick. *In the Circles of Fire and Desire.* Chicago: University of Chicago Press, 1985.

Dolvers, Horst. *Der Erzähler Robert Louis Stevenson: Interpretationen.* Berne: Francke, 1969.

Douglas, James. *Theodore Watts-Dunton.* New York: John Lane, n.d.

Egan, Joseph J. "The Relationship of Theme and Art in *The Strange Case of Dr. Jekyll and Mr. Hyde.*" *English Literature in Transition* 9 (1966): 28–32.

Eigner, Edwin M. *Robert Louis Stevenson and Romantic Tradition*. Princeton, N.J.: Princeton University Press, 1966.

Elwin, Malcolm. *The Strange Case of Robert Louis Stevenson*. London: Macdonald, 1950.

Fraustino, Daniel V. "*Dr. Jekyll and Mr. Hyde:* Anatomy of Misperception." *Arizona Quarterly* 38 (1982): 235–40.

Furnas, J. C. "Full Circle: Stevenson and His Critics." *Atlantic Monthly* 188 (October 1951): 67–71.

———. *Voyage to Windward: The Life of Robert Louis Stevenson*. New York: William Sloane, 1951.

Geduld, Harry M., ed. *The Definitive* Dr. Jekyll and Mr. Hyde *Companion*. New York: Garland Publishing, 1983.

Girling, H. K. "The Strange Case of Dr. James and Mr. Stevenson." *Wascana Review* 3 (1968): 65–76.

Good, Graham. "Rereading Robert Louis Stevenson." *Dalhousie Review* 62 (1982): 44–59.

Guerard, Albert J. "Concepts of the Double." In *Stories of the Double*, edited by Albert J. Guerard. Philadelphia: J. B. Lippincott, 1967.

Gwynn, Stephen. *Robert Louis Stevenson*. London: Macmillan Publishing Co., 1939.

Hammerton, J. A. *Stevensoniana: An Anecdotal Life and Appreciation of Robert Louis Stevenson*. Edinburgh: John Grant, 1907.

Hannah, Barbara. *Striving toward Wholeness*. New York: G. P. Putnam's Sons, 1971.

Harvie, Christopher. "The Politics of Stevenson." In *Stevenson and Victorian Scotland*, edited by Jenni Calder. Edinburgh: Edinburgh University Press, 1981.

Heath, Stephen. "Psychopathia sexualis: Stevenson's *Strange Case*." *Critical Quarterly* 28 (1986): 93–108.

Hellman, George S. *The True Stevenson: A Study in Clarification*. Boston: Little, Brown and Co., 1925.

Henley, W. E. "R.L.S." *Pall Mall Gazette* 25 (April 1901): 505–14.

Hennelly, Mark M., Jr. "Stevenson's 'Silent Symbols' of the 'Fatal Cross Roads' in *Dr. Jekyll and Mr. Hyde*." *Gothic* 1 (1979): 10–16.

Jackson, Rosemary. *Fantasy: The Literature of Subversion*. London: Methuen, 1981.

James, Henry. "Robert Louis Stevenson." In Maixner, 290–311.

Jefford, Andrew. "Dr. Jekyll and Professor Nabokov: Reading a Reading." In Noble, 47–72.

Kanzer, Mark. "The Self-Analytic Literature of Robert Louis Stevenson." In *Psychoanalysis and Culture*, edited by George B. Wilbur and Warner Muensterberger, 425–35. New York: International Universities Press, 1951; reprinted in Geduld, 118–126.

Keating, Peter. "The Fortunes of RLS." *Times Literary Supplement*, 26 June 1981, 715–16.

Keith, C. "Stevenson To-day." *Queen's Quarterly* 57 (1950): 452–58.

Kiely, Robert. "Robert Louis Stevenson." In *Victorian Fiction: A Second Guide to Research*, edited by George H. Ford, 333–47. New York: Modern Language Association, 1978.

————. *Robert Louis Stevenson and the Fiction of Adventure.* Cambridge, Mass.: Harvard University Press, 1964.

Leonelli, Michele. "Jekyll, Hyde & Co.: Un passo in avanti?" *Annali della Scuola Normale Superiore di Pisa* 38 (1969): 295–301.

Limedorfer, Eugene. "The Manuscript of *Dr. Jekyll and Mr. Hyde*." *Bookman* 12 (1900): 52–58; reprinted in Geduld, 99–102.

Luhr, William, and Peter Lehman. *Authorship and Narrative in the Cinema: Issues in Contemporary Aesthetics and Criticism.* New York: Putnam's, 1977.

Mackay, Margaret. *The Violent Friend: The Story of Mrs. Robert Louis Stevenson.* Garden City, N.Y.: Doubleday and Co., 1968.

MacPherson, Harriet D. *R. L. Stevenson: A Study in the French Influence.* New York: Publications of the Institute of French Studies, 1930.

Maixner, Paul, ed. *Robert Louis Stevenson: The Critical Heritage.* London: Routledge and Kegan Paul, 1981.

McKay, George L. *A Stevenson Library: Catalogue of a Collection of Writings by and about Robert Louis Stevenson formed by Edwin J. Beinecke.* 6 vols. New Haven, Conn.: Yale University Press, 1951–64.

Midgley, Mary. "Selves and Shadows." *Times Literary Supplement,* 30 July 1982, 821.

Miller, Karl. *Doubles: Studies in Literary History.* New York: Oxford University Press, 1985.

Miyoshi, Masao. "Dr. Jekyll and the Emergence of Mr. Hyde." *College English* 27 (1966): 470–474, 479–80; republished in revised form in *The Divided Self* (New York: New York University Press, 1969), 294–301.

Mulder, Elisabeth. "Robert Louis Stevenson: Fantasia y conciencia de escritor." *Cuadernos Hispano-Americanos* (Madrid) 28 (1956): 197–207.

Nabokov, Vladimir. "The Strange Case of Dr. Jekyll and Mr. Hyde (1885)." In *Lectures on Literature,* edited by Fredson Bowers, 179–205. New York: Harcourt Brace Jovanovich, 1980.

Noble, Andrew, ed. *Robert Louis Stevenson.* London: Vision Press, 1983.

Osbourne, Lloyd. *An Intimate Portrait of R.L.S.* New York: Charles Scribner's Sons, 1924.

Philmus, Robert. *Into the Unknown: The Evolution of Science Fiction from Francis Godwin to H. G. Wells.* Berkeley: University of California Press, 1970.

Prawer, S. S. "Book into Film: *Dr. Jekyll and Mr. Hyde*." *Times Literary Supplement,* 21 December 1979, 161–64.

Praz, Mario. *The Romantic Agony.* Trans. Angus Davidson. London: Oxford University Press, 1933.

Punter, David. *The Literature of Terror.* London: Longmans, 1979.

Richard, Anne Brigitte. "Forvandling og destruktion." *Vindrosen* 20 (1973): 36–46.

Rogers, Robert. *A Psychoanalytic Study of the Double in Literature.* Detroit: Wayne State University Press, 1970.

Sanchez, Nellie Van de Grift. *The Life of Mrs. Robert Louis Stevenson.* New York: Charles Scribner's Sons, 1920.

Saposnik, Irving S. "The Anatomy of *Dr. Jekyll and Mr. Hyde.*" *Studies in English Literature* 11 (1971): 715–31; reprinted in *Robert Louis Stevenson* (see next entry).

———. *Robert Louis Stevenson.* New York: Twayne Publishers, 1974.

Schultz, Myron G. "The 'Strange Case' of Robert Louis Stevenson." *Journal of the American Medical Association* 216 (5 April 1971): 90–94.

Silverman, Kaja. *The Subject of Semiotics.* New York: Oxford University Press, 1983.

Smith, Ralph. "*Jekyll and Hyde* and Victorian Science Fiction." *Sphinx* 4 (1975): 62–70.

Stevenson, W. H. "The Surname Jekyll." *Notes and Queries* 4 (1899): 415; reprinted in Geduld, 103.

Stone, Donald David. *Novelists in a Changing World.* Cambridge, Mass.: Harvard University Press, 1972.

Strathdee, R. B. "Robert Louis Stevenson as a Scientist." *Aberdeen University Review* 36 (1956): 268–75.

Swearingen, Roger G. *The Prose Writings of Robert Louis Stevenson.* Hamden, Conn.: Archon Books, 1980.

Swinnerton, Frank. *R. L. Stevenson: A Critical Study.* New York: George H. Doran, 1923.

Twitchell, James B. *Dreadful Pleasures.* New York: Oxford University Press, 1985.

Tymms, Ralph. *Doubles in Literary Psychology.* Cambridge: Bowes and Bowes, 1949.

Wainwright, Alexander D., comp. *Robert Louis Stevenson: A Catalogue of the Henry E. Gerstley Stevenson Collection, the Stevenson Section of the Morris L. Parrish Collection of Victorian Novelists, and Items from Other Collections in the Department of Rare Books and Special Collections of the Princeton University Library.* Princeton, N.J.: Princeton University Library, 1971.

Welsch, Janice R. "The Horrific and the Tragic." In *The English Novel and the Movies* edited and introduced by Michael Klein and Gillian Parker, 165–79. New York: Unger Publishing Co., 1981.

Wirth-Nesher, Hana. "The Stranger Case of *The Turn of the Screw* and *Heart of Darkness.*" *Studies in Short Fiction* 16 (1979): 317–25.

Woolf, Leonard. "The Fall of Stevenson." In *Essays on Literature, History, Politics, Etc.,* 33–43. London: Hogarth, 1927.

Zaic, Franz. "Robert Louis Stevenson: *Strange Case of Dr. Jekyll and Mr. Hyde.*" In *Der Englische Roman im 19. Jahrhundert: Interpretationen. Zu Ehren von Horst Oppel,* edited by Paul Goetsch, Heinz Kosok, and Kurt Otten, 243–52. Berlin: E. Schmidt, 1973.